GREEN CAREERS IN BUILDING AND LANDSCAPING

PETERSON'S

A ⓝelnet COMPANY

About Peterson's

To succeed on your lifelong educational journey, you will need accurate, dependable, and practical tools and resources. That is why Peterson's is everywhere education happens. Because whenever and however you need education content delivered, you can rely on Peterson's to provide the information, know-how, and guidance to help you reach your goals. Tools to match the right students with the right school. It's here. Personalized resources and expert guidance. It's here. Comprehensive and dependable education content—delivered whenever and however you need it. It's all here.

For more information, contact Peterson's, 2000 Lenox Drive, Lawrenceville, NJ 08648; 800-338-3282 Ext. 54229.

Stephen Clemente, Managing Director, Publishing and Institutional Research; Bernadette Webster, Director of Publishing; Jill C. Schwartz, Editor; Ray Golaszewski, Manufacturing Manager; Linda M. Williams, Composition Manager; Practical Strategies, LLC: Contributing Researchers: Barbara Jani, Libby Romero; Contributing Writers: Margaret C. Moran, Judy Johnson, Rita A. Read

ISBN-13: 978-0-7689-2911-9
ISBN-10: 0-7689-2911-3

Printed in the United States of America

10 9 8 7 6 5 4 3 2 1   12 11 10

CONTENTS

PART II: COLLEGES AND UNION ORGANIZATIONS WITH GREAT GREEN PROGRAMS

A NOTE FROM THE PETERSON'S EDITORS

If you are a high school or college student thinking about your future—and the future of our planet—or if you are a career changer wondering what you need to do to get a job in the new green economy, *Peterson's Green Careers in Building and Landscaping* can offer you the information you need. Throughout the book, you will find details on numerous building and landscaping–related jobs and careers as well as programs offered at two-year and four-year colleges and universities and through trade unions and specialized organizations.

If, like most people, you need a better understanding of what being green or living a green lifestyle means and how to begin your search for a green job, you've come to the right place! In **What Is the New Green Economy?,** you'll find out why we're seeing an increase in the current interest in sustainability and what the New Energy for America Plan and the 2009 Stimulus Plan mean in terms of your green job search.

Next, **Essays on the Importance of Sustainability** features insightful and inspirational articles by individuals who are at the forefront of this exciting field:

- Julia Feder, Director, Education/Technology, U.S. Green Building Council; Amy Seif Hattan, Director of Strategic Initiatives, Second Nature; and Ashka Naik, Program Manager, Advancing Green Building Initiative, Second Nature
- Jennifer Berry, Public & Strategic Relations Manager, Earth911.com
- Deborah J. Hanson, ASID, AUID; Project & Environmental Coordinator, University of Arizona, Residence Life
- Robert Fleming, Director, Sustainable Design Program, Philadelphia University
- Alyce Engle, Environmental Health & Safety Director, Skanska USA Building Inc., Oakland, California

If you are seeking a professional or skilled job in the new green economy, check out **Part I (chapters 1–5)** for details on jobs in building design and construction; installation and energy efficiency; commercial, industrial, and residential design; landscaping, groundskeeping, and turf care; and policy, analysis, advocacy, and regulatory affairs. You can search by field for information on job trends, career paths, earning potential, education/licensure requirements, and where to get additional information. Each job profile includes professional and trade associations that may have special interest groups or sections related to energy and sustainability. In addition, you'll find fascinating interviews with individuals in certain green careers. These folks offer great advice and insight, which is tremendously beneficial to anyone thinking about their particular field. Finally, as an added benefit, you will find links to videos on

CareerOneStop.org for many of the careers mentioned throughout these chapters—links that look like this:

 http://bit.ly/career1

CareerOneStop's Web site is sponsored by the U.S. Department of Labor Employment and Training Administration and offers career resources and workforce information to job seekers, students, businesses, and workforce professionals to foster talent development in a global economy.

To locate some of the great four-year and/or graduate programs or some of the outstanding two-year (including community colleges) and union programs, check out **Part II (chapters 6 and 7).** The colleges and universities profiled here support innovative programs in building and landscaping, have vibrant on-campus sustainability programs and organizations, and have made a commitment to making their campus communities sustainable. Both chapters highlight degrees offered, including distance learning opportunities, and green campus organizations and activities.

Don't want to leave your carbon footprint traveling to see colleges or universities and want to save some green in the process? Check out the videos and educational resources on YOUniversityTV.com. You'll find easy-to-use links to videos that look like this:

http://bit.ly/collvid2

YOUniversityTV.com assists students with the college-selection process by providing access to videos and educational resources for colleges across the United States. YOUniversityTV.com is free-of-charge and does not receive compensation from any of the universities it features.

Chapter 8 features labor unions that offer energy-related apprenticeship and training programs. In **Chapter 9's State and Federal Workforce Training,** you'll discover what each state's One-Stop Career Center offers in terms of help with job search, resume writing, training programs, and more. Simply find your state, and you'll uncover a wealth of information, including phone numbers and Web site.

In the **Appendixes,** you'll learn how to find and search "green" job boards and how to "green" your vocabulary—what all of the new terms actually mean. You'll also find a list of organizations in the United States and abroad that support sustainability through education, research, and activities. Finally, for additional help, we've provided an index of the interviews, feature articles, and "About" boxes that appear in this book, alphabetically and with page numbers.

Throughout the book, you'll find feature pages offering extra "green" tips and advice, with such topics as *Recyclable Materials, Tips for Retrofitting a Bathroom for Green Design, How to Recycle,* and *Greenscaping with Native Plants.* "About" boxes that are scattered throughout the chapters provide even more information and explanations to help you succeed on your way to a green job—and a green life.

Join Peterson's *Green Careers* conversation on Facebook® and Twitter™ at www.facebook.com/green.series and www.twitter.com/green_series. Peterson's resources are available to help you with your "green" job and college search.

Peterson's publishes a full line of books—education exploration, career preparation, test prep, and financial aid. Peterson's publications can be found at high school guidance offices, college libraries and career centers, and your local bookstore and library. Peterson's books are now also available as eBooks.

We welcome any comments or suggestions you may have about this publication. Your feedback will help us make educational dreams possible for you—and others like you.

Colleges and universities will be pleased to know that Peterson's helped you in your selection. Admissions and Sustainability Office staff members are more than happy to answer questions and help in any way they can. The editors at Peterson's wish you great success in your search for a great *green* career in building and landscaping!

WHAT IS THE
NEW GREEN ECONOMY?

Once upon a time, the only thing that was green was Kermit the Frog. Now, it seems as though everywhere you turn, all you see and hear is "green." Eat organically grown food. Use only low- or no-VOC paint. (What's VOC?) Trade in your gas-guzzler for a hybrid. Have a fuel-efficient car? Buy an even more fuel-efficient car. Wear clothes made from renewable sources such as cotton or bamboo. (Bamboo? For clothes?) Recycle your computer, your cell phone, and even your sneakers. On and on goes the list of do's and don'ts in this new sustainable, eco-friendly, twenty-first century. But what does it mean to you—the student, the worker, the consumer, and the citizen?

Why the Interest in Sustainability Now?

First, the fear of global warming and climate change as well as national security issues are driving the push to conserve energy and become less dependent on foreign oil. Second, the recession that began in 2007 turned the spotlight on the consumption patterns of Americans. Our savings rate had fallen into the negative zone as we borrowed against the equity in our homes to buy boats, electronics, the latest hot trends in clothes, gas-hungry SUVs, and crossovers—generally whatever we wanted until we reached our credit limits. And when we did, some of us just got another credit card. Whereas our great-grandparents may have darned a hole in a sock, shortened a hem on a dress, or had their shoes resoled, we just tossed out old items and bought new ones.

New Energy for America

Certainly a number of Americans did practice "recycle, reuse, reduce" since the first Earth Day in 1970, but the nation as a whole had not embraced the mantra of conservationists and environmentalists until the recent recession—which brings us to the third point. The election of Barack Obama in 2008 served to crystallize the need to do something about our profligate attitude toward the environment. As a candidate, President Obama had promised to reduce the nation's dependence on nonrenewable sources of energy and fight climate change. As President, he launched his "New Energy for America" program that is intended to

- "Chart a new energy future: . . . by embracing alternative and renewable energy, ending our addiction to foreign oil, addressing the global climate crisis, and creating millions of new jobs that can't be shipped overseas."

- "Invest in clean, renewable energy: To achieve our goal of generating 25 percent of our energy from renewable sources by 2025, we will make unprecedented investments in clean, renewable energy—solar, wind, biofuels, and geothermal power."
- "Fight climate change: We will invest in energy efficiency and conservation, two sure-fire ways to decrease deadly pollution and drive down demand. . . ."

The 2009 Stimulus Plan

Within a month of Obama's inauguration, Congress passed a $787-billion stimulus package, officially called the American Recovery and Reinvestment Act (ARRA) of 2009, to help the nation dig itself out of the recession. One goal of the act was to put the nation on the course to achieve the President's energy plan for the nation, including creating 3.5 million "green jobs." Among the programs included in the stimulus package were the following:

- $32 billion to transform the nation's energy transmission, distribution, and production system
- $6 billion to weatherize low-income homes
- $16 billion to repair and retrofit public housing for energy efficiency
- $30 billion for highway construction
- $31 billion to modernize federal and other public buildings for energy efficiency
- $19 billion for clean water, flood control, and environmental restoration
- $10 billion for transit and rail expansion
- $20 billion for health information technology
- $1.5 billion for biomedical research
- $3.95 billion for the Workforce Investment Act, which includes money available to community colleges for worker-training programs

- $25 billion in Recovery Zone bonds to states with high unemployment rates for job training, infrastructure construction and repair, and economic development
- $20 billion in tax incentives for installing solar and wind systems in homes and businesses

In July 2009, the President proposed another $12 billion to fund workforce training through the nation's network of community colleges. In his speech at Macomb Community College in Warren, Michigan, Obama said, "This is training to install solar panels and build those wind turbines and develop a smarter electricity grid. And this is the kind of education that more and more Americans are using to improve their skills and broaden their horizons." (http://www.whitehouse.gov/the_press_office/Remarks-by-the-President-on-the-American-Graduation-Initiative-in-Warren-MI/)

Focusing much of the stimulus package on energy conservation, infrastructure, and work force training has meant an immediate impact on people's lives. It has also helped to reorient our thinking about how the choices we make about food, clothing, housing, and the use of discretionary income affect others and the environment.

About Committing to Climate Change

". . . Colleges and universities must exercise their leadership in their communities and throughout society by modeling ways to eliminate global warming emissions, and by providing the knowledge and the educated graduates to achieve climate neutrality. . . ."
—The Signatories of the American College & University Presidents' Climate Commitment

2010 and Beyond

ARRA funding was structured so that grants to states and research institutes continued throughout 2010. Many of the awards went for development of renewable energy resources such as biofuel, wind, and solar power systems. The Department of Energy (DOE) also announced several loan guarantees in the millions and even a billion dollars to underwrite the construction of new power plants by private companies.

By investing in energy research, developing power systems based on that research, and then constructing devices and systems to enable consumers to tap into those power sources, the nation underscores its obligation to be a good steward of the environment, create jobs, and to expand the economy—a win-win for everyone, even the polar bears.

Where to Look for More Information

To find out more about federal energy programs, visit the U.S. Department of Energy, the Department of Transportation, and the Environmental Protection Agency Web sites:

> www.doe.gov
> www.dot.gov
> www.epa.gov

To find what your state is doing to reduce energy consumption and support the environment, go online to www.state.<insert state abbreviation>.us

For example for New Jersey, it would be:

> www.state.nj.us.

Check the state's home page as well as its environmental protection agency or department and its department of transportation.

Greenest Places to Live and Work in the United States

Every year, a number of magazines and Web sites report on the top 10, 25, or 50 greenest places to live in the United States. The criteria for what makes a city "green" vary somewhat from source to source, but, in general, criteria include factors such as the following:

- Air and water quality
- Amount of mass transit
- Green initiatives
- Level of alternative energy use
- Number of green-certified buildings
- Recycling and waste reduction programs

No two sources assign the same ratings to criteria, but there are similarities in the listings of green cities, as you can see from the following lists of green "big" cities:

From the National Resources Defense Council:

1. Seattle, Washington
2. San Francisco, California
3. Portland, Oregon
4. Oakland, California
5. San Jose, California
6. Austin, Texas
7. Sacramento, California
8. Boston, Massachusetts
9. Denver, Colorado
10. Chicago, Illinois

From *MSN City Guides:*

1. Austin, Texas
2. Berkeley, California
3. Boston, Massachusetts
4. Chicago, Illinois
5. Minneapolis, Minnesota
6. New York City, New York
7. Philadelphia, Pennsylvania
8. Portland, Oregon
9. San Francisco, California
10. Seattle, Washington

The U.S. Green Building Council compiled a list of the top cities with the most LEED-certified buildings:

1. Chicago, Illinois: 88
2. Portland, Oregon: 73
3. Seattle, Washington: 63
4. Washington, D.C.: 57
5. Atlanta, Georgia: 53
6. San Francisco, California: 50
7. New York City, New York: 46
8. Grand Rapids, Michigan: 44
9. Los Angeles, California: 40
10. Boston, Massachusetts: 38

ESSAYS ON THE IMPORTANCE OF SUSTAINABILITY

TEACHING THE CONCEPTS OF GREEN BUILDING TO ALL STUDENTS: A CALL TO ACTION

by Julia Feder, LEED Green Associate,
Director, Educational Technology, U.S. Green Building Council

Amy Seif Hattan, Director of Strategic Initiatives, Second Nature

Ashka Naik, Program Manager, Advancing Green Building Initiative,
Second Nature

How will we ensure that current and future generations will be healthy and have strong, secure, thriving communities and economic opportunity for all?

Create a Foundation

Buildings and communities set the foundation for an increasingly urbanized, global population. At the most basic level, these structures provide shelter and protection. In increasingly complex scenarios, the design, construction, operation, and occupancy of both new and retrofitted buildings and communities can model a sustainable paradigm for the structure of our social systems—from college campuses to suburban neighborhoods and urban centers.

The planning, design, construction, and operations of buildings and communities can aptly exemplify the intersection of sustainability's three tenets as they:

- Reduce the ecological footprint of the built environment.
- Produce healthy, vibrant places for people to live and work.
- Make sound economic sense by reducing the cost to operate and maintain these spaces.

As pioneers of innovation and often trendsetters within our society, higher education serves as a critical leverage point for making education about sustainability a part of every student's academic course. The goal is simple and attainable: Today's students will emerge from higher education institutions as leaders of the green economy. They will be the innovators and the problem solvers, building thriving communities, new economic opportunities, and a healthy regenerative environment.

What Is Sustainable Building Education?

Increasingly, colleges and universities are embracing sustainable design, construction, and building operation and maintenance as an essential element of their plans to "go green," achieve carbon neutrality, and fulfill sustainability commitments. However, the construction and operation of sustainable buildings can only take us part way to answering the questions of both today's and tomorrow's generations. How do we make sure the students, faculty, and staff living, learning, and working in these buildings and on these campuses recognize, understand, and practice the foundational principles of sustainable building? How can the members of today's campus communities become the leaders and spokespeople for building and maintaining strong, sustainable communities tomorrow? How do we ensure that today's students have the proficiency needed to enter the growing green workforce?

Sustainable building education cannot be divorced from the broad teachings of ecological literacy, which imparts the values and knowledge necessary to understand construction, renovation, and operations as mechanisms functioning within a larger system that determines human health, quality of life, and biodiversity. Ecological literacy, or "Education for Sustainability," which encompasses the three-legged stool of ecology, economics, and society, is the lens through which students will bring sustainable building education into their professional and personal lives. Lessons in sustainable building education start with this wider perspective but must also impart more specific concepts pertaining to the built environment.

Education for sustainability addresses broad concepts, but it also represents a shift in the educational methods by: (1) setting the *context of education* in a foundation of human/environment interdependence, values and ethics; (2) ensuring the *content of learning* reflects interdisciplinary, systems thinking across professional fields; and (3) developing a *process of education* that is grounded in active, experiential, inquiry-based learning and real-world problem solving.

With these processes in mind, sustainable building education specifically provides students with the skills and knowledge needed to

- Speak the language of sustainable building.
- Understand the systems behind a sustainable built environment.
- Make informed decisions about building design and operation.

As all students are exposed to education about sustainable building, they will develop problem solving and critical thinking skills. As students acquire these skills, they will be prepared to meet the great challenges of this century, understand and apply smart solutions to help solve complex problems, and be ready to enter a newly defined professional landscape.

A Call to Action

Despite the growing opportunities in green professions and the promise of sustainable building to reduce and avert impacts of climate change, few colleges and universities are educating all students about how sustainability applies to the built environment. Most of the best practices for teaching the concepts of sustainable building now lie within the specialized niche of design programs and schools, but even there, much progress is still needed.

Ironically, many schools have the tools for educating their students about sustainable building, but these resources are not being fully utilized. According to the U.S. Green Building Council (USGBC), colleges and universities are registering their buildings for LEED certification at an average rate of growth of 82 percent a year. These buildings are tangible demonstrations of the concepts of sustainable building and provide a great educational opportunity for students, if the buildings are used as teachers.

Institutions of higher education must utilize their physical resources and the increasing green building expertise of administrators and faculty and staff members to educate all students—in a wide range of disciplines—in the basic concepts of sustainable building. In return, with these learning opportunities, students will gain the knowledge and skills that they need to be proficient building occupants, informed professionals, and responsible citizens in an era of climate change. A scan of current practices at higher education institutions in this regard revealed a suite of best practices for sustainable building education—strategies that can be applied at any college and university and across disciplines. Practical strategies for integrating sustainable building curriculum throughout higher education include the following:

Strategy #1: Integrate sustainable building principles into course work. Schools across the country have revamped existing curriculum and created new courses to address growing student demand. Successful curriculum reorientation efforts typically reach across multiple disciplines. These courses emulate the holistic approach to understanding challenges, principles, and solutions sustainable building encapsulates.

Strategy #2: Introduce service learning requirements. Community and residential projects teach students the benefits of sustainable buildings and development, as well as provide opportunities to work with sustainable building industry experts. In addition, academic courses imbedded with service learning components have the potential to disseminate awareness and teach practical skills.

Strategy #3: Apply real-world problem solving. At colleges and universities, student competitions and experiential learning opportunities such as internships and research programs are platforms that offer real-world understanding of the sustainable building techniques and tools. Using the campus as a teaching tool allows students to get their hands on sustainable building projects, while furthering institutional initiatives.

Strategy #4: Connect higher education with future employers. Connecting colleges and universities with future employers provides students, faculty, and administrators with an authentic framework to understand concepts. Innovative programs can expose students to sustainable building and other sustainability topics through internships, practicums, or simply opportunities to interact with experts in the field, thus enabling them to find their niche in the competitive job market.

Strategy #5: Learn from what others are doing. In many ways, the United States has been slower to integrate these approaches into academic curriculum than other countries. Exploring the creative initiatives undertaken around the world can help form strategies for the integration of sustainable building lessons into the educational experience in the United States.

Higher education institutions from Maine to New Mexico are experimenting with new strategies and approaches to integrating sustainable building principles into their curriculum. The full text from which this essay has been adapted includes numerous examples and case studies, providing detailed accounts of successful efforts on campuses throughout the world.

On a daily basis, we must face the unprecedented crossroads we are at today. With biodiversity in decline and consumption rising steadily, the crucial question we must ask ourselves is: What can I do to build thriving communities and ensure economic opportunity for all, both today and tomorrow? This is arguably the greatest challenge human civilization has ever faced, and higher education institutions are poised to be the innovators of a sustainable response.

It is obvious that we need a transformative shift in the way we think and act. *Teaching the Concepts of Sustainable Building to All Students* is the first step in the process of developing strategies specific to an education that highlights the built environment as a critical piece of achieving sustainability. We invite you to work with us on this important effort. To get involved, please read the full text this essay was adapted from at www.campusgreenbuilder.org/Curriculum.

Julia Feder is the Director of Educational Technology for the U.S. Green Building Council (USGBC) and leads USGBC's efforts to bring high-quality, green building education to broad audiences, utilizing dynamic delivery platforms and technology resources. Julia has supervised the development of green building case studies and a variety of publications, and she led USGBC's efforts to support the integration of green building and sustainability concepts into K–12, undergraduate, and graduate curriculum in 2008–09. Prior to joining USGBC, Julia worked with the Missouri Botanical Garden EarthWays Center in St. Louis, coordinating the organization's sustainability education programs for K–12, higher education, and adult audiences. Julia has also taught fourth grade and helped start a farmers' market serving an urban neighborhood. Julia holds a Master of Science in Environmental Studies from Antioch University New England and a B.A. from the University of Michigan.

Amy Seif Hattan is Director of Strategic Initiatives at Second Nature. She directs the program to advance green building among under-resourced higher education institutions and has developed new initiatives in renewable energy and other areas. She has over twelve years' experience working in the field of environmental sustainability. Amy was the sustainability coordinator for Middlebury College and had earlier worked to initiate the sustainability program at the University of New Hampshire. At Middlebury, Amy advanced green building and provided leadership on addressing climate change. She was formally a senior research associate at Rocky Mountain Institute and a science writer for the Institute for the Study of Earth, Oceans, and Space, which houses the Climate Change Research Center. While working with Dennis Meadows of Limits to Growth, she co-authored the workbook, Creating High Performance Teams for Sustainable Development. *Amy has a Master in Public Administration degree from the Harvard University Kennedy School of Government and a master's degree in journalism and mass communications from the University of Wisconsin–Madison. She earned a B.S. in environmental conservation at the University of New Hampshire.*

Ashka Naik joined Second Nature in January 2009 as a program manager for the Advancing Green Building in Higher Education Initiative, which helps build the capacity of under-resourced colleges and universities to construct and renovate campus green buildings that can also serve as community models for sustainability. Before joining Second Nature, she worked for the Office for Sustainability (OFS) at Harvard University where she acted as Project Coordinator for the High Performance Building Services. Ashka has worked extensively in India and the UK for last ten years on various building design and research projects. Following her passion for sustainability issues in the developing countries, in 2007 she co-founded a sustainable design company (Artha Studio) in India that works on community development projects addressing social justice and environmental wellbeing. Ashka received her bachelor's degree in interior architecture from the Center for Environmental Planning and Technology (India), and a Master of Arts in Product Design from the Birmingham Institute of Art and Design (UK).

FORM, FUNCTION, AND THOSE WITHIN

How Green Buildings are Revolutionizing Our Experience in the Work Environment

by Jennifer Berry, Public & Strategic Relations Manager, Earth911.com

Sustainability. Green. Eco-friendly. Environmentally conscious.

Of all the words that portray the worldwide movement towards more ecologically sound living, "thoughtful" is an often overlooked phrase.

The concept of thoughtfulness in this arena moves beyond typical applications, opening a new door to considering how our everyday actions and decisions contribute to our quality of life and the health of our environment.

With almost a quarter of our time spent at our places of work, the marriage of design and ecology is becoming an increasingly crucial element of construction, to say the least. Recent research shows that the U.S. green building market is set to grow 146 percent by 2013 from 2009 levels. This could move the sector into a market worth of $128 billion.

A landmark study by CB Richard Ellis and the University of San Diego found that tenants in green buildings (such as LEED-certified or Energy Star–labeled buildings) experienced increased productivity and fewer sick days. According to the report, "natural light, good ventilation, and the absence of organic compounds ensure happier, healthier workers."[1]

In addition, businesses within these structures see added benefits, as "public image, recruitment and retention of employees are enhanced in green buildings."

Deliberate Design

Earth911.com is no stranger to green spaces. Moving into LEED Silver-certified SkySong, the Arizona State University Scottsdale Innovation Center, allowed our company an ideal opportunity to try green building and design for ourselves.

Tony Ash, operations director, was tasked with creating an eco-conscious space that aligned our organization's goals with our new office setting.

Ash's design carefully considered, above all other elements, the overall well-being of the people who would use it on a daily basis and the tasks they would be carrying out.

"When planning a green office move or remodel, the primary concern should be for the individuals working within the space, how they will interact with the space and materials, and how the space and materials will interact with them," said Ash. "With an emphasis on the latter, planning for environmental sustainability comes organically. We are what we eat and breathe, after all."

This attention to form and function created a symbiotic relationship between our staff and our office, rather than a forced, traditional work environment typically not conducive to creative endeavors.

---

[1]*CB Richard Ellis and Burnham-Moores, Center for Real Estate, University of San Diego. Do Green Buildings Make Dollars and Sense? USD-BMC Working Paper 09-11. Draft: November 6, 2009. http://catcher.sandiego.edu/items/business/Do_Green_Buildings_Make_Dollars_and_Sense_draft_Nov_6_2009.pdf.*

Common Misconceptions

There are some challenges, however, to continuing to advance this "thoughtful" design concept. However, through research and the cooperation of contractors, Ash found there is more flexibility in green materials than may be apparent at first blush. "There are so many options available for every type of material and product, that my creativity was almost entirely uninhibited," said Ash.

"Office furniture, flooring, and wall covering manufacturers seem to have realized a few years ago that to remain competitive they would need to start creating 'green' product lines," he added.

However, with the creation of an increasing number of product lines marketed as 'green,' careful attention to detail is key. "There seems to be an ever growing mass of buildings, products, and materials claiming to be 'green,' but when you look past the label, they are not," said Ash. "That being said, the most important lesson I learned was to do some of my own research and double-check things. Reading past the label and seeking independent, third-party opinions helped immensely."

Beyond a perceived restriction in available materials to execute design, cost is often misconstrued as prohibitive to eco-friendly construction as well. This concept, however, is rapidly changing, with many environmentally friendly product lines gaining traction in the market, subsequently lowering their price points. And although some green upgrades may still run as much as 5 to 10 percent higher than their traditional counterparts, their long-term benefits generally overshadow this initial investment. For example, replacing twenty traditional light bulbs with energy-efficient compact fluorescents can save $800 over their collective lifetime, yielding a return on investment of over 133 percent[2].

Real Results

Since this redesign, our company has grown, evolved, focused, and become more cohesive in our mission and work efforts.

Coincidence? Perhaps. But we would like to think that these marked improvements are not only a product of our hard work and diligence, but also of the freedom to think organically that our new space allows.

Earth911.com is an environmental services company that addresses product end-of-life solutions for businesses and consumers.

Jennifer Berry works in public relations, social media, sales, and editorial for Earth911.com. Joining the team in 2008, she utilizes her love for writing and communications in a number of facets to support the company's growth and reach into new arenas.

Jennifer also enjoys an active, green lifestyle outside of work, including swimming, cycling, hiking and being vegan. After completing a double-major in Psychology and Public Relations from Baylor University, Jennifer continues to explore the relationship between people and the environment, both at work and home.

[2]GREENandSAVE.com. Master ROI Table. http://www.greenandsave.com/master_roi_table.html

GREEN JOBS FOR THE INTERIOR DESIGNER

Deborah J. Hanson, ASID, AUID, Project & Environmental Coordinator, University of Arizona, Residence Life

Professional interior designers utilize their education, experience, and examination to protect and enhance the health, life safety, and welfare of the public. This means they create interior spaces that are not just aesthetically pleasing, but also functional and safe. Utilizing sustainable green products is becoming a norm for designers and will be even more important in the future. We spend approximately 80 to 90 percent of our time indoors. Therefore, interior designers must understand the importance of air quality and circulation, temperature control, ergonomic layout, effects from lighting, off-gassing, and other related matters in regard to the interior environment. In doing so, resources must be considered that are capable of being continued with minimal long-term effects on the environment.

While the main concern of an interior designer may appear to be how different colors, textures, furniture, and space work together to meet the needs of a building's occupants, all interior designers' knowledge in today's world—and the future—must expand into the green and sustainable field. Similar to the medical field where a doctor cannot be expected to be an expert in every area, with the introduction of green and sustainable design, the interior design field is also making a shift to specialization.

One area of specialization for interior designers is building space—usually residential or commercial or specialty areas such as lighting, kitchen and bath, or closet design. Green design is increasing in popularity. Green design for these spaces involves selecting furniture, flooring materials, and other interior finishes that are hypoallergenic and free of chemicals. It includes selecting construction materials that are energy-efficient or are made from renewable resources. Extensive knowledge of green design will be in demand and incorporated into design fields such as health care, hotels, resorts, restaurants, casinos, conference facilities, public buildings, homes, spas and exercise facilities, outdoor living spaces, and indoor gardens.

One third of today's interior designers are working in a specialized design field. With the employment of interior designers expected to grow anywhere from 14 to 19 percent between now and 2018, green design jobs and expertise in the "green" field will become a norm. There is an increasing interest in interior design and its benefits; therefore, we should see an increased demand for interior designers. Businesses are beginning to realize the improvements that can be made for workers and customer satisfaction created through good design and the implementation of a healthy environment. As this knowledge increases, more interior designers should be hired to redesign offices and stores. In addition, the general public's growing awareness of environmental quality along with the number of individuals developing allergies and asthma will no doubt help to increase the demand for environmentally savvy interior designers. Interior designers with formal training or experience in green and energy-efficient design will certainly have better job prospects. And, as interest in the design field continues to grow, there will be keen competition. It is clear that it will become essential for the designer to be either LEED (Leadership in Energy and Environmental Design) accredited or certified by other environmental credentials to work in the area of green and sustainable design.

I believe that niches for interior designers will be created not only by our environment but by our population. As the Baby Boomer generation grows older, demand of interior design services from the health-care industry is expected to be high. As new facilities will be built for this generation, interior designers will be charged with providing a healthy environment for them—and generations to come.

As healthy living and working interior environments become more important, you can expect to see an increase of specialization within the interior design field. The American Recovery and Reinvestment Act was just the beginning. The U.S. Green Building Council recently released a Top 10 list of green building legislation in the House and Senate. As these Federal bills, along with state and local bills, have greater impacts on the environment, design professionals will need to demonstrate their expertise in improving indoor environmental quality to maintain a competitive edge in their career field. For example, if you were to ask most people, including designers, if bamboo flooring is an environmentally good product to install, most of them would say "yes." The correct answer is both yes and no. The designer needs to be aware that many sources for bamboo actually introduce more toxins into the interior of a space than hardwood products. This is just one example of how specialization of interior designers will become necessary in the future.

As it becomes more important to utilize more natural daylight within interior spaces, there will also be an increased need for interior designers with lighting expertise. Understanding the measurement of light within each space and how it is impacted by different materials will be essential, along with the understanding of the impact of occupants' behavior. Knowing how to optimize energy performance with lighting control systems will play a strong role for the interior designer who wants to work in the green field of design. Knowing how to select lighting that maximizes the efficiency of a building's HVAC system, along with creating carbon emission credits, will benefit the designer who is looking for a specialty niche.

Another area of specialization for an interior designer is with HVAC systems and the usage of live plants. Most designers know the general benefits of live plants in terms of their filtering the air within a space, and most designers will utilize plants to provide an aesthetic quality. With so many people spending so much time indoors, the air quality within these areas is crucial. What many designers may not understand is the impact of certain plants within an environment. Not all plants are good for our indoor environments, and some can even produce extremely harmful toxins into the air or when touched. A designer in this field will need the knowledge to ensure that plants providing the healthiest filtration system for the space will be utilized. The designer who can combine this understanding with knowledge of HVAC systems and air circulation will be able to provide his or her client with an indoor space free of toxins and pollutants. This literal green niche is another great area for interior designers to develop their unique talents.

Recycling is also a sustainable avenue for interior designers to consider—whether it involves recycling certain materials and offering them for reuse or actually reusing items as design elements within a space. The development of stores for the collection of salvaged materials and reclaimed products is only beginning to be tapped, and this is yet another avenue for a designer to pursue.

To ensure the health, welfare, and safety of those who may live or work in the building space the interior designer is creating, he or she has to know the products that are involved. A well-educated designer knows whether a manufacturer is truly "green," or whether the company is simply greenwashing its practices—misleading consumers regarding the environmental practices and benefits of a product or service. Thus it is essential for the interior designer to have accredited specialties.

As described in this article, the world of interior design is evolving and developing new facets in the new green economy. Interior designers have new opportunities and can make a tremendous difference in their clients' lives. New green specialties are out there and are in demand. Whether it involves natural lighting, the use of plants, or placement of recycled materials, interior designers play an important role in creating indoor living environments that promote the health of individuals, as well as the health of our planet today and for generations to come.

Debbie Hanson is the interior designer for Facility Operations in Residence Life at the University of Arizona. She has spent the last seventeen years in Residence Life managing design projects from initial concept to final completion. In addition, Debbie developed a program to walk through residence halls on a regular basis with maintenance and custodial managers to ensure the buildings are clean and well maintained and that no furniture, fixtures, and equipment (FF&E) items are damaged or missing. Debbie is a professional member of the American Society of Interior Designers (ASID) and the Association of University Interior Designers (AUID). She also enjoys being part of the jury team for the National Council for Interior Design Qualification (NCIDQ) exam. After many years of travel during her husband's career in the Air Force, Debbie is happy to call Tucson, Arizona, home.

SUSTAINABILITY: A PARADIGM, NOT A PRACTICE

by Robert Fleming, Director, Sustainable Design Program,
Philadelphia University

In 2005, Hurricane Katrina ravaged New Orleans, gasoline prices hit $3 per gallon, President Bush declared that the United States must "end its addiction to foreign oil," and Al Gore's movie *An Inconvenient Truth* all combined to radically reshape how our society views its relationship to the natural world, to each other, and to shake the very foundations of western thought. These four profound events marked the end of the industrial age and the beginning of the age of ecology. In 2005, sustainability stopped being an esoteric and elitist concept and became an accepted tenant within the collective conscious of our society. The great recession of 2007, the Massey coal mine explosion, and the Gulf oil spill of 2010 have further heightened the public's perception of the importance of sustainability. The business world is taking notice with increasing commitments to carbon neutrality, full life-cycle accountability, and triple bottom line thinking. Sustainability has moved from the superficial pages of marketing brochures to the threshold of widespread implementation by corporate culture. On the surface, it would seem that career opportunities would abound in the new green economy, but before jumping in, there are several key knowledge sets that must be in place before making the leap:

1. Sustainability is a paradigm, not a practice. This means that simply deciding to be sustainable is not enough. Job-seekers must begin with a mind shift to embrace sustainability as a holistic model that is radically reshaping our natural, economic, and civic systems.

2. Green training does not necessarily equal green jobs. While the public sector is moving forward to prepare future workers for new opportunities, the slow economy has compromised the ability of the private sector to create enough jobs for everyone who has been trained.

3. Gaining education should be done carefully and with a plan. While passing the LEED® exam is certainly a step forward, it will not be enough to separate you from the masses—many of whom passed the exam years back when the test was easier.

4. If the goal is to find employment with a decidedly dedicated green company, employers can identify a padded resume a mile away. Just saying that you are "eager to learn" is not enough, as it costs firms significant investment in training new employees.

5. Volunteer experiences are a key route to gaining workforce credibility in the sustainability market. Doing work for your local green building council or local environmental group will help. Traveling to Haiti or other significant contributions are highly prized.

6. Remember that green jobs are still jobs. Many young green job-seekers enter the market starry eyed and excited about the prospect of "doing good for the world" and getting paid, but work is still work. It's important to maintain the vision while digging trenches for rain gardens.

7. For some, a master's degree is a good route, but it is recommended to wait a few years before going directly for a degree. However, if persistent unemployment continues to exist, direct enrollment in a master's degree program may be necessary.

8. Not all master's degrees are created equal. When looking for a degree program, step clear of courses that look like the same courses a university has always offered but with a twist of sustainability. Better find sustainability programs that started from scratch. Remember:

Sustainability is a paradigm. Twentieth-century educational approaches simply don't work for the twenty-first century. Find the educational innovators, visit their programs, and attempt to ascertain whether sustainability is taught as an add-on to existing curricula or if the program is truly embracing the paradigm of sustainability. Beware of programs stating, "Sustainability is integrated into our curriculum." This is a tell-tale sign of trouble, as it is impossible to integrate a holistic concept such as sustainability into a typical curriculum that fostered unsustainable behavior throughout the twentieth century.

In conclusion, our society has entered the new millennium and with that has a come a new and powerful worldview that sees humanity as part of nature and our activities as not only non-damaging, but regenerative. It tells us that things don't have to be done the way they were done before simply for the sake of convenience, but rather that hard work and perseverance can have a legitimate and long-lasting impact. Women's rights and civil rights marked the contribution of the previous generation; before that, World War II was the call to action. Today, our society is heeding the call to action by contributing our time, our creativity, and our energy to restoring the health and vitality of the Earth in order to create a higher and more sustainable quality of life—not just for the affluent class but for everyone. This is a noble vision to be sure, but one worth fighting for and certainly one worth getting a weekly paycheck, a roof over the head, and three square meals per day.

Rob Fleming is a registered architect and LEED® Accredited Professional who founded and directs the Master of Science in Sustainable Design Program at Philadelphia University. This trans-disciplinary program accepts students from a wide variety of backgrounds including engineering, construction, design, business, and more. The Sustainable Design Program, now entering its fourth year, has seen a dramatic increase in the number of students and great success in job placement; it is also gaining a foothold in the new academic realm of sustainability.

THE TRIPLE BOTTOM LINE OF SUSTAINABILITY

by Alyce Engle, Environmental Health & Safety Director,
Skanska USA Building Inc., Oakland, California

When I grew up, we were only beginning to understand what it meant to be good stewards of the environment. It was not until I went to work that I understood how I could personally affect it.

I didn't always work for a progressively minded construction firm. In fact, at my first job in the 1980s, I found myself at a Class I hazardous waste landfill in the Environmental Department. As you might imagine, I was exposed to a lot of environmental issues at a hazardous waste landfill. My experiences there drove me to begin taking university courses that were directly related to environmental issues, such as groundwater contamination, air quality, hazardous waste, and more.

The seeds were planted. I felt empowered. The more I learned, the more interested I became in teaching my family how to conserve as a means of contributing positively to a future society. I knew that American grassroots efforts to promote conservation, much like I started to do in my home, can help change our culture from one of consumption to one of sustainability. For real change to take place, I realized that businesses had to be empowered to do the same … all without affecting the bottom line.

At Skanska, we often talk about the "triple bottom line" of sustainability. It's more than a catchphrase, though. This bottom line looks, of course, at the dollars-and-cents business case for being green. And, obviously, there is a strong environmental aspect to sustainability. But at Skanska, we consider the social responsibility that people working in business will have to address in the years to come. For instance, when you consider the topic of climate change, it usually sparks a passionate, heated debate. However, this is an example of "environmental" and "social" aspects of the triple bottom line framed around a flashpoint issue that misses the real point.

Here in California, as in many other areas of the country, water quality and quantity is a major issue. There is a strong environmental case to be made to conserve water. After all, clean water is a basic need—and we don't have enough of it. But there is also a social responsibility that businesses need to address. The rules of supply and demand say that if water demand increases (as California's population certainly will) and the water resource diminishes (as it will through use by more and more people), the price of water will eventually go up. How high a price do businesses want to pay for water, or any another limited natural resource? How will we support growth, both in population and—to the business case—economically if we cannot *sustain* growth?

In 1995, my career transitioned to the waste and recycling industry where I learned which materials could be profitably recycled and how the local municipalities work with recycling service providers to ensure residential and commercial waste is recycled at levels required by state regulations. During that time, I learned that businesses could place recycling containers in place of trash containers, diverting trash from the landfill, but also eliminating the business overhead cost of disposal.

Along the way, I added safety to my area of expertise in managing environmental issues in waste, recycling, readymix concrete, and mining. Through an industry associate, and now long-time friend, I found myself at Skanska. Skanska is a large construction company with local offices around the country. We build everything from hospitals to college campuses. Our civil construction unit has built highways and bridges you've probably driven on. It is possible you are reading this article in a library on a campus we have worked on.

At Skanska, we are very proud of our commitment to protecting the environment. Skanska doesn't just talk about environmental stewardship; we hold a Certificate of Registration in conformance to the ISO 14001:2004 standard. This means a lot of things, but it also means that, every year, Skanska is audited to ensure the highest level of environmental practices. We also have a comprehensive Environmental Policy that includes a commitment to continuously improve through internal assessments, management review, and the prevention of environmental pollution, as well as through a commitment to comply with relevant environmental legislation, regulations, and customer requirements. It is through the Environmental Policy and strong commitment from the leadership at Skanska that we have built a culture rich in environmental ethics and focus on sustainability.

This is reflected in the way we choose the right kinds of materials in advance of construction, manage our projects so that we eliminate the potential for a hazardous material release, recycle during demolition and construction, and choose subcontractors and service providers that have the same environmental values as Skanska and the clients we serve.

Most businesses understand there are clear holistic benefits of not harming our environment. However, we have just now reached a point economically in business where we recognize that natural resources are no longer unlimited. This is reflected in the price of consumer goods and supplies, the cost of environmental remediation, and the economic downfall we are now facing worldwide. Through working closely with our clients, Skanska advises them on how to lower overhead operating costs through water and energy efficiency achieved by using environmental building strategies such as building orientation to take advantage of sunlight or harvesting rainwater for use in landscape irrigation or toilets.

It should come as no surprise to today's students that sustainability is found in every career. From where I sit, I recommend that one not focus solely on sustainability, but on sustainability in career, home, and family. Whether students aspire to become a veterinarian or a commercial builder, they should also become an expert in how their chosen career will impact the environment in areas such as procurement of supplies, implementing the service or operation, and finally disposing or recycling of the waste generated as a result of the job, while finding ways to do it so that they can reap not only the holistic benefits, but the very real business benefits as well.

Alyce Engle is a LEED AP, CHST and holds a Certificate in Environmental Auditing. She is the Environmental Health and Safety (EHS) Director for Skanska USA Building, Inc, based in Oakland, California. Alyce chairs Skanska's Environmental Leadership Team, manages Skanska's national ISO 14001 and OHSAS 18001 Certification programs, and, with her team of EHS professionals, manages EHS activities on Skanska's construction projects in California.

Skanska USA is one of the largest, most financially sound construction networks in the country consisting of four business units: Skanska USA Building, which specializes in building construction; Skanska USA Civil, which is focused on civil infrastructure; Skanska Infrastructure Development, which develops public-private partnerships; and, Skanska Commercial Development, which pursues commercial development initiatives in select U.S. markets. Headquartered in New York with thirty-three offices across the country, Skanska USA has approximately 7,000 employees.

HOW TO USE THIS GREEN CAREER GUIDE

Peterson's Green Careers in Building and Landscaping contains a wealth of information for anyone interested in a career in the green building and building industry. This book includes an extensive number of great green careers and the undergraduate, graduate, or training programs that can lead to these green careers. The following section details what you will find in each part of this book.

PART I: PROFESSIONAL AND SKILLED JOBS

Part I is divided into five chapters:

- Chapter 1: Building Design and Construction Jobs
- Chapter 2: Installation, Operations, and Energy Efficiency Jobs
- Chapter 3: Commercial, Industrial, and Residential Design Jobs
- Chapter 4: Landscaping, Groundskeeping, and Turf Care Jobs
- Chapter 5: Policy, Analysis, Advocacy, and Regulatory Affairs Jobs

The different jobs featured represent a variety of interests, education, and training.

As you read through Part I, you will see that occupations may be designated as "Bright Outlook" and/ or "Green New and Emerging" or "Green Enhanced-Skills" occupations. These are categories used by O*NET, which stands for Occupational Information Network (O*NET), a joint effort of the U.S. Department of Labor/Employment and Training Administration (USDOL/ETA) and the North Carolina Employment Security Commission. "Bright Outlook" occupations are those that are expected to have a large number of new job openings, and "Green" jobs are those that require enhanced or new skill sets because technology, sustainability, and economic incentives are changing the nature of the occupation. The estimates of job growth and job opportunities between 2008 and 2018 are based on data and projections of the U.S. Bureau of Labor Statistics.

Details on industry overview, job trends, job duties, career paths, earning potential, education and licensure, and trade and professional organizations follow each job listed. Information on how the information was obtained for each of these sections—and what this data means to you as a job seeker—can be found at the beginning of Part I.

PART II: COLLEGES AND UNION ORGANIZATIONS WITH GREAT GREEN PROGRAMS

Chapters 6 and 7 describe innovative programs related to architecture, design, construction, and landscaping at both the undergraduate and graduate levels. Four-year colleges and universities are highlighted in Chapter 6. Chapter 7 features two-year schools. The programs were chosen to reflect a broad range of majors related to building, design, and landscaping topics across all regions of the country, public and private schools, and large and small schools. The "Fast Facts" feature in each profile underscores on-campus sustainability programs, awards that schools have won, research facilities, and other notable highlights of the schools' efforts to be good citizens of the local and global communities.

Chapter 8 contains information on union-training programs including apprenticeships for a variety of green jobs.

PART III: WORKFORCE TRAINING

Chapter 9 contains a list of the One-Stop Career Centers for training, job search, and career assistance information that are available in each of the fifty states and the District of Columbia. Under each state's name, you will find important contact information and a brief description of the job-related training services that each state offers. Information for veterans is highlighted.

PART IV: APPENDIXES

The appendixes in Part IV provide additional information that can help you in your search for a great green job. *Appendix A: Building, Design, and Landscaping Jobs by Industry* is a handy tool to help you navigate the jobs listed in Chapters 1 through 5. In addition to the main job title, the alternate job titles and related careers for each job are included. *Appendix B: Green Job Boards* lists some job boards that specialize in green industry jobs. *Appendix C: "Green" Your Vocabulary for a Sustainable Future* provides a list with definitions of many of the terms that you will find on TV and Websites and in magazines and newspapers that discuss the environment, sustainability, and renewable and alternative sources of energy. *Appendix D: Green Features in this Guide* provides an index of the interviews, feature articles, and "About" boxes that appear in this book, listed alphabetically and with page numbers.

SPECIAL FEATURES THROUGHOUT THIS GUIDE

All of the chapters in this guide also provide full-length features that offer tips on what you can do now to make a difference for the environment, where the greenest places are to live, how to find out if a potential employer is socially responsible, and how to dress fashionably in eco-friendly clothing, including clothes made from bamboo fiber (actually softer than rayon!). There are also features related specifically to building and landscaping such as the advantages of using native plants for landscaping, what LEED certification is, and what to consider in "greening" a bathroom, new and retrofit.

Chapters 1 through 5 also have informational interviews. Each chapter has at least two interviews with practitioners of careers described in the chapter. For example, Chapter 2, which is about energy efficiency, has an interview with a weatherization specialist, and Chapter 4, about landscaping and turfgrass care, includes an interview with a turfgrass specialist.

In addition, in shaded boxes throughout this guide, you will find useful information called "About . . ." that will help you find out what others are doing to live more eco-friendly lives and how to make your own life greener. Tips include where to recycle your old computer, cell phone, tennis balls, and even your sneakers; why you should be careful about how you fertilize your garden and lawn; and what community colleges, colleges, and universities are doing to commit to campus sustainability.

Some Numbers to Consider— Even in a Recession

- The commercial construction industry had revenue of $152 billion in 2009, according to ibisworld.com, an industry analyst.
- There were 438,000 new housing starts in May.
- The interior design industry had revenue of $11 billion in 2009, according to ibisworld.com.
- The landscaping services industry had revenues of $50 billion in 2008, according to Hoovers.com, an industry analyst group.
- 200 to 300 new golf courses a year are built according to the North Dakota State University's Sports and Urban Turfgrass Management program.

PART I

PROFESSIONAL AND SKILLED JOBS

CHAPTER 1

BUILDING DESIGN AND CONSTRUCTION JOBS

The *Occupational Outlook Handbook* reports that 9 million people were employed in the construction industry in 2008, and the number of jobs is predicted to increase by 19 percent by 2018. This number includes those who are employed by companies and those who are self-employed or work for family businesses.

About 64 percent of those who worked for companies were employed by contractors in specialty trades such as plumbing, heating and air conditioning, electrical, and masonry. Heavy and civil engineering construction employed about 77 percent of construction workers. About 23 percent worked in residential and nonresidential building construction.

Three factors are driving demand for construction workers in the short and long term:

- The nation's growing—and at the same time aging—population.
- The need to expand and improve housing and the nation's crumbling and insufficient infrastructure to bring them into line with the population changes.
- The funding from the American Recovery and Reinvestment Act (ARRA), also known as the stimulus package, to expand and improve the infrastructure and energy efficiency.

Heavy construction, including roads, bridges, and tunnels as well as repairs to existing highways and bridges, is expected to generate most of the demand for construction workers. However, green nonresidential and residential building should experience an increase in demand, even though construction of new residential and commercial buildings overall slowed during the recession that lasted from 2007 to 2009. As the economy continues to recover, the construction industry, especially the housing sector, is expected to bounce back.

In an April 2009 summary, the U.S. Green Building Council (USGBC) reported that green building is expected to more than double by 2013. Green building is projected to add $554 billion to the U.S. gross domestic product in the five-year period between 2009 and 2013. USGBC estimated in 2010, that if the nation committed to green building, some 2.5 million jobs could be added to the economy.

Major growth in nonresidential green building is expected in the education, office, and health-care sectors as well as increased demand in the government, industrial, hospitality, and retail sectors. Government initiatives along with increased interest in residential green building are encouraging energy-efficient, environmentally sustainable green construction. Remodeling of existing structures especially to retrofit them as green buildings is expected to generate additional demand for construction workers.

JOBS PROFILED HERE

The following occupations are profiled in this chapter:

- Architect
- Architectural Drafter
- Carpenter Helper
- Cement Mason/Concrete Finisher
- Civil Engineer
- Civil Engineering Technician
- Civil Drafter
- Construction Carpenter
- Construction Manager
- Construction Worker
- Cost Estimator
- Electrical Engineer
- Engineering Manager
- Operating Engineer/Construction Equipment Operator
- Pipefitter and Steamfitter
- Plumber
- Property/Real Estate/Community Association Manager
- Real Estate Agent
- Roofer
- Rough Carpenter
- Sheet Metal Worker
- Structural Iron and Steel Worker
- Surveyor
- Surveying Technician
- Welder, Cutter, and Welder Fitter

KEY TO UNDERSTANDING THE JOB PROFILES

The job profiles are classified according to one or more of the following categories:

⚙ Bright Outlook

☀ Green Occupation

The classifications "Bright Outlook" and "Green Occupation" are taken from the National Center for O*NET Development's O*NET OnLine job site. O*NET, which is sponsored by the U.S. Department of Labor/Employment and Training Administration (USDOL/ETA), has broken green jobs into three categories:

- Green Increased-Demand occupations
  - o These are occupations that are likely to see job growth, but the work and worker requirements are unlikely to experience significant changes.
- Green Enhanced-Skills occupations
  - o These occupations are likely to experience significant changes in work and worker requirements. Workers may find themselves doing new tasks requiring new knowledge, skills, and credentials. Current projections do not project increased demand for workers in these occupations, but O*NET notes that an increase is possible.
- Green New and Emerging occupations
  - o These are new occupations—not growth in existing jobs—that are created as a result of activity and technology in green sectors of the economy.

Video Links

We've provided easy-to-use links that will take you directly to a particular career video from the One-Stop Career System Multimedia Career Video Library at CareerOneStop.org. The links will look like this:

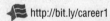 http://bit.ly/career1

Note that videos are not available for all jobs listed here. The videos come in QuickTime and Mpeg formats, with and without captions; download times may vary. CareerOneStop.org is sponsored by the U.S. Department of Labor/Employment and Training Administration.

Architect 🌐

Alternate Titles and Related Careers

- Architectural Engineer
- Architectural Engineering Consultant
- Architectural and Engineering Manager
- Architectural Project Manager
- Design Architect
- Green Building and Retrofit Architect
- Project Architect
- Project Manager
- Industrial Green Systems and Retrofit Designer

Architect is a "Green Enhanced-Skills" occupation with demand in green construction and also research, design, and consulting services.

 http://bit.ly/career15

Job Trends

The rate of job growth for architects is projected to be faster than average at 14 to 19 percent. In 2008, there were 141,000 architects, and job openings between then and 2018 are estimated to be 46,800. According to the *Occupational Outlook Handbook,* two main forces are driving the need for more architects, namely, population growth and the interest in eco-friendly "green" buildings—residential and commercial. Not only is the size of the population growing, but it is also aging, which results in the need for more health-care facilities, assisted-living complexes, nursing homes, and retirement communities. Population growth also leads to the need for more schools at all levels, kindergarten through university.

The interest in building or retrofitting existing construction to follow green design principles is also an important source of new jobs for architects. Green design, or sustainable design, emphasizes the efficient use of resources, including energy- and eco-friendly specifications and materials.

Nature of the Work

Architects design houses, schools, hospitals, office buildings, churches, college buildings, urban centers, and industrial parks. In addition to the structure itself, architects also design the electrical system; heating, air conditioning, and ventilation system; plumbing; and communication system. The structures must be safe, functional, and cost-effective. Architects work with many other professionals, such as engineers, landscape architects, interior designers, and urban planners.

In creating their plans, architects must consider federal, state, and local regulations; building codes; zoning laws; and fire codes. Much of their work is done using building information modeling (BIM) and computer-aided design (CAD). Their work also includes preparing reports, cost estimates, environmental impact studies, land-use studies, models and presentations for clients, and plans for regulatory approvals. During construction, architects monitor the work being done by construction contractors.

Green building and sustainable design require the expertise of architects. The U.S. Green Building Council LEED (Leadership in Energy and Environmental Design) building certification program includes credit for energy-efficient systems for heating and cooling, lighting, and water usage and disposal; clean renewable energy use; natural and sustainably produced materials; indoor air quality; innovative design; educating the people who use the building; location to transportation and services; and a sustainable site. This is a great deal of expertise for architects to master.

Based on the O*NET database, architects may also perform the following tasks:

- Consult with clients to determine functional and spatial requirements of the construction
- Integrate engineering elements such as the heating and air conditioning and wiring systems into the design
- Prepare scale drawings or direct staff in preparing drawings and specifications

- Plan layout of the project
- Prepare information regarding design, specifications, materials, color, equipment, estimated costs, and construction time
- Represent the client in obtaining bids and awarding contracts
- Prepare and administer contracts for contractors

Career Path

Architecture graduates usually begin a three-year intern program, working under the supervision of a licensed architect. After completing that program, they are eligible to take licensing exams. After passing the exams, they become licensed and gain responsibility for projects. With greater experience, they may become managers or partners in an architecture firm.

About 21 percent of architects are self-employed, and about 69 percent work for architectural, engineering, and related services companies according to the *Occupational Outlook Handbook*. The remainder work for construction firms and government agencies that deal with housing, community planning, and construction of government buildings.

Earning Potential

Median hourly wage (2009): $34.95

Median annual wage (2009): $72,700

Education/Licensure

A bachelor's degree is the minimum required for architects. Bachelor of Arts or Bachelor of Science in architecture, Bachelor of Environmental Design, and Bachelor of Architectural Studies are considered preprofessional degrees. A preprofessional bachelor's degree may qualify a person for licensure in some states, but in most states, further education is required to get a professional degree. Professional degrees are Bachelor of Architecture (B.Arch.), which usually requires five years; Master of Architecture (M.Arch.); and Doctor of Architecture (D.Arch.) from an architectural program that is accredited by the National Architectural Accrediting Board (NAAB). However, state architectural registration boards set their own standards, so a nonaccredited program may meet the educational requirements in a few states. Most architects, though, earn their professional degree through the five-year bachelor of architecture degree program.

All fifty states and the District of Columbia require architects to be licensed. Licensing normally requires a professional degree from an accredited school, completion of a three-year intern program, and passing a national exam. The National Council of Architectural Registration Boards (NCARB) administers the exam. There are some alternate provisions for those who do not have a professional degree. Only Arizona does not require the three-year intern program. Students who complete part of their internship while in school will have an advantage.

The NCARB offers certification that allows an architect licensed in one state to become licensed in another state through reciprocity.

Most states require continuing education to maintain a license. From 2009 through 2012, The American Institute of Architects (AIA) requires 4 hours of continuing education in sustainable design every year to maintain membership. The Green Building Certification Institute, affiliated with the U.S. Green Building Council, offers LEED (Leadership in Energy and Environmental Design) credentials in green building.

For More Information

American Institute of Architects
1735 New York Avenue NW
Washington, DC 20006
202-626-7300
www.aia.org

Association of Collegiate Schools of Architecture
1735 New York Avenue, NW
Washington, DC 20006
202-785-2324
www.asca-arch.org

National Architectural Accrediting Board (NAAB)
1735 New York Avenue NW
Washington, DC 20006
202-783-2007
www.naab.org

National Council of Architectural Registration
  Boards
Suite 700K
1801 K Street NW
Washington, DC 20006
202-783-6500
www.ncarb.org

U.S. Green Building Council (USGBC)
2101 L Street, NW, Suite 500
Washington, DC 20037
800-795-1747 (toll-free)
www.usgbc.org

Architectural Drafter 🌐

Alternate Titles and Related Careers
- Architectural Drafter
- CAD Technician (Computer-Aided Design)
- CADD Operator (Computer-Aided Design
  and Drafting)
- Designer
- Drafter
- Intern Architect
- Project Manager
- Project Architect

This is considered a "Green Increased-Demand"
occupation in the green construction sector of the
economy.

Job Trends

The Bureau of Labor Statistics forecasts a 7 to 13
percent growth for jobs in the architectural and
civil drafting category. This is average for all occupations. The total number of new jobs in the combined category is 36,200.

Employment opportunities will be best for those
with two years of postsecondary training, strong
technical skills, and computer-aided design (CAD)

experience. The majority of architectural and civil
drafters are currently employed by architecture and
engineering services.

About Green Roofs

Green roofs incorporate landscaping into the roofing.
Roofers lay waterproofing material and test it to make
sure it's waterproof. Then a root barrier is applied and
layers of soil added. Landscapers then plant trees,
shrubs, and flowering plants. The result is a rooftop
garden that is helping the environment.

Demand for architectural drafters will be mainly in
nonresidential construction. Construction of new
schools at all levels is expected in order to meet
the educational needs of the expanding population.
Green building design is also expected to generate
demand as environmental concerns and energy
costs increase.

Nature of the Work

Green building and sustainable design require
the expertise of architectural drafters to prepare
the drawings for approvals and construction. The
U.S. Green Building Council LEED (Leadership in
Energy and Environmental Design) building certification encourages innovative designs for energy-
efficient systems. It also encourages use of natural
and sustainably produced materials. These design
considerations add new challenges for architectural
drafters.

Architectural drafters prepare detailed drawings of
structures and buildings, based on specifications
provided by architects. Drafters may specialize in
residential or commercial buildings, and they may
specialize in the type of material used such as concrete or steel. Using computer-aided design and
drafting (CADD) systems, they prepare drawings
that contain all of the details and specifications for
the project, such as dimensions and materials. To
do their jobs, architectural drafters must understand standard building techniques.

According to O*NET, architectural drafters may perform the following tasks:

- Analyze building codes, by-laws, space and site requirements, and other technical documents and reports to determine their effect on architectural designs
- Obtain and assemble data to complete architectural designs, visiting job sites to compile measurements as necessary
- Analyze technical implications of architect's design concept, calculating weights, volumes, and stress factors
- Coordinate structural, electrical, and mechanical designs and determine a method of presentation to graphically represent building plans
- Operate computer-aided drafting (CAD) equipment or conventional drafting station to produce designs, working drawings, charts, forms and records
- Prepare colored drawings of landscape and interior designs for presentation to client
- Build landscape, architectural, and display models
- Draw rough and detailed scale plans for foundations, buildings and structures, based on preliminary concepts, sketches, engineering calculations, specification sheets and other data
- Lay out and plan interior room arrangements for commercial buildings using computer-assisted drafting (CAD) equipment and software
- Determine procedures and instructions to be followed, according to design specifications and quantity of required materials
- Represent architect on construction site, ensuring builder compliance with design specifications and advising on design corrections, under architect's supervision
- Check dimensions of materials to be used and assign numbers to lists of materials
- Calculate heat loss and gain of buildings and structures to determine required equipment specifications, following standard procedures
- Create freehand drawings and lettering to accompany drawings
- Reproduce drawings on copy machines or trace copies of plans and drawings using transparent paper or cloth, ink, pencil, and standard drafting instruments
- Prepare cost estimates, contracts, bidding documents, and technical reports for specific projects under an architect's supervision
- Supervise, coordinate, and inspect the work of draftspersons, technicians, and technologists on construction projects

Career Path

The entry-level position of junior drafter is closely supervised. As junior drafters gain experience, they become intermediate drafters and are expected to make more calculations and judgments independently. Eventually they become senior drafters and may become designers or supervisors. Some continue their education, which may be paid for by their employers, and become engineers, engineering technicians, or architects.

Earning Potential

Median hourly wage (2009): $21.92

Median annual wage (2009): $45,600

Education/Licensure

Although drafting is offered in some high schools, individuals who complete an associate degree or postsecondary technical program have much better job opportunities. Programs are offered at community colleges, technical institutes, and some four-year colleges and universities.

The Accrediting Commission of Career Schools and Colleges of Technology (ACCSCT) accredits drafting programs. Its Web site provides links to accredited programs. The American Design Drafting Association (ADDA) also accredits and certifies schools with drafting programs and provides a list on its Web site, but some are high schools. There are seven recognized apprenticeable specialties associated with this occupation: Drafter, Architectural; Drafter, Commercial; Drafter, Heating and Ventilating; Drafter, Landscape; Drafter, Marine; Drafter, Plumbing; and Drafter, Structural.

Certification is voluntary but may be an asset in getting a job. The ADDA offers certification as a Certified Drafter, which requires passing an exam. There are different exams for different specializations including apprentice, architectural, mechanical, and digital imaging. Certification must be renewed every five years.

For More Information

Accrediting Commission of Career Schools and
   Colleges of Technology (ACCSCT)
2101 Wilson Blvd.
Suite 302
Arlington, Virginia 22201
703-247-4212
www.accsct.org

American Design Drafting Association (ADDA)
105 East Main Street
Newbern, Tennessee 38059
731-627-0802
www.adda.org

U.S. Green Building Council (USGBC)
2101 L Street, NW
Suite 500
Washington, DC 20037
800-795-1747 (toll-free)
www.usgbc.org

Carpenter Helper ☼ 🌐

Alternate Titles and Related Careers
- Carpenter Apprentice
- Carpenter Frame Helper
- Formwork Carpenter Helper
- Industrial Carpenter Helper
- Industrial Scaffold Carpenter Helper

This is considered a "Bright Outlook" and "Green Increased-Demand" occupation in the green construction sector of the economy.

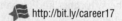 http://bit.ly/career17

Job Trends

The Bureau of Labor Statistics projects a much faster than average rate of growth for this occupation. At 20 percent or higher, the rate of growth translates into 35,300 job openings between 2008 and 2018. About 90 percent of all carpenter helpers are employed in construction. Long-term job opportunities will be best for those who can acquire the training and skills to move up to carpenter.

A number of market forces are driving the demand for carpenters and with them, their helpers. One market force is the growing U.S. population that requires additional housing stock. A second factor is energy conservation. Businesses and individuals are seeking buildings that are more energy efficient. Other factors are home remodeling and government spending on repairs and expansion of the nation's infrastructure, including the construction of new bridges, tunnels, and highways.

Nature of the Work

Carpenter helpers assist carpenters by performing tasks that require less skill than that of a carpenter. These duties include using, supplying, or holding materials or tools, and cleaning work areas and equipment. Depending on the field such as residential construction or public works, carpenter helpers may work with many types of tools and materials or just a few.

Based on O*NET surveys, carpenter helpers may perform the following tasks:

- Position and hold timbers, lumber, and paneling in place for fastening or cutting
- Erect scaffolding, shoring, and braces
- Fasten timbers or lumber with glue, screws, pegs, or nails, and install hardware
- Hold plumb bobs, sighting rods, or other equipment to aid in establishing reference points and lines
- Align, straighten, plumb, and square forms for installation
- Cut timbers, lumber and/or paneling to specified dimensions, and drill holes in timbers or lumber
- Smooth and sand surfaces to remove ridges, tool marks, glue, or caulking
- Perform tie spacing layout and measure, mark, drill or cut
- Secure stakes to grids for constructions of footings, nail scabs to footing forms, and vibrate and float concrete
- Construct forms and assist in raising them to the required elevation
- Install handrails under the direction of a carpenter
- Glue and clamp edges or joints of assembled parts
- Cut and install insulating or sound-absorbing material
- Cut tile or linoleum to fit and spread adhesives on flooring for installation
- Cover surfaces with laminated plastic covering material
- Select tools, equipment, and materials from storage and transport items to work site
- Clean work areas, machines, and equipment, to maintain a clean and safe jobsite

Career Path

Typically, carpentry requires a high school diploma or equivalent. The carpenter helper occupation is an entry-level position working under the supervision of an experienced carpenter. Helpers enrolled in formal apprentice programs may advance with experience and training over a period of years to carpenter journeyman.

Experienced carpenters may advance to general construction supervisor and some may become building inspectors or sales representatives or purchasing agents for building products companies. Others become teachers in vocational or technical schools. With additional education and experience, there are opportunities for carpenters in management, including becoming self-employed contractors. Note that contractors must be licensed.

Speaking both English and Spanish can be an advantage for those who wish to advance.

Earning Potential

Median hourly wage (2009): $12.43

Median annual wage (2009): $25,860

Education/Licensure

The majority of currently employed carpenter helpers have a high school diploma or equivalent. About 13 percent have some college such as an associate degree and 3 percent have a bachelor's degree. Carpenter is an apprenticeable occupation.

About Carpentry Opportunities for Students

The Associated Builders and Contractors trade organization has a special Web site for high school students interested in learning more about the carpentry trade. Visit www.trytools.org.

Carpenter helpers need some type of formal instruction to advance. Attending a trade or vocational school or a community college and enrolling in an apprenticeship program are two main opportunities that helpers have to become skilled. Apprenticeship programs are offered by some employers and by trade associations and unions as well as some trade and vocational schools. These programs may last three to five years and include both classroom and on-the-job training. Upon completing an apprenticeship program, a person becomes a journeyman carpenter.

Some carpenters work toward voluntary certifications in specialized construction techniques such as building scaffolds. These certifications typically enable them to earn additional responsibilities and money. The Green Building Certification Institute, affiliated with the U.S. Green Building Council, offers LEED (Leadership in Energy and Environmental Design) credentials in green building.

For More Information

Associated Builders and Contractors (ABC)
4250 North Fairfax Drive
9th Floor
Arlington, Virginia 22203-1607
703-812-2000
www.abc.org

Associated General Contractors of America, Inc. (AGC)
2300 Wilson Boulevard
Suite 400
Arlington, Virginia 22201-5426
703-548-3118
www.agc.org

Home Builders Institute (HNI)
1201 15th Street, NW
Washington, DC 20005
202-266-8927
www.buildingcareers.org

National Association of Home Builders (NAHB)
1201 15th Street, NW
Washington, DC 20005
800-368-5242 (toll-free)
www.nahb.org

National Center for Construction Education and Research (NCCER)
3600 Northwest 43rd Street
Building G
Gainesville, Florida 32606-8134
www.nccer.org

United Brotherhood of Carpenters and Joiners of America
International Training Center
6801 Placid Street
Las Vegas, Nevada 89119
702-938-1111
www.carpenters.org

U.S. Green Building Council (USGBC)
2101 L Street, NW
Suite 500
Washington, DC 20037
800-795-1747 (toll-free)
www.usgbc.org

Cement Mason / Concrete Finisher ⊕

Alternate Titles and Related Careers

- Cement Finisher
- Concrete Mason
- Mason
- Terrazzo Worker

These are considered "Green Increased-Demand" occupations in the green construction sector of the economy.

Job Trends

The Bureau of Labor Statistics projects that this occupational category will grow at an average rate of 7 to 13 percent. This would be 76,400 new jobs between 2008 and 2018. About 90 percent of currently employed masons and finishers work in construction. The *Occupation Outlook Handbook* notes that a significant number of masons and finishers will be retiring over the coming decade.

In the long term, job growth will be fueled by both the nation's rising population that will require additional housing and the nation's need to repair and expand its infrastructure. In addition, government spending at all levels is being directed to renovation and building projects that require cement masons and concrete finishers. The use of concrete for buildings is increasing because of its strength to withstand severe weather.

Job opportunities will be good, especially for those with the most experience and skills. Job candidates who have taken masonry courses at technical schools will have an advantage when looking for a job. Employers are having difficulty finding workers with the right skills because qualified job seekers often prefer work that is less strenuous and has more comfortable working conditions. Masonry can be a demanding physical job.

Nature of the Work

Cement masons and concrete finishers work with concrete, one of the most common and durable of building materials. Once set, concrete becomes the foundation for everything from decorative patios to office buildings to huge dams to miles of roads. Cement masons and concrete finishers smooth and finish surfaces of poured concrete such as floors, walks, sidewalks, roads, and curbs. They also align forms for sidewalks, curbs, and gutters and patch voids. In their work they use a variety of hand and power tools including saws to cut expansion joints, rakes to smooth wet concrete, straightedges to mold expansion joints, and hand or power trowels spread wet concrete. Other tools include pneumatic chisels and power grinders.

According to O*NET, cement masons and concrete finishers may perform the following:

- Check the forms that hold the concrete to see that they are properly constructed
- Set the forms that hold concrete to the desired pitch and depth, and align them
- Spread, level, and smooth concrete

- Mold expansion joints and edges, using edging tools, jointers, and straightedge
- Signal truck driver to position truck to facilitate pouring concrete, and move chute to direct concrete on forms
- Produce rough concrete surface, using broom
- Operate power vibrator to compact concrete
- Monitor how the wind, heat, or cold affect the curing of the concrete throughout the entire process
- Direct the casting of the concrete and supervise laborers who use shovels or special tools to spread it
- Mix cement, sand, and water to produce concrete, grout, or slurry, using hoe, trowel, tamper, scraper, or concrete-mixing machine
- Cut out damaged areas, drill holes for reinforcing rods, and position reinforcing rods to repair concrete, using power saw and drill
- Wet concrete surface, and rub with stone to smooth surface and obtain specified finish
- Wet surface to prepare for bonding, fill holes and cracks with grout or slurry, and smooth, using trowel
- Clean chipped area, using wire brush, and feel and observe surface to determine if it is rough or uneven
- Apply hardening and sealing compounds to cure surface of concrete, and waterproof or restore surface
- Chip, scrape, and grind high spots, ridges, and rough projections to finish concrete
- Build wooden molds, and clamp molds around area to be repaired, using hand tools
- Fabricate concrete beams, columns, and panels
- Waterproof or restore concrete surfaces, using appropriate compounds

Working with terrazzo marble is a specialty. Those workers may perform the following additional tasks:

- Spread roofing paper on surface of foundation, and spread concrete onto roofing paper with trowel to form terrazzo base
- Sprinkle colored marble or stone chips, powdered steel, or coloring powder over surface to produce prescribed finish
- Cut metal division strips, and press them into terrazzo base so that top edges form desired design or pattern
- Install anchor bolts, steel plates, door sills and other fixtures in freshly poured concrete or pattern or stamp the surface to provide a decorative finish
- Apply muriatic acid to clean surface, and rinse with water
- Push roller over surface to embed chips in surface
- Polish surface, using polishing or surfacing machine

Career Path

Entry-level workers begin work under experienced cement masons and concrete finishers. Their first tasks are relatively simple such as edging, joining, and using a straightedge on fresh concrete. As they gain experience, newer workers are given more complex tasks and allowed to work with less direct supervisions.

In time, some cement masons and concrete finishers may become supervisors or move into jobs as construction managers, building inspectors, or cost estimators. Certification is helpful when seeking advancement. Some masons and finishers choose to open their own businesses.

Earning Potential

Median hourly wage (2009): $17.04

Median annual wage (2009): $35,440

Education/Licensure

Typically, cement masons and concrete finishers have high school diplomas or the equivalent. About 86 percent of cement masons and concrete finishers employed in 2009 had high school diplomas or the equivalent. About 12 percent had some college such as an associate degree or a certificate from a technical school, whereas 2 percent had a bachelor's degree.

Most workers learn their trade on the job as helpers or apprentices. Cement mason and concrete finisher are apprenticeable trades. Most on-the-job training programs are informal, but some programs include taking courses at a community college or technical school. Some entry-level workers have already attended trade or vocational-technical schools when looking for their first job.

Formal apprenticeship programs combine both on-the-job training with a minimum of 144 hours of classroom instruction for each of three or four years that the program takes. Apprentices learn applied mathematics, blueprint reading, safety measures, layout work, and cost estimation.

The National Concrete Masonry Association (NCMA) offers voluntary certification as Certified Concrete Masonry Testing Technician (CCMTT) for product and Certified Concrete Masonry Testing Technician (CCMTT) for testing and quality control. NCMA also offers the Certified Consultant of Concrete Masonry (C3M) for sales, and the Certified SRW Installer (CSRWI) and Certified SRW Installer Advanced (segmental retaining wall).

For More Information

Associated Builders and Contractors (ABC)
4250 North Fairfax Drive
9th Floor
Arlington, Virginia 22203-1607
703-812-2000
www.abc.org

Associated General Contractors of America, Inc. (AGC)
2300 Wilson Boulevard
Suite 400
Arlington, Virginia 22201-5426
703-548-3118
www.agc.org

International Masonry Institute
International Union of Bricklayers and Allied
   Craftworkers
The James Brice House
42 East Street
Annapolis, Maryland 21401-1731
410-280-1305
www.imiweb.org

Mason Contractors Association of America
   (MCAA)
33 South Roselle Road
Schaumburg, Illinois 60193-1646
800-536-2225 (toll-free)
www.masoncontractors.org

National Center for Construction Education and
   Research (NCCER)
3600 Northwest 43rd Street
Building G
Gainesville, Florida 32606-8134
www.nccer.org

National Concrete Masonry Association (NCMA)
13750 Sunrise Valley Drive
Herndon, Virginia 20171-4662
703-713-1900
www.ncma.org

National Terrazzo and Mosaic Association
   (NTMA)
P.O. Box 2605
Fredericksburg, Texas 78624
800-323-9736 (toll-free)
www.ntma.com

Operative Plasterers' and Cement Masons'
   International Association of the United States
   and Canada (OPCMIA)
11720 Beltsville Drive
Suite 700
Beltsville, Maryland 20705-3104
301-623-1000
ww.opcmia.org

Civil Engineer ☼ ⑤

Alternate Titles and Related Careers

- Architectural Engineer
- City Engineer
- Civil Engineering Manager
- Design Engineer
- Project Engineer
- Project Manager
- Research Hydraulic Engineer
- Structural Engineer

This is considered a "Bright Outlook" and "Green Enhanced-Skills" occupation in the green construction, energy efficiency, and research, design, and consulting services sectors of the economy.

Job Trends

Civil engineering occupational category is estimated to grow much faster-than-average at 20 percent or higher. This would be 114,600 more job opening between 2008 and 2018 for civil engineers. Slightly more than half work in businesses that provide professional, scientific, or technical services. About 27 percent are employed by government agencies, and another 11 percent in construction.

Environmental regulations and considerations increase the demand by requiring more engineers to expand existing transportation systems or to design and build new systems. Engineers are also needed to repair existing roads and bridges and design and build new water supply and wastewater treatment systems.

Nature of the Work

Civil engineers plan, design, and oversee construction and maintenance of building structures an facilities such as roads, tunnels, railroads, airports, bridges, harbors, channels, dam, irrigation projects, pipelines, power plants, water and sewage systems, and waste disposal units. Just about anything that is built in the way of public works like bridges or that affects the public like power plants involves civil engineers.

Among the tasks that civil engineers may perform according to O*NET are the following:

- Analyze survey reports, maps, drawings, blueprints, aerial photography, and other topographical or geologic data to plan projects
- Provide technical advice regarding design, construction, or program modifications and structural repairs to industrial and managerial personnel
- Estimate quantities and cost of materials, equipment, or labor to determine project feasibility
- Test soils and materials to determine the adequacy and strength of foundations, concrete, asphalt, or steel
- Compute load and grade requirements, water flow rates, and material stress factors to determine design specifications
- Plan and design transportation or hydraulic systems and structures, following construction and government standards, using design software and drawing tools
- Direct or participate in surveying to lay out installations and establish reference points, grades, and elevations to guide construction
- Conduct studies of traffic patterns or environmental conditions to identify engineering problems and assess the potential impact of projects
- Manage and direct staff members and the construction, operations, or maintenance activities at project site
- Inspect project sites to monitor progress and ensure conformance to design specifications and safety or sanitation standards
- Prepare or present public reports on topics such as bid proposals, deeds, environmental impact statements, or property and right-of-way descriptions

Career Path

As civil engineers gain experience, they become specialists and advance into positions where they supervise a team of engineers and other staff members. Some eventually become managers. Some go on to earn an MBA degree to prepare them for high-level managerial and executive positions.

About Types of Electrical Engineers

Electrical engineers work in a wide variety of industries including automotive, aerospace, bioengineering, computers, construction, information technology, manufacturing, nanotechnology, semiconductors, and telecommunications. Some are even hired by the service, financial, and entertainment industries.

Earning Potential

Median hourly wage (2009): $36.82

Median annual wage (2009): $76,590

Education/Licensure

For entry-level positions, a bachelor's degree in engineering from a college or university program that is accredited by the Accreditation Board for Engineering and Technology (ABET) is required. In some cases, engineers with degrees in one type of engineering may qualify for jobs in other areas of engineering. Most colleges and universities offer transportation engineering as a specialty in civil engineering.

Some colleges and universities offer five-year programs that culminate in a master's degree. Some offer five- or six-year programs that include cooperative experience. Some four-year schools have arrangements with community colleges or liberal arts colleges that allow students to spend two or three years at the initial school and transfer for the last two years to complete their engineering degree.

All fifty states and the District of Columbia require engineers to be licensed as professional engineers (PE) if they serve the public directly. In most states, licensure requires graduation from a four-year engineering program accredited by ABET, four years of experience, and passing the state exam. Many engineers take the Fundamentals of Engineering portion of the exam upon graduation. They are then engineers in training (EIT). After obtaining appropriate work experience, they take the Principles and Practice of Engineering exam to complete their professional license. Most states recognize licenses from other states, as long as the requirements are the same or more stringent. Some states have continuing education requirements.

For More Information

Accreditation Board for Engineering and
    Technology (ABET)
111 Market Place
Suite 1050
Baltimore, Maryland 21202
410-347-7700
www.abet.org

American Society of Civil Engineers (ASCE)
Transportation and Development Institute
1801 Alexander Bell Drive
Reston, Virginia 20191-4400
800-548-2723 (toll-free)
www.asce.org

National Society of Professional Engineers
    (NSPE)
1420 King Street
Alexandria, Virginia 22314
703-684-2800
www.nspe.org

Civil Engineering Technician ✿

Alternate Titles and Related Careers

- Civil Designer
- Civil Engineering Assistant
- Civil Engineering Designer
- Construction Analyst
- Construction Technician
- Design Technician

- Engineering Assistant
- Engineering Specialist
- Engineering Technician
- Transportation Engineering Technician

The civil engineering technician occupation is related to civil engineering, which is a "Bright Outlook" occupation.

Job Trends

The civil engineering occupation is projected by the Bureau of Labor Statistics to grow faster than the average of all occupations between 2008 and 2018. The rate is estimated to be 14 to 19 percent and result in 32,800 new jobs. Employment is about evenly divided between professional, scientific, and technical services and government agencies, 47 percent and 45 percent respectively.

The same forces that are driving the demand for civil engineers will fuel the demand for civil engineering technicians. Population growth and the resulting need to improve and expand the nation's infrastructure including its transportation, water, and pollution control systems and to construct large energy efficient buildings and building complexes will result in excellent job opportunities for civil engineering technicians. Those with associate degrees or other postsecondary training in engineering technology will be the most employable.

Nature of the Work

Civil engineering technicians apply the theory and principles of civil engineering in the planning, design, and oversight of the construction and maintenance of structures and facilities. They work under the supervision of engineering staff and their work is more narrowly focused than that of the engineers and scientists with whom they work. Generally, engineering technicians specialize so that some will do cost estimating and materials selection, whereas others will set up and monitor instruments used to study traffic patterns. Still others will perform land surveys.

O*NET has tracked the following tasks as those that civil engineering may perform:

- Plan and conduct field surveys to locate new sites and analyze details of project sites
- Analyze proposed site factors and design maps, graphs, tracings, and diagrams to illustrate findings
- Draft detailed dimensional drawings and design layouts for projects and to ensure conformance to specifications
- Calculate dimensions, square footage, profile and component specifications, and material quantities using calculator or computer
- Read and review project blueprints and structural specifications to determine dimensions of structure or system and material requirements
- Confer with supervisor to determine project details such as plan preparation, acceptance testing, and evaluation of field conditions
- Develop plans and estimate costs for installation of systems, utilization of facilities, or construction of structures
- Prepare reports and document project activities and data
- Inspect project site and evaluate contractor work to detect design malfunctions and ensure conformance to design specifications and applicable codes
- Report maintenance problems occurring at project site to supervisor and negotiate changes to resolve system conflicts
- Evaluate facility to determine suitability for occupancy and square footage availability
- Conduct materials test and analysis using tools and equipment and applying engineering knowledge
- Respond to public suggestions and complaints

Career Path

The *Occupational Outlook Handbook* notes that opportunities are best for those who possess an associate degree or other postsecondary training in engineering technology. Engineering technicians usually begin their careers working under an experienced technician, technologist, or engineer. Over time, engineering technicians take on more responsibility with less supervision. In time, some may become supervisors.

Earning Potential

Median hourly wage (2009): $22.10

Median annual wage (2009): $45,970

> **About Green Building in Washington, DC**
>
> According to the U.S. Green Building Council in 2009, the District of Columbia had seventy LEED-certified projects and 522 LEED-registered projects. This placed our nation's capital first among cities of comparable size in North America.

Education/Licensure

Typically, entry-level positions require that candidates have associate degrees or other postsecondary training in engineering technology. Workers who have less formal training need more time to learn skills while on the job, which interferes with productivity.

A number of community colleges, technical institutes, extension divisions of colleges and universities, and public and private vocational-technical schools offer degree and certification programs to train mechanical engineering technologists. Technical institutes offer less general education and less theory than community or technical colleges. However, they tend to focus more on intensive technical training, and may be part of a community college or state university system.

The Technology Accreditation Commission of the Accreditation Board for Engineering and Technology (ABET) accredits two-year associate degree programs in engineering technology. Typically, ABET requires that these programs include at least college algebra and trigonometry, and one or two basic science courses. Graduates of these programs are considered to have an acceptable level of competence.

The National Institute for Certification in Engineering Technologies provides voluntary technician certification in civil engineering technology for water/wastewater plant construction; asphalt, concrete, and soil materials testing; generalist and construction geotechnical; erosion and sediment control for land management and water control; bridge safety inspection, highway construction, highway design, highway materials, high surveys, highway traffic operations, highway system maintenance and preservation; and water and sewer lines

For More Information

Accreditation Board for Engineering and
    Technology (ABET)
111 Market Place
Suite 1050
Baltimore, Maryland 21202
410-347-7700
www.abet.org

American Society of Certified Engineering
    Technicians (ASCET)
P.O. Box 1536
Brandon, Mississippi 39043
601-824-8991
www.ascet.org

National Institute for Certification in Engineering
    Technologies (NICET)
1420 King Street
Alexandria, Virginia 22314
888-476-4238 (toll-free)
www.nicet.org

Civil Drafter ☼

Alternate Titles and Related Careers
- Civil CAD Designer (Computer-Aided Design)
- Civil CAD Technician (Computer-Aided Design)
- Computer-Aided Design Designer (CAD)
- Computer-Aided Design Operator (CAD)
- Computer-Aided Design Technician (CAD)
- Computer-Aided Drafting and Design Drafter (CADD)
- Drafting Technician

The civil drafter occupation is related to civil engineering, which is a "Bright Outlook" occupation.

Job Trends

The overall category of architectural and civil drafter is estimated by the Bureau of labor Statistics to grow by 7 to 13 percent between 2008 and 2018, which is about average for all occupations. The total job growth is projected to 36,200. About 80 percent of currently employed civil and architectural drafters work in professional, scientific, and technical services. The best opportunities for employment will be for candidates who have at least two years of postsecondary training.

Job growth will result from the increase in the U.S. population and the need to improve and expand the nation's infrastructure including highways, roads, bridges, tunnels, harbors, railroad network, wastewater facilities, power plants, and similar large buildings and building complexes.

Nature of the Work

Civil drafters prepare drawings and topographical and relief maps needed for civil engineering projects such as highways, bridges, pipelines, flood control projects, and water and sewage control systems. The ability to use computer-aided drafting and design (CADD) software is an important skill for anyone interested in this occupation. CADD software has increased the complexity of drafting applications, but also increased productivity. In addition to using (CADD) software, civil drafters must still be able to use compasses, dividers, protractors, triangles, and other manual drafting devices.

The following are among the tasks that civil drafters may perform according to O*NET:

- Draw maps, diagrams, and profiles, using cross-sections and surveys, to represent elevations, topographical contours, subsurface formations and structures
- Draft plans and detailed drawings for structures, installations, and construction projects such as highways, sewage disposal systems, and dikes, working from sketches or notes
- Determine the order of work and method of presentation, such as orthographic or isometric drawing
- Finish and duplicate drawings and documentation packages, according to required mediums and specifications for reproduction using blueprinting, photography, or other duplicating methods
- Review rough sketches, drawings, specifications, and other engineering data received from civil engineers to ensure that they conform to design concepts
- Calculate excavation tonnage and prepare graphs and fill-hauling diagrams for use in earth-moving operations
- Correlate, interpret, and modify data obtained from topographical surveys, well logs, and geophysical prospecting reports
- Locate and identify symbols located on topographical surveys to denote geological and geophysical formations or oil field installations
- Calculate weights, volumes, and stress factors and their implications for technical aspects of designs
- Plot characteristics of boreholes for oil and gas wells from photographic subsurface survey recordings and other data, representing depth, degree and direction of inclination
- Supervise or conduct field surveys, inspections or technical investigations to obtain data required to revise construction drawings
- Explain drawings to production or construction teams and provide adjustments as necessary
- Determine quality, cost, strength and quantity of required materials, and enter figures on materials lists
- Supervise and train other technologists, technicians and drafters

Career Path

The entry-level position of junior drafter is closely supervised. As junior drafters gain experience, they become intermediate drafters and are expected to make more calculations and judgments independently. Eventually they become senior drafters and may become designers or supervisors. Some continue their education, which may be paid for by their employers, and become engineers, engineering technicians, or architects.

Earning Potential

Median hourly wage (2009): $21.92

Median annual wage (2009): $45,600

Education/Licensure

Although drafting is offered in some high schools, individuals who complete an associate degree or postsecondary technical program have much better job opportunities. Programs are offered at community colleges, technical institutes, and some four-year colleges and universities.

The Accrediting Commission of Career Schools and Colleges of Technology (ACCSCT) accredits drafting programs. Its Web site provides links to accredited programs. The American Design Drafting Association (ADDA) also accredits and certifies schools with drafting programs and provides a list on its Web site, but some are high schools. There are seven recognized apprenticeable specialties associated with this occupation: Drafter, Architectural; Drafter, Commercial; Drafter, Heating and Ventilating; Drafter, Landscape; Drafter, Marine; Drafter, Plumbing; and Drafter, Structural.

Certification is voluntary but may be an asset in getting a job. The ADDA offers certification as a Certified Drafter, which requires passing an exam. There are different exams for different specializations including apprentice, architectural, mechanical, and digital imaging. Certification must be renewed every five years.

For More Information

Accrediting Commission of Career Schools and
  Colleges of Technology (ACCSCT)
2101 Wilson Blvd.
Suite 302
Arlington, Virginia 22201
703-247-4212
www.accsct.org

American Design Drafting Association (ADDA)
105 East Main Street
Newbern, Tennessee 38059
731-627-0802
www.adda.org

U.S. Green Building Council (USGBC)
2101 L Street, NW
Suite 500
Washington, DC 20037
800-795-1747 (toll-free)
www.usgbc.org

Construction Carpenter ✿ ⑤

Alternate Titles and Related Careers
- Assembler
- Concrete Carpenter
- Construction Worker
- Custom Stair Builder
- Finish Carpenter
- Installer
- Lead Carpenter
- Trim Carpenter

This is considered a "Bright Outlook" and "Green Increased-Demand" occupation in the green construction sector of the economy. Carpentry crosses a number of industries in addition to building construction, but demand for carpenters will grow in green building construction.

 http://bit.ly/career17

About Air Quality in Schools

The U.S. Environmental Protection Agency has developed a kit for developing a school-based indoor air quality initiative. For a downloadable copy of the program, go to www.epa.gov/iaq/schools/tfs/coord_section_2.html.

Job Trends

Carpentry is the largest building trade occupation. According to the *Occupational Outlook Handbook,* there were about 1.5 million jobs in 2006 and 1.2 million in 2008 after the recession began. However, that number is expected to increase by 2018 at a rate that is average for all occupations—7 to 13 percent. This category includes both construction carpenters and rough carpenters. The job market is expected to be best for those with the most training and skills.

In addition to population growth, the increasing interest in energy efficiency among both individuals and companies will stimulate demand for new energy efficient homes and buildings. Besides the demand for new construction, the market for home remodeling is currently strong and will be for some time. This is partially driven by economic conditions, but also by environmental concerns. Retrofitting and remodeling homes to improve energy efficiency is increasing as is retrofitting industrial plants, schools, and government buildings for energy efficiency. All these factors will provide job opportunities for carpenters.

Nature of the Work

Carpenters need knowledge of tools, materials, blueprints, sketches, building plans, and basic math as well as safety rules and regulations and local building codes. Those who are self-employed must be able to estimate materials, time, and cost to complete a job. Today, carpenters must also be aware of the latest in energy-efficient doors, windows, and sealants as well as environmentally friendly building products such as bamboo.

Specifically, construction carpenters may do any or all of the following tasks as listed on O*NET:

- Study specifications in blueprints, sketches, and building plans to prepare project layout and determine dimensions and materials required
- Shape or cut materials to specified measurements, using hand tools, machines, or power saw
- Follow established safety rules and regulations and maintain a safe and clean environment
- Measure and mark cutting lines on materials, using ruler, pencil, chalk, and marking gauge
- Install structures and fixtures, such as windows, frames, floorings, and trim, or hardware, using carpenter's hand and power tools
- Verify trueness of structure, using plumb bob and level
- Build or repair cabinets, doors, frameworks, floors, and other wooden fixtures used in buildings, using woodworking machines, carpenter's hand tools, and power tools
- Assemble and fasten materials to make framework or props, using hand tools and wood screws, nails, dowel pins, or glue
- Remove damaged or defective parts or sections of structures and repair or replace, using hand tools
- Inspect ceiling or floor tile, wall coverings, siding, glass, or woodwork to detect broken or damaged structures
- Erect scaffolding and ladders for assembling structures above ground level
- Finish surfaces of woodwork or wallboard in houses and buildings, using paint, hand tools, and paneling

- Fill cracks and other defects in plaster or plasterboard and sand patch, using patching plaster, trowel, and sanding tool
- Select and order lumber and other required materials
- Maintain records, document actions and present written progress reports
- Construct forms and chutes for pouring concrete
- Cover subfloors with building paper to keep out moisture and lay hardwood, parquet, and wood-strip-block floors by nailing floors to subfloor or cementing them to mastic or asphalt base
- Apply shock-absorbing, sound-deadening, and decorative paneling to ceilings and walls
- Perform minor plumbing, welding or concrete mixing work
- Prepare cost estimates for clients or employers

Construction carpenters who are self-employed or become supervisors may also:

- Prepare project layout and determine dimensions and materials that will be needed
- Prepare cost estimate for clients
- Select and order materials
- Arrange for subcontractors for special area such as heating
- Maintain records, document activities, and present written progress reports

Career Path

Experienced carpenters may become carpentry supervisors. Because they are involved in all aspects of the construction process, they also have opportunities to advance to general construction supervisor. Some may become building inspectors or sales representatives or purchasing agents for building products. Others become teachers in vocational or technical schools. With additional education and experience, there are opportunities for carpenters in management, including becoming self-employed contractors. States require that contractors be licensed to do business.

Because of the number of Latinos in construction, speaking both English and Spanish can be an advantage for those who wish to advance.

Earning Potential

Median hourly wage (2009): $18.98

Median annual wage (2009): $39,470

Education/Licensure

Typically, carpentry requires a high school diploma. Carpenters may begin as carpenter's helpers working with experienced carpenters, but they also need some type of formal instruction to become skilled. There are two main options for formal instruction: attending a trade or vocational school or a community college, or enrolling in an apprenticeship program. Usually, trade or vocational schools confer a certificate of achievement (not the same as certification), and community colleges confer an associate degree in carpentry.

Carpentry is an apprenticeable trade. Apprenticeship programs are offered by some employers and by trade associations and unions as well as some trade and vocational schools. These programs may last three to five years and include both classroom and on-the-job training. Upon completing an apprenticeship program, a person becomes a journeyman carpenter.

Some carpenters obtain certifications in specialized construction techniques. Certification may enable them to earn additional responsibilities and money. The Green Building Certification Institute, affiliated with the U.S. Green Building Council, offers LEED (Leadership in Energy and Environmental Design) credentials in green building.

For More Information

Associated General Contractors of America, Inc. (AGC)
2300 Wilson Boulevard
Suite 400
Arlington, Virginia 22201-5426
703-548-3118
www.agc.org

Home Builders Institute
1201 15th Street, NW
Washington, DC 20005
202-266-8927
www.buildingcareers.org

National Association of Home Builders
1201 15th Street, NW
Washington, DC 20005
800-368-5242 (toll-free)
www.nahb.org

United Brotherhood of Carpenters and Joiners of America
International Training Center
6801 Placid Street
Las Vegas, Nevada 89119
702-938-1111
www.carpenters.org

U.S. Green Building Council (USGBC)
2101 L Street, NW
Suite 500
Washington, DC 20037
800-795-1747 (toll-free)
www.usgbc.org

Construction Manager ☼ ⊕

Alternate Titles and Related Careers

- Construction Area Manager
- Construction Foreman
- Construction Superintendent
- General Contractor
- Job Superintendent
- Project Manager
- Project Superintendent

This is considered a "Bright Outlook" and "Green Enhanced-Skills" occupation in the green construction and environment protection sectors of the economy. All kinds of building projects—schools to highways—need construction manager.

 http://bit.ly/career18

Job Trends

According to the Bureau of Labor Statistics, employment growth of 14 to 19 percent is expected for this occupation by 2018. This is faster-than-average for all occupations. Job opportunities should be excellent because the need is expected to exceed the number of qualified persons entering this profession.

Demand for construction managers is generated by increasing construction of homes, offices, schools, hospitals, restaurants, and retail spaces as a result of population growth. In addition, the need to replace and repair roads, highways, and bridges will also generate demand. Increasing complexity of projects along with more laws and regulations regarding energy efficiency, environmental protection, worker safety, and environmentally friendly construction processes and materials also contribute to the demand for construction managers.

About Green Building Materials

The Green Guard Institute tests and certifies building products and materials that are low in harmful emissions. You can find listings of these products and materials, a number of which are used in school construction, on the Institute's Web site www.greenguard.org.

Nature of the Work

Construction managers oversee and coordinate the entire construction process from planning and development through the completion of the project. They are responsible for making sure that the work gets done within budget and on schedule. On a very large project, different construction managers may handle different portions of the project.

The majority of construction managers work on residential and nonresidential construction such as homes, apartment buildings, commercial buildings, schools, and hospitals. However, construction managers also work on large industrial complexes, bridges, highways, and wastewater treatment plants.

O*NET lists the following as among the tasks of construction managers:

- Evaluate construction methods and determine cost-effectiveness of plans and construction for projects
- Select, contract, and oversee general and trades contractors
- Prepare contracts and negotiate changes to contracts with clients, architects, consultants, suppliers, and subcontractors
- Prepare and submit budget estimates and cost and tracking reports
- Schedule projects in logical steps and time periods to meet deadlines
- Obtain necessary permits and licenses
- Interpret and explain plans and contract terms to all necessary parties
- Plan, organize, and direct activities involved in the construction
- Confer with supervisory personnel, owners, contractors, and design professionals to resolve issues related to work process, complaints, and construction problems
- Take actions to deal with the results of delays, bad weather, or emergencies at construction sites
- Inspect and review projects to monitor compliance with all regulations including building and safety codes
- Arrange delivery of materials, tools, and equipment
- Develop and implement quality control programs

- Investigate damage, accidents, and delays at construction sites to ensure proper procedures are being carried out

Career Path

Experienced construction managers in large companies may become high-level managers or administrators. An additional degree in business administration, finance, or accounting may be necessary for the highest positions. Many construction managers are self-employed in their own small construction or consulting companies.

Earning Potential

Median hourly wage (2009): $39.58

Median annual wage (2009): $82,330

Education/Licensure

Traditionally, trades workers such as carpenters, electricians, and plumbers with significant construction experience could advance to construction managers. According to the *Occupational Outlook Handbook,* only about 31 percent of currently employed construction managers have college degrees. However, the trend is for employers to hire people as construction managers with bachelor's degrees or higher in construction management, construction science, construction engineering, or civil engineering. In addition to education, construction industry experience is critical in getting a job. For those in college and university programs, internships are a good way to gain experience.

The American Council for Construction Education (ACCE) provides links to accredited bachelor's and associate degree programs in construction sciences. The National Center for Construction Education and Research (NCCER) also provides links to accredited programs. In addition, the latter organization sponsors Construction Management Academies that offer professional training and certifications. The American Institute of Constructors (AIC) offers online continuing education courses through www.RedVector.com. Many are green construction courses.

Certification is voluntary for construction managers, but is a growing trend. Employers value certification because it ensures a certain level of training and experience. The Construction Management Association of America (CMAA) offers the Construction Manager in Training (CMIT) certification for college juniors, seniors, and recent graduates and the Certified Construction Manager (CCM) for those with experience. The CCM requires a combination of education and experience plus passing an exam. The American Institute of Constructors also offers certification for construction managers. The Green Building Certification Institute also provides a credential in LEED construction.

For More Information

American Council for Construction Education
1717 North Loop 1604 E
Suite 320
San Antonio, Texas 78232-1570
210-495-6161
www.acce-hq.org

American Institute of Constructors (AIC)
P.O. Box 26334
Alexandria, Virginia 22314
703-683-4999
www.aicnet.org

Construction Management Association of America (CMAA)
7926 Jones Branch Drive
Suite 800
McLean, Virginia 22102-3303
703-356-2622
www.cmaanet.org

Green Building Certification Institute
2101 L Street, NW
Suite 650
Washington, DC 20037
800-795-1746 (toll-free)
www.gbci.org

National Center for Construction Education and
    Research (NCCER)
3600 NW 43rd Street
Building G
Gainesville, Florida 32606
888-622-3720 (toll-free)
www.nccer.org

Construction Worker ☼⑤

Alternate Titles and Related Careers
- Construction Laborer
- Curb and Gutter Laborer
- Drain Layer
- Drop Crew Laborer
- Finisher
- Helper
- Post Framer
- Punch Out Crew Member

This is considered a "Bright Outlook" and "Green Enhanced-Skills" occupation in the green construction sector of the economy. Some workers specialize in "green" energy-efficient construction or environmental remediation of hazardous materials.

Job Trends
The Bureau of Labor Statistics estimates that the construction laborer occupation will see a much faster than average job growth between 2008 and 2018. The 20 percent or higher projected growth rate will translate into 339,400 openings. About 62 percent of currently employed workers are employed by construction companies and another 21 percent are self-employed. Those with few skills will face competition for jobs, but laborers with specialized skills or who can move to areas with new construction should have the best job opportunities.

Because of the large variety of tasks that construction laborers perform, demand will mirror the level of overall construction activity, which is expected to recover from the downturn in the nation's economy during the recession of 2007 to 2009. An important factor in the recovery of the construction industry is the amount of spending that the federal government has poured into infrastructure improvement and expansion and new alternative sources of energy. Getting these new sources online requires building factories and power plants. Because laborers make up a significant portion of workers on construction projects, the demand for this type of worker should see an increase.

Nature of the Work
Construction laborers perform tasks involving physical labor at building, highway, and heavy construction projects; tunnel and shaft excavations; and demolition sites. Among the tools that they may use on the job are air hammers, earth tampers, cement mixers, small mechanical hoists, surveying and measuring equipment, rakes, picks, shovels, and a variety of other equipment and instruments. Construction laborers work along side craftworkers such as carpenters, plasterers, and masons and assist them.

Construction workers may perform the following tasks according to O*NET:
- Clean and prepare construction sites to eliminate possible hazards
- Read and interpret plans, instructions, and specifications to determine work activities
- Control traffic passing near, in, and around work zones
- Signal equipment operators to facilitate alignment, movement, and adjustment of machinery, equipment, and materials
- Dig ditches or trenches, backfill excavations, and compact and level earth to grade specifications
- Position, join, align, and seal structural components, such as concrete wall sections and pipes
- Measure, mark, and record openings and distances to lay out areas where construction work will be performed

- Load, unload, and identify building materials, machinery, and tools, and distribute them to the appropriate locations, according to project plans and specifications
- Erect and disassemble scaffolding, shoring, braces, traffic barricades, ramps, and other temporary structures
- Build and position forms for pouring concrete, and dismantle forms after use
- Lubricate, clean, and repair machinery, equipment, and tools
- Operate jackhammers and drills to break up concrete or pavement
- Smooth and finish freshly poured cement or concrete
- Install sewer, water, and storm drain pipes, using pipe-laying machinery and laser guidance equipment
- Transport and set explosives for tunnel, shaft, and road construction
- Tend pumps, compressors, and generators to provide power for tools, machinery, and equipment, or to heat and move materials such as asphalt
- Mop, brush, or spread paints, cleaning solutions, or other compounds over surfaces to clean them or to provide protection
- Shovel cement and other materials into portable cement mixers; and mix, pour, and spread concrete
- Place, consolidate, and protect case-in-place concrete or masonry structures
- Grind, scrape, sand, or polish surfaces such as concrete, marble, terrazzo, or wood flooring, using abrasive tools or machines
- Mix ingredients to create compounds for covering or cleaning surfaces
- Tend machines that pump concrete, grout, cement, sand, plaster or stucco through spray-guns for application to ceilings and walls

- Spray materials such as water, sand, steam, vinyl, paint, or stucco through hoses to clean, coat, or seal surfaces
- Apply caulking compounds by hand or using caulking guns
- Operate, read, and maintain air monitoring and other sampling devices in confined and/or hazardous environments
- Identify, pack, and transport hazardous and/or radioactive materials
- Use computers and other input devices to control robotic pipe cutters and cleaners
- Raze buildings and salvage useful materials

Career Path

Most construction laborers start by getting a job with a contractor who provides on-the-job training. Typically, entry-level workers help more experienced workers by performing routine tasks. When the opportunities arise, they learn how to do more difficult tasks. Construction laborers may also choose or be required by their employers to attend a trade or vocational school, association training class, or community college for further trade-related training.

Through training and experience, laborers can move into other construction occupations. Some may advance over time to become construction supervisors or general contractors. States require that contractors be licensed.

About Habitat for Humanity and Green Building

Habitat for Humanity and The Home Depot announced a five-year program in 2009 to build 5,000 sustainable homes across the country. The $30 million program will channel funds to 120 Habitat affiliates to expand the "Partners in Sustainable Building" program. The new homes will be energy efficient and use water-conserving plumbing fixtures.

Because of the number of Latinos in construction, speaking both English and Spanish can be an advantage for those who wish to advance.

Earning Potential

Median hourly wage (2009): $14.01

Median annual wage (2009): $29,150

Education/Licensure

Most construction laborers learn on the job, but formal apprenticeship programs provide the most thorough preparation. Although some construction laborer jobs have no specific educational qualifications or entry-level training, apprenticeships for laborers usually require a high school diploma or the equivalent. High school classes in English, math, physics, mechanical drawing, blueprint reading, welding, and general provide a good foundation for the variety of tasks that construction laborers may perform.

Some laborers may choose or be required to attend formal instruction at a community college or trade or vocational school. They may receive certification in specialties such as welding, scaffold erection, and concrete finishing. Certification can be an advantage when seeking advancement.

A small percentage of laborers enter formal apprenticeship programs that take two to four years to complete and combine classroom instruction with on-the-job training. Typically, the curriculum consists of skills training in the three largest segments of the construction industry: building construction, heavy and highway construction, and environmental remediation. The latter may involve lead or asbestos abatement and mold or hazardous waste remediation.

Workers who handle toxic chemicals or operate dangerous equipment receive specialized safety training. Those who remove hazardous materials are required to take union- or employer-sponsored Occupational Safety and Health (OSHA) safety training.

The Laborers' International Union of North America (LIUNA) offers a lead renovator training program that is accredited by the U.S. Environmental Protection Agency. This is one of fifty training programs that LIUNA offers for workforce advancement.

For More Information

Laborers' International Union of North America (LIUNA)
905 16th Street, NW
Washington, DC 2006
202-737-8320
www.liuna.org

National Center for Construction Education and Research (NCCER)
3600 Northwest 43rd Street
Building G
Gainesville, Florida 32606-8134
888-622-3720 (toll-free)
www.nccer.org

Occupational Safety and Health Administration (OSHA)
200 Constitution Avenue, NW
Washington, DC 20210
800-321-6742 (toll-free)
www.osha.gov

Cost Estimator ☼

Alternate Titles and Related Careers

- Construction Estimator
- Cost Analyst
- Estimator
- Estimator Project Manager
- Operations Manager
- Project Manager
- Sales Engineer

This is a "Bright Outlook" occupation in a variety of fields, including product manufacturing and services as well as construction. Regardless of the field, cost estimators perform the same type of work.

Job Trends

This occupation will grow much faster than average at 20 percent or higher according to projections of the Bureau of Labor Statistics. Between 2008 and 2018, about 103,600 new jobs will be added to the occupation. About 59 percent of cost estimators work in construction and 15 percent in manufacturing. The remainder are spread across a variety of industries. Employment opportunities should be very good especially for those with bachelor's degrees and industry experience.

Most of the growth in this occupation is expected in the construction sector. The need to repair highways, bridges, water and sewer systems, airports, and subways will generate jobs for cost estimators. Increasing population will generate the need for homes, schools, and offices, while the aging population contributes to the need for hospitals, extended care facilities, and nursing homes. In addition, the market for home remodeling is currently strong. This is partially driven by economic conditions, but also by environmental concerns. Retrofitting and remodeling to improve energy efficiency is increasing. Also retrofitting of industrial plants, government buildings, and schools will provide job opportunities for people who can analyze resource factors and estimate project costs.

Nature of the Work

Cost estimators use mathematics, engineering, technology, economics, and accounting in their work. They estimate the costs, scope, and duration of construction projects, product manufacturing, or services. These estimates are used to prepare bids and to decide if a project will be profitable. Cost estimators must be familiar with spreadsheet software and software for accounting and financials.

Construction estimators must analyze all factors that affect a project's cost including location, site, materials, machinery, labor, and length of the project. Estimators may work for the construction company, the architect, or the owner. In large companies, estimators may specialize in the type of work they estimate. For example, some may specialize in estimating electrical work only or the plumbing.

According to O*NET, cost estimators may perform the following tasks:

- Analyze blueprints and other documentation to prepare time, cost, materials, and labor estimates
- Visit site and record information about access, drainage and topography, and availability of services such as water and electricity
- Prepare estimates used by management for purposes such as planning, organizing, and scheduling work
- Consult with clients, vendors, personnel in other departments, or construction foremen to discuss and formulate estimates and resolve issues
- Prepare estimates for use in selecting vendors or subcontractors
- Confer with engineers, architects, owners, contractors and subcontractors on changes and adjustments to cost estimates
- Set up cost monitoring and reporting systems and procedures
- Prepare cost and expenditure statements and other necessary documentation at regular intervals for the duration of the project
- Assess cost effectiveness of products, projects, or services, tracking actual costs relative to bids as the project develops
- Conduct special studies to develop and establish standard hour and related cost data or to effect cost reduction
- Review material and labor requirements to decide whether it is more cost-effective to produce or purchase components
- Prepare and maintain a directory of suppliers, contractors, and subcontractors
- Establish and maintain tendering process, and conduct negotiations

Career Path

Cost estimators generally advance by receiving higher pay. However, some become project managers in construction or engineering managers in manufacturing. Some start their own consulting firms to provide services to construction or manufacturing companies or to the government.

Earning Potential

Median hourly wage (2009): $27.55

Median annual wage (2009): $57,300

Education/Licensure

About 40 percent of currently employed cost estimators have some college education, but less than a bachelor's degree. Those with bachelor's degrees, about 32 percent, have the best job prospects now and in the future. However, colleges and universities do not offer degree programs in cost estimating. Instead a bachelor's degree in construction management, construction science, or building science is preferred for the construction industry. Most colleges and universities include cost estimating in the curriculum for civil and industrial engineering and construction management. Associate degree programs in construction engineering technology also include cost estimating.

Experience is critical for job candidates. Students can gain valuable experience through internships and cooperative education experiences while working toward their degrees. Those already working in other areas of the construction industry can gain practical experience and knowledge of costs, materials, and procedures that they can translate into a cost estimation job. On-the-job training is also important because each company has its own methods for cost estimating.

Certification is voluntary, but is valuable for job candidates, and some employers require certification. The Society of Cost Estimating and Analysis (SCEA) and the Association for the Advancement of Cost Engineering (AACE International) offer certifications that require two to eight years of experience and passing an exam. These organizations also offer professional development opportunities. Many community colleges, technical schools, and universities offer specialized courses in cost estimation procedures and techniques.

For More Information

Association for the Advancement of Cost Engineering (AACE International)
209 Prairie Avenue
Suite 100
Morgantown, West Virginia 26501-5934
(800) 858–2678 (toll-free)
www.aacei.org

Society of Cost Estimating and Analysis (SCEA)
527 Maple Avenue East
Suite 301
Vienna, Virginia 22180
(703) 938–5090
www.sceaonline.net

Electrical Engineer 🌍

Alternate Titles and Related Careers

- Circuits Engineer
- Electrical and Instrument Maintenance Supervisor (E and I)
- Electrical Controls Engineer
- Electrical Design Engineer
- Electrical Project Engineer
- Electro-Mechanical Engineer
- Project Engineer
- Test Engineer

This is considered a "Green Enhanced-Skills" occupation in a variety of sectors of the green economy: energy efficiency, green construction, renewable energy generation, and research, design, and consulting services.

Job Trends

The *Occupational Outlook Handbook* lists a growth of about 2 percent for electrical engineers between 2008 and 2018. This reflects a small change in the total of jobs for electrical engineers. Replacement of engineers reaching retirement or transferring into sales and management, however, will add to the number of jobs.

About Calgreen

Calgreen is the name of California's mandatory statewide green building code, the first in the nation. The California Air Resources Board estimated that three million metric tons of emissions will be removed from the air by 2020, which will help Californians meet the state's goal of reducing greenhouse gas emissions by 33 percent by 2020.

Nature of the Work

Electrical engineers design, develop, test, or supervise the manufacturing and installation of electrical equipment, components, or systems for commercial, industrial, military, or scientific use. Equipment includes motors, devices for generating power, controls, and transmission devices, and systems include navigational systems, and wiring in buildings, aircraft, and automobiles.

Among the tasks that electrical engineers may perform according to O*NET are the following:

- Prepare and study technical drawings, specifications of electrical systems, and topographical maps to ensure that installation and operations conform to standards and customer requirements
- Operate computer-assisted engineering and design software and equipment to perform engineering tasks
- Confer with engineers, customers, and others to discuss existing or potential engineering projects and products
- Direct and coordinate manufacturing, construction, installation, maintenance, support, documentation, or testing activities to ensure compliance with specifications, codes, and customer requirements
- Prepare specifications for purchase of materials and equipment

- Perform detailed calculations to compute and establish manufacturing, construction, and installation standards and specifications
- Oversee project production efforts to assure projects are completed satisfactorily, on time and within budget
- Plan and implement research methodology and procedures to apply principles of electrical theory to engineering projects
- Plan layout of electric power generating plants and distribution lines and stations
- Inspect completed installations and observe operations to ensure conformance to design and equipment specifications and compliance with operational and safety standards
- Collect data relating to commercial and residential development, population, and power system interconnection to determine operating efficiency of electrical systems
- Assist in developing capital project programs for new equipment and major repairs
- Investigate customer or public complaints, determine nature and extent of problem, and recommend remedial measures
- Develop budgets, estimating labor, material, and construction costs
- Compile data and write reports regarding existing and potential engineering studies and projects
- Investigate and test vendors' and competitors' products
- Supervise and train project team members as necessary

Career Path

As electrical engineers gain experience, they become specialists and advance into positions where they supervise a team of engineers and other staff. Some eventually may become managers or move into sales jobs where their technical background is particularly useful. Some go on to earn a master's in business administration (MBA) to prepare them for high-level managerial positions.

Earning Potential

Median hourly wage (2009): $39.96

Median annual wage (2009): $83,110

Education/Licensure

For entry-level positions, a bachelor's degree in engineering from a college or university program that is accredited by the Accreditation Board for Engineering and Technology (ABET) is required. In some cases, engineers with degrees in one type of engineering may qualify for jobs in other areas of engineering.

Some colleges and universities offer five-year programs that culminate in a master's degree. Some offer five-or six-year programs that include cooperative experience. Some four-year schools have arrangements with community colleges or liberal arts colleges that allow students to spend two or three years at the initial school and transfer for the last two years to complete their engineering degree.

All fifty states and the District of Columbia require engineers to be licensed as professional engineers (PE) if they serve the public directly. In most states, licensure requires graduation from a four-year engineering program accredited by ABET, four years of experience, and passing the state exam. Many engineers take the Fundamentals of Engineering portion of the exam upon graduation. They are then engineers in training (EIT). After obtaining appropriate work experience, they take the Principles and Practice of Engineering exam to complete their professional license. Most states recognize licenses from other states, as long as the requirements are the same or more stringent. Some states have continuing education requirements.

For More Information

Accreditation Board for Engineering and
   Technology (ABET)
111 Market Place
Suite 1050
Baltimore, Maryland 21202
(410) 347–7700
www.abet.org

American Society for Engineering Education
   (ASEE)
1818 N Street, NW
Suite 600
Washington, DC 20036-2479
(202) 331–3500
www.asee.org

Institute of Electrical and Electronics Engineers
   (IEEE)
445 Hoes Lane
Piscataway, New Jersey 08854-4141
(732) 981–0060
www.ieee.org

National Society of Professional Engineers
   (NSPE)
1420 King Street
Alexandria, Virginia 22314
(703) 684–2800
www.nspe.org

Engineering Manager ☉

Alternate Titles and Related Careers

- Chief Engineer
- Civil Engineering Manager
- Director of Engineering
- Principal Engineer
- Process Engineering Manager
- Project Engineer
- Project Engineering Manager
- Project Manager
- Supervisory Civil Engineer

This is considered a "Green Enhanced-Skills" occupation in the environment protection and research, design, and consulting green sectors of the economy.

Job Trends

Job growth is projected to be as fast as average for all occupations at 8 percent between 2008 and 2018 according to the *Occupational Outlook Handbook*. Job opportunities will be best for engineers with strong communication and business management skills. In addition to openings created by employment growth, openings will result from the need to replace managers who retire or move into other occupations.

Nature of the Work

Engineering managers plan, direct, or coordinate activities or research and development in fields such as architecture and engineering. They may supervise the work of engineers, scientists, and technicians as well as support staff. Managers decide what should be done and how. Knowledge of administrative procedures and strong analytical skills are needed. For example, managers may develop the overall concepts of a new product or identify the technical problems that prevent the completion of a project.

According to O*NET, engineering managers may perform the following tasks, depending on the field in which they work:

- Coordinate and direct projects, making detailed plans to accomplish goals and directing the integration of technical activities
- Set scientific and technical goals within broad outlines provided by top management
- Consult or negotiate with clients to prepare project specifications
- Present and explain proposals, reports, and findings to clients
- Confer with management, production, and marketing staff to discuss project specifications and procedures
- Direct, review, and approve product design and changes

- Analyze technology, resource needs, and market demand, to plan and assess the feasibility of projects
- Develop and implement policies, standards, and procedures for the engineering and technical work performed in the department, service, laboratory or firm
- Plan and direct the installation, testing, operation, maintenance, and repair of facilities and equipment
- Administer highway planning, construction, and maintenance
- Direct the engineering of water control, treatment, and distribution projects
- Plan, direct, and coordinate survey work with other staff activities, certifying survey work, and writing land legal descriptions
- Prepare budgets, bids, and contracts, and direct the negotiation of contracts
- Review and recommend or approve contracts and cost estimates
- Confer with and report to officials and the public to provide information and solicit support for projects
- Recruit employees, assign, direct, and evaluate their work, and oversee the development and maintenance of staff competence
- Perform administrative functions such as reviewing and writing reports, approving expenditures, enforcing rules, and making decisions about the purchase of materials or services

Career Path

Most engineering managers have formal education and work experience as engineers and typically advance to management positions only after years of employment as engineers. Engineering managers may advance to progressively higher leadership positions within their disciplines. Some may become managers in nontechnical areas such as marketing or sales.

Some engineering firms prefer to hire experienced engineers as sales representatives because of the technical knowledge required to adequately explain the products and services. Over time, a sales representative may advance to a regional sales manager's job or even a national sales manager position.

Earning Potential

Median hourly wage (2009): $56.25

Median annual wage (2009): $117,000

Education/Licensure

Because almost all engineering managers begin their careers as practicing engineers, the job typically requires at least a bachelor's degree in some engineering specialty from a college or university program that is accredited by the Accreditation Board for Engineering and Technology (ABET).

Some colleges and universities offer five-year programs that culminate in a master's degree. Some offer five- or six-year programs that include cooperative experience. Some four-year schools have arrangements with community colleges or liberal arts colleges that allow students to spend two or three years at the initial school and transfer for the last two years to complete their engineering degree.

Many engineering managers also gain business management skills by earning either a master's in engineering management degree (MEM) or a master's in business administration (MBA). Employers often pay for such training and some large companies offer some courses onsite. Typically, engineers who prefer to manage in technical areas pursue the MEM, whereas those more interested in the business side earn an MBA.

All fifty states and the District of Columbia require engineers to be licensed as professional engineers (PE) if they serve the public directly. In most states, licensure requires graduation from a four-year engineering program accredited by ABET, four years of experience, and passing the state exam. Many engineers take the Fundamentals of Engineering portion of the exam upon graduation. They are then engineers in training (EIT). After obtaining appropriate work experience, they take the Principles and Practice of Engineering exam to complete their professional license. Most states recognize licenses from other states, as long as the requirements are the same or more stringent. Some states have continuing education requirements.

The American Society for Engineering Management (ASEM) at the University of Missouri offers two voluntary certifications: Associate Engineering Manager (AEM) and Professional Engineering Manager (PEM). Its Web site also lists universities that offer engineering management programs at the undergraduate and graduate levels.

For More Information

Accreditation Board for Engineering and
 Technology (ABET)
111 Market Place
Suite 1050
Baltimore, Maryland 21202
410-347-7700
www.abet.org

American Council of Engineering Companies
 (ACEC)
1015 15th Street, NW
8th Floor
Washington, DC 20005-2605
202-347-7474
www.acec.org

American Society for Engineering Management
 (ASEM)
614 North Pine Street
Suite 206
P.O. Box 206
Rolla, Missouri 65402-0820
www.netforumondemand.com

National Society of Professional Engineers
 (NSPE)
1420 King Street
Alexandria, Virginia 22314
703-684-2800
www.nspe.org

Operating Engineer/Construction Equipment Operator ✿ ⊕

Alternate Titles and Related Careers
- Back Hoe Operator
- Equipment Operator
- Excavator Operator
- Grader Operator
- Heavy Equipment Operator
- Loader Operator
- Machine Operator
- Motor Grader Operator
- Track Hoe Operator

This is considered a "Bright Outlook" and "Green Increased-Demand" occupation in the green construction sector of the economy.

Job Trends

The Bureau of Labor Statistics rates the job growth for the operating engineer and other construction equipment operator category as average at 7 to 13 percent. The overall projected job openings is estimated at 118,200. About 63 percent of currently employed operating engineers and operators of other types of construction equipment work in construction, and 18 percent work for government agencies.

Nature of the Work

Operating engineers operate one or several types of power construction equipment such as motor graders, bulldozers, scrapers, compressors, pumps, derricks, shovels, tractors, or front-end loaders. Their jobs may include excavating, moving, and grading earth; erecting structures; and pouring concrete or other hard surface pavement. In addition to their other duties, operating engineers may also repair and maintain the equipment.

According to O*NET, operating engineers and other construction equipment operators may perform the following tasks:

- Learn and follow safety regulations and monitor operations to ensure that health and safety standards are met
- Take actions to avoid potential hazards and obstructions, such as utility lines, other equipment, other workers, and falling objects
- Locate underground services, such as pipes and wires, prior to beginning work
- Start engines; move throttles, switches, and levers; and depress pedals to operate machines
- Adjust handwheels and depress pedals to control attachments, such as blades, buckets, scrapers, and swing booms
- Align machines, cutterheads, or depth gauge makers with reference stakes and guidelines or ground or position equipment, following hand signals of other workers
- Coordinate machine actions with other activities, positioning or moving loads in response to hand or audio signals from crew members
- Load and move dirt, rocks, equipment, and materials, using trucks, crawler tractors, power cranes, shovels, graders, or related equipment
- Drive and maneuver equipment equipped with blades in successive passes over working areas to remove topsoil, vegetation, and rocks, and to distribute and level earth or terrain
- Operate tractors and bulldozers to perform such tasks as clearing land, mixing sludge, trimming backfills, and building roadways and parking lots
- Select and fasten bulldozer blades or other attachments to tractors, using hitches
- Connect hydraulic hoses, belts, mechanical linkages, or power takeoff shafts to tractors
- Operate loaders to pull out stumps, rip asphalt or concrete, rough-grade properties, bury refuse, or perform general cleanup

- Operate compactors, scrapers, or rollers to level, compact, or cover refuse at disposal grounds
- Operate equipment to demolish and remove debris and to remove snow from streets, roads, and parking lots
- Operate road watering, oiling, and rolling equipment, or street sealing equipment, such as chip spreaders
- Perform specialized work, using equipment such as pile drivers, dredging rigs, drillers, and concrete pumpers
- Drive tractor-trailer trucks to move equipment from site to site
- Check fuel supplies at sites to ensure adequate availability
- Repair and maintain equipment, making emergency adjustments or assisting with major repairs as necessary
- Keep records of material and equipment usage and problems encountered
- Talk to clients and study instructions, plans, and diagrams to establish work requirements
- Compile cost estimates for jobs

Career Path

Entry-level positions typically require a high school diploma or equivalent, although some employers may hire and train nongraduates to operate certain types of equipment. Typically, entry-level workers begin by operating light equipment under the supervision of an experience operator. With experience, they may operate heavier equipment. Because of the computerization of construction equipment, operators may need more training and some understanding of electronics to advance.

Construction equipment operators may advance in time to become supervisors. Some become trainers and other open their own contracting businesses. Contractors must be licensed.

Earning Potential

Median hourly wage (2009): $19.12

Median annual wage (2009): $39,770

Education/Licensure

Entry-level construction equipment operators may receive training through a formal apprenticeship program, on-the-job training, a paid training program, or a combination of the three. Typically, entry-level personnel have a high school diploma or the equivalent. High school courses in automotive mechanics, science, mechanical drawing, and computers are helpful.

Formal operating engineer apprenticeship programs offer the most comprehensive training. Administered by union-management committees of the International Union of Operating Engineers (IUOE), the apprenticeship offers candidates three years, or 6,000 hours, of on-the-job training for which they are paid. In addition to work experience, apprentices also receive 144 hours of classroom instruction during each of the three years.

Private vocational schools may also training in certain types of construction equipment. An important factor to consider is whether a particular school offers the opportunity to work on actual machines in realistic situations. The alternative is sophisticated simulators similar to the ones used in IUOE apprenticeship programs.

The IUOE offers the Operating Engineers Certification (OEC) in several five crane types: boom truck, lattice boom, overhead, telescopic, and tower. Earning a certification can be an advantage in seeking advancement by demonstrating competency and also commitment.

For More Information

Associated General Contractors of America, Inc. (AGC)
2300 Wilson Boulevard
Suite 400
Arlington, Virginia 22201-5426
703-548-3118
www.agc.org

International Union of Operating Engineers (IUOE)
1125 17th Street, NW
Washington, DC 20036
202-429-9100

National Center for Construction Education and Research (NCCER)
3600 Northwest 43rd Street
Building G
Gainesville, Florida 32606-8134
888-622-3720 (toll-free)
www.nccer.org

Pipefitter and Steamfitter ✿ 🌐

Alternate Titles and Related Careers
- Equipment Service Associate (ESA)
- Industrial Pipefitter
- Journeyman Pipe Fitter
- Lead Pipefitter
- Lead Steamfitter
- Machine Repairman
- Mechanical Pipefitter
- Millwright
- Pipefitting Tradesman
- Pipefitter Helper
- Plumber and Steamfitter
- Senior Steamfitter
- Service Technician
- Sprinkler Fitter
- Steamfitter Foreman
- Welder

This is considered a "Bright Outlook" and "Green Enhanced-Skills" occupation in the green construction sector of the economy.

Job Trends

The Bureau of Labor Statistics includes pipefitters and steamfitters with plumbers in a single category and estimates that the overall category will grow faster than the average of all occupations at 14 to 19 percent. Projected job openings for the total category are 175,500. About 72 percent are currently employed in construction and another 12 percent are self-employed.

According to the *Occupational Outlook Handbook,* demand for pipefitters and steamfitters will be driven by maintenance and construction of power plants, water and wastewater treatment plants, office buildings, and factories, all of which have extensive pipe systems. The need to improve and expand the nation's infrastructure is prompting this construction.

About Green Office Buildings

In 2009, the University of San Diego and the commercial real estate broker CB Richard Ellis Group conducted a survey of 2,000 tenants in 154 buildings managed by the company. All the buildings had either Energy Star ratings from the Environmental Protection Agency or LEED certification. The results showed that employees took 2.9 fewer sick days, 55 percent of employers noted a rise in productivity among their staffs, and employers saved on average 21 percent on their energy bills.

Job opportunities are expected to outpace the supply of skilled pipefitters and steamfitters. In addition, many people currently working in this field are expected to retire over the next decade and their jobs will need to be filled. Generally, the jobs of pipefitters and steamfitters are less sensitive to changes in economic conditions than are other jobs in construction. Also, the growing emphasis on energy and water conservation is opening up opportunities for pipefitters and steamfitters who become proficient in new green technologies.

Nature of the Work

Pipefitters and steamfitters lay out, assemble, install, and maintain pipe systems, pipe supports, and related hydraulic and pneumatic equipment for steam, hot water, heating, cooling, lubricating, sprinkling, and industrial production and processing systems. Among the tools that pipefitters and steamfitters use are saws, cutting torches, pipe threaders and benders, valve keys, and wrenches. They may weld, braze, cement, solder, and thread pipe joints.

Based on O*NET surveys, pipefitters and steamfitters may perform the following tasks:

- Measure and mark pipes for cutting and threading and cut, thread, and hammer pipe to specifications
- Assemble and secure pipes, tubes, fittings, and related equipment, according to specifications
- Attach pipes to walls, structures and fixtures, such as radiators or tanks, using brackets, clamps, tools, or welding equipment
- Inspect, examine, and test installed systems and pipe lines, using pressure gauge, hydrostatic testing, observation, or other methods
- Lay out full-scale drawings of pipe systems, supports, and related equipment, following blueprints
- Plan pipe system layout, installation, and repair work according to specifications
- Select pipe sizes and types and related materials, such as supports, hangers, and hydraulic cylinders, according to specifications
- Cut and bore holes in structures, such as bulkheads, decks, walls, and mains, prior to pipe installation
- Modify, clean, and maintain pipe systems, units, fittings, and related machines and equipment, following specifications
- Install automatic controls used to regulate pipe systems
- Turn valves to shut off steam, water, or other gases or liquids from pipe sections
- Remove and replace worn components
- Inspect work sites for obstructions and to ensure that holes will not cause structural weakness
- Operate motorized pumps to remove water from flooded manholes, basements, or facility floors
- Dip nonferrous piping materials in a mixture of molten tin and lead to obtain a coating that prevents erosion or galvanic and electrolytic action
- Prepare cost estimates for clients

Career Path

Entry-level pipefitters and steamfitters begin as apprentices under the supervision of experienced workers. The apprentices learn basic skills and do low-level tasks. As they gain experience, apprentices are given more difficult tasks and work with less supervision. At the end of the apprenticeship—typically four or five years—a pipefitter or steamfitter is a journeyman and able to work independently.

With experience and additional training, pipefitters and steamfitters can become supervisors for mechanical and plumbing contractors. Some move into related fields such as construction management or building inspection. Some may open their own businesses as contractors, which may require a license.

Because of the increasing number of Spanish-speaking workers in the construction industry, being able to speak Spanish is a useful skill for those who wish to move into supervision and management.

Earning Potential

Median hourly wage (2009): $22.27

Median annual wage (2009): $46,320

(Based on "Plumbers, Pipefitters, and Steamfitters")

Education/Licensure

Typically, a high school diploma or equivalent is required. Most pipefitters and steamfitters learn their trade through apprenticeship programs or by earning a certificate or associate degree from a technical school or community college. A formal apprenticeship lasts four or five years and consists of paid on-the-job training and at least 144 hours of classroom instruction each year of the apprenticeship. Training as a pipefitter or steamfitter in the U.S. military is good preparation for civilian jobs.

The Green Building Institute affiliated with the U.S. Green Building Council offers LEED credentialing appropriate for mechanical service contractors.

Pipefitters must be licensed in some states.

For More Information

American Fire Sprinkler Association (AFSA)
12750 Merit Drive
Suite 350
Dallas, Texas 75251
214-349-5965
www.sprinklernet.org

Mechanical Contractors Association of America (MCAA)
1385 Piccard Drive
Rockville, Maryland 20850
301-869-5800
www.mcaa.org

National Fire Sprinkler Association (NFSA)
40 Jon Barrett Road
Patterson, New York 12563
845-878-4200
www.nfsa.org

Plumbing-Heating-Cooling Contractors National Association (PHCC)
180 South Washington Street
Falls Church, Virginia 22046
800-533-7694 (toll-free)
www.phcc.org

United Association of Journeymen and Apprentices of the Plumbing and Pipe Fitting Industry
Three Park Place
Annapolis, Maryland 21401-3687
410-269-2000
www.ua.org

U.S. Green Building Council (USGBC)
2101 L Street, NW
Suite 500
Washington, DC 20037
800-795-1747 (toll-free)
www.usgbc.org

Plumber ☼ⓖ

Alternate Titles and Related Careers
- Commercial Plumber
- Drain Technician
- Journeyman Plumber
- Plumber Gasfitter
- Plumbing and Heating Mechanic
- Residential Plumber
- Service Plumber

This is considered a "Bright Outlook" and "Green Enhanced-Skills" occupation in the green construction sector of the economy.

Job Trends

The Bureau of Labor Statistics includes plumbers with pipefitters and steamfitters in a single category and estimates that the overall category will grow faster than the average of all occupations at 14 to 19 percent. Projected job openings for the total category are 175,500. About 72 percent are currently employed in construction and another 12 percent are self-employed.

The demand for plumbers will be driven by several factors: new construction and the renovation of existing buildings as well as the repair and maintenance of plumbing systems in existing homes, according to the *Occupational Outlook Handbook*. A growing concern about conserving water, particularly in drier parts of the country, will require retrofitting plumbing systems to conserve water in new ways, which will also increase the demand for plumbers.

Job opportunities are expected to outpace the supply of skilled plumbers. In addition, many people currently working in this field are expected to retire over the next decade and their jobs will need to be filled. Generally, the jobs of plumbers like those of pipefitters and steamfitters are less sensitive to changes in economic conditions than are other jobs in construction. Also, the growing emphasis on conservation of energy and water is opening up opportunities for plumbers who become proficient in new green technologies.

Nature of the Work

Plumbers assemble, install, and repair pipes, fittings, and fixtures used in heating, water, and drainage systems. Plumbers have to follow the specifications as laid out for a job and also plumbing codes. They work with a variety of hand and power tools such as pipe cutters, pipe-threading machines, pipe-bending machines, rulers, levels, and pressure gauges. In their work, they may install dishwashers, water heaters, clothes washers and dryers, sinks, and toilets. Plumbers may work for construction companies or plumbing contractors, or be self-employed.

According to O*NET, plumbers may perform the following tasks:

- Study building plans and inspect structures to assess material and equipment needs, to establish the sequence of pipe installations, and to plan installation around obstructions such as electrical wiring
- Review blueprints and building codes and specifications to determine work details and procedures
- Locate and mark the position of pipe installations, connections, passage holes, and fixtures in structures
- Fill pipes or plumbing fixtures with water or air and observe pressure gauges to detect and locate leaks
- Measure, cut, thread, and bend pipe to required angle
- Assemble pipe sections, tubing and fittings, using couplings, clamps, screws, bolts, cement, plastic solvent, caulking, or soldering, brazing and welding equipment

- Install pipe assemblies, fittings, valves, appliances, and fixtures
- Cut openings in structures to accommodate pipes and pipe fittings
- Install underground storm, sanitary, and water piping systems and extend piping to connect fixtures and plumbing to these systems
- Repair and maintain plumbing, replacing defective washers, replacing or mending broken pipes, and opening clogged drains
- Hang steel supports from ceiling joists to hold pipes in place
- Clear away debris in a renovation
- Use specialized techniques, equipment, or materials, such as performing computer-assisted welding of small pipes, or working with the special piping used in microchip fabrication
- Direct workers engaged in pipe cutting and preassembly and installation of plumbing systems and components
- Prepare written work cost estimates and negotiate contracts
- Perform complex calculations and planning for special or very large jobs
- Keep records of assignments and produce detailed work reports

Career Path

Entry-level plumbers begin as apprentices under the supervision of experienced workers. The apprentices learn basic skills and do low-level tasks. As they gain experience, apprentices are given more difficult tasks and work with less supervision. At the end of the apprenticeship—typically four or five years—a plumber is a journeyman and able to work independently.

With experience and additional training, plumbers can become supervisors for mechanical and plumbing contractors. Some move into related fields such as construction management or building inspection. Many open their own plumbing businesses, starting out on their own, and slowly building a business that employs a number of plumbers and apprentices.

Because of the increasing number of Spanish-speaking workers in the construction industry, being able to speak Spanish is a useful skill for those who wish to move into supervision and management.

Earning Potential

Median hourly wage (2009): $22.27

Median annual wage (2009): $46,320

Education/Licensure

Typically, a high school diploma or equivalent is required. Most plumbers learn their trade through apprenticeship programs or by earning a certificate or associate degree from a technical school or community college. A formal apprenticeship lasts four or five years and consists of paid on-the-job training and at least 144 hours of classroom instruction each year of the apprenticeship. Training as a plumber in the U.S. military is good preparation for civilian jobs.

Most states and municipalities require that plumbers be licensed. Requirements vary from place to place, but typically plumbers must have two to five years' experience and pass an exam that includes questions on local plumbing codes as well as on plumbing. Once plumbers pass the test, they can work independently. Several states require a separate license for plumbers to work on gas lines, such as installing a gas clothes dryer.

The Plumbing-Heating-Cooling Contractors National Association formed a partnership with GreenPlumbers USA to train and certify plumbers on water-saving technologies and energy efficiency. Because of the growing concern over water conservation, this certification is expected to open up job and advancement opportunities for plumbers who are trained in these methods.

The Green Building Institute affiliated with the U.S. Green Building Council offers LEED credentialing appropriate for mechanical service contractors.

For More Information

American Fire Sprinkler Association (AFSA)
12750 Merit Drive
Suite 350
Dallas, Texas 75251
214-349-5965
www.sprinklernet.org

GreenPlumbers USA
4153 Northgate Boulevard
Suite 1
Sacramento, California 95834
888-929-6207 (toll-free)
www.greenplumbersusa.com

Mechanical Contractors Association of America (MCAA)
1385 Piccard Drive
Rockville, Maryland 20850
301-869-5800
www.mcaa.org

National Fire Sprinkler Association (NFSA)
40 Jon Barrett Road
Patterson, New York 12563
845-878-4200
www.nfsa.org

Plumbing-Heating-Cooling Contractors National Association (PHCC)
180 South Washington Street
Falls Church, Virginia 22046
800-533-7694 (toll-free)
www.phcc.org

United Association of Journeymen and Apprentices of the Plumbing and Pipe Fitting Industry
Three Park Place
Annapolis, Maryland 21401-3687
410-269-2000
www.ua.org

Property, Real Estate, or Community Association Manager

Alternate Titles and Related Careers

- Apartment Manager
- Community Manager
- Concierge
- Lease Administration Supervisor
- Leasing Manager
- On-Site Manager
- Resident Manager

Good opportunities will exist for those with experience managing housing for older people or health-care facilities, both of which are expected to experience growth as the nation's population ages.

Job Trends

The Bureau of Labor Statistics projects that this occupational category will increase by 8 percent between 2008 and 2018. The rate is as fast average for all occupations and translates into around 78,000 job openings in addition to those openings that will occur as people retire or move into other occupations. About 46 percent of currently employed managers are self-employed, and another 40 percent work for real estate, rental, and leasing companies.

Candidates with a degree in business administration, real estate, or a related field or who earn professional certificates or designations in property management should have the best job opportunities. The job growth will result from a growing population that will increasingly live in developments—apartment buildings, condominiums, homeowner associations, and senior housing—managed by third-party property management companies. A smaller increase in the number of commercial and retail buildings will also generate a need for additional property managers.

Nature of the Work

Property, real estate, and community association managers plan, direct, or coordinate the selling, buying, leasing, or governance activities of commercial, industrial, or residential real estate properties. By running efficient, well-maintained properties, managers raise the value of real estate investments. This is true for real estate holding companies as well as for housing developments of individual homeowners. For rental managers, an important part of the job is staying up-to-date on building codes and housing laws related to nondiscrimination laws in advertising and renting property.

O*NET lists the following tasks as those that property, real estate, and community association managers may perform:

- Market vacant space to prospective tenants through leasing agents, advertising, or other methods
- Meet with prospective tenants to show properties, explain terms of occupancy, and provide information about local areas
- Determine and certify the eligibility of prospective tenants, following government regulations
- Direct collection of monthly assessments, rental fees, and deposits and payment of insurance premiums, mortgage, taxes, and incurred operating expenses
- Investigate complaints, disturbances, and violations and resolve problems following management rules and regulations
- Inspect grounds, facilities, and equipment routinely to determine necessity of repairs or maintenance
- Plan, schedule, and coordinate general maintenance, major repairs, and remodeling or construction projects for commercial or residential properties
- Solicit and analyze bids from contractors for repairs, renovations, and maintenance
- Prepare and administer contracts for provision of property services such as cleaning, maintenance, and security services
- Manage and oversee operations, maintenance, administration, and

improvement of commercial, industrial, or residential properties

- Direct and coordinate the activities of staff and contract personnel and evaluate their performance
- Maintain contact with insurance carriers, fire and police departments, and other agencies to ensure protection and compliance with codes and regulations
- Maintain records of sales, rental or usage activity, special permits issued, maintenance and operating costs, or property availability
- Prepare detailed budgets and financial reports for properties
- Review rents to ensure that they are in line with rental markets
- Purchase building and maintenance supplies, equipment, or furniture
- Clean common areas, change light bulbs, and make minor property repairs
- Act as liaisons between on-site managers or tenants and owners
- Confer regularly with community association members to ensure their needs are being met
- Meet with boards of directors and committees to discuss and resolve legal and environmental issues or disputes between neighbors
- Confer with legal authorities to ensure that renting and advertising practices are not discriminatory and that properties comply with state and federal regulations
- Meet with clients to negotiate management and service contracts, determine priorities, and discuss the financial and operational status of properties
- Contract with architectural firms to draw up detailed plans for new structures
- Negotiate with government leaders, businesses, special interest representatives, and utility companies to gain support for new projects and to eliminate potential obstacles

- Analyze information on property values, taxes, zoning, population growth, and traffic volume and patterns to determine if properties should be acquired
- Negotiate the sale, lease, or development of property and complete or review appropriate documents and forms
- Negotiate short- and long-term loans to finance construction and ownership of structures

Career Path

Many property, real estate, and community association managers begin their careers as assistants, working in an office with a property manager to learn the business. They will assist in preparing budgets, analyzing insurance coverage and risk options, collecting overdue rents, and similar tasks. With experience, they may advance to property manager.

Some managers instead begin their careers as onsite managers of apartment buildings, office complexes, and community associations. Typically, they work under the supervision of a more experienced property manager. In time, assistants may advance to positions with greater responsibilities and may transfer to assistant offsite property manager jobs. In these jobs—for example, for a large real estate holding company that manages shopping malls—they gain experience in a broad range of property management responsibilities. Managers advance by taking on more responsibilities and managing larger and more properties.

Many managers specialize in a particular type of property. Some manage office buildings only or only homeowners' associations. Some property managers open their own property management firms, contracting to manage properties for building or complex owners or homeowners' associations.

Earning Potential

Median hourly wage (2009): $23.30

Median annual wage (2009): $48,460

Education/Licensure

Typically, employers prefer to hire college graduates for property management positions. A bachelor's degree or master's degree in business administration, accounting, finance, real estate, or public administration is the norm for off-site positions that deal with a property's finances and contract management, and for most commercial properties, according to the *Occupation Outlook Handbook*. Those with liberal arts degrees may also qualify, especially if they have relevant coursework. Most new managers also participate in on-the-job training.

All states require that real estate managers who buy or sell property be licensed. In some states, community association managers must also be licensed. Anyone who manages public housing subsidized by the federal government must be certified.

The Institute of Real Estate Management (IREM) offers certification programs in Certified Property Manager (CPM), Accredited Residential Manager (ARM), and Accredited Commercial Manager (ACoM) for individuals and Accredited Management Organization (AMO) for management firms.

The Building Owners and Managers Institute (BOMI) offers both designations and certificate programs. The certificate programs offered are Property Administrator Certification (PAC), Facilities Management Certificate (FMC), Building Systems Management Certificate (SMC), and Property Management Financial Proficiency Certificate (PMFP). The professional designations build on these certificates.

The National Board of Certification for Community Association Managers (NBC-CAM) administers the Certified Manager of Community Associations (CMCA).

For More Information

Building Owners and Managers Institute (BOMI)
One Park Place
Suite 475
Annapolis, Maryland 21401
800-235-2664 (toll-free)
www.bomi.org

Community Associations Institute
225 Reinekers Lane
Suite 300
Alexandria, Virginia 22314
886-224-4321 (toll-free)
www.caionline.org

Institute of Real Estate Management (IREM)
430 North Michigan Avenue
Chicago, Illinois 60611
800-837-0706 (toll-free)
www.irem.org

National Board of Certification for Community Association Managers (NBC-CAM)
225 Reinekers Lane
Suite 310
Alexandria, Virginia 22314
886-779-2622 (toll-free)
www.nbccam.org

Real Estate Agent ☼

Alternate Titles and Related Careers

- Associate Broker
- Broker Associate
- Real Estate Broker
- Real Estate Broker Associate
- Real Estate Sales Agent
- Real Estate Salesperson
- Broker in Charge
- Realtor
- Sales Agent

This is considered a "Bright Outlook" occupation. Although economic conditions affect employment opportunities in this field, the stock of existing homes and commercial properties as well as other factors indicate that prospects are good for this occupation in the long term.

Job Trends

The Bureau of Labor Statistics projects job openings for real estate agents of 128,300 between 2008 and 2018, which represents a growth rate of between 14 and 19 percent, faster than average of all occupations. About 58 percent of currently employed real estate agents are self-employed and about 32 percent work for real estate and rental and leasing companies.

While jobs openings are expected to grow at a faster than average rate for real estate agents, entry-level agents will face competition for jobs from more experienced agents. A growing population, especially among young adults forming house-holds, will drive the demand for agents. Empty-nesters downsizing and moving into smaller homes, apartments, and over-55 communities will also be a factor. A negative is the use of the Internet to locate and preview homes. While this improves the productivity of agents, it changes the way they do business—and removes a real estate broker's need for having so many agents. Agents no longer have to spend hours driving customers from home to home because the customers have preselected properties to view.

However, the *Occupational Outlook Handbook* notes that Realtors are typically older on average than most other workers. The need to replace retiring agents will add to the number of jobs available.

Nature of the Work

Real estate agents rent, buy, or sell property for clients. They perform duties such as study property listings, interview prospective clients, show property to clients, discuss conditions of sale, and may draw up real estate contracts. Agents may represent either the buyer or seller, or both in a sales transaction, depending on a state's real estate laws and regulations.

According to O*NET, Realtors may perform the following tasks, depending on what their job is:

- Act as an intermediary in negotiations between buyers and sellers, generally representing one or the other
- Advise clients on market conditions, prices, mortgages, legal requirements, and related matters
- Compare a property with similar properties that have recently sold to determine its competitive market prices
- Advise sellers on how to make homes more appealing to potential buyers
- Promote sales of properties through advertisements, open houses, and participation in multiple listing services (MLS)
- Interview clients to determine what kinds of properties they are seeking
- Generate lists of properties that are compatible with buyers' needs and financial resources
- Accompany buyers during visits to and inspections of property, advising them on the suitability and value of the homes they are visiting
- Answer clients' questions regarding construction work, financing, maintenance, repairs, and appraisals
- Evaluate mortgage options to help clients obtain financing at the best prevailing rates and terms
- Arrange meetings between buyers and sellers when details of transactions need to be negotiated
- Prepare documents such as representation contracts, purchase agreements, closing statements, deeds, and leases, depending on the state's real estate laws and customs
- Present purchase offers to sellers for consideration
- Confer with escrow companies, lenders, home inspectors, and pest control operators to ensure that terms and conditions of

purchase agreements are met before closing dates

- Arrange for title searches to determine whether clients have clear property titles
- Coordinate property closings, overseeing signing of documents and disbursement of funds
- Display commercial, industrial, agricultural, and residential properties to clients and explain their features
- Inspect condition of premises, and arrange for necessary maintenance or notify owners of maintenance needs
- Solicit and compile listings of available rental properties
- Rent or lease properties on behalf of clients
- Secure construction or purchase financing with own firm or mortgage company
- Review plans for new construction with clients, enumerating and recommending available options and features
- Locate and appraise undeveloped areas for building sites, based on evaluations of area market conditions
- Develop networks of attorneys, mortgage lenders, and contractors to whom clients may be referred
- Contact property owners and advertise services to solicit property sales listings Visit properties to assess them before showing them to clients
- Review property listings, trade journals, and relevant literature, and attend conventions, seminars, and staff and association meetings to remain knowledgeable about real estate markets

Career Path

Real estate agents must work under the supervision of a real estate broker in all fifty states. As agents gain knowledge and experience, they become more productive and make more money. In large firms, experienced agents may advance to sales manager or the firm's general manager. Some agents choose to earn a broker's license and open their own real estate agency.

Because of the many aspects of real estate that agents come into contact with while performing their jobs, some agents move out of selling real estate to related occupations. They may become real estate appraisers, property managers, or real estate investment counselors. Some may go into banking and work on mortgage financing with property buyers.

Earning Potential

Median hourly wage (2009): $19.28

Median annual wage (2009): $40,100

Education/Licensure

Because of the growing complexity of real estate laws including antidiscrimination rules and regulations, more real estate firms are now hiring college graduates. Most universities, colleges, and community colleges offer courses in real estate, and some offer associate and bachelor's degrees, but most offer only certificate programs, according to the *Occupational Outlook Handbook.* Coursework in finance, business administration, statistics, economics, and law are helpful, and for agents interested in going into business for themselves, courses in marketing and accounting would also be useful.

Local real estate associations that are members of the National Association of Realtors (NAR) often sponsor courses for agents. Topics typically include real estate law, mortgage financing, and property development. Some real estate brokers also off formal training programs for their agents. Much of the practical skills needed in the job are learned on the job under the guidance of an experienced agent.

Real estate agents must be licensed in all fifty states and the District of Columbia. In addition to passing a licensing exam, agents must complete between 30 and 90 hours of classroom instruction, depending on the state. Licenses must be renewed every one or two years, again depending on the state. Continuing education is typically required for license renewal.

Real estate brokers must pass an exam also to be licensed and must have 60 to 90 hours of classroom instruction as well as a certain number of years of selling real estate. Depending on the state, the requirement may be one to three years.

For More Information

National Association of Real Estate Brokers (NAREB)
9831 Greenbelt Road
Lanham, Maryland 20706
301-552-9340
www.nareb.com

National Association of Realtors
430 North Michigan Avenue
Chicago, Illinois 60611
800-874-6500 (toll-free)
www.realtor.org

Roofer ✪

Alternate Titles and Related Careers

- Industrial Roofer
- Metal Roofing Mechanic
- Residential Roofer
- Roof Mechanic
- Roof Service Technician
- Roofing Technician
- Sheet Metal Roofer

This is considered a "Green Enhanced-Skills" occupation in the green construction sector of the economy.

Job Trends

The Bureau of Labor Statistics projects a 4 percent growth rate for this occupation between 2008 and 2018. This is slower than the average of all occupations. However, this translates into 30,100 job openings. About 76 percent of currently employed roofers work in the construction industry, and about 21 percent are self-employed.

Roofs deteriorate more quickly than most other parts of a building, so they need to be replaced or repaired more often, notes the *Occupational Outlook Handbook*. This results in a certain amount of work for roofers as does roofing new construction. As the economy recovers from the recession of 2007 through 2009, and new housing and commercial building starts increase, the demand for roofers is anticipated to increase. Most roofing work, however, involves repair and replacement of existing roofs, so roofing is less sensitive to the ups and downs of the construction industry than some other building trades.

Most openings occur because of the shift of roofers into other occupations within construction. Roofing is strenuous, hot, and dirty.

Nature of the Work

Roofers cover the roofs of structures with a variety of materials: tar, shingles, slate, rubber, thermoplastic, asphalt, and wood. They may also spray roofs, sidings, and walls with material to bind, seal, insulate, or soundproof sections of structures. Among the tools that roofers use are spray guns, air compressors, heaters, knives, chisels, punches, and hammers.

Roofs may be low-slope or steep-slope; some roofers work on both roof types, and others specialize in one or the other type. Some are beginning to work on "green" roofs where they are responsible for ensuring that a roof is watertight and can bear the weight and water needs of the plantings.

Based on O*NET surveys, roofers may perform the following tasks:

- Inspect problem roofs to determine the best procedures for repairing them
- Set up scaffolding to provide safe access to roofs
- Remove snow, water, or debris from roofs prior to applying roofing materials
- Cement or nail flashing-strips of metal or shingle over joints to make them watertight
- Cover exposed nailheads with roofing cement or caulking to prevent water leakage and rust

- Install, repair, or replace single-ply roofing systems, using waterproof sheet materials such as modified plastics, elastomeric, or other asphaltic composition
- Cut felt, shingles, and strips of flashing, and fit them into angles formed by walls, vents, and intersecting roof surfaces
- Install vapor barriers and/or layers of insulation on the roof decks of flat roofs, and seal the seams
- Cut roofing paper to size, and nail or staple roofing paper to roofs in overlapping strips to form bases for other materials
- Install partially overlapping layers of material over roof insulation surfaces, determining distance of roofing material overlap using chalk lines, gauges on shingling hatchets, or lines on shingles
- Cover roofs and exterior walls of structures with slate, asphalt, aluminum, wood, gravel, gypsum, and/or related materials
- Apply alternate layers of hot asphalt or tar and roofing paper to roofs, according to specification
- Spray roofs, sidings, and walls with material to bind, seal, insulate, or soundproof sections of structures
- Hammer and chisel away rough spots or remove them with rubbing bricks to prepare surfaces for waterproofing
- Waterproof and damp-proof walls, floors, roofs, foundations, and basements by painting or spraying surfaces with waterproof coatings, or by attaching waterproofing membranes to surfaces
- Mop or pour hot asphalt or tar onto roof bases
- Apply plastic coatings and membranes, fiberglass, or felt over sloped roofs before applying shingles
- Glaze top layers to make a smooth finish, or embed gravel in the bitumen for rough surfaces

- Apply gravel or pebbles over top layers of roofs, using rakes or stiff-bristled brooms
- Estimate roofing materials and labor required to complete jobs, and provide price quotes
- Clean and maintain equipment

Career Path

Roofers begin as trainees or apprentices under the supervision of experienced workers. Trainees start by carrying equipment and materials and erecting scaffolds. Within two or three months, they begin to learn basic skills, graduating to progressively more difficult work with less supervision.

Some roofers will advance to become supervisors themselves. Some move into cost estimating for a roofing company, whereas others go into business for themselves as roofing contractors.

About C&D Materials

Reduce, reuse, and recycle isn't just a policy for homeowners. It's the policy that the U.S. Environmental Protection Agency wants construction and demolition companies to follow, too. More than 160 million tons of building-related construction and demolition (C&D) materials were generated in a recent year and about 60 percent went to landfills. Check out www.epa.gov/epawaste/conserve/rrr/imr/index.htm for information on the EPA's waste reduction programs for C&D materials.

Earning Potential

Median hourly wage (2009): $16.33

Median annual wage (2009): $33,970

Education/Licensure

Typically, roofers have high school diplomas or the equivalent. Although most workers learn roofing on the job, some enroll in three-year apprenticeship programs administered by union-management committees representing roofing contractors and locals of the United Union of Roofers,

Waterproofers, and Allied Workers. The programs typically include 2,000 hours of on-the-job training for which apprentices are paid combined with a minimum of 144 hours of classroom instruction during each year of the apprenticeship.

For More Information

National Roofing Contractors Association
10255 West Higgins Road
Suite 600
Rosemont, Illinois 60018-5607
847-299-9070
www.nrca.net

Center for Environmental Innovation in Roofing
    (CEIR)
866-928-2347 (toll-free)
www.roofingcenter.org

United Union of Roofers, Waterproofers, and
    Allied Workers
1660 L Street, NW
Suite 800
Washington, DC 20036
202-463-7663
www.unionroofers.com

Rough Carpenter ✿ 🌎

Alternate Titles and Related Careers

- Apprentice Carpenter
- Carpenter
- Framer Rough Carpenter
- Journeyman Carpenter

This is considered a "Bright Outlook" and "Green Increased-Demand" occupation in the green construction sector of the economy.

 http://bit.ly/career17

Job Trends

The Bureau of Labor Statistics groups rough carpenters with the general carpenter occupation and estimates an average growth rate of 7 to 13 percent. The total of projected job openings is 325,400.

Currently, about 56 percent of all carpenters are employed in the construction industry, and another 32 percent are self-employed.

Job opportunities will be best for those with the most training and skills. Unlike other carpentry specialties, how quickly the housing market rebounds from the recession of 2007 through 2009 will not affect job opportunities for rough carpenters. The amount of spending by federal, state, and local governments on the expansion and improvement of the nation's infrastructure will affect the number of job openings for rough carpenters.

> **About Construction and the Environment**
>
> One reason to renovate rather than tear down buildings and start over is the environment. Construction creates more carbon dioxide than any other industry.

Nature of the Work

Rough carpenters build wooden structures such as forms for poured concrete, scaffolds, billboard signs, temporary frame shelters, and supports for tunnels, bridges, and sewers. Rough carpenters must be able to read sketches and blueprints and follow oral instructions. Among the tools that rough carpenters use are measuring tape, plumb rule, level, handsaw, power saw, woodworking machine, anchor rods, steel cables, planks, wedges, and power drill.

According to O*NET, rough carpenters may perform the following tasks:

- Study blueprints and diagrams to determine dimensions of structure or form to be constructed
- Measure materials or distances to lay out work
- Cut or saw boards, timbers, or plywood to required size
- Assemble and fasten material together to construct wood or metal framework of structure

- Anchor and brace forms and other structures in place
- Mark cutting lines on materials
- Erect forms, framework, scaffolds, hoists, roof supports, or chutes
- Install rough door and window frames, subflooring, fixtures, or temporary supports in structures undergoing construction or repair
- Examine structural timbers and supports to detect decay, and replace timbers as required
- Bore boltholes in timber, masonry, or concrete walls
- Fabricate parts, using woodworking and metalworking machines
- Dig or direct digging of post holes and set poles to support structures
- Build sleds from logs and timbers for use in hauling camp buildings and machinery through wooded areas
- Build chutes for pouring concrete

Career Path

Experienced carpenters may become carpentry supervisors. Because they are involved in all aspects of the construction process, they also have opportunities to advance to general construction supervisor. With additional education and experience, there are opportunities for carpenters in management, including becoming self-employed contractors. States require that contractors be licensed to do business.

Because of the number of Latinos in construction, speaking both English and Spanish can be an advantage for those who wish to advance.

Earning Potential

Median hourly wage (2009): $18.98

Median annual wage (2009): $39,470

Education/Licensure

Typically, carpentry requires a high school diploma. Carpenters may begin as carpenter's helpers working with experienced carpenters, but they also need some type of formal instruction to become skilled. There are two main options for formal instruction: attending a trade or vocational school or a community college, or enrolling in an apprenticeship program. Usually, trade or vocational schools confer a certificate of achievement (not the same as certification), and community colleges confer an associate degree in carpentry.

Carpentry is an apprenticeable trade. Apprenticeship programs are offered by some employers and by trade associations and unions as well as some trade and vocational schools. These programs may last three to five years and include both classroom and on-the-job training. Upon completing an apprenticeship program, a person becomes a journeyman carpenter.

Some carpenters obtain certifications in specialized construction techniques such as scaffold building or high torque bolting. Certification may enable them to earn additional responsibilities and money.

For More Information

Associated General Contractors of America, Inc. (AGC)
2300 Wilson Boulevard
Suite 400
Arlington, Virginia 22201-5426
703-548-3118
www.agc.org

United Brotherhood of Carpenters and Joiners of America
International Training Center
6801 Placid Street
Las Vegas, Nevada 89119
702-938-1111
www.carpenters.org

Sheet Metal Worker 🌱

Alternate Titles and Related Careers
- Crew Leader
- Fabricator
- Geothermal Heat Pump Fabricator
- Journeyman Sheetmetal Worker
- Machinist
- Project Manager
- Sheet Metal Apprenctice
- Sheet Metal Lay Out Mechanic
- Sheet Metal Mechanic

This is considered a "Green Enhanced-Skills" occupation in the green construction sector of the economy. Depending on the job description, the occupation may also be found in manufacturing and renewable energy generation.

Job Trends

This occupation is rated as having a slower-than-average job growth of 3 to 6 percent between 2008 and 2018, according to the Bureau of Labor Statistics. Total projected job openings are 51,700.

As interest and investment in geothermal power both as a source of power generation for the electricity grid and heat and air conditioning for residential and commercial properties grow, the need for fabricators of geothermal equipment should also expand. According to the *Occupational Outlook Handbook,* job prospects should be especially good for sheet metal workers with apprenticeship training and a welding certification.

Nature of the Work

Sheet metal workers may fabricate, assemble, install, or repair heating, ventilation, and air-conditioning duct systems; piping; siding, rain gutters and downspouts; skylights; restaurant equipment; outdoor signs; furnace casings; customized precision equipment; and many other products made from sheet metal. They may also work with fiberglass and plastic materials.

Although some workers specialize in fabrication, installation, or maintenance, most do all three types of work, according to the *Occupational Outlook Handbook.* Depending on their interests and job availability, sheet metal workers may work in construction or in manufacturing. One area of green manufacturing that employs sheet metal workers is the production of geothermal heat pumps.

Sheet metal workers must be able to read and follow blueprints, drawings, templates, and written and oral instructions and convert blueprints into shop drawings. They must be able to use calculators, scribes, dividers, squares, rulers, calipers, scales, and micrometers.

According to O*NET, the following are the tasks that a sheet metal worker may perform:
- Determine project requirements including scope, assembly sequence, and required methods and materials
- Lay out, measure, and mark dimensions and reference lines on material
- Maneuver completed units into position for installation
- Install assemblies in supportive frameworks
- Select gauges and types of sheet metal or nonmetallic material according to the product specifications
- Drill and punch holes in metal, for screws, bolts, and rivets
- Fasten seams and joints together with welds, bolts, cement, rivets, solder, cauls, metal drive clips, and bonds to assemble components
- Fabricate or alter parts at construction sites, using shears, hammers, punches, and drills
- Trim, file, grind, deburr, buff, and smooth surfaces, seams, and joints of assembled parts
- Maintain equipment making repairs and modifications when necessary
- Transport prefabricated parts to construction sites for assembly and installation
- Develop and lay out patterns that use materials most efficiently, using

computerized metalworking equipment to experiment with different layouts

- Inspect individual parts, assemblies, and installation for conformance to specifications and building codes

Career Path

Entry-level workers begin working under the supervision of an experienced worker, either for informal on-the-job training or through a formal apprenticeship program. Sheet metal workers in the construction industry may become supervisors themselves. Some take additional training in welding and do more specialized work. Workers who perform building and system testing may become construction and building inspectors. Others open their own contracting businesses, which is expensive because of the need to purchase sheet metal fabrication machinery.

Sheet metal workers who work in manufacturing may advance to supervisory roles. Some become quality control inspectors.

Earning Potential

Median hourly wage (2008): $19.37

Median annual wage (2008): $40,290

Education/Licensure

Sheet metal construction workers are more likely to learn their trade through a formal apprenticeship program. Other sheet metal workers typically learn the trade through informal on-the-job training. Some employers may send their employees to trade or vocational schools or to community colleges for further training. Becoming proficient in manufacturing methods takes less time than gaining proficiency in construction.

Apprenticeship programs for sheet metal construction workers take between four and five years and combine classroom instruction with paid on-the-job training. The length of the program varies with an apprentice's skills. These programs are administered by local joint committees of the Sheet

Metal Workers International Association (SMWIA) and local chapters of the Sheet Metal and Air-Conditioning Contractors' National Association (SMACNA).

Regardless of training, sheet metal workers may choose to specialize. Among their choices are commercial and residential HVAC installation and maintenance, exterior or architectural sheet metal installation, service and refrigeration, industrial welding and fabrication, and testing and balancing of building systems.

The Fabricators and Manufactures Association (FMA) offers the Precision Sheet Metal Operator (PSMO) Certification for sheet metal workers, and the International Training Institute for the Sheet Metal and Air-Conditioning Industry (ITI) offers certification programs for welding; testing, adjusting, and balancing (TAB); life safety; detailing; and HVAC.

For More Information

Fabricators and Manufacturers Association (FMA)
833 Featherstone Road
Rockford, Illinois 61107
815-399-8700
www.fmanet.org

International Training Institute for the Sheet Metal and Air-Conditioning Industry
601 North Fairfax Street
Suite 24
Alexandria, Virginia 22314-2083
703-739-7200
www.sheetmetal-iti.org

National Center for Construction Education and Research (NCCER)
3600 Northwest 43rd Street
Building G
Gainesville, Florida 32606-8134
888-622-3720 (toll-free)
www.nccer.org

Sheet Metal and Air-Conditioning Contractors'
National Association (SMACNA)
4201 Lafayette Center Drive
Chantilly, Virginia 20151-1209
703-803-2980
www.smacna.rog

Sheet Metal Workers International Association
(SMWIA)
1750 New York Avenue, NW
6th Floor
Washington, DC 20006-5301
ww.smwia.org

Structural Iron and Steel Worker 🌐

Alternate Titles and Related Careers

- Fitter/Welder
- Ironworker
- Ornamental Ironworker
- Reinforcing Iron and Rebar Worker
- Rod Buster
- Steel Fabricator
- Steel Worker
- Structural Steel Erector
- Tower Hand

This is considered a "Green Increased-Demand" occupation in the green construction sector of the economy. Depending on the job description, the occupation is also found in manufacturing.

Job Trends

The Bureau of Labor Statistics projects a growth rate of 12 percent for structural iron and steel workers between 2008 and 2018, which is about as fast as the average for all occupations. About 85 percent of currently employed workers are employed in construction.

The repair, maintenance, and replacement of a growing number of older buildings, power plants, highways, and bridges are expected to create employment opportunities for some time. A problem for employers and a boost for skilled job applicants is the difficulty in finding qualified candidates. Additional jobs will open up because of the shift of structural iron and steel workers into other occupations and from the retirement of older workers. Like all construction industry jobs, this one is sensitive to economic conditions and also seasonal and geographic variations in employment needs.

Nature of the Work

Structural iron and steel workers raise, place, and unite iron or steel girders and other structural elements such as columns to form completed structures or structural frameworks. They may also erect metal storage tanks and assemble prefabricated metal buildings as well as position and secure steel bars or mesh in concrete forms to reinforce the concrete. The latter workers are known as reinforcing and rebar workers.

There are several specialties in the structural iron and steel worker category. For example, while most workers do structural work on highways, office and apartment buildings, bridges, tunnels, and other large structures, some ironworkers install ornamental ironwork such as handrails. Others make structural metal in fabricating shops that are not on the building site.

Among the tools that structural iron and steel workers use are plumb bobs, laser equipment, transits, and levels for alignment. For cutting and bending steel pieces, they use metal shears, torches, and welding equipment and to force structural steel into place, turnbuckles, crowbars, jacks, and hand tools are used.

Based on O*NET surveys, structural iron and steel workers may perform the following tasks, depending on their job descriptions:

- Read specifications and blueprints to determine the locations, quantities, and sizes of materials required
- Verify vertical and horizontal alignment of structural-steel members
- Connect columns, beams, and girders with bolts, following blueprints and instructions from supervisors

- Hoist steel beams, girders, and columns into place, using cranes, or signal hoisting equipment operators to lift and position structural-steel members
- Assemble hoisting equipment and rigging, such as cables, pulleys, and hooks, to move heavy equipment and materials
- Fasten structural-steel members to hoist cables, using chains, cables, or rope
- Ride on girders or other structural-steel members to position them, or use rope to guide them into position
- Bolt aligned structural-steel members in position for permanent riveting, bolting, or welding into place
- Pull, push, or pry structural-steel members into approximate positions for bolting into place
- Cut, bend, and weld steel pieces
- Force structural-steel members into final positions
- Fabricate metal parts such as steel frames, columns, beams, and girders, according to blueprints or instructions from supervisors
- Erect metal and precast concrete components for structures such as buildings, bridges, dams, towers, storage tanks, fences, and highway guard rails
- Unload and position prefabricated steel units for hoisting as needed
- Insert sealing strips, wiring, insulating material, ladders, flanges, gauges, and valves, depending on types of structures being assembled
- Drive drift pins through rivet holes in order to align rivet holes in structural-steel members with corresponding holes in previously placed members
- Catch hot rivets in buckets, and insert rivets in holes, using tongs
- Hold rivets while riveters use air-hammers to form heads on rivets
- Place blocks under reinforcing bars used to reinforce floors

Career Path

Many entry-level workers begin their careers in formal apprenticeship programs. They work under the supervision of experienced workers and at the end of their apprenticeships are qualified journeymen structural iron and steel workers, which enhances their opportunities for jobs and promotions. Typically, apprenticeships include certification as a welder, which is also an advantage when seeking a job or advancement.

Some experienced workers become supervisors, whereas others open their own contracting businesses. Contractors must be licensed. Knowledge of Spanish is increasingly important for managers because of the large numbers of Spanish-speaking workers in the construction industry.

Earning Potential

Median hourly wage (2009): $21.40

Median annual wage (2009): $44,500

Education/Licensure

Employers prefer to hire entry-level candidates with high school diplomas or the equivalent. The best route to employment and advancement is a formal apprenticeship program, which lasts from three to four years and combines classroom instruction and paid on-the-job training. The programs are administered by committees of the local unions of the International Association of Bridge, Structural, Ornamental, and Reinforcing Iron Workers (Iron Workers) or the local chapters of contractors associations.

An apprenticeship program ends with certification as a journeyman. Many local apprenticeship programs include certification in welding offered by the American Welding Society. This expertise adds to a worker's job options because many ironworker tasks include welding.

Some structural iron and steel workers learn their trade through informal on-the-job training under the supervision of experienced ironworkers. The trainees begin by doing simple tasks and move up to more difficult jobs.

For More Information

Associated General Contractors of America, Inc. (AGC)
2300 Wilson Boulevard
Suite 400
Arlington, Virginia 22201-5426
703-548-3118
www.agc.org

International Association of Bridge, Structural, Ornamental, and Reinforcing Iron Workers (Iron Workers)
1750 New York Avenue, NW
Suite 400
Washington, DC 20006
202-383-4800
www.ironworkers.org

Surveyor

Alternate Titles and Related Careers

- County Surveyor
- Geodesist
- Land Surveyor
- Licensed Land Surveyor
- Professional Land Surveyor
- Survey Engineer
- Survey Party Chief

While not specifically a green job, surveying is the basis of projects in the green construction industry.

Job Trends

The Bureau of Labor Statistics lists the surveying occupation among those jobs that will grow at a faster than average rate of 14 to 19 percent. The number of job openings is expected to around 23,300. About 78 percent of currently employed surveyors work for architectural, engineering, and related services companies and about 10 percent for government agencies. Opportunities will be best for surveyors with a bachelor's degree and strong technical skills.

According to the *Occupational Outlook Handbook,* the demand for surveyors is driven by the need for new construction as the nation's population grows and for improvements to and expansion of the infrastructure to meet the demands of that growing population. Surveyors and their survey teams are usually the first people to arrive at a site at the start of a major construction project. Throughout the project, they continue to provide information and recommendations to engineers, architects, contractors, and others developing the project.

About GIS

"GIS " technology, which stands for "geographic information systems," can be applied to problems across a number of fields related to the green economy, including environmental, conservation, and urban planning, and all types of organizations, from government and private firms to nonprofit advocacy organizations. Urban and regional planners use GIS to model urban growth. In natural resource management, GIS technology is used to manage forests and rangelands, preserve wetlands and wildlife habitats, model migration of toxic chemicals, and assess groundwater contamination and air quality. Public health officials use it to track the incidence of certain diseases in relation to natural and environmental factors.

The demand for traditional surveying services is strongly tied to construction. Job opportunities vary by season and geographic region of the country, and according to economic conditions. However, surveyors can work on many different types of projects, so they may have less difficulty in finding work in slow economic times than workers in other construction occupations.

Nature of the Work

Surveyors make exact measurements and determine official land, airspace, and water boundaries. Data may indicate shape, contour, gravitation, location, elevation, or dimension of land or land features near the surface of the earth. Surveyors write descriptions of land for deeds, leases, and other legal documents. Some define airspace for airports and others take measurements of construction and mineral sites. The information that surveyors provide is used for engineering, mapmaking, mining, land evaluation, and construction among other purposes.

Specialties include geodetic surveying (large areas of the earth), geophysical prospecting surveying (usually for petroleum deposits), and marine or hydraulic surveying (harbors, rivers, and other bodies of water). Global Positioning System (GPS) and Geographic Information Systems (GIS) are important technologies for surveyors and other professionals such as cartographers and photo-grammetrists involved in measuring and mapping the Earth's surface.

According to O*NET, surveyors may perform the following tasks:

- Search legal records, survey records, and land titles to obtain information about property boundaries in areas to be surveyed
- Direct or conduct surveys to establish legal boundaries for properties, based on legal deeds and titles
- Calculate heights, depths, relative positions, property lines, and other characteristics of terrain
- Prepare and maintain sketches, maps, reports, and legal descriptions of surveys to describe, certify, and assume liability for work performed
- Verify the accuracy of survey data including measurements and calculations conducted at survey sites
- Prepare or supervise preparation of all data, charts, plots, maps, records, and documents related to surveys
- Write descriptions of property boundary surveys for use in deeds, leases, or other legal documents

- Plan and conduct ground surveys designed to establish baselines, elevations, and other geodetic measurements
- Compute geodetic measurements and interpret survey data to determine positions, shapes, and elevations of geomorphic and topographic features
- Determine longitudes and latitudes of important features and boundaries in survey areas using theodolites, transits, levels, and satellite-based global positioning systems (GPS)
- Record the results of surveys including the shape, contour, location, elevation, and dimensions of land or land features
- Coordinate findings with the work of engineering and architectural personnel, clients, and others concerned with projects
- Establish fixed points for use in making maps, using geodetic and engineering instruments
- Survey bodies of water to determine navigable channels and to secure data for construction of breakwaters, piers, and other marine structures
- Locate and mark sites selected for geophysical prospecting activities such as efforts to locate petroleum or other mineral products
- Direct aerial surveys of specified geographical areas
- Determine specifications for photographic equipment to be used for aerial photography, as well as altitudes from which to photograph terrain
- Analyze survey objectives and specifications to prepare survey proposals or to direct others in survey proposal preparation
- Develop criteria for survey methods and procedures
- Adjust surveying instruments to maintain their accuracy

- Develop criteria for the design and modification of survey instruments
- Conduct research in surveying and mapping methods using knowledge of techniques of photogrammetric map compilation and electronic data processing
- Train assistants and helpers, and direct their work in such activities as performing surveys or drafting maps

Career Path

Entry-level surveyors must pass the first of two exams to be licensed and work independently. After taking and passing the Fundamentals of Surveying, an entry-level surveyor begins working under the supervision of an experienced surveyor. After gaining four years of experience, the new surveyor may take the second exam, Principles and Practice of Surveying. By passing this exam and one administered by the state's licensing board, the surveyor may work independently.

Surveyors may advance to higher levels of management within companies; go to work for a government agency such as the Army Corps of Engineers on the federal level, or an urban planning and development agency on the municipal government level; or start their own consulting and service business.

Earning Potential

Median hourly wage (2009): $26.05

Median annual wage (2009): $54,180

Education/Licensure

Today, most surveyors have a bachelor's degree in surveying or a related field. Many states now require that surveyors have a bachelor's degree in surveying or a closely related field such as civil engineering or forestry. Some states require that the degree be from a school accredited by the Accreditation Board for Engineering and Technology (ABET). Most states also have a continuing education requirement.

All states require that surveyors be licensed. Most state licensing boards have their own examination and also require that surveyor candidates pass a series of written exams administered by the National Council of Examiners for Engineering and Surveying (NCEES). The process involves taking and passing two exams over the space of four years: Fundamentals of Surveying and Principles and Practice of Surveying.

For More Information

Accreditation Board for Engineering and
    Technology (ABET)
111 Market Place
Suite 1050
Baltimore, Maryland 21202
410-347-7700
www.abet.org

American Association for Geodetic Surveying
    (AAGS)
6 Montgomery Village Avenue
Suite 403
Gaithersburg, Maryland 20879
240-632-9716
www.aagsmo.org

American Congress on Surveying and Mapping
6 Montgomery Village Avenue
Suite 403
Gaithersburg, Maryland 20879
240-632-9716
www.acsm.net

National Council of Examiners for Engineering
    and Surveying (NCEES)
280 Seneca Creek Road
Seneca, South Carolina 29678
800-250-3196 (toll-free)
www.ncees.org

National Society of Professional Surveyors
    (NSPS)
6 Montgomery Village Avenue
Suite 403
Gaithersburg, Maryland 20879
240-632-9716
www.nspsmo.org

Surveying Technician ✿

Alternate Titles and Related Careers

- Chainman
- Engineering Assistant
- Engineering Technician
- Field Crew Chief
- Instrument Man (I-Man)
- Instrument Operator
- Rodman
- Survey Crew Chief
- Survey Party Chief
- Survey Technician

Surveying technician is considered a "Bright Outlook" occupation with an impact on the construction industry.

Job Trends

According to the Bureau of Labor Statistics, employment for surveying and mapping technicians, BLS's overall occupational category, is expected to increase by 20 percent or more between 2008 and 2018, which is faster than average for all occupations.

Most currently employed surveying and mapping technicians work for engineering services firms. About 15 percent work for governmental agencies. Some work for local governments, and fewer work for federal and state governments. Engineering firms should continue to provide the best job opportunities for surveying technicians.

According to the *Occupational Outlook Handbook,* the need for new construction as the nation's population grows and for improvements to and expansion of the infrastructure to meet the demands of that growing population will drive the demand for surveying technicians. Surveyors and surveying technicians are usually the first people there at the start of major construction projects and continue to provide information and recommendations to engineers, architects, contractors, and other professionals during all phases of the project.

The demand for traditional surveying services is strongly tied to construction and opportunities vary by season and geographic region of the country, and by economic conditions. However, because surveying technicians can work on many different types of projects from highways to housing developments to shopping malls, they may find steadier work than other construction occupations when the economy takes a downturn.

Nature of the Work

Surveying technicians adjust and operate surveying instruments, compile notes, make sketches, and enter data into computers. They work under the direction of surveyors or senior survey technicians called a party chief to collect data in the field, make calculations, and use computer-aided drafting (CAD) software. Much of their work is used in geographic information systems (GIS) to construct digital maps that can be manipulated in many ways. Among the tools that surveying technicians use are theodolites, electronic distance measuring equipment, and prisms.

Among the tasks surveying technicians perform are the following, according to O*NET:

- Perform calculations to determine Earth curvature corrections, atmospheric impacts on measurements, traverse closures and adjustments, azimuths, level runs, and placement of markers
- Record survey measurements and descriptive data using notes, drawings, sketches, and inked tracings
- Search for section corners, property irons, and survey points
- Position and hold the vertical rods, or targets, that theodolite operators use for sighting to measure angles, distances, and elevations
- Lay out grids, and determine horizontal and vertical controls
- Compare survey computations with applicable standards to determine adequacy of data

- Set out and recover stakes, marks, and other monumentation
- Conduct surveys to ascertain the locations of natural features and artificial structures on the Earth's surface, underground, and underwater using electronic distance-measuring equipment and other surveying instruments
- Compile information necessary to stake projects for construction, using engineering plans
- Prepare topographic and contour maps of land surveyed, including site features and other relevant information such as charts, drawings, and survey notes
- Place and hold measuring tapes when electronic distance-measuring equipment is not used
- Run rods for benches and cross-section elevations
- Perform manual labor as needed, such as cutting brush for lines, carrying stakes, rebar, and other heavy items, and stacking rods
- Operate and manage land-information computer systems, performing tasks such as storing data, making inquiries, and producing plots and reports
- Maintain equipment and vehicles used by surveying crews
- Collect information needed to carry out new surveys using source maps, previous survey data, photographs, computer records, and other relevant information
- Provide assistance in the development of methods and procedures for conducting field surveys
- Direct and supervise work of subordinate members of surveying parties

Career Path

High school graduates with no formal training in surveying usually begin as apprentices working under supervision. As they gain more experience, they become involved in more difficult projects with less supervision. As they gain experience, they may advance to senior survey technician and then to party chief, the person in charge of a survey team.

Some survey technicians will choose to continue their educations and earn bachelor's degrees. Because technology is advancing rapidly, those with bachelor's degrees and technical skills will have the best opportunities for jobs and advancement.

Earning Potential

Median hourly wage (2009): $17.88

Median annual wage (2009): $37,190

(Based on "Surveying and Mapping Technicians")

Education/Licensure

An associate degree or training program is generally required to become a surveying technician. Many vocational and technical schools and community colleges have programs in surveying and surveying technology. These may take from one to three years to complete. Some offer an associate degree. Some colleges and universities offer bachelor's degree programs.

The Accreditation Board for Engineering and Technology (ABET) accredits surveying and mapping technology programs. The American Congress on Surveying and Mapping Web site provides a list of and links to junior colleges, community colleges, colleges, and universities that have programs in surveying technology, surveying engineering technology, and geomatics technology. They have lists for both ABET-accredited and non-accredited programs.

The National Society of Professional Surveyors offers the Certified Survey Technician (CST) certification program that certifies technicians at four levels of expertise, each building on the previous level. This program is part of the National Apprenticeship Program sponsored by the U.S. Department of Labor. Apprenticeship specialties for surveying technicians are Geodetic Computator and Surveyor Assistant (Instruments).

For More Information

Accreditation Board for Engineering and
  Technology (ABET)
111 Market Place
Suite 1050
Baltimore, Maryland 21202
410-347-7700
www.abet.org

American Association for Geodetic Surveying
  (AAGS)
6 Montgomery Village Avenue
Suite 403
Gaithersburg, Maryland 20879
240-632-9716
www.aagsmo.org

American Congress on Surveying and Mapping
6 Montgomery Village Avenue
Suite 403
Gaithersburg, Maryland 20879
240-632-9716
www.acsm.net

National Society of Professional Surveyors
  (NSPS)
6 Montgomery Village Avenue
Suite 403
Gaithersburg, Maryland 20879
240-632-9716
www.nspsmo.org

Welder, Cutter, and Welder Fitter ✿ ⊕

Alternate Titles and Related Careers

- Maintenance Welder
- Sub Arc Operator
- Welder-Brazier
- Welder-Cutter
- Welder-Fitter
- Welder/Solderer
- Welding Inspector
- Welding Supervisor

There are 100 methods of welding, but the most common uses an electric current and is called arc welding. This is considered a "Bright Outlook" "Green Increased Demand" occupation in the green construction sector of the economy. Depending on the job description, it may also fit in the green manufacturing sector of the economy.

Job Trends

The Bureau of Labor Statistics includes welders, cutters, and welder fitters in the overall occupational category of welding, soldering, and brazing workers and sees little or no change for this category between 2008 and 2018. This still translates into a total of 126,300 job openings for the overall category.

The basic skills involved in welding are the same regardless of the industry, so welders can shift more easily than other workers from one industry to another based on job availability. There are two other factors that play into the job market for welders. Even though semi-automated and automated welding machines are used for many types of welds, welders are still need to operate the machines, inspect the welds, and make machine adjustments accordingly. Construction welding work like making repairs in factories using welding is known as custom applications, and these can't be easily automated or automated at all.

Nature of the Work

Welding, soldering, and brazing are all methods of joining two pieces of metal using extreme heat. Welding may be done manually or it may be automated using machines. In either case, the experience of the welder is critical to achieving a joint of sufficient strength. These processes are used in the manufacturing and construction industries. About two thirds of jobs are in manufacturing; transportation equipment manufacturing is a major industry segment. The rest are employed mostly in construction.

A major concern is safety, so welders must know safety procedures and follow them while working. Among the process that welders use are gas tungsten arc, gas metal arc, flux-cored arc, plasma arc, shielded metal arc, resistance welding, and submerged arc welding. In addition to welding equipment, the tools that welders use include straightedges, combination squares, calipers, rulers, hand scrapers or power chippers, portable grinders, hand files, scrapers, hoists, cranes, banding machines, wire brushes, cutting torches, and straightening presses.

According to O*NET, welders may perform the following tasks:

- Analyze engineering drawings, blueprints, specifications, sketches, work orders, and material safety data sheets to plan layout, assembly, and welding operations
- Determine required equipment and welding methods, applying knowledge of metallurgy, geometry, and welding techniques
- Weld components in flat, vertical, or overhead positions
- Ignite torches or start power supplies and strike arcs by touching electrodes to metals being welded, completing electrical circuits
- Clamp, hold, tack-weld, heat-bend, grind or bolt component parts to obtain required configurations and positions for welding
- Detect faulty operation of equipment or defective materials and notify supervisors
- Operate manual or semi-automatic welding equipment to fuse metal segments
- Monitor the fitting, burning, and welding processes to avoid overheating of parts or warping, shrinking, distortion, or expansion of material
- Examine workpieces for defects and measure workpieces with straightedges or templates to ensure conformance with specifications
- Recognize, set up, and operate hand and power tools common to the welding trade
- Lay out, position, align, and secure parts and assemblies prior to assembly

- Chip or grind off excess weld, slag, or spatter
- Weld separately or in combination, using aluminum, stainless steel, cast iron, and other alloys
- Mark or tag material with proper job number, piece marks, and other identifying marks as required
- Prepare all material surfaces to be welded, ensuring that there is no loose or thick scale, slag, rust, moisture, grease, or other foreign matter
- Select and install torches, torch tips, filler rods, and flux, according to welding chart specifications or types and thicknesses of metals
- Remove rough spots from workpieces
- Position and secure workpieces
- Repair products by dismantling, straightening, reshaping, and reassembling parts
- Dismantle metal assemblies or cut scrap metal
- Check grooves, angles, or gap allowances
- Signal crane operators to move large workpieces
- Guide and direct flames or electrodes on or across workpieces to straighten, bend, melt, or build up metal
- Cut, contour, and bevel metal plates and structural shapes to dimensions as specified by blueprints, layouts, work orders, and templates, using powered saws, hand shears, or chipping knives
- Preheat workpieces prior to welding or bending
- Melt lead bars, wire, or scrap to add lead to joints or to extrude melted scrap into reusable form
- Join parts such as beams and steel reinforcing rods in buildings, bridges, and highways, bolting and riveting as necessary.
- Hammer out bulges or bends in metal workpieces

- Mix and apply protective coatings to products
- Operate metal shaping, straightening, and bending machines and brazing and soldering equipment
- Estimate materials needed for production and manufacturing and maintain required stocks of materials
- Develop templates and models for welding projects

Career Path

An entry-level welder works under the supervision of an experienced welder. Over time with experience and additional training, welders may advance to jobs as supervisor, sales representative, or welding inspector. Some welders open their own repair shops. Some choose to earn a bachelor's degree and become welding engineers.

Earning Potential

Median hourly wage (2009): $16.71

Median annual wage (2009): $34,750

Education/Licensure

Training for welders, solders, and braziers depends on the skill level of the position. The lowest levels may require on-the-job training or a few weeks in school. Highly skilled positions may require several years of school and experience. High schools, vocational and technical schools, community colleges, the armed forces, and private welding schools offer formal training. Computer knowledge is becoming more important as more processes are done by computerized machines or robots. The American Welding Society has a welding school locator on its Web site.

Some positions require certifications. These may be a general welding certification or a specialization. The American Welding Society offers a variety of certifications, including Certified Welder, Certified Welding Supervisor, Certified Welding Inspector, and some specialized certifications such as robotics.

For More Information

American Welding Society
550 NW LeJeune Road
Miami, Florida 33126
800-443-9353 (toll-free)
www.aws.org

Fabricators and Manufactures Association (FMA)
833 Featherstone Road
Rockford, Illinois 61107
888-394-4362 (toll-free)
www.fmanet.org

Welding Research Council
P.O. Box 1942
New York, New York 10156
212-658-3847
http://www.forengineers.org/wrc

How Green Is a Prospective Employer?

Today, just about any company that you interview with will say it is eco-conscious, but how do you know for sure? Here are some things to look for as you do your due diligence on prospective employers. Remember to look at the "small" picture—the daily culture of the company—not just the big picture, its social responsibility report.

1. Does the company have a social responsibility officer? Does the company issue a social responsibility report?

2. Does the company show up in the news as eco-friendly?

3. Depending on the type of company, what is its policy on carbon neutrality? How is it moving toward becoming carbon neutral?

4. If it has separate offices or manufacturing plants, what is the company's environmental policy toward new construction and/or toward retrofitting older sites?

5. If the company leases autos for employees, does it lease fuel-efficient ones?

6. If the company is in a suburban setting, does it encourage carpooling by setting aside special parking close to the building? Does it reimburse drivers of carpools for part of the mileage or tolls?

7. If the company is in a suburban setting with nearby train service, does it run a van or bus to meet trains to pick up and drop off employees?

8. What is the company's policy on telecommuting? What is its policy on flextime? Both cut down on auto emissions.

9. If there's a cafeteria, does it serve locally grown foods? Does it use paper, plastic, or ceramic dishes? Does it use metal or plastic utensils? What kind of take-out containers does it use?

10. What is the policy on printing e-mail? What is the policy on copying: single-sided or double-sided?

11. Does it have recycle bins for paper and plastic goods in convenient places for employees to use?

12. If the company is in retail sales, does it use paper or plastic bags? Does it encourage customers to use recyclable bags? How?

13. If it's a manufacturing company, what is its policy on the amount of packaging it uses for its products?

14. Does the company support green causes in its locations like the Great American Cleanup™? Does it have a foundation that makes grants to local environmental efforts?

LEED Certification

LEED stands for Leadership in Energy and Environmental Design and designates the green building certification program of the U.S. Green Building Council (USGBC). The USGBC is a nonprofit organization with the goal of making green buildings available to all by the next generation. Through its LEED certification program, it offers independent, third-party certification of residential, commercial, and institutional construction as "green." Through the Green Building Certification Institute (GBCI), individuals can become credentialed as green building professionals.

The goal of the LEED program is to integrate sustainable standards of design, construction, and operations into the construction of new buildings and the retrofitting of existing buildings. Several thousand projects worldwide have been LEED-certified. To gain certification, a building must be designed and built keeping the following criteria in mind:

- Sustainable site
- Materials and resources
- Indoor environmental quality
- Water efficiency
- Energy and atmosphere

Using a 100-point scale, green raters assess how well a building matches each criterion. Different scales have been developed for different kinds of buildings: schools, retail stores, health-care facilities, homes, commercial interiors, new construction, and neighborhood development. To become certified, projects must earn a minimum number of points. Four levels of certification exist.

- Platinum   80+ points
- Gold   60+ points
- Silver   50+ points
- Certified   40+ points

In addition, projects may earn up to ten bonus points for innovation and for taking into account regional priorities. Six key environmental concerns have been identified for each region of the country. These have been further refined by ZIP Code to lessen the environmental impact of building as much as possible.

The GBCI oversees the process for credentialing individuals working in the construction field including interior design. Becoming credentialed requires completing a number of hours of coursework, successfully passing examinations, and working on green projects. Classes are taught traditionally or online. In 2010, the Veterans Administration began contributing to the cost of credentialing for veterans through the GI Bill. The three tiers of credential are:

- *LEED Green Associate:* Demonstrates basic knowledge and skills of green building. Areas of knowledge include design, construction, and operations.
- *LEED AP:* In addition, demonstrates skill in specialty areas such as building and design, interior design and construction, homes, neighborhood development, and operations and maintenance.
- *LEED Fellow:* Highest level of experience and contribution to the field of green building.

Over 144,000 individuals have attained LEED professional credentials.

In 2009, the USGBC established the USGBC Students program for college and university groups. The purpose is "to educate students as well as empower them to get engaged in green building and sustainability on their campuses."

How Being Breen Works for
Jake Pederson, Project Manager

Jake Pederson, 27, works as a project engineer for a general contractor and construction management firm in Bellingham, Washington. Pederson has been working on green projects for the past five years. While visiting a job site, Pederson checks storm water runoff, completes erosion control reports, and reviews details of an upcoming concrete pour with the superintendent.

Describe your job, including common daily tasks and long-term projects that you have worked on or are working on now. What, specifically, about your job makes it green?

As a project manager, my daily tasks are always different because no two projects are the same. Checking e-mails and staying in contact with the clients, architects, superintendents, subcontractors, and suppliers is paramount to the success of the project and should occur as often as possible.

The degree to which I am directly involved with procurement of materials, scheduling, and on-site supervision depends on the size of a project. As the size of the project increases, the tasks mentioned above are typically turned over to the on-site superintendent. A few of the major tasks that I am generally responsible for are writing subcontracts and purchase orders, material submittals, shop drawing approvals, and tracking costs.

Long-term projects would include taking a project from design to final construction. Although contractors are not often involved heavily in the design phase, it can be very helpful and financially beneficial to bring them on board as early as possible. Contractors can help with design issues such as value engineering and constructability analysis, as well as green building methods and materials.

The greenest part of my job centers around the LEED projects that we do. Becoming a LEED AP has greatly expanded my knowledge of green building practices. Our company has implemented some of the green building practices into all of our projects, whether they are going for LEED certification or not. In my opinion, LEED and other green building practices are still a bit of a mystery to many people, and it can be very frustrating if you are not educated about them. I would recommend to anyone going into the construction industry to become educated in green building practices.

Why/how did you decide to work in a green industry?

When I was in college, green building practices were beginning to gain attention. Soon after college, I decided to become a LEED AP to boost my resume and help my company with our LEED projects. Since I started in May 2007, I have been involved with the construction of five LEED-certified buildings.

How did you prepare for your current position?

I have been around the construction industry my entire life. When I was old enough to come on job sites, my first job was sweeping and clean-up duty. Later, during high school, I became more involved with the actual carpentry part. I spent six summers working full-time as an apprentice carpenter during high school and college.

After earning a degree in construction management from Washington State University, my intention was to come back home and work for a few more years as a carpenter to gain more field knowledge. However, the company I work for needed me to work full-time as a project manager, and I have been in the office ever since.

When I decided to pursue the LEED accreditation, I took a one-day class to help familiarize myself with LEED. Then, I chose to focus on a specific sector of LEED—new construction. I studied until I felt I was ready to take the test. The test was difficult, but I passed it on my first attempt.

Which aspect of your education and/or training do you think has been the most helpful and/or useful to you? Why?

I think all my training has been equally important. In my opinion, project managers who have had hands-on field experience have a much better idea of what it actually takes to build a project. However, without my degree in construction management, I would lack the project management skills necessary to run a smooth and successful project.

Do you find that the skills and/or knowledge required for your job continue to evolve? If so, what have you done to keep up to date?

Green building practices are constantly evolving, and it is necessary to keep up with them. I attend green seminars and classes as often as possible. Formal training and education for LEED usually takes place on an annual cycle.

How have continuing education and/or training impacted the way you do your job?

Continuing education has increased my knowledge of current green building practices and has allowed me to pass this knowledge on to clients and architects I work with. New and improved methods and materials hit the market every day. It is critical to stay up-to-date on these methods and materials in order to better serve our clients.

What is the most rewarding part of your work, and what do you find to be the most challenging?

Nothing is more rewarding than seeing a happy client at the end of the project. While we are in business to make a profit, making a profit feels a lot better when the client is happy.

With the current economy [recession of 2007 through 2009], the most challenging part of my job is finding the next project. Being an accredited LEED builder has helped us find work during these troubled times. Marketing and staying in contact with architects is also very important and should not be overlooked.

What advice would you give to people interested in pursuing your career?

When I talk to people who are interested in the construction industry—and more specifically, construction management—I offer the following advice: Get as much field experience as possible. Interview (in person) experienced project managers to get a feel for what a career in construction management is really like. Obtain a degree in construction management or business management. Become LEED accredited, or at least well educated in green building practices.

How Being Green Works for
Jim Adrian,
Architectural Designer

Jim Adrian, 32, is an architectural designer for a global architectural, engineering, and consulting firm in Omaha, Nebraska. The firm he works for completes many sustainable projects. Adrian has been working in this green industry for the past eight years. Here, Adrian creates a stair section on his computer. The stair is a metal channel and treads with a picket handrail system.

Describe your job, including common daily tasks and long-term projects that you have worked on or are working on now. What, specifically, about your job makes it green?

My tasks vary across a wide spectrum. At the start of a new project, I may attend a design charrette [design workshop involving all stakeholders in a project] with the client for several days. On some projects, I could be generating a full set of contract documents to be used by contractors. Or one day, I could be designing a wall section using CAD software to determine what sustainable products best fit the project.

A lot of coordination occurs between architectural, mechanical, structural, and electrical people working on a project. This is needed to make sure we understand what each group is doing and to ensure that there is no interference with one another's work. For example, the architects provide mechanical engineers with R-values of different products they want to use on a project. This allows the engineers to provide an energy model or analysis in order to determine energy efficiency.

One task that happens very early on is generating a list of sustainable items or approaches in order to achieve a LEED rating for the project. I use the LEED checklist as a guide for projects that do not require an official LEED registration. I use CAD as a tool to create floor plans and details for the construction documents.

Why/how did you decide to work in a green industry?

Some influence came from my professors while attending the University of Nebraska. After learning more about sustainability, it only seemed to make sense to do work that betters one's living environment. As architects, we design spaces that affect others' "well being," whether it's for shelter, entertainment, or somewhere in between. If we can create space that is better for people, then we are all better off. Many times, people don't even realize how the space is affecting them, and they may take a space for granted.

How did you prepare for your current position?

I received an associate degree in architectural drafting from the High Tech Institute in Phoenix, Arizona, in 1997. In 2004, I received a bachelor of science in design, and in 2006 I earned my Masters of Architecture. Both of these degrees are from the University of Nebraska in Lincoln. I am a current member of Construction Specification Institute (CSI).

In addition, I am currently a LEED AP (Accredited Professional).

Right out of college, you think you know a lot about your field. But when you get out in the practicing world, you find the truth very quickly. I think one just grows into the position over time. It's not as if you simply take a class or read a book and you become an expert. You can never be fully prepared or know everything. There is such a wealth of information at your fingertips with the Internet and other sources. Exposure to both new and old things has been a key to learning for me.

Which aspect of your education and/or training do you think has been the most helpful and/or useful to you? Why?

I think getting exposure to as many things as possible is the most helpful—even if it's just a little bit of information—because it can be enough to intrigue you to research more on a topic that interests you or to make a decision that the subject is not for you. I call it the sponge effect; soaking up everything and anything.

Do you find that the skills and/or knowledge required for your job continue to evolve? If so, what have you done to keep up-to-date?

For me, being involved in an organization helps me to stay current with this ever-changing field. Every project seems to focus on a different set of skills. I am constantly building on what I know—and don't know, for that matter. I am always researching products or seeking advice from senior design members.

How have continuing education and/or training impacted the way you do your job?

With the ever-changing nature of the business, one must stay current with products and codes and so forth. Continuing education is a great way to stay current and to learn about new products being introduced into the field. A lot of product reps provide learning credits for little or no cost. Seminars are a great way to network with peers, too. Every year, there are more computer software updates, and I am learning new ways to use CAD to better what we produce for our clients.

What is the most rewarding part of your work, and what do you find to be the most challenging?

I really enjoy seeing the work I have spent months designing and drawing come to life when projects reach the construction phase. It's fun to explain to people who know little about green design how a sustainable element came to be in a project and watch their reaction of "Wow, that's really cool!" or "I didn't know that!"

What advice would you give to people interested in pursuing your career?

Be open-minded, because you never know where your path will lead you!

CHAPTER 2

INSTALLATION, OPERATIONS, AND ENERGY-EFFICIENCY JOBS

Energy efficiency is an important component of the federal government's commitment to reducing the nation's dependence on foreign oil and cutting greenhouse gas emissions. The U.S. Department of Energy's Energy Star® program to identify energy-efficient appliances is one example of how businesses, homeowners, and individuals save energy. According to the Energy Star® Web site, Americans in 2009 "saved enough energy to power 10 million homes and avoid greenhouse gas emissions from 12 million cars." In the process of being proactive about energy, Americans saved $6 billion.

In addition to replacing energy-inefficient and out-of-date appliances such as refrigerators and clothes washers, Americans in greater numbers are replacing old heating and cooling systems, adding insulation to attics, weather stripping doors and windows, replacing non-E windows and glass doors, replacing old lighting systems, and installing new technologies, such as solar-powered heat and hot water tanks. These actions represent jobs in greening industries or clean technology now.

In terms of the future, the Department of Energy's Office of Energy Efficiency and Renewable Energy (EERE) sponsors the "Building Technologies Program," which works with the construction industry and educational partners to find cost-effective methods "to improve the efficiency of buildings and the equipment, components, and systems within them." This is where building management and operations become important. By improving the efficiency of heating, air conditioning, and lighting, building operations personnel in office buildings, apartment houses, and department and big box stores can save energy and water. Managers can also improve the air quality by their choices of cleaning products, paint, flooring, and floor coverings.

One aspect of the "Building Technologies" umbrella program is "Building America," which seeks to reduce the average energy use of housing. The goal is to reduce energy use by 40 to 100 percent. Ultimately, EERE hopes the research will lead to net energy homes—homes that produce as much energy as they use. A similar EERE program aimed at commercial construction is the "Net-Zero Energy Commercial Building Initiative."

About Building Operations

The Service Employees International Union (SEIU) has a model green training program for its members who represent a variety of facilities jobs, including maintenance workers, superintendents, and resident managers. The goal of the 11-session program is to teach them how to make their buildings more eco-friendly.

JOBS PROFILED HERE

The following occupations are profiled in this chapter:

- Boilermaker
- Electrician
- Energy Auditor
- Energy Broker
- Energy Engineer
- Facility Manager
- Geothermal Technician
- Heating, Air Conditioning, and Refrigeration Mechanic and Installer
- Insulation Worker: Floor, Ceiling, and Wall
- Insulation Worker, Mechanical
- Maintenance and Repair Worker, General
- Mechanical Engineer
- Refrigeration Mechanic and Installer
- Solar Energy Installation Manager
- Solar Photovoltaic Installer
- Solar Sales Representative and Assessor
- Solar Thermal Installer and Technician
- Stationary Engineer and Boiler Operator
- Weatherization Installer and Technician

KEY TO UNDERSTANDING THE JOB PROFILES

The job profiles are classified according to one or more of the following categories:

✿ Bright Outlook
🌐 Green Occupation

The classifications "Bright Outlook" and "Green Occupation" are taken from the National Center for O*NET Development's O*NET OnLine job site. O*NET, which is sponsored by the U.S. Department of Labor/Employment and Training Administration (USDOL/ETA), has broken green jobs into three categories:

- Green Increased-Demand occupations
  - o These are occupations that are likely to see job growth, but the work and worker

requirements are unlikely to experience significant changes.
- Green Enhanced-Skills occupations
  - o These occupations are likely to experience significant changes in work and worker requirements. Workers may find themselves doing new tasks requiring new knowledge, skills, and credentials. Current projections do not anticipate increased demand for workers in these occupations, but O*NET notes that an increase is possible.
- Green New and Emerging occupations
  - o These are new occupations—not growth in existing jobs—that are created as a result of activity and technology in green sectors of the economy.

Boilermaker 🌐

Alternate Titles and Related Careers

- Boilermaker Mechanic
- Boilermaker Pipefitter
- Boilermaker Welder
- Boiler Mechanic
- Boiler Technician
- Boiler Welder
- Service Technician

This is considered a "Green Increased-Demand" occupation in the green construction sector of the economy. It also has ramifications in terms of energy efficiency.

About the Many Jobs That Boilermakers Do

The *Occupational Outlook Handbook* lists a variety of fields in which boilermakers construct, repair, and maintain equipment, including blast furnaces, water treatment plants, air pollution equipment, storage and process tanks, and the pipes used in dams to send water to and from hydroelectric power generation turbines.

Job Trends

The boilermaker occupation is projected to have a faster-than-average growth rate of 14 to 19 percent between 2008 and 2018. The Bureau of Labor Statistics anticipates that the occupation will experience projected job openings of 8,100 during that period. The number of openings will be due in part to an increase in the demand for boilermakers and in part because of the retirement of workers and the movement of workers out of this highly physical and demanding occupation.

According to the *Occupational Outlook Handbook,* job opportunities are expected to be favorable and driven in large part by the need to maintain and upgrade aging boilers. Typically, boilers last 50 years, but they require maintenance work on a regular and ongoing basis. In addition, the nation's growing population requires increasingly greater amounts of energy, and because of the Clean Air Act, utility companies must upgrade their boiler systems. Federal clean energy policies also encourage the construction of new, more environmentally friendly and efficient clean-burning coal, wind, and solar power plants that will also spur the demand for boilermakers.

Nature of the Work

Boilermakers construct, assemble, maintain, and repair stationary steam boilers and boiler house auxiliaries. Boilers heat water or other fluids under extreme pressure for use in generating electric power and to provide heat and power in buildings, factories, and ships. In addition to those who fabricate and assemble boilers, the occupation includes those who assist in testing assembled vessels, direct the cleaning of boilers and boiler furnaces, and inspect and repair boiler fittings. These fittings include safety valves, regulators, automatic-controlled mechanisms, water columns, and auxiliary machines.

According to O*NET, boilermakers who are employed in repair and service positions may perform the following tasks:

- Examine boilers, pressure vessels, tanks, and vats to locate defects such as leaks, weak spots, and defective sections so that they can be repaired
- Inspect assembled vessels and individual components, such as tubes, fittings, valves, controls, and auxiliary mechanisms to locate any defects
- Repair or replace defective pressure vessel parts, such as safety valves and regulators, using torches, jacks, caulking hammers, power saws, threading dies, welding equipment, and metalworking machinery
- Study blueprints to determine locations, relationships, and dimensions of parts
- Straighten or reshape bent pressure vessel plates and structure parts, using hammers, jacks, and torches
- Clean pressure vessel equipment, using scrapers, wire brushes, and cleaning solvents
- Install refractory bricks and other heat-resistant materials in fireboxes of pressure vessels

Based on O*NET's list of tasks, boilermakers who fabricate and assemble stationary steam boilers and boiler house auxiliaries may perform the following tasks:

- Attach rigging and signal crane or hoist operators to lift heavy frame and plate sections and other parts into place
- Bolt or arc-weld pressure vessel structures and parts together, using wrenches and welding equipment
- Bell, bead with power hammers, or weld pressure vessel tube ends, in order to ensure leakproof joints
- Lay out plate, sheet steel, or other heavy metal, and locate and mark bending and cutting lines, using protractors, compasses, and drawing instruments or templates
- Install manholes, handholes, taps, tubes, valves, gauges, and feedwater connections

in drums of water tube boilers, using hand tools

- Shape seams, joints, and irregular edges of pressure vessel sections and structural parts in order to attain specified fit of parts, using cutting torches, hammers, files, and metalworking machines
- Position, align, and secure structural parts and related assemblies to boiler frames, tanks, or vats of pressure vessels, following blueprints
- Locate and mark reference points for columns or plates on boiler foundations, following blueprints and using straightedges, squares, transits, and measuring instruments
- Shape and fabricate parts, such as stacks, uptakes, and chutes, in order to adapt pressure vessels, heat exchangers, and piping to premises, using heavy-metalworking machines such as brakes, rolls, and drill presses
- Assemble large vessels in an on-site fabrication shop prior to installation, in order to ensure proper fit

Career Path

Boilermakers typically learn their trade through an apprenticeship that begins with an entry-level position as helper. As the new hire moves through the apprenticeship program, the type of work and the salary level increase over time. Some boilermakers will become supervisors. Having successfully completed an apprenticeship is an advantage in moving from company to company and in being promoted.

Earning Potential

Median hourly wage (2009): $26.97

Median annual wage (2009): $56,100

Education/Licensure

Boilermaker is a formal apprenticeship occupation and most boilermakers learn through an apprenticeship. To be eligible for an apprenticeship, a candidate must have a high school diploma or equivalent. A welding certificate or some training in welding can be an advantage in seeking an apprenticeship.

The apprenticeship is typically provided by a union or an employer, or a combination of a trade or technical school program and employer training. An apprenticeship typically consists of four years of paid on-the-job training, as well as a minimum of 144 hours of classroom instruction each of the four years. At the completion of the apprenticeship, graduates are fully qualified journey-level workers.

For More Information

International Brotherhood of Boilermakers, Iron Ship Builders, Blacksmiths, Forgers, and Helpers (IBB)
753 State Avenue
Suite 570
Kansas City, Kansas 66101
913-371-2640
www.boilermakers.org

Electrician ✿⦿

Alternate Titles and Related Careers

- Commercial Electrician
- Electrical Systems Installer
- Electrician Technician
- Inside Wireman
- Journeyman Electrician
- Journeyman Wireman
- Maintenance Electrician

This is considered a "Bright Outlook" and "Green Increased-Demand" occupation in the green construction sector of the economy.

 http://bit.ly/career19

Job Trends

According to the Bureau of Labor Statistics, there were 695,000 electricians in 2008. Of those,

70 percent were employed in the construction industry. Others work in manufacturing, the motion picture and video industry, and power generation. Approximately 80 percent of electricians working in construction are self-employed.

Employment is expected to increase 7 to 13 percent by 2018, which is about average for all occupations. However, job prospects are very good. By 2018, about 250,900 new jobs are projected. New residential and commercial construction, power plant construction to meet increasing energy demands, computers, telecommunications, and manufacturing automation are all expected to create new jobs during the coming decade. Remodeling homes and retrofitting buildings—public and private—to meet increasing concerns about the environment are also driving demand for construction workers, including electricians.

Nature of the Work

Electricians install, test, maintain, and repair wiring and electrical systems in residential and commercial buildings. Systems may include lighting, security, climate control, communications, or other control systems. Electricians also install electrical equipment and fixtures, like circuit breakers, switches, and fuses. Knowledge of tools, blueprints, materials, and basic mathematics is required. Electricians must also know the National Electrical Code and state and local codes. They must also maintain their electrician's license. If self-employed, they must be able to estimate materials, time, and cost to complete a job.

Some electricians install other types of wiring, such as low-voltage wiring used for voice, data, and video transmission. Others install fiber optic and coaxial cables. In factories, electricians wire and maintain more complex equipment, including generators, transformers, motors, and robots.

O*NET lists the following as among the jobs that electricians perform who work on residential and commercial electrical systems, equipment, and fixtures:

- Connect, repair, or replace wiring, equipment, and fixtures
- Assemble, install, test, and maintain electrical or electronic wiring, equipment, appliances, apparatus, and fixtures
- Inspect electrical and electronic systems to diagnose malfunctions
- Plan layout and installation of electrical wiring, equipment, and fixtures
- Install ground leads and connect power cables
- Fabricate parts
- Place conduit, pipes, or tubing inside partitions, walls, and other concealed areas
- Perform physically demanding tasks such as digging trenches and moving heavy objects

About Air Quality Standards

In 2007, California became the first state to require that the construction industry retrofit heavy equipment to cut down on toxic fumes from diesel engines.

Electricians who go into business for themselves also may do the following:
- Prepare cost estimates
- Prepare sketches and read blueprints
- Direct and train workers
- Maintain records and files, prepare reports, and order supplies and equipment

Career Path

Experienced electricians may become supervisors, and they also have opportunities to advance to construction managers. Many become electrical inspectors, and many start their own businesses as electrical contractors. Speaking both English and Spanish is an advantage for those who wish to advance.

Earning Potential

Median hourly wage (2009): $22.68

Median annual wage (2009): $47,180

Education/Licensure

Most electricians get training and skills through apprenticeship programs that take between four and five years to complete. These programs consist of classroom instruction and supervised training on the job with pay. The Independent Electrical Contractors (IEC) group offers apprenticeship programs, continuing education, and online courses. The National Electrical Contractors Association (NECA) and the International Brotherhood of Electrical Workers (IBEW) jointly sponsor apprenticeship programs. Technical and vocational schools and training academies also offer training programs. All programs require a high school diploma or GED.

Continuing education is important for electricians, so that they can keep up with changes to the National Electrical Code. Many electricians also take courses on contracting and management in preparation for starting their own businesses or for advancing within a company.

Most states require electricians to be licensed. Obtaining a license requires passing an exam about the National Electrical Code, local building and electric codes, and electrical theory. Most states also require electricians who do public work to hold a special license. In some cases, this requires that a person be certified as a master electrician. This process requires seven years or more experience in most states. Some states require a bachelor's degree in electrical engineering.

For More Information

Green Building Certification Institute
2101 L Street, NW
Suite 650
Washington, DC 20037
800-795-1746 (toll-free)
www.gbci.org

Illuminating Engineering Society of North America (IES)
120 Wall Street
Floor 17
New York, New York 10005-4001
212-248-5000
www.ies.org

Independent Electrical Contractors (IEC)
4401 Ford Avenue
Suite 1100
Alexandria, Virginia 22302
703-549-7351
www.ieci.org

International Brotherhood of Electrical Workers (IBEW)
900 Seventh Street, NW
Washington, DC 20001
202-833-7000
www.ibew.org

National Association of Home Builders (NAHB)
1201 15th Street, NW
Washington, DC 20005
800-368-5242 (toll-free)
www.nahb.org

National Electrical Contractors Association (NECA)
3 Bethesda Metro Center
Suite 1100
Bethesda, Maryland 20814
301-657-3110
www.necanet.org

U.S. Green Building Council (USGBC)
2101 L Street, NW
Suite 500
Washington, DC 20037
800-795-1747 (toll-free)
www.usgbc.org

Energy Auditor ☼🌎

Alternate Titles and Related Careers
- Building Performance Consultant
- Energy Consultant
- Energy Rater
- Home Energy Rater
- Home Performance Consultant

This is both a "Bright Outlook" and "Green New and Emerging" occupation. Workers are employed in both the energy efficiency sector and in governmental and regulatory administration.

Job Trends

The Bureau of Labor Statistics considers this occupation part of the "all other business operations specialists" and projects an average growth rate of 7 to 13 percent. However, energy auditor is a "Green New and Emerging" occupation. People's interest in going "green" and saving money on the cost of energy is expected to increase the number of job openings. Energy auditors have a positive impact on the environment because their work directly impacts the amount of energy that their customers consume in their homes or businesses.

Nature of the Work

Energy auditors conduct energy audits of buildings, building systems, and process systems. Among the tools they use are air velocity and temperature monitors, catalytic combustion analyzers, psychrometers, gas monitors, and leak testing equipment. They must be able to use analytical and scientific software, as well as CAD, database, graphics, and spreadsheet software. Knowledge of engineering, energy production, energy use, construction, maintenance, system operation, and process systems can be useful.

Energy auditors may perform any or all of the following tasks according to O*NET:
- Perform tests and collect and analyze field data

- Analyze energy bills including utility rates or tariffs to gather historical energy usage data
- Measure energy usage
- Determine patterns of building use to show annual or monthly needs for heating, cooling, lighting, or other energy needs
- Compare existing energy consumption levels to normative data
- Recommend energy-efficient technologies or alternate energy sources
- Identify opportunities to improve the operation, maintenance, or energy efficiency of building or process systems
- Analyze technical feasibility of energy-saving measures
- Calculate potential energy savings
- Prepare audit reports
- Identify and prioritize energy-saving measures
- Educate customers on energy efficiency strategies
- Prepare job specifications for home energy improvements
- Oversee installation of equipment such as pipe insulation and weatherstripping

Career Path

Because of the newness of the field, it is hard to say how much education will be required, but in general, it appears that many companies are looking for entry-level candidates with a bachelor's degree in engineering. Entry-level employees work under the supervision of an experienced energy auditor. After a certain amount of on-the-job training and experience, support energy auditors are given assignments on their own and over time begin to supervise entry-level workers. Some companies may require that energy auditors earn a business administration degree (MBA) to advance to higher-level management positions. Some may move into sales jobs selling the company's services.

Earning Potential

Median hourly wage (2009): $29.14

Median annual wage (2009): $60,610

Education/Licensure

For entry-level positions, a bachelor's degree in engineering from a college or university program that is accredited by the Accreditation Board for Engineering and Technology (ABET) may be required.

About Energy in Existing Buildings

Reducing energy consumption in the existing building stock in the United States offers the biggest opportunity for reducing our CO_2 emissions, according to the Intergovernmental Panel on Climate Change (IPCC). The U.S. Green Building Council provides a rating system, LEED Existing Building Operations and Maintenance (LEED-EB-O&M), for certifying energy efficiency in existing buildings.

Some colleges and universities offer five-year programs that culminate in a master's degree. Some offer five- or six-year programs that include cooperative experience. Some four-year schools have arrangements with community colleges or liberal arts colleges that allow students to spend two or three years at the initial school and transfer for the last two years to complete their engineering degree.

All fifty states and the District of Columbia require engineers to be licensed as professional engineers (PE) if they serve the public directly. In most states, licensure requires graduation from a four-year engineering program accredited by ABET, four years of experience, and passing the state exam. Many engineers take the Fundamentals of Engineering portion of the exam upon graduation. They are then engineers in training (EIT). After obtaining appropriate work experience, they take the Principles and Practice of Engineering exam to complete their professional license. Most states recognize licenses from other states as long as the requirements are the same or more stringent. Some states have continuing education requirements.

The Association of Energy Engineers (AEE) offers three certificate programs for energy auditors: Certified Energy Auditor (CEA), Certified Energy Auditor in Training (CEAIT), and Certified Residential Energy Auditor. The Building Performance Institute (BPI) offers a certification as building analyst. Some states have their own certification programs. The Residential Energy Services Network (RESNET)* offers programs for Certified In-Home Energy Survey Professional and Diagnostic Home Energy Survey Professional.

For More Information

Accreditation Board for Engineering and
    Technology (ABET)
111 Market Place
Suite 1050
Baltimore, Maryland 21202
410-347-7700
www.abet.org

Association of Energy Engineers (AEE)
4025 Pleasantdale Road
Suite 420
Atlanta, Georgia 30340
770-447-5083
www.aeecenter.org

Building Performance Institute (BPI)
107 Hermes Road
Suite 110
Malta, New York 12020
877-274-1274 (toll-free)
www.bpi.org

California Building Performance Contractors
    Association (CBPCA)
1000 Broadway
Suite 410
Oakland, California 94607
888-352-2272 (toll-free)
www.cbpca.org

Residential Energy Services Network (RESNET)
PO Box 4561
Oceanside, California 92052-4561
760-806-3448
www.resnet.us

U.S. Green Building Council (USGBC)
2101 L Street, NW
Suite 500
Washington, DC 20037
800-795-1747 (toll-free)
www.usgbc.org

About the Next Cool Thing

Dark roofs will be a thing of the past if the scientists at Lawrence Berkeley Laboratory and other researchers have their way. They have been experimenting with light-colored roofs for years. According to various studies, air conditioning use can be reduced by as much as 20 percent with white roofs. Roofs needn't be white to result in energy—and cost—savings, but a lemon-yellow roof won't save as much as a white roof.

Energy Broker ✿ 🌍

Alternate Titles and Related Careers
- Account Executive: Energy Sales
- Energy Consultant
- Energy Sales Consultant
- Energy Sales Representative

This is a "Bright Outlook" and "Green New and Emerging" occupation in the energy trading sector of the financial services industry. Although included under the electricity industry, energy brokers may also work in the natural gas and propane/liquid fuels sectors.

Job Trends

The Bureau of Labor Statistics includes this occupation in "Sales Representatives, Services, All Other" and rates the category as having a 14 to 19 percent growth rate between 2008 and 2018. This is faster than average for all occupations.

Energy deregulation, which began in the late 1990s, created this job by creating competition among companies to sell energy to consumers—residential and commercial. Under energy deregulation, states decide if they want to allow consumers to choose from whom they buy their power. They can choose to keep their current utility or buy from a new supplier that has bought the power from a power-generation company. The power is delivered over existing power lines by a third-party distributor, which charges a fee to its competitor for the service. As the companies that produce power proliferate, the need for energy brokers as intermediaries to buy power from generation companies and sell it to consumers should grow as well.

Nature of the Work

Energy brokers buy and sell energy for customers. They buy from energy generators and sell to consumers. The goal is to help consumers realize savings from energy deregulation by creating a competitive marketplace. Each company tries to provide the best pricing terms and conditions for consumers, while making a profit.

Among the tasks that an energy broker who interacts with consumers performs are the following, according to O*NET:
- Contact prospective buyers or sellers of power to arrange transactions
- Create product packages based on assessment of customers' or potential customers' needs
- Educate customers and answer questions related to the buying or selling of energy, energy markets, or alternative energy sources
- Explain contract and related documents to customers
- Analyze customer bills and utility rate structures to select optimal rate structures for customers

About Federal Clean Energy Resources

EREN stands for Efficiency and Renewable Energy Network, the U.S. Department of Energy's Web site on renewable energy issues. Visit www.eren.gov to see what the network has to offer. Also check out the National Renewable Energy Laboratory at www.nrel.org for information about alternative energy research studies. The Green Power Network at http://apps3.eere.energy.gov is the U.S. Department of Energy's Web site for information on green power markets, green power providers, products, consumer protection issues, and policies.

Energy brokers who deal with purchasing energy from electric power companies or natural gas and propane/liquid gas providers may perform the following tasks:

- Contact prospective buyers or sellers of power to arrange transactions
- Purchase or sell energy or energy derivatives for customers
- Explain contract and related documents to customers
- Forecast energy supply and demand to minimize the cost of meeting load demands and to maximize the value of supply resources
- Negotiate prices and contracts for energy sales or purchases
- Price energy based on market conditions
- Develop and deliver proposals or presentations on topics such as the purchase and sale of energy
- Facilitate the delivery or receipt of wholesale power or retail load scheduling
- Monitor the flow of energy in response to changes in consumer demand

Career Path

After a probationary period with greater supervision, an entry-level energy broker will work on his/her own. Advancement typically takes the form of being assigned to a larger account or territory,

where commissions are likely to be greater. Brokers with good sales records and leadership ability may advance to higher level positions, such as sales supervisor, district manager, territory manager, or vice president of sales. Some may become sales trainers working with new employees on selling techniques and company policies. Others may strike out on their own as independent sales agents or consultants.

Earning Potential

Median hourly wage (2009): $23.76

Median annual wage (2009): $49,410

Education/Licensure

Those engaged in financial sales (energy derivatives) require a bachelor's degree in business, finance, accounting, or economics. A master's in business (MBA) can be helpful for advancement. For other energy brokers, there is no formal educational requirement. Regardless of educational background, factors such as communication skills, the ability to sell, and knowledge of the products are key components for success.

Some states such as Massachusetts require licensing of energy brokers. Energy brokers who deal in derivatives must register with the Financial Industry Regulatory Authority (FINRA) and comply with exam and licensing requirements.

The Association of Energy Engineers (AEE) offers the Certified Energy Procurement Professional (CEP) program for energy brokers. The American Public Power Association offers the e-Learning course "Solving Your Customer's Energy Concerns" as initial training or a refresher.

For More Information

American Public Power Association (APPANET)
1875 Connecticut Avenue, NW
Suite 1200
Washington, DC 20009-5715
www.appanet.org

Association of Energy Engineers (AEE)
4025 Pleasantdale Road
Suite 420
Atlanta, Georgia 30340
770-447-5083
www.aeecenter.org

Electric Power Supply Association (EPSA)
1401 New York Avenue, NW
11th Floor
Washington, DC 20005-2110
www.epsa.org

Financial Industry Regulatory Authority (FINRA)
1735 K Street, NW
Washington, DC 20006
www.finra.org

National Energy Marketers Association (NEMA)
3333 K Street, NW
Suite 110
Washington, DC 20007
202-333-3288
www.energymarketers.com

Security Industries and Financial Markets
   Association (SIFMA)
120 Broadway
35th Floor
New York, New York 10271-0080
212-313-1200
AND
1101 New York Avenue, NW
Washington, DC 20005
202-962-7300
www.sifma.org

Energy Engineer ✿⊛

Alternate Titles and Related Careers

- Distributed Generation Project Manager
- Energy Efficiency Engineer
- Energy Manager
- Environmental Solutions Engineer
- Industrial Energy Engineer
- Measurement and Verification Engineer
- Test and Balance Engineer

This is a "Bright Outlook" and "Green New and Emerging" occupation in the green construction sector of the economy. It is also a "Green New and Emerging" occupation in the energy efficiency and research, design, and consulting services sectors.

Job Trends

The Bureau of Labor Statistics includes this in the engineering category and indicates an average rate of job growth in the 7- to 13-percent range. However, as a "new and emerging" occupation in several green sectors of the economy, it may see a higher growth rate.

Nature of the Work

An energy engineer designs, develops, and evaluates energy-related projects and programs to reduce energy costs or improve energy efficiency during the design, building, or remodeling stages of construction. Energy engineers may specialize in electrical systems; heating, ventilation, and air-conditioning systems; green buildings; lighting; air quality; or energy procurement. They may consult with clients and other engineers on topics such as climate control systems, energy modeling, data logging, energy management control systems, lighting or day-lighting design, sustainable design, energy auditing, LEED principles, and green buildings. In the course of their work, energy engineers ensure acceptability of budgets and time lines, conformance to federal and state laws and regulations, and adherence to approved job specifications.

Among the tasks that energy engineers perform, according to O*NET, are the following:

- Conduct energy audits to evaluate energy use, costs, or conservation measures
- Monitor and analyze energy consumption
- Perform energy modeling, measurement, verification, commissioning, or retro-commissioning
- Oversee design or construction aspects related to energy such as energy engineering, energy management, and sustainable design

- Conduct job site observations, field inspections, and sub-metering to collect data for energy conservation analyses
- Review architectural, mechanical, and electrical plans and specifications to evaluate energy efficiency or determine economic, service, or engineering feasibility
- Inspect or monitor energy systems to determine energy use or potential energy savings
- Direct the work of contractors or staff in the implementation of energy management projects
- Prepare project reports and other program or technical documentation
- Analyze, interpret, and create graphical representations of data using engineering software
- Promote awareness or use of alternative and renewable energy sources
- Conduct research or collect data on renewable or alternative energy systems or technologies such as solar thermal energy

If an energy engineer is involved in the procurement of energy sources, the engineer may also

- Make recommendations regarding fuel selection
- Review and negotiate energy purchase agreements

Career Path

Entry-level energy engineers typically begin work under the supervision of experienced engineers. They may also participate in a formal training program if offered by their employer. As they gain knowledge and experience, they are assigned to more complex projects with less supervision. In time, they may become supervisors or team leaders. Some may become engineering managers or choose to enter sales or start their own businesses.

Earning Potential

Median hourly wage (2009): $43.06

Median annual wage (2009): $89,560

About Cutting the Nation's Energy Use

Two reports released in 2009 estimated that the nation could cut energy use between 15 and 23 percent by 2020 by instituting energy efficiencies such as sealing air ducts and replacing energy inefficient electrical appliances. The study done by the consulting firm McKinsey estimated the cost for a 23 percent decline in energy use at $520 billion. Savings realized in the long term: $1.2 trillion.

Education/Licensure

This occupation requires a bachelor's degree in engineering from an institution accredited by the Accreditation Board for Engineering and Technology (ABET). While many colleges and universities offer the major branches of engineering, only a few offer programs in the smaller specialties. However, graduates with a degree in one branch of engineering may qualify for jobs in other branches.

Some colleges and universities offer five-year programs that culminate in a master's degree. Some offer five- or six-year programs that include cooperative experience. Some four-year schools have arrangements with community colleges or liberal arts colleges that allow students to spend two or three years at the initial school and transfer for the last two years to complete their engineering degree.

All fifty states and the District of Columbia require engineers to be licensed as professional engineers (PE) if they serve the public directly. In most states, licensure requires graduation from a four-year engineering program accredited by the Accreditation Board for Engineering and Technology (ABET), four years of experience, and passing the state exam. Many engineers take the Fundamentals of Engineering portion of the exam upon graduation. They are then engineers in training (EIT). After obtaining appropriate work experience, they take the Principles and Practice of Engineering exam to complete their professional license. Most states recognize licenses from other states, as long as the requirements are the same or more stringent. Some states have continuing education requirements.

The Association of Energy Engineers (AEE) offers several certification programs for energy engineers, including Certified Measurement and Verification Professional (CMVP), Certified Lighting Efficiency Professional (CLEP), Certified Building Commissioning Professional (CBCP), and Existing Building Commissioning Professional (EBCP) programs. For those who procure energy, AEE offers the Certified Energy Procurement Professional (CEP) program.

For More Information

Accreditation Board for Engineering and
   Technology (ABET)
111 Market Place
Suite 1050
Baltimore, Maryland 21202
410-347-7700
www.abet.org

Association of Energy Engineers (AEE)
4025 Pleasantdale Road
Suite 420
Atlanta, Georgia 30340
770-447-5083
www.aeecenter.org

U.S. Green Building Council (USGBC)
2101 L Street, NW
Suite 500
Washington, DC 20037
800-795-1747 (toll-free)
www.usgbc.org

Facilities Manager ⊕

Alternate Titles and Related Careers
- Administrative Services Manager
- Building Manager
- Building Operations Manager
- Energy Manager
- Maintenance and Operations Manager
- Maintenance Engineer
- Maintenance Manager

Facilities manager belongs to a "Green Increased-Demand" category. Rising energy costs to heat and cool buildings is making the job of facilities manager increasingly important.

 http://bit.ly/career21

Job Trends

According to the *Occupational Outlook Handbook,* administrative managers, the category that includes facilities managers, should rise about as fast as average for all occupations between 2008 and 2018. However, demand for facilities managers is expected to be strong.

Businesses and educational institutions are facing rising energy costs and are concerned about maintaining, securing, and operating their facilities as efficiently as possible. Cost-cutting and streamlining operations will be of increasing importance to organizations and primary goals of their facilities managers.

However, the rebound of the economy from the recession will affect job openings. Companies and organizations will not build new facilities until they feel more confident about the economy.

One trend that is evident in this field is the outsourcing of facilities management and operations to private firms.

About Energy Savings and Profit Margins

Energy savings from buildings is the lowest-cost method of reducing greenhouse gas emissions, according to the consulting firm McKinsey & Company. In addition, greener buildings could save the New York real estate industry alone as much as $230 million a year in operating expenses.

Nature of the Work

Facilities managers "ensure the optimal operation of plants [physical buildings], grounds, and offices," according to the mission statement of the

Association of Facilities Engineering. Facilities managers work in manufacturing plants, hospitals, office buildings, apartment buildings, government agencies, and industrial parks. They plan, design, and manage buildings, grounds, equipment, and supplies. Typically, the job involves mechanical, electrical, safety, and building management control systems as well as managing people. Facilities managers' duties increasingly include developing and implementing energy efficiency strategies.

Among the specific tasks of facilities managers are the following:

- Monitor the facility to ensure that it is safe, secure, and well-maintained
- Recommend energy-saving alternatives or production efficiencies
- Coordinate repair activities
- Oversee renovation projects
- Ensure that renovations meet codes and environmental, health, and security standards
- Improve operations including energy efficiency
- Hire and train staff
- Manage staff, including maintenance, grounds, custodial, and office personnel
- Prepare budgets and reports including energy use

Facility managers who work for large companies or for colleges and universities may also be involved in

- Purchase and sale of real estate
- Lease management
- Architectural planning and design

Career Path

Some facilities managers begin by specializing in one area of expertise to gain experience and then move to another field for more experience. In this way, they work their way up within a company or move from company to company gaining more experience, greater responsibilities, and higher pay with each move. Certifications can also help a facilities manager in seeking promotions. Knowledge of business administration, information technology, and architecture, as well as engineering, is useful as facilities managers gain higher-level jobs. Some experienced managers may become consultants, working for themselves or for facilities management and operations consulting firms.

Earning Potential

Mean hourly wage (2009): $36.31

Mean annual wage (2009): $75,520
(Based on "Administrative Services Manager")

Education/Licensure

Facilities managers typically have at least a bachelor's degree in engineering, and some have an undergraduate or graduate degree in engineering, architecture, construction management, business administration, or facility management. A background in real estate, construction, or interior design can also be helpful.

All fifty states as well as the District of Columbia require engineers to be licensed as professional engineers (PE) if they serve the public directly. In most states, licensure requires graduation from a four-year engineering program accredited by the Accreditation Board for Engineering and Technology (ABET), four years of experience, and passing the state exam. Many engineers take the Fundamentals of Engineering portion of the exam upon graduation. They are then engineers in training (EIT). After obtaining appropriate work experience, they take the Principles and Practice of Engineering exam to complete their professional license. Most states recognize licenses from other states as long as the requirements are the same or more stringent. Some states have continuing education requirements.

The International Facility Management Association (IFMA) offers two credentials, the Facility Management Professional (FMP) as the first step and the Certified Facility Manager (CFM) for those with experience in the facility management field.

Additional certifications in Facilities Management, Facility Management: Principles, Facility Management: Practices, and Facilities and Environmental Management are available online through IFMA partners.

The Association of Facilities Engineering (AFE) offers three certifications: Certified Plant Engineer (CPE), Certified Plant Maintenance Manager (CPMM), and Certified Plant Supervisor (CPS).

The American Society of Heating, Refrigerating and Air-Conditioning Engineers (ASHRAE) offers professional certificates in Building Energy Modeling, High Performance Building Design, Operations and Performance Management, and Healthcare Facility Design. In addition to general facilities management associations, there are also specific organizations like the Association of Physical Plant Administrators (APPA), which is an organization of managers of educational facilities such as university campuses. It offers two credentials: Educational Facilities Credential (EFC) and the Certified Educational Facilities Professional (CEFP) for experienced managers.

About Changing Filters

Manufacturers typically recommend that air filters for furnaces and air conditioners be changed every thirty days. The reason is that filters become clogged with the dust and dirt that circulate in your home. The heater and air conditioning units then have to work harder for the air to flow through the dirty filter. The result is more wear and tear on the unit and higher utility bills.

For More Information

Accreditation Board for Engineering and
    Technology (ABET)
111 Market Place
Suite 1050
Baltimore, Maryland 21202
410-347-7700
www.abet.org

American Society of Heating, Refrigerating and
    Air-Conditioning Engineers (ASHRAE)
1791 Tullie Circle NE
Atlanta, Georgia 30329
404-636-8400
www.ashrae.org

Association for Facilities Engineering (AFE)
12801 Worldgate Drive
Suite 500
Herndon, Virginia 20170
571-203-7171
www.afe.org

Association of Physical Plant Administrators
    (APPA)
1643 Prince Street
Alexandria, Virginia 22314
703-684-1446
www.appa.org

International Facility Management Association
    (IFMA)
1 E. Greenway Plaza
Suite 1100
Houston, Texas 77046-0104
713-623-4362
www.ifma.org

National Association of State Facilities
    Administrators (NASFA)
c/o The Council of State Governments
PO Box 11910
Lexington, Kentucky 40578-1910
859-244-8181
www.nasfa.net

Geothermal Technician ☼ 🌎

Alternate Title and Related Career

- Geothermal Installer

This is a "Bright Outlook" and "Green New and Emerging" occupation in the renewable energy generation sector. Geothermal technicians will also find work in green construction.

Job Trends

The Bureau of Labor Statistics equates this occupation with "Installation, Maintenance, and Repair Workers, All Other" and estimates an average rate of growth of 7 to 13 percent for the category. However, two factors may increase the rate of growth for geothermal technicians: the investment in geothermal research and ultimately power-generation plants and the growth of geothermal technology for home heating.

Nature of the Work

Geothermal technicians monitor and control operating activities at geothermal power generation facilities and perform maintenance and repairs as necessary. They may also install, test, and maintain residential and commercial geothermal heat pumps. Their areas of responsibilities include geothermal heating, air-conditioning, and hot water utilities in new construction and retrofits.

According to O*NET, geothermal technicians who work in geothermal power plants may perform the following tasks:

- Identify and correct malfunctions of geothermal plant equipment, electrical systems, instrumentation, or controls
- Monitor and adjust operations of the geothermal power plant equipment or systems
- Adjust power production systems to meet load and distribution demands
- Maintain, calibrate, or repair plant instrumentation, control, and electronic devices in geothermal plants
- Apply coating or operate system to mitigate corrosion of geothermal plant equipment or structures
- Collect and record data associated with geothermal power plants or well fields
- Install and maintain geothermal plant electrical protection equipment
- Prepare and maintain logs, reports, or other documentation of work performed
- Test water sources for factors such as flow volume and contaminant presence

Geothermal technicians who install residential or commercial geothermal systems may perform the following functions:

- Install, maintain, or repair ground or water source-coupled heat pumps to heat and cool residential or commercial building air or water
- Calculate heat loss and heat gain factors for residential properties to determine heating and cooling required by installed geothermal systems
- Design and lay out geothermal heat systems according to property characteristics, heating an cooling requirements, piping and equipment requirements, applicable regulations, or other factors
- Determine the type of geothermal loop system most suitable to a specific property and its heating and cooling needs
- Perform pre- and post-installation pressure, flow, and related tests of vertical and horizontal loop piping
- Dig trenches for system piping to appropriate depths and lay piping in trenches
- Backfill piping trenches to protect pipes from damage
- Prepare newly installed geothermal heat systems for operation by flushing, purging, or other actions
- Identify equipment options, such as compressors, and make appropriate selections
- Install and maintain geothermal system instrumentation or controls
- Place geothermal system pipes in bodies of water, weighting them to allow them to sink into position
- Verify that piping placed in bodies of water is situated to prevent damage to aquaculture and away from potential sources of harm

- Integrate hot water heater systems with geothermal heat exchange systems
- Prepare and maintain logs, reports, or other documentation of work performed
- Test water sources for factors such as flow volume and contaminant presence

Career Path

Typically, technicians begin as helpers working under the supervision of experienced employees. Several months or even a year of on-the-job training may be required to move to the next level of responsibility. Workers may advance through several levels of experience and responsibility to become supervisors themselves. In time, some geothermal technicians start their own businesses installing residential and commercials systems or consulting with homeowners and businesses.

Earning Potential

Median hourly wage (2009): $17.08

Median annual wage (2009): $35,520

Education/Licensure

Most employers prefer entry-level workers to have high school diplomas or the equivalent. Typically, workers in geothermal power plants undergo on-the-job training working under experienced technicians.

The same is true for technicians who work as commercial and residential installers of geothermal systems. States and municipalities may require licensing as plumbers, electricians, or HVAC (heating, ventilation, air-conditioning) installers.

Some community colleges and a variety of for-profit institutes and training providers are now offering short-course training opportunities for geothermal technicians. Some of these are online courses.

The International Ground Source Heat Pump Association (IGSHPA), in partnership with the HeatSpring Learning Institute, offers the Accredited Geothermal Installer Certification.

HeatSpring also offers an online Entry Level Geothermal Professional Certificate. The Green Building Certification Institute, affiliated with the U.S. Green Building Council, offers LEED (Leadership in Energy and Environmental Design) credentials in green building that are applicable for geothermal technicians.

For More Information

Geothermal Energy Association (GEA)
209 Pennsylvania Avenue, SE
Washington, DC 20003
202-454-5261
www.geo-energy.org

Geothermal Heat Pump Consortium (GHPC)
1050 Connecticut Avenue, NW
Suite 1000
Washington, DC 20036
888-255-4436 (toll-free)
www.geoexchange.org

Geothermal Resources Council (GRC)
2001 Second Street
Suite 5
Davis, California 95617
www.geothermal.org

HeatSpring Learning Institute
220 Concord Avenue
Cambridge, Massachusetts 02138
800-393-2044 (toll-free)
www.heatspring.com

International Ground Source Heat Pump
Association (IGSHPA)
374 Cordell South
Stillwater, Oklahoma 74078
405-744-5175
www.igshpa.okstate.edu

U.S. Green Building Council (USGBC)
2101 L Street, NW
Suite 500
Washington, DC 20037
800-795-1747 (toll-free)
www.usgbc.org

Heating, Air Conditioning, and Refrigeration Mechanic and Installer ✿⊕

Alternate Titles and Related Careers

- Air Conditioning Technician (AC Tech)
- Commercial Service Technician
- Field Service Technician
- Heating, Air Conditioning, and Refrigeration Mechanic and Installer ✿ ⊕
- HVAC Installer (Heating, Ventilation, and Air Conditioning)
- HVAC Specialist (Heating, Ventilation, and Air Conditioning)
- HVAC Technician (Heating, Ventilation, and Air Conditioning)
- HVAC/R Service Technician (Heating, Ventilation, and Air Conditioning/Refrigeration)
- Refrigeration Mechanic and Installer ✿⊕
- Refrigeration Operator
- Refrigeration Technician
- Service Manager
- Service Technician

This is both a "Bright Outlook" and "Green Enhanced-Skills" occupation. Workers may be required to obtain new skills, knowledge, and credentials to fulfill new job tasks. The two sectors that employ most HVAC/R mechanics and installers are energy efficiency and green construction.

 http://bit.ly/career21

Job Trends

According to the Bureau of Labor Statistics, employment for heating, air conditioning, and refrigeration mechanics and installers is expected to increase by 20 percent or more by 2018. This is much faster than average for all occupations. Numerous workers are expected to retire and the number of people entering the occupation is low, so job prospects are expected to be excellent for this trade. By 2018, some 136,200 new employees will be needed.

One area in particular that is driving the demand for HVAC/R mechanics and technicians is home remodeling and retrofitting public and private buildings as the population becomes more energy conscious. The need for people who are able to install new, efficient climate-control systems will increase demand for HVAC/R technicians with knowledge of the latest in HVAC/R technology. New residential and commercial construction also requires skilled HVAC/R technicians and installers.

Retrofitting the HVAC systems in residential, commercial, and industrial buildings can result in significant reduction in energy use. HVAC systems can account for as much as half the energy use in homes and 40 percent of electricity use in commercial buildings. Replacing units that are over ten years old can reduce energy costs between 20 and 50 percent.

Nature of the Work

This job, like a number of construction and building occupations, requires a personable manner in dealing with the public, because much of the job involves face-to-face contact with customers. Heating and air conditioning technicians install and service heating and air conditioning systems in residential and commercial buildings. They test and inspect systems to verify that they comply with specifications and to detect malfunctions if they don't comply. They test all components of a system, including electrical circuits and pressure testing pipes and joints, to ensure that the system meets all standards and that it follows manufacturer's procedures and safety precautions while working.

Refrigeration technicians, another specialty in the category of heating, air conditioning, and refrigeration mechanics and installers, build refrigeration systems that are often used for air conditioning in commercial buildings and are now beginning to be used in residences. They connect pipes, install the refrigerant, test for leaks, connect the electric power source, and check to ensure that the system meets specifications. Reclaiming and recycling the refrigerant is critical, because it is harmful to the environment.

Among specific tasks, according to O*NET, are the following:

- Test electrical circuits and components, piping, tubing, and connections
- Repair or replace defective equipment, components, and wiring
- Reassemble and test equipment after repairs
- Inspect and test systems to verify system compliance with plans and specifications and to detect and locate malfunctions
- Discuss system malfunctions with users to isolate problems or verify the malfunctions have been corrected
- Recommend, develop, and perform preventive and general maintenance
- Lay out and install wiring and components according to wiring diagrams and blueprints
- Assist with other work in coordination with repair and maintenance teams
- Fabricate, assemble, and install metal work such as ducts
- Comply with all applicable standards, policies, and procedures
- Record the nature of a job, and time and materials used

Career Path

For most HVAC/R technicians, advancement is in the form of higher pay. Some technicians will become supervisors or managers. Others will advance by moving into other positions in the industry, such as sales representative, building supervisor, or contractor.

Earning Potential

Median hourly wage (2009): $19.76

Median annual wage (2009): $41,100

Education/Licensure

Heating, ventilation, air conditioning, and refrigeration technicians may still be able to learn this trade on the job, but those who have completed a formal apprenticeship or postsecondary training program—and may have earned an associate degree—have better opportunities. Community colleges, junior colleges, vocational and trade schools, and the armed forces offer programs, some of which lead to an associate degree. The programs take from six months to two years to complete.

Some states and municipalities require HVAC/R technicians to be licensed. Requirements vary, but all include passing an exam. Some require an apprenticeship, which is another way to be trained. Formal apprenticeship programs last from three to five years. They are often given by local chapters of trade organizations. There are five apprenticeships for heating and air conditioning technicians:

- Air and Hydronic Balancing Technician
- Furnace Installer
- Furnace Installer-and-Repairer, Hot Air
- Heating-and-Air-Conditioning Installer-Servicer
- Oil-Burner-Servicer-and-Installer

There are two apprenticeships for refrigeration technicians:

- Refrigeration Mechanic
- Refrigeration Unit Repairer

Under Section 608 of the Clean Air Act, the U.S. Environmental Protection Agency (EPA) requires anyone who handles ozone-depleting refrigerants to be properly trained. This includes technicians who work on refrigeration systems and stationary air conditioners. The Air-Conditioning Contractors of America offers training.

The North American Technician Excellence (NATE) certification program for HVAC/R technicians is recognized nationwide. HVAC Excellence offers a number of technician certifications at the professional and master levels. The Building Performance Institute offers certifications in Heating and Air Conditioning and Heat Pump. The U.S.

Green Building Council offers the LEED (Leadership in Energy and Environmental Design) Associate and LEED AP credentials that may be appropriate for some HVAC/R technicians.

For More Information

Air-Conditioning, Heating and Refrigeration Institute
2111 Wilson Blvd.
Suite 500
Arlington, Virginia 22201
703-524-8800
www.ari.org

Building Performance Institute (BPI)
107 Hermes Road
Suite 110
Malta, New York 12020
877-274-1274 (toll-free)
www.bpi.org

HVAC Excellence
1701 Pennsylvania Avenue, NW
Washington, DC 20006
800-394-5268 (toll-free)
www.hvacexcellence.org

North American Technician Excellence
2111 Wilson Blvd. #510
Arlington, Virginia 22201
703-276-7247
www.natex.org

Refrigeration Service Engineers Society
1666 Rand Road
Des Plaines, Illinois 60016
847-759-4051
www.rses.org

Sheet Metal and Air Conditioning Contractors' National Association
4201 Lafayette Center Drive
Chantilly, Virginia 20151-1209
703-803-2980
www.smacna.org

U.S. Green Building Council (USGBC)
2101 L Street, NW
Suite 500
Washington, DC 20037
800-795-1747 (toll-free)
www.usgbc.org

The following organizations sponsor apprenticeships:

Air-Conditioning Contractors of America
2800 Shirlington Road
Suite 300
Arlington, Virginia 22206
703-575-4477
www.acca.org

Associated Builders and Contractors
Workforce Development Department
4250 North Fairfax Drive
9th Floor
Arlington, Virginia 22203
703-812-2000
www.abc.org

Home Builders Institute
National Association of Home Builders
1201 15th Street, NW
6th Floor
Washington, DC 20005
800-795-7955 (toll-free)
www.hbi.org

Mechanical Contractors Association of America
Mechanical Service Contractors of America
1385 Piccard Drive
Rockville, Maryland 20850
301-869-5800
www.mcaa.org
www.mcaa.org/msca

Plumbing-Heating-Cooling Contractors
180 S. Washington Street
P.O. Box 6808
Falls Church, Virginia 22046
703-237-8100
www.phccweb.org

United Association of Journeymen and
   Apprentices of the Plumbing and Pipefitting
   Industry
United Association Building
Three Park Place
Annapolis, Maryland 21401
410-269-2000
www.ua.org

Insulation Worker: Floor, Ceiling, and Wall 💲

Alternate Titles and Related Careers
- Insulation Installer
- Installer
- Insulation Estimator
- Insulation Mechanic
- Insulation Worker, Mechanical
- Retrofit Installer

This is a "Green Increased-Demand" occupation found in the energy efficiency and green construction sectors of the economy. While demand may increase because of activities in the green economy and new technologies, there will probably not be significant changes in the work or in the skills and knowledge required of workers.

 http://bit.ly/career22

Job Trends
The need for insulation workers is expected to grow at the rate of 14 to 19 percent between 2008 and 2018. This translates into 13,200 job openings over the time period. However, as a "Green Increased-Demand" job, growth may be higher. Proper insulation can cut down on energy usage and, therefore, costs for both residential and commercial buildings. Much will depend on the rebound in the housing market—how long it takes and how high it goes—although retrofitting existing buildings also generates business for insulation installers.

Nature of the Work
Insulation workers cover structures with insulating materials to cover flooring, ceilings, and walls. The insulation may be in roll form or blown material—fiberglass, cork, calcium, silicate, foamglass, expanded silicate, and spray insulation—and installers may need to wear protective clothing. Physical abilities such as coordination, strength, and flexibility are important. Depending on their job, insulation workers may need to use analytical or scientific and project management software.

Among the tasks that an insulation installer may perform are the following, according to O*NET:
- Read blueprints and select appropriate insulation based on the space and heat characteristics of insulating materials
- Measure and cut insulation
- Cover and line structures with insulation
- Fit, wrap, staple, or glue insulation
- Distribute blown insulating materials evenly
- Cover, seal, or finish insulated surfaces or access holes
- Prepare surfaces for insulation application
- Remove old insulation

Career Path
Entry-level employees work under the supervision of experienced workers. On-the-job training may take up to four years, depending on whether the company installs insulation in residential or

commercial buildings. Over the training period, entry-level workers are given more responsibility with less supervision and earn more money.

Skilled insulation workers may become supervisors, shop superintendents, or estimators working with clients to determine insulation needs. Some experienced insulation workers with continuing education in business organization and finance may start their own businesses. The ability to speak English and Spanish is important for anyone wishing to advance to supervisor in the construction trades.

Earning Potential

Median hourly wage (2009): $15.65

Median annual wage (2009): $32,550

Education/Licensure

Typically, entry-level jobs require a high school diploma or equivalent. "Insulation worker" is an apprenticeship category recognized by the U.S. Department of Labor. Usually, insulation companies that install and maintain mechanical industrial insulation offer apprenticeships, sometimes in conjunction with the local of the International Association of Heat and Frost Insulators and Allied Workers. An apprenticeship usually lasts four or five years and combines classroom instruction with on-the-job training.

The National Insulation Association (NIA) offers an Insulation Energy Appraisal Program that results in a certification as an insulation energy appraiser meant for workers in the industrial insulation sector.

Under the rules of the Environmental Protection Agency (EPA), workers in the asbestos industry must be certified. This includes anyone who removes or handles asbestos; is involved in operations and maintenance, management planning, project design, and project monitoring related to asbestos; and conducts asbestos project air sampling and asbestos inspections. To become certified, workers must complete a training program accredited by their state and pay a license fee.

For More Information

International Association of Heat and Frost Insulators and Allied Workers (AWIU)
9602 Martin Luther King, Jr. Highway
Lanham, Maryland 20706-1839
301-731-9101
www.insulators.org

National Insulation Association (NIA)
12100 Sunset Hills Road
Suite 330
Reston, Virginia 20190-3295
703-464-6422
www.insulation.org

North American Insulation Manufacturers' Association (NAIMA)
44 Canal Center Plaza
Suite 310
Alexandria, Virginia 22314-1548
703-684-0084
www.naima.org

Insulation Worker, Mechanical

Alternative Titles and Related Careers

- Commercial Insulator
- Heat and Frost Insulator
- Industrial Insulator
- Insulation Installer
- Insulation Mechanic
- Insulation Worker
- Mechanical Insulator

The International Association of Heat and Frost Insulators and Allied Workers (AWIU) and the National Insulation Association (NIA) have studied the impact of proper insulation on energy conservation and emission reduction and estimated that 89,000 new jobs would be created just by repairing and replacing mechanical insulation on piping and duct work in industrial facilities and on HVAC equipment in commercial buildings.

Job Trends

The Bureau of Labor Statistics projects that job growth for mechanical insulators will increase faster than average between 2008 and 2018 at a rate of 14 to 19 percent. The *Occupational Outlook Handbook* rates job prospects as excellent. The actual number of projected openings is 15,500 new jobs. Approximately 91 percent of mechanical insulators are employed in the construction industry.

Nature of the Work

Mechanical insulators apply insulation materials to pipes, ductwork, and other mechanical systems in order to help control and maintain temperature. Workers must follow safety guidelines to protect themselves from irritants, such as fiberglass and cork, present in various forms. They use a variety of hand tools, including handsaws, knives, and scissors.

Mechanical insulators perform tasks that are different from those performed by floor, ceiling, and wall insulation workers. According to O*NET, mechanical insulators may perform the following tasks:

- Measure and cut insulation for covering surfaces
- Fit insulation around obstructions and shape insulating materials and protective coverings as required
- Determine the amounts and types of insulation needed and methods of installation, based on factors such as location, surface shape, and equipment use
- Install sheet metal around insulated pipes with screws in order to protect the insulation from weather conditions or physical damage
- Apply, remove, and repair insulation on industrial equipment, pipes, ductwork, or other mechanical systems, such as heat exchangers, tanks, and vessels, to help control noise and maintain temperatures
- Select appropriate insulation such as fiberglass, Styrofoam, or cork, based on the heat-retaining or -excluding characteristics of the material
- Read blueprints and specifications to determine job requirements
- Cover, seal, or finish insulated surfaces or access holes with plastic covers, canvas strips, sealants, tape, cement, or asphalt mastic
- Prepare surfaces for insulation application by brushing or spreading on adhesives, cement, or asphalt, or by attaching metal pins to surfaces
- Remove or seal off old asbestos insulation, following safety procedures
- Distribute insulating materials evenly into small spaces within floors, ceilings, or walls, using blowers and hose attachments or cement mortar

Career Path

Entry-level employees work under the supervision of experienced workers. On-the-job training may take up to four years depending on whether the company installs insulation in residential or commercial buildings. Over the training period, entry-level workers are given more responsibility with less supervision and earn more money. Entry-level employees in mechanical insulation typically participate in formal apprenticeship programs that take four or five years.

Skilled insulation workers may become supervisors, shop superintendents, or estimators working with clients to determine insulation needs. Some experienced insulation workers with continuing education in business organization and finance may start their own businesses. The ability to speak English and Spanish is important for anyone wishing to advance to supervisor in the construction trades.

Earning Potential

Median hourly wage (2009): $17.81

Median annual wage (2009): $37,040

Education/Licensure

Typically, entry-level jobs require a high school diploma or equivalent. Mechanical insulators typically participate in formal apprenticeships, unlike floor, ceiling, and wall insulators who typically learn on the job. The typical apprenticeship program lasts 4 or 5 years and combines classroom instruction with on-the-job training. "Insulation worker" is an apprenticeship category recognized by the U.S. Department of Labor.

The National Insulation Association (NIA) offers an Insulation Energy Appraisal Program that results in a certification as an insulation energy appraiser meant for workers in the industrial insulation sector.

Under the rules of the Environmental Protection Agency (EPA), workers in the asbestos industry must be certified. This includes anyone who removes or handles asbestos; is involved in operations and maintenance, management planning, project design, and project monitoring related to asbestos; and conducts asbestos project air sampling and asbestos inspections. To become certified, workers must complete a training program accredited by their state and pay a license fee.

For More Information

International Association of Heat and Frost Insulators and Allied Workers (AWIU)
9602 Martin Luther King, Jr. Highway
Lanham, Maryland 20706-1839
301-731-9101
www.insulators.org

National Insulation Association (NIA)
12100 Sunset Hills Road
Suite 330
Reston, Virginia 20190-3295
703-464-6422
www.insulation.org

North American Insulation Manufacturers' Association (NAIMA)
44 Canal Center Plaza
Suite 310
Alexandria, Virginia 22314-1548
703-684-0084
www.naima.org

Maintenance and Repair Worker, General ✿⑬

Alternate Titles and Related Careers
- Building Maintenance Mechanic
- Building Mechanic
- Equipment Engineering Technician
- I&C Technician (Instrument and Controls)
- Maintenance Technician
- Maintenance Mechanic
- Maintenance Supervisor
- Maintenance Electrician
- Maintenance Engineer
- Process Technician

This is considered a "Bright Outlook" and "Green Enhanced-Skills" occupation in the following green sectors of the economy: energy efficiency, environmental protection, green construction, manufacturing, and renewable energy generation.

Job Trends

The Bureau of Labor Statistics projects a 7 to 13 percent growth rate for jobs in this category. This is about average for all occupations. However, the actual number of expected job openings is 357,500 between 2008 and 2018. About 18 percent of current maintenance workers are employed in real estate and rental and leasing, another 18 are employed in manufacturing facilities, and about 11 percent work for government agencies. The remainder is divided among a variety of other industries.

Job opportunities are considered to be excellent, especially for those with experience. Some growth will result from the construction of new buildings, including hospitals, office buildings, hotels, and schools. Other jobs will result from the retirement of experienced maintenance workers. However, the use of computers to operate building systems will limit job growth to some degree.

Nature of the Work

Most craft workers like plumbers and carpenters specialize in one kind of work. General maintenance and repair workers perform work involving the skills of two or more craft occupations to keep machines, mechanical equipment, or the structure of a building in repair. According to the *Occupational Outlook Handbook,* general maintenance and repair workers may work on plumbing, electrical, and air-conditioning and heating systems, as well as build partitions, repair drywall, paint ceilings, and repair floors and stairs. Their duties may involve pipe fitting, boiler making, insulating, welding, machining, carpentry, and repairing electrical or mechanical equipment. Maintenance workers also install, align, and balance new equipment. They use tools ranging from common hand and power tools, such as hammers, hoists, saws, drills, and wrenches, to precision measuring instruments and electrical and electronic testing devices. They also use welding equipment and cutting torches. The ability to read diagrams, drawings, blueprints, maintenance manuals, and schematic diagrams is important.

According to O*NET, maintenance and repair workers may perform the following tasks:

- Repair or replace defective equipment parts, using hand tools and power tools, and reassemble equipment
- Perform routine preventive maintenance to ensure that machines continue to run smoothly, building systems operate efficiently, or the physical condition of buildings does not deteriorate
- Inspect drives, motors, and belts, check fluid levels, replace filters, or perform other maintenance actions, following checklists

- Assemble, install, or repair wiring, electrical and electronic components, pipe systems and plumbing, machinery, and equipment
- Diagnose mechanical problems and determine how to correct them, checking blueprints, repair manuals, and parts catalogs as necessary
- Inspect, operate, and test machinery and equipment to diagnose machine malfunctions
- Dismantle devices to access and remove defective parts, using hoists, cranes, hand tools, and power tools
- Clean and lubricate shafts, bearings, gears, and other parts of machinery
- Plan and lay out repair work order parts, supplies, and equipment from catalogs and suppliers, or obtain them from storerooms
- Adjust functional parts of devices and control instruments, using hand tools, levels, plumb bobs, and straightedges
- Paint and repair roofs, windows, doors, floors, woodwork, plaster, drywall, and other parts of building structures
- Align and balance new equipment after installation
- Inspect used parts to determine changes in dimensional requirements, using rules, calipers, micrometers, and other measuring instruments
- Set up and operate machine tools to repair or fabricate machine parts, jigs and fixtures, and tools
- Maintain and repair specialized equipment and machinery found in cafeterias, laundries, hospitals, stores, offices, or factories
- Fabricate and repair counters, benches, partitions, or other wooden structures, such as sheds and outbuildings
- Lay brick to repair and maintain buildings, walls, arches and other structures
- Grind and reseat valves, using valve-grinding machines

- Estimate and record type and cost of maintenance or repair work

Career Path

Entry-level positions are typically as helpers to experienced maintenance and repair workers. New hires begin by observing and then performing simple jobs such as fixing leaky faucets and replacing light bulbs. With experience, they move up to more difficult tasks, such as building partitions and overhauling machinery.

Obtaining certification can aid in advancement, especially in larger firms. Many general maintenance and repair workers in large organizations advance to supervisor jobs. Others decide to specialize in a particular craft such as plumbing, HVAC, or carpentry.

Earning Potential

Median hourly wage (2009): $16.65

Median annual wage (2009): $34,620

Education/Licensure

Typically, employers hiring for entry-level positions look for candidates with high school diplomas or the equivalent. Coursework in mechanical drawing, electricity, woodworking, blueprint reading, and computers are useful preparation for this occupation. Most training takes place on the job. Certification can be useful in demonstrating competency to prospective and current employers.

The International Maintenance Institute (IMI) offers three levels of Certified Maintenance Technician I-III, Certified Maintenance Professional (CMP), and Certified Maintenance Manager (CMM). IMI also offers four levels of Certified Water/Wastewater Maintenance Technician I-IV.

The Society for Maintenance and Reliability Professionals offers the Certified Industrial Maintenance Mechanic (CIMM) and the Certified Maintenance and Reliability Professional certifications.

Some states and municipalities require that workers who perform electrical or plumbing work be licensed.

For More Information

International Maintenance Institute
P.O. Box 751896
Houston, Texas 77275-1896
888-207-1773 (toll-free)
www.imionline.org

Society for Maintenance and Reliability
  Professionals
8400 Westpark Drive
2nd Floor
McLean, Virginia 22102-3570
800-950-7354 (toll-free)
www.smrp.org

Mechanical Engineer 🌐

Alternate Titles and Related Careers
- Commissioning Engineer
- Design Engineer
- Design Maintenance Engineer
- Equipment Engineer
- Mechanical Design Engineer
- Process Engineer
- Product Engineer
- Systems Engineer

This is considered a "Green Enhanced-Skills" occupation with demand in the following green sectors of the economy: energy efficiency; green construction; renewable energy generation; research, design, and consulting services; and transportation.

Job Trends

The Bureau of Labor Statistics projects that employment for the mechanical engineering occupation will grow at the rate of 7 to 13 percent between 2008 and 2018. This translates into 75,700 job openings. Openings will come from retirements and shifts of engineers into sales and management, as well as growth in sectors that employ mechanical engineers.

Nature of the Work

Mechanical engineering is a very broad discipline, and mechanical engineers perform a variety of tasks and work in a variety of industries, including the transportation and automobile industries where they plan and design tools, engines, and machinery. But mechanical engineers also play a role in the installation, operation, maintenance, and repair of equipment such as centralized heating, gas, water, and steam systems.

Among the skills that mechanical engineers need are the ability to read and interpret blueprints, technical drawings, schematics, and computer-generated reports. They also must be able to use drafting tools, computer-aided design (CAD), or drafting equipment and software.

O*NET lists the following as tasks that mechanical engineers may perform:

- Research, design, evaluate, install, operate, and maintain mechanical products, equipment, systems and processes to meet requirements, applying knowledge of engineering principles
- Confer with engineers and other personnel to implement operating procedures, resolve system malfunctions, and provide technical information
- Recommend design modifications to eliminate machine or system malfunctions
- Conduct research that tests and analyzes the feasibility, design, operation, and performance of equipment, components, and systems
- Investigate equipment failures and difficulties to diagnose faulty operation and to make recommendations to maintenance crew
- Research and analyze customer design proposals, specifications, manuals, and other data to evaluate the feasibility, cost, and maintenance requirements of designs or applications
- Develop and test models of alternate designs and processing methods to assess feasibility, operating condition effects, possible new applications and necessity of modification
- Oversee installation, operation, maintenance, and repair to ensure that machines and equipment are installed and functioning according to specifications
- Develop, coordinate, and monitor all aspects of production, including selection of manufacturing methods, fabrication, and operation of product designs
- Specify system components or direct modification of products to ensure conformance with engineering design and performance specifications
- Write performance requirements for product development or engineering projects
- Design test control apparatus and equipment and develop procedures for testing products
- Provide feedback to design engineers on customer problems and needs
- Establish and coordinate the maintenance and safety procedures, service schedule, and supply of materials required to maintain machines and equipment in the prescribed condition
- Apply engineering principles and practices to emerging fields such as robotics and waste management
- Study industrial processes to determine where and how application of equipment can be made
- Perform personnel functions such as supervision of production workers, technicians, technologists, and other engineers or design evaluation programs
- Solicit new business and provide technical customer service
- Estimate costs and submit bids for engineering, construction, or extraction projects and prepare contract documents

Career Path

As mechanical engineers gain experience, they may become specialists or advance into positions where they supervise a team of engineers and other staff members. Some eventually become managers. Some go on to earn a master's in business administration (MBA) degree to prepare them for high-level managerial positions. Some move into technical sales.

Earning Potential

Median hourly wage (2009): $37.03

Median annual wage (2009): $77,020

Education/Licensure

For entry-level positions, a bachelor's degree in engineering from a college or university program that is accredited by the Accreditation Board for Engineering and Technology (ABET) is required. In some cases, engineers with degrees in one type of engineering may qualify for jobs in other areas of engineering. Most colleges and universities offer mechanical engineering degrees.

Some colleges and universities offer five-year programs that culminate in a master's degree. Some offer five- or six-year programs that include cooperative experience. Some four-year schools have arrangements with community colleges or liberal arts colleges that allow students to spend two or three years at the initial school and transfer for the last two years to complete their engineering degree.

All fifty states and the District of Columbia require engineers to be licensed as professional engineers (PE) if they serve the public directly. In most states, licensure requires graduation from a four-year engineering program accredited by ABET, four years of experience, and passing the state exam. Many engineers take the Fundamentals of Engineering portion of the exam upon graduation. They are then engineers in training (EIT). After obtaining appropriate work experience, they take the Principles and Practice of Engineering exam to complete their professional license. Most states recognize licenses from other states, as long as the requirements are the same or more stringent. Some states have continuing education requirements.

The American Society of Mechanical Engineers (ASME) offers a number of specialized short courses, Internet seminars, and online courses as part of continuing education and licensure for mechanical engineers. ASME also offers the Geometric Dimensioning and Tolerancing Professional Certification (GDTP).

For More Information

Accreditation Board for Engineering and
   Technology (ABET)
111 Market Place
Suite 1050
Baltimore, Maryland 21202
410-347-7700
www.abet.org

American Society of Mechanical Engineers
   (ASME)
3 Park Avenue
New York, New York 10016-5990
800-843-2763 (toll-free)
www.asme.org

National Society of Professional Engineers
   (NSPE)
1420 King Street
Alexandria, Virginia 22314
703-684-2800
www.nspe.org

Refrigeration Mechanic and Installer ☼🌐

Alternative Titles and Related Careers

- Refrigeration Mechanic
- Refrigeration Operator
- Refrigeration Technician
- Service Technician
- VRT Mechanic (Variable Retention Time Mechanic)

This is a "Bright Outlook" and "Green Increased-Demand" occupation. The majority of jobs are in green construction, with additional jobs in the energy efficiency sector of the economy.

Job Trends

The Bureau of Labor Statistics includes the Refrigeration Mechanic and Installer occupation in the "Heating, Air Conditioning, and Refrigeration Mechanics and Installers" category, which is expected to grow at a much faster than average rate of 20 percent or higher. The total projected job openings are 136,200.

Nature of the Work

Refrigeration mechanics and installers install and repair industrial and commercial refrigeration systems and a variety of refrigeration equipment. They build refrigeration systems that are often used for air conditioning in commercial buildings and are now beginning to be used in residences. Refrigeration technicians connect pipes, install the refrigerant, test for leaks, connect the electric power source, and check to ensure that the system meets specifications. Reclaiming and recycling the refrigerant in cooling systems is a critical part of their jobs because refrigerant is harmful to the environment.

Among the tasks that refrigeration mechanics and installers perform are the following, according to O*NET:

- Observe and test system operation, including lines, components, and connections for leaks
- Dismantle malfunctioning systems and test components, using electrical, mechanical, and pneumatic testing equipment
- Adjust or replace worn or defective mechanisms and parts and reassemble repaired systems
- Braze or solder parts to repair defective joints and leaks
- Install wiring to connect components to an electric power source
- Perform mechanical overhauls and refrigerant reclaiming

- Adjust valves according to specifications and charge system with proper type of refrigerant by pumping the specified gas or fluid into the system
- Install expansion and control valves, using acetylene torches and wrenches
- Mount compressor, condenser, and other components in specified locations on frames, using hand tools and acetylene welding equipment
- Lay out reference points for installation of structural and functional components, using measuring instruments
- Fabricate and assemble structural and functional components of refrigeration system, using hand tools, power tools, and welding equipment
- Cut, bend, thread, and connect pipe to functional components and water, power, or refrigeration system
- Insulate shells and cabinets of systems
- Read blueprints to determine location, size, capacity, and type of components needed to build refrigeration system
- Schedule work with customers and initiate work orders, house requisitions, and orders from stock
- Estimate, order, pick up, deliver, and install materials and supplies needed to maintain equipment in good working condition
- Keep records of repairs and replacements made and causes of malfunctions

Career Path

Employers prefer to hire those who have completed technical school training or a formal apprenticeship or have been certified as competent. For most technicians, advancement is in the form of higher pay. Some technicians will become supervisors or managers. Others will advance by moving into other positions in the industry, such as sales representative, building supervisor, or contractor. Some open their own contracting businesses.

Earning Potential

Median hourly wage (2009): $19.76

Median annual wage (2009): $41,100

(Based on the "Heating, Air Conditioning, and Refrigeration Mechanics and Installers" occupation)

Education/Licensure

Refrigeration technicians may still be able to learn this trade on the job, but those who have completed a formal apprenticeship or postsecondary training program have better opportunities. Community colleges, junior colleges, vocational and trade schools, and the armed forces offer programs, some of which lead to an associate degree. The programs take from 6 months to 2 years to complete.

Some states and municipalities require refrigeration mechanics and installers to be licensed. Requirements vary, but all include passing an exam. Some require an apprenticeship, which is another way to be trained. Formal apprenticeship programs last from 2 to 5 years. They are often given by local chapters of trade organizations. There are two apprenticeships for refrigeration technicians:

- Refrigeration Mechanic
- Refrigeration Unit Repairer

Under Section 608 of the Clean Air Act, the U.S. Environmental Protection Agency (EPA) requires anyone who handles ozone-depleting refrigerants to be properly trained. This includes technicians who work on refrigeration systems and stationary air conditioners. To become certified to purchase and handle refrigerants, technicians must pass a written exam specific to their type of work: small appliances, high-pressure refrigerants, or low-pressure refrigerants. Trade schools, unions, contractor associations, and building groups are authorized by the EPA to administer these certifying exams.

The refrigeration industry has a series of competency exams that individuals with the appropriate coursework and less than 2 years of experience may take for Entry-Level Certifications. The Air Conditioning, Heating, and Refrigeration Institute offers a Secondary Employment Ready Exam as does the National Occupational Competency Testing Institute. The Refrigeration Service Engineers Society also offers certification.

The North American Technician Excellence (NATE) certification program for HVAC/R technicians is recognized nationwide. The U.S. Green Building Council offers the LEED (Leadership in Energy and Environmental Design) Associate and LEED AP credentials that may be appropriate for some HVAC/R technicians.

For More Information

Air-Conditioning, Heating and Refrigeration Institute
2111 Wilson Blvd
Suite 500
Arlington, Virginia 22201
703-524-8800
www.ari.org

Building Performance Institute (BPI)
107 Hermes Road
Suite 110
Malta, New York 12020
877-274-1274 (toll-free)
www.bpi.org

National Occupational Competency Testing Institute
500 North Bronson Avenue
Big Rapids, Michigan 49307-2737
800-334-6283 (toll-free)
www.nocti.org

North American Technician Excellence
2111 Wilson Blvd. #510
Arlington, Virginia 22201
703-276-7247
www.natex.org

Refrigeration Service Engineers Society
1666 Rand Road
Des Plaines, Illinois 60016
847-759-4051
www.rses.org

U.S. Green Building Council (USGBC)
2101 L Street, NW
Suite 500
Washington, DC 20037
800-795-1747 (toll-free)
www.usgbc.org

The following organizations sponsor apprenticeships:

Air-Conditioning Contractors of America
2800 Shirlington Road
Suite 300
Arlington, Virginia 22206
703-575-4477
www.acca.org

Associated Builders and Contractors
Workforce Development Department
4250 North Fairfax Drive
9th Floor
Arlington, Virginia 22203
703-812-2000
www.abc.org

Mechanical Contractors Association of America
Mechanical Service Contractors of America
1385 Piccard Drive
Rockville, Maryland 20850
301-869-5800
www.mcaa.org
www.mcaa.org/msca

Plumbing-Heating-Cooling Contractors
180 S. Washington Street
P.O. Box 6808
Falls Church, Virginia 22046
703-237-8100
www.phccweb.org

United Association of Journeymen and
   Apprentices of the Plumbing and Pipefitting
   Industry
United Association Building
Three Park Place
Annapolis, Maryland 21401
410-269-2000
www.ua.org

> ### About Calculating Your Energy Use
> At www.1.eere.energy/.gov/calculator, you will find calculators to help you figure out your energy use at home and in your car, SUV, or truck. The site also has calculators for buildings and industry and tips on how to save energy.

Solar Energy Installation Manager ☼ ⊕

Alternate Titles and Related Careers
- Foreman
- Project Manager

This is a "Bright Outlook" and "Green New and Emerging" occupation in renewable energy generation.

Job Trends

This occupation is expected to grow at a faster-than-average rate of 14 to 19 percent between 2008 and 2018. The expansion of the solar photovoltaic and CSP sectors is driving this growth. The Bureau of Labor Statistics groups this occupation in the category of "First-Line Supervisors/Managers."

Nature of the Work

Solar energy installation managers direct work crews that install residential or commercial solar photovoltaic or thermal systems. They estimate materials, equipment, and personnel needs for residential and commercial solar installation projects. Among the tasks that solar energy installation managers may perform, according to O*NET, are the following:

- Assess potential solar installation sites to determine feasibility and design requirements
- Plan and coordinate installations of photovoltaic (PV) solar and solar thermal systems to ensure conformance to codes
- Prepare solar installation project proposals, quotes, budgets, or schedules

- Evaluate subcontractors or subcontractor bids for quality, cost, and reliability
- Supervise solar installers, technicians, and subcontractors for solar installation projects to ensure compliance with safety standards
- Monitor work of contractors and subcontractors to ensure projects conform to plans, specifications, schedules, or budgets
- Perform start-up of systems for testing or customer implementation
- Assess system performance or functionality at the system, subsystem, and component levels
- Coordinate or schedule building inspections for solar installation projects
- Develop and maintain system architecture, including all piping, instrumentation, or process flow diagrams
- Identify means to reduce costs, minimize risks, or increase efficiency of solar installation projects
- Provide technical assistance to installers, technicians, or other solar professionals in areas such as solar electric systems, solar thermal systems, electrical systems, and mechanical systems

Career Path

New employees begin work as helpers to experienced solar panel installers. Over time they take on more responsibility on projects and work their way up to installation manager.

Over time, some experienced installation managers may move into sales, and others may become consultants to homeowners or businesses interested in converting to solar power. Some may start their own solar panel or thermal installation companies. Coursework in management, accounting, and marketing can be useful for new business owners.

Earning Potential

Median hourly wage (2009): $28.04

Median annual wage (2009): $58,330

Education/Licensure

About 60 percent of first-line managers have a high school diploma or less. Thirty percent have some college, and 10 percent have a bachelor's degree or higher.

Community colleges, technical colleges, and vocational institutes, as well as private, for-profit training organizations offer training for a variety of solar PV and thermal degrees and certificates. The North American Board of Certified Energy Practitioners offers both the Solar Thermal Installer Certificate and the Photovoltaic Installer Certification. These can be useful in demonstrating an individual's competence in the field.

For More Information

American Solar Energy Society (ASES)
2400 Central Avenue
Suite A
Boulder, Colorado 80301
303-443-3130
www.ases.org

North American Board of Certified Energy
    Practitioners (NABCEP)
634 Plank Road
Suite 102
Clifton Park, New York 12065
800-654-0021 (toll-free)
www.nabcep.org

Solar Electric Power Association (SEPA)
1220 19th Street, NW
Suite 401
Washington, DC 20036-2405
202-857-0898
www.solarelectricpower.org

Solar Industries Association (SEIA)
575 7th Street, NW
Suite 400
Washington, DC 20009
202-682-0556
www.seia.org

Solar Living Institute (SLI)
13771 South Highway 101
P.O. Box 836
Hopland, California 95449
707-472-2450
www.solarliving.org

Solar Photovoltaic Installer ✿⑤

Alternate Titles and Related Careers
- Solar Field Service Technician
- Solar Installation Electrician
- Solar Installation Technician Commercial
- Solar Installation Technician Residential
- Solar and PV Installation Roofer

This is a "Bright Outlook" and "Green New and Emerging" occupation in the renewable energy-generation sector of the economy.

Job Trends

The statistics are based on the Bureau of Labor's category of "Construction and Related Workers, All Other," which projects an average growth rate of 7 to 13 percent for this category between 2008 and 2018. This translates into 26,600 new employees overall. However, as a "Bright Outlook" occupation in the renewable energy sector, it may require more workers more quickly than anticipated.

Nature of the Work

Solar photovoltaic installers assemble, install, or maintain solar photovoltaic (PV) systems on roofs or other structures in compliance with site assessments and schematics. These systems may include solar collectors, concentrators, pumps, and fans. In the course of their jobs, solar photovoltaic installers may work with modules, arrays, batteries, power conditioning equipment, safety systems, structural systems, and weather sealing.

Their work may include measuring, cutting, assembling, and bolting structural framing and solar modules. They may also perform minor electrical work such as current checks.

According to O*NET, solar photovoltaic installers may perform the following duties:
- Diagram layouts and locations for photovoltaic (PV) arrays and equipment, including existing building or site features
- Examine designs to determine current requirements for all parts of the photovoltaic (PV) system electrical circuit
- Identify electrical, environmental, and safety hazards associated with photovoltaic (PV) installations
- Identify installation locations with proper orientation, area, solar access, or structural integrity for photovoltaic (PV) arrays
- Identify methods for laying out, orienting, and mounting modules or arrays to ensure efficient installation, electrical configuration, or system maintenance
- Assemble solar modules, panels, or support structures
- Install photovoltaic (PV) systems in accordance with codes and standards using drawings, schematics, and instructions
- Determine appropriate sizes, ratings, and locations for all system overcurrent devices, disconnect devices, grounding equipment, and surge suppression equipment
- Determine connection interfaces for additional subpanels or for connecting photovoltaic (PV) systems with utility services or other power-generation sources
- Determine photovoltaic (PV) system designs or configurations based on factors such as customer needs, expectations, and site conditions
- Perform routine photovoltaic (PV) system maintenance and balance of systems equipment
- Activate photovoltaic (PV) systems to verify system functionality and conformity to performance expectations
- Apply weather sealing to array, building, or support mechanisms

- Check electrical installation for proper wiring, polarity, grounding, or integrity of terminations
- Identify and resolve any deficiencies in photovoltaic (PV) system installation or materials
- Install module array interconnect wiring, implementing measures to disable arrays during installation
- Install required labels on solar system components and hardware
- Measure and analyze system performance and operating parameters to assess operating condition of systems or equipment
- Program, adjust, or configure inverters and controls for desired set points and operating modes
- Select mechanical designs, installation equipment, or installation plans that conform to environmental, architectural, structural, site, and code requirements
- Test operating voltages to ensure operation within acceptable limits for power-conditioning equipment, such as inverters and controllers
- Visually inspect and test photovoltaic (PV) modules or systems
- Compile or maintain records of system operation, performance, and maintenance
- Demonstrate system functionality and performance, including start-up, shut-down, normal operation, and emergency or bypass operations
- Determine materials, equipment, and installation sequences necessary to maximize installation efficiency

Career Path

Entry-level solar photovoltaic technicians begin work under the supervision of more experienced workers. Over time, they are given more complex work and more independence in accomplishing it. Some become supervisors or become electrical inspectors. Others start their own businesses as consultants or as solar panel installation contractors.

Earning Potential

Median hourly wage (2009): $16.34

Median annual wage (2009): $33,980

Education/Licensure

Entry-level jobs in construction typically require a high school diploma or equivalent and generally start workers as laborers, helpers, or apprentices. Skilled occupations such as solar photovoltaic technician require classroom instruction and on-the-job training that may be gotten by attending a technical or trade school, participating in an apprenticeship, or taking part in an employer-provided training program. Some community colleges, technical schools and institutes, and trade associations offer short-term online training programs.

Apprenticeships are administered by local employers, trade associations, and trade unions and provide the most thorough training. Typically, they last between three and five years and combine on-the-job training and 144 hours or more of related classroom instruction for each year of the program. The Independent Electrical Contractors (IEC) operates apprenticeship training programs for individuals wishing to become electricians, as does the International Brotherhood of Electrical Workers (IBEW).

Solar power training certification is currently voluntary, but some states are looking into requiring it. The North American Board of Certified Energy Practitioners (NABCEP) provides the Solar Photovoltaic Installer Certification program. Most states require licensing for electricians.

For More Information

American Solar Energy Society (ASES)
2400 Central Avenue
Suite A
Boulder, Colorado 80301
303-443-3130
www.ases.org

Independent Electrical Contractors (IEC)
4401 Ford Avenue
Suite 1100
Alexandria, Virginia 22303
703-549-7351
www.ieci.org

International Brotherhood of Electrical Workers
(IBEW)
900 Seventh Street, NW
Washington, DC 20001
202-833-7000
www.ibew.org

North American Board of Certified Energy
Practitioners (NABCEP)
634 Plank Road
Suite 102
Clifton Park, New York 12065
800-654-0021 (toll-free)
www.nabcep.org

Solar Electric Power Association (SEPA)
1220 19th Street, NW
Suite 401
Washington, DC 20036-2405
202-857-0898
www.solarelectricpower.org

Solar Industries Association (SEIA)
575 7th Street, NW
Suite 400
Washington, DC 20009
202-682-0556
www.seia.org

Solar Living Institute (SLI)
13771 South Highway 101
P.O. Box 836
Hopland, California 95449
707-472-2450
www.solarliving.org

Solar Sales Representative and Assessor ☼ ⑨

Alternate Titles and Related Careers

- Account Manager
- Assistant Sales Manager
- Director, Regional Sales
- Independent Sales Representative, Solar
- Outside Solar Energy Sales Representative
- Outside Solar Sales Representative
- Outside Sales Representative, Residential Solar
- PV Sales Representative, Commercial
- Senior Account Executive
- Solar Account Executive
- Solar PV Sales Representative

This is a "Bright Outlook" and "Green New and Emerging" occupation in the renewable energy generation sector of the economy. The term "outside," also called "field sales," means that the sales job requires traveling to customers' sites rather than phone sales, which is also known as "inside" sales.

Job Trends

Using information for "Sales Representatives, Wholesale and Manufacturing, Technical and Scientific Products" as the basis, the Bureau of Labor Statistics projects an average growth of 7 to 13 percent for this category. This translates into 42,000 estimated job openings between 2008 and 2018 for all technical and scientific salespeople. However, as a "Bright Outlook" occupation in the renewable energy generation sector, it may see faster growth and a greater expansion of job opportunities. Job prospects will be best for those with a college degree, the appropriate technical experience, and an outgoing personality with good communication skills.

Nature of the Work

Sales representatives may work for large manufacturers or wholesalers, or in the case of solar sales representatives/assessors, they may work for small companies that install the end product—solar panels or solar thermal systems. In the distribution chain, the small company that does the installation is probably visited by a sales representative from a manufacturer of solar panels who wants the installer to buy panels only from his/her employer. Some sales representatives who have been successful working for manufacturers or wholesalers may start their own independent agencies and represent several different manufacturers or wholesalers. Regardless of for whom the sales representative works, the goal is the same: to convince the customer to buy from the sales representative.

Solar sales representatives and assessors contact new or existing customers to determine their solar equipment needs. They analyze, or assess, the site and suggest systems or equipment and estimate the costs for purchase and installation. It is important that they stay current with the latest products and trends in the industry as well as the changing needs of the marketplace.

According to O*NET, a solar sales representative and assessor may perform the following tasks:

- Develop marketing or strategic plans for sales territories
- Generate solar energy customer leads to develop new accounts
- Assess sites to determine suitability for solar equipment
- Calculate potential solar resources or solar array production for a particular site, considering issues such as climate, shading, and roof orientation
- Gather information from prospective customers to identify their solar energy needs
- Select solar energy products, systems, or services for customers based on electrical energy requirements, site conditions, price, or other factors
- Create customized energy management packages to satisfy customer needs
- Prepare proposals, quotes, contracts, or presentations for potential solar customers

- Provide customers with information such as quotes, orders, sales, shipping, warranties, credit, funding options, incentives, or tax rebates
- Prepare or review detailed design drawings, specifications, or lists related to solar installations
- Provide technical information about solar power, solar systems, equipment, and services to potential customers or dealers
- Demonstrate use of solar and related equipment to customers or dealers

Career Path

While sales jobs in general do not have formal educational requirements, technical and scientific product sales jobs typically require a degree. A beginning salesperson may ride along with an experienced sales representative for a short period to become familiar with the product line, how customers react to the product, and the questions they ask.

Promotion typically means taking on bigger accounts or a larger territory. Individuals with good sales records and leadership abilities may advance to management jobs such as sales supervisor, district manager, or vice president of sales. Some may move into other areas of the business such as marketing and advertising or become trainers for new sales employees. Others may start their own businesses as independent representatives.

Earning Potential

Median hourly wage (2009): $34.30

Median annual wage (2009): $71,340

(Based on "Sales Representatives, Wholesale and Manufacturing, Technical and Scientific Products")

Education/Licensure

Typically, technical and scientific sales jobs require a degree. Some employers may accept an associate degree, and others may require a bachelor's degree in a technical or scientific discipline.

New employees typically undergo training on the product they will sell. Companies also train all sales personnel on a new product as it is introduced. In addition, sales representatives may attend seminars and webinars on sales techniques.

There are no licensing requirements for this occupation, but the Manufacturer's Representatives Education Research Foundation offers two certifications, the Certified Professional Manufacturers' Representative (CPMR) and the Certified Sales Professional (CSP). The North American Board of Certified Energy Practitioners (NABCET) is working on a Photovoltaic Technical Sales Certification program.

For More Information

American Solar Energy Society (ASES)
2400 Central Avenue
Suite A
Boulder, Colorado 80301
303-443-3130
www.ases.org

Manufacturers' Agents National Association (MANA)
16A Journery
Suite 200
Aliso Viejo, California 92656-3317
877-626-2776 (toll-free)
www.manaonline.org

Manufacturer's Representatives Education Research Foundation (MRERF)
8329 Cole Street
Arvada, Colorado 80005
303-463-1801
www.mrerf.org

North American Board of Certified Energy Practitioners (NABCEP)
634 Plank Road
Suite 102
Clifton Park, New York 12065
800-654-0021 (toll-free)
www.nabcep.org

Solar Electric Power Association (SEPA)
1220 19th Street, NW
Suite 401
Washington, DC 20036-2405
202-857-0898
www.solarelectricpower.org

Solar Industries Association (SEIA)
575 7th Street, NW
Suite 400
Washington, DC 20009
202-682-0556
www.seia.org

Solar Living Institute (SLI)
13771 South Highway 101
P.O. Box 836
Hopland, California 95449
707-472-2450
www.solarliving.org

Solar Thermal Installer and Technician ✿⑤

Alternate Titles and Related Careers
- Solar Field Service Technician
- Solar Installation Technician Commercial
- Solar Installation Technician Residential

These two jobs are "Bright Outlook" and "Green New and Emerging" occupations in the renewable energy generation sector of the economy.

Job Trends

The statistics are based on the Bureau of Labor's category of "Construction and Related Workers, All Other," which projects an average growth rate of 7 to 13 percent for this category between 2008 and 2018. This translates into 26,600 new employees overall. However, as a "Bright Outlook" occupation in the renewable energy sector, the solar thermal installer and technician jobs may require more workers more quickly than anticipated.

Nature of the Work

Solar thermal installers install energy systems designed to collect, store, and circulate solar-heated water for residential, commercial, or industrial use. Solar thermal technicians repair these systems.

Both occupations deal with piping, water heaters, valves, tanks, pipefittings, and auxiliary equipment. Solar thermal installers and technicians work with soldering equipment, pipe cutters, acetylene torches, wire brushes, sand cloths, plastic glue, brackets, and struts. They have to be able to read manufacturer specifications as well as flow meters and temperature and pressure gauges.

According to O*NET, solar thermal installers may perform the following tasks:

- Design active direct or indirect, passive direct or indirect, or pool solar systems
- Apply operation or identification tags or labels to system components, as required
- Assess collector sites to ensure structural integrity of potential mounting surfaces or the best orientation and tilt for solar collectors
- Connect water heaters and storage tanks to power and water sources
- Determine locations for installing solar subsystem components
- Fill water tanks and check for leaks
- Identify plumbing, electrical, environmental, or safety hazards associated with solar thermal installations
- Install circulating pumps; copper or plastic plumbing; flat-plat, evacuated glass, or concentrating solar collectors; heat exchangers and heat exchanger fluids; monitoring system components; and plumbing
- Install solar collector mounting devices on tile, asphalt, shingle, or built-up gravel roofs, using appropriate materials and penetration methods
- Install solar thermal system controllers and sensors

- Test operation or functionality of mechanical, plumbing, electrical, and control systems
- Apply ultraviolet radiation protection to prevent degradation of plumbing
- Apply weather seal, such as pipe flashings and sealants, to roof penetrations and structural devices
- Cut, miter, and glue piping insulation to insulate plumbing pipes and fittings
- Demonstrate start-up, shut-down, maintenance, diagnostic, and safety procedures to thermal system owners
- Solar thermal technicians specifically perform routine maintenance or repairs to restore solar thermal systems to baseline operating conditions

Career Path

Entry-level solar thermal installers begin work under the supervision of more experienced workers. Over time, they are given more complex work and more independence in accomplishing it. After several years of experience installing thermal systems, the installer may become a technician. Installers and technicians with more experience may become supervisors. Others start their own businesses as consultants or as solar panel installation and service contractors.

Earning Potential

Median hourly wage (2009): $16.34

Median annual wage (2009): $33,980

Education/Licensure

Entry-level jobs in construction typically require a high school diploma or equivalent and generally start workers as laborers, helpers, or apprentices. Skilled occupations such as solar thermal installer and technician require classroom instruction and on-the-job training that may be acquired by attending a community college or technical or trade school, participating in an apprenticeship, or taking part in an employer-provided training program.

Some community colleges, technical schools and institutes, and trade associations offer short-term online training programs.

Apprenticeships are administered by local employers, trade associations, and trade unions and provide the most thorough training. Typically, they last between three and five years and combine on-the-job training and 144 hours or more of related classroom instruction for each year of the program. The Independent Electrical Contractors (IEC) operates apprenticeship training programs for individuals wishing to become electricians, as does the International Brotherhood of Electrical Workers (IBEW). Most states require licensing for plumbers and electricians.

Solar power training certification is currently voluntary, but some states are looking into requiring it. The North American Board of Certified Energy Practitioners (NABCEP) provides the Solar Thermal Installer Certification program.

For More Information

American Solar Energy Society (ASES)
2400 Central Avenue
Suite A
Boulder, Colorado 80301
303-443-3130
www.ases.org

North American Board of Certified Energy
    Practitioners (NABCEP)
634 Plank Road
Suite 102
Clifton Park, New York 12065
800-654-0021 (toll-free)
www.nabcep.org

Solar Electric Power Association (SEPA)
1220 19th Street, NW
Suite 401
Washington, DC 20036-2405
202-857-0898
www.solarelectricpower.org

Solar Industries Association (SEIA)
575 7th Street, NW
Suite 400
Washington, DC 20009
202-682-0556
www.seia.org

Solar Living Institute (SLI)
13771 South Highway 101
P.O. Box 836
Hopland, California 95449
707-472-2450
www.solarliving.org

Stationary Engineer and Boiler Operator ⑤

Alternate Titles and Related Careers
- Boiler Engineer
- Boiler Inspector
- Building Manager
- Boiler Operator
- Building Superintendent
- Boiler Tender
- Chief Plant Engineer
- Fireman
- Operating Engineer
- Plant Operator
- Plant Superintendent
- Plant Utilities Engineer
- Stationary Engineer
- Stationary Steam Engineer
- Utility Operator

This is considered a "Green Increased-Demand" occupation in the green energy-efficiency sector of the economy.

Job Trends

The *Occupational Outlook Handbook* projects a slower-than-average growth rate of 5 percent for the stationary engineer/boiler operator category, which translates into 9,200 jobs between 2008 and 2018. Current jobs are about evenly divided among government, manufacturing, and educational services facilities at 22, 20, and 19 percent, respectively. The remaining 39 percent are spread across all other industries.

Retirements and continuing commercial and industrial facilities development will fuel demand for new workers. The greatest growth is expected in industries in which precise temperature control is required, such as hospitals.

New automated systems and computerized controls require fewer workers, but this is offset by the need for experienced workers to maintain and repair the equipment. Competition will be stiff for these relatively high-paying jobs so that individuals who have completed a training course or an apprenticeship will have the best chance for entry-level employment.

Nature of the Work

Stationary engineers and boiler operators operate or maintain stationary engines, boilers, or other mechanical equipment to provide utilities—heat, hot water, electricity, and air conditioning—for buildings or industrial processes. The equipment may be steam engines, generators, motors, turbines, and steam boilers.

According to O*NET, stationary engineers and boiler operators may perform the following tasks:

- Operate or tend stationary engines, boilers, and auxiliary equipment, such as pumps, compressors, and air-conditioning equipment, to supply and maintain steam or heat
- Observe and interpret readings on gauges, meters, and charts registering various aspects of boiler operation to ensure that boilers are operating properly
- Test boiler water quality or arrange for testing and take necessary corrective action, such as adding chemicals to prevent corrosion and harmful deposits
- Activate valves to maintain required amounts of water in boilers, to adjust supplies of combustion air, and to control the flow of fuel into burners

- Monitor boiler water, chemical, and fuel levels, and make adjustments to maintain required levels
- Fire coal furnaces by hand or with stokers and gas- or oil-fed boilers, using automatic gas feeds or oil pumps
- Monitor and inspect equipment, computer terminals, switches, valves, gauges, alarms, safety devices, and meters to detect leaks or malfunctions and to ensure that equipment is operating efficiently and safely
- Analyze problems and take appropriate action to ensure continuous and reliable operation of equipment and systems
- Adjust controls and/or valves on equipment to provide power and to regulate and set operations of system or industrial processes
- Switch from automatic to manual controls and isolate equipment mechanically and electrically to allow for safe inspection and repair work
- Clean and lubricate boilers and auxiliary equipment and make minor adjustments as needed, using hand tools
- Check the air quality of ventilation systems and make adjustments to ensure compliance with mandated safety codes
- Weigh, measure, and record fuel used
- Test electrical systems to determine voltages, using voltage meters
- Develop operation, safety, and maintenance procedures or assist in their development
- Install burners and auxiliary equipment, using hand tools
- Perform or arrange for repairs, such as complete overhauls, replacement of defective valves, gaskets, or bearings, or fabrication of new parts
- Contact equipment manufacturers or appropriate specialists when necessary to resolve equipment problems
- Provide assistance to plumbers in repairing or replacing water, sewer, or waste lines, and in daily maintenance activities

- Operate mechanical hoppers and provide assistance in their adjustment and repair
- Receive instructions from steam engineers regarding steam plant and air compressor operations
- Supervise the work of assistant stationary engineers, turbine operators, boiler tenders, or air conditioning and refrigeration operators and mechanics
- Investigate and report on accidents
- Maintain daily logs of operation, maintenance, and safety activities, including test results, instrument readings, and details of equipment malfunctions and maintenance work.

Career Path

Stationary engineers and boiler operators may begin as helpers and receive on-the-job training or enroll in an apprenticeship program. The latter is an advantage when looking for an entry-level position.

The stationary engineer and boiler operator occupation requires licensure in some states, and the requirements may include different classes of licensure—each class allowing an individual to work with larger, more powerful or more types of equipment. In state without licensing requirements, stationary engineers and boiler operators may be required to pass company-sponsored testing to advance.

Over time, experienced workers may become supervisors, boiler inspectors, chief plant engineers, building or plant superintendents, or building managers.

Earning Potential

Median hourly wage (2009): $24.70

Median annual wage (2009): $51,370

Education/Licensure

Entry-level positions typically require a high school diploma or equivalent. Stationary engineers and boiler operators either begin as helpers under the supervision of experienced engineers or enter a formal training program or apprenticeship. Becoming an engineer or operator without completing a formal apprenticeship takes many years of work experience.

The International Union of Operating Engineers (IUOE) sponsors apprenticeship programs through its local unions. The programs usually last four years and include 6,000 hours of on-the-job training supplemented by 600 hours of classroom instruction. In addition to the practical experience of learning how to operate boilers, generators, compressors, and air-conditioning and refrigeration equipment, apprentices study physics, practical chemistry, and instrumentation. Apprentices earn while they learn and at the successful completion of the program become journey-level engineers/operators.

Many states and municipalities require licensing of stationary engineers and boiler operators and some employers require that applicants already be licensed. Typically, there are four or five classes of licensure, and each class specifies the type and size of the equipment that can be operated under that license.

For More Information

International Union of Operating Engineers (IUOE)
1125 17th Street, NW
Washington, DC 20036
202-429-9100
www.iuoe.org

National Association of Power Engineers, Inc.
1 Springfield Street
Chicopee, Massachusetts 01018
413-592-6273
www.napenational.org

Weatherization Installer and Technician ☼ ⊕

Alternate Titles and Related Careers

- Residential Air Sealing Technician
- Weatherization Crew Chief
- Weatherization Field Technician
- Weatherization Operations Manager
- Window/Door Retrofit Technician

This is a "Bright Outlook" and "Green New and Emerging" occupation. This is an example of an occupation that has developed as a result of peoples' concerns about the environment and the high cost of home heating.

Job Trends

The Bureau of Labor Statistics estimated in 2008 that the growth rate for the category would be about average at 7 to 13 percent. However, as a "Green New and Emerging" job, growth may be faster. In promoting his jobs programs, President Barack Obama stressed the importance of weatherization as one way to stimulate job growth during the recession.

One factor driving jobs in this category is the U.S. Department of Energy's (DOE) Weatherization Assistance Program. Although the program has been around since the late 1970s—the last energy crisis—it benefited from the $5 billion allocated to it in the American Recovery and Reinvestment Act of 2009. The Weatherization Assistance Program provides weatherization services to low-income families. Since its inception, the program has helped more than 6.4 million families save on their energy bills by weatherizing their homes.

The interest in saving energy costs on residential and commercial heating and air conditioning is also a spur to weatherization projects. ENERGY STAR estimates that sealing and insulating homes can save homeowners as much as 20 percent on their heating and air-conditioning bills. Building codes in many municipalities now include energy efficiency requirements.

Nature of the Work

Weatherization installers and technicians weatherize homes to make them more energy-efficient and improve indoor air quality. They may repair windows, insulate heating and air-conditioning ducts, and perform maintenance on the heating, ventilation, and air-conditioning (HVAC) system. They may also perform energy audits and must know applicable energy regulations, codes, policies, and statutes.

O*NET lists the following as among the tasks that a weatherization installer and technician may perform:

- Inspect buildings to identify weatherization strategies such as repair, modification, or replacement
- Test and diagnose air flow systems
- Recommend and explain weatherization and energy conservation measures, policies, procedures, and requirements to clients
- Apply insulation materials
- Install and seal air ducts, combustion air openings, or ventilation openings
- Install storm windows or storm doors and verify proper fit
- Prepare and apply weather-stripping, glazing, caulking, or door sweeps to reduce energy losses
- Wrap air ducts and water lines and water heaters
- Apply spackling, compounding, or other materials to repair holes
- Prepare cost estimates and specifications
- Maintain activity logs and financial records
- Prepare or assist in the preparation of bids, contracts, or written reports

Career Path

Entry-level employees work under the supervision of experienced workers. Over the training period, entry-level workers are given more responsibility with less supervision and earn more money. With experience, weatherization installers and technicians may become supervisors themselves. With training in business and finance, some may start their own businesses. The ability to speak both English and Spanish is important for anyone wishing to advance to supervisor in the construction trades.

Earning Potential

Median hourly wage (2009): $16.34

Median annual wage (2009): $33,980

Education/Licensure

Typically, employers prefer employees with high school diplomas or the equivalent. Some prior experience in construction, inspection, or energy conservation is useful. States may also have their own training and certification programs for weatherization technicians. Some of these programs may be through community colleges and others through community action associations within states. For example, the Indiana Community Action Association (www.incap.org) has more than a dozen introductory and advanced training classes for weatherization installers and technicians.

The Home Builders Institute of the National Association of Home Builders (NAHB) offers a Green/Weatherizing and ESL certification for native Spanish speakers. The Building Performance Institute (BPI) offers an Envelope Certificate, which includes such topics as stopping air leaks and ensuring the best performance from heating and air-conditioning systems.

For More Information

Building Performance Institute (BPI)
107 Hermes Road
Suite 110
Malta, New York 12020
877-274-1274 (toll-free)
www.bpi.org

National Association of Home Builders (NAHB)
1201 15th Street, NW
Washington, DC 20005
800-368-5242 (toll-free)
www.nahb.org

Can This Be Recycled?

Depending on the municipality, the answer may be "no." What's recyclable and how recyclables are collected vary from community to community.

Recyclable Materials

Some communities accept paper, glass bottles and jars, plastic bottles, and aluminum cans. Other communities collect all kinds of metal and also cardboard. Some accept chipboard, but other communities don't. As the recycling technology available to each municipality improves, the items that can be recycled increases over time. In general, paper, plastics, glass, and aluminum cans are typically recyclable.

One of the greatest concerns is recycling plastics. Recyclable plastics are marked with the symbol of a round-edged triangle made of three chasing arrows, and within the symbol is a number from 1 to 7. The following is the list of the plastic codes developed by the Society of Plastics Industry and recognized by the majority of states:

1 PET (PETE) *Polyethylene terephthalate:* Water bottles, audio/videotapes, 2-liter soda bottles, peanut butter jars

2 HDPE *High-density polyethylene:* Laundry detergent bottles, milk containers, Tyvek, plastic lumber

3 PVC *Polyvinyl chloride:* Siding, household product containers, plastic piping, water bottles, salad dressing bottles, plastic bags

4 LDPE *Low-density polyethylene:* Garbage bags, six-pack soda rings, dry cleaner bags

5 PP *Polypropylene:* Photo album page protectors, bottle caps, drinking straws, ID badge protectors

6 PS *Polystyrene:* Styrofoam products such as packing peanuts and "clam shell" containers; plastic tableware

7 Other *Made from a resin other than ones used in 1 through 6 or made from a combination of resins:* Some kinds of food containers, Tupperware

Municipalities determine which classes of plastics they will accept for recycling, usually determined by the technology available for recycling materials. Generally, #1 and #2 plastic items are the most frequently accepted for recycling. However, #5 items are usually not accepted for recycling. Keep this in mind the next time you toss an empty bottle into a recycling bin—the cap is not the same recycling number as the bottle. Although this may be changing soon, most bottles can't be recycled when the caps are still on. So, take the cap off first. What can you do to avoid throwing bottle caps in the trash? You can take #5 bottle caps to any Aveda salon, which turns them into new packaging for their products. The program accepts caps that twist on with a threaded neck (caps on shampoo, water, soda, milk, and other beverage bottles), flip-top caps on tubes and food product bottles (ketchup and mayonnaise bottles), laundry detergent caps, and some lids like those on peanut butter jars. For more information, visit www.aveda.com/aboutaveda/caps.tmpl. In addition, Whole Foods is another national retailer that collects #5 plastic products.

Packaging stores will often accept bags of clean packing peanuts (#6) for reuse in packing, and supermarkets may accept for recycling clean plastic bags (#4 or #2), such as ones that produce and home-delivered newspapers come in. Some dry cleaners will recycle their used bags (4). For more information on recycling plastic bags, check out www.plasticbagrecycling.org.

How to Recycle

As to the method of recycling, any of the following four methods of recycling may be used alone or in combination:

- Curbside
- Drop-off center
- Buy-back centers
- Deposit or refund programs

In curbside recycling, households put their recyclables out on a schedule set by the municipality, which may be the town or city or the county. Some localities use drop-off centers for hazardous materials such as motor oil, and other municipalities, typically small towns and villages, have a central location where households drop off all recyclables. In some places, sorting and separating is required, while other municipalities do not mandate this practice.

Some municipalities operate buy-back centers, where households can sell their aluminum cans and glass bottles and sometimes other materials for salvage value. Some states have deposit, also called refund, programs for glass and/or plastic bottles and aluminum cans. The states that use the deposit program for aluminum cans average an 80 percent recycling rate. States without a deposit program average 46 percent.

How Being Green Works for Russ Hellem, Energy Efficiency Expert

Russ Hellem, 31, works as an energy efficiency expert in Missoula, Montana. Hellem owns a company that offers everything from whole-house energy audits to passive house design. He has worked in this green industry for the past ten years. In the photo here, Hellem sets up a blower door test, which allows him to measure the air leakage rate of a building.

Describe your job, including common daily tasks and long-term projects that you have worked on or are working on now. What, specifically, about your job makes it green?

I work directly with building owners, builders, and architects to help them design, build, and occupy buildings that are durable, healthy, and energy efficient. The primary area of focus on energy savings is to address how a building is designed. The more complicated and larger a building is, the harder it is to insulate and air seal.

The first item that we address is the site where a building is to be built. In northern climates, access to solar exposure is a must. Taking advantage of free heat through passive solar (not active PV panels) design is the cheapest way to build green. For architects, we provide valuable information on how to improve the design process to accommodate for energy efficiency features. For example, we might recommend simple building shapes that allow for easy insulation and air sealing details. We also provide information on different types of heating, cooling, and ventilation systems. These systems are a vital component to energy-efficient construction and must be given consideration from the very beginning of the project. With builders, we help them implement proper construction methods to meet the energy and green goals established during the design process.

I spend time consulting with people and providing education to help further the green building industry. Our main focus is to help our customers to begin thinking about their green goals as early as possible. Once the goals are established, they shape how the building is designed and built. We start by focusing on site selection, building design, and energy efficiency goals. Then we move to the more detailed discussions of water management, heating and cooling systems, and product selection. Unfortunately, the majority of our customers contact us too late in the process for us to have a major impact on the "greenness" of their project. Often times, we meet with clients after they have already designed the building, and at this point the advice we can offer is limited. If customers come to us early enough, we can help them establish and attain a high level of "green" construction and high-performance energy goals. Our green goals are to reduce energy and material consumption by providing input and commissioning services to test how energy-efficiently a building is operating.

Why/how did you decide to work in a green industry?

My passion for resource conservation teamed with my background in building homes made it an easy fit.

How did you prepare for your current position?

I started building homes with my father, Tom Hellem, at a young age. After high school, I pursued a degree in forestry and natural resource management. Although this degree did not prepare me for green building, it did solidify and deepen my commitment to environmental stewardship.

Which aspect of your education and/or training do you think has been the most helpful and/or useful to you? Why?

Building homes has definitely given me a background in construction that allows me to understand how buildings and the systems within them function together. Without this background, it would be very difficult for me to provide insight on how to improve upon what we currently have.

Do you find that the skills and/or knowledge required for your job continue to evolve? If so, what have you done to keep up-to-date?

The green building industry continues to evolve. However, the basics are still the same as they have been forever. For example, the physics of how heat, moisture, and energy move in a building has not changed. However, the methods by which we address these issues have. I always try to bring it back to the basics of physical science and look at how what we do can be verified and tested for quality performance. If something cannot be measured, we cannot tell if it is working correctly. I continually strive to learn more and more about building science and green building practices, but I always weigh what I am learning against the basic physics principles that I already know.

How have continuing education and/or training impacted the way you do your job?

We have been sought out to provide continuing education and training for other younger companies and organizations. We also seek continuing education opportunities for ourselves. Recently, we went through Passive House Training, which has elevated our knowledge of and commitment to super-insulated, energy-efficient construction details. By taking this additional training, we have continued to remain at the cutting edge of "green building" by expanding our knowledge base and experience to where our nation should be going with building methods.

What is the most rewarding part of your work, and what do you find to be the most challenging?

The most rewarding part is to see someone we are talking to fully understand the basics behind green building. The most challenging part is that most people are not committed at a gut level to saving resources. This leads to compromises in quality in order to have fancier finishes, larger buildings, and inefficiencies.

What advice would you give to people interested in pursuing your career?

Figure out why you want to go into this industry. If you want to get into it for the money or the recognition, you will not last.

Pursue a green career because you are committed to making the planet a better place. Once you have figured out why, then jump in and get your hands dirty. Get out and get some real-world experience in building so you understand how things work within a building. Once you have a basic understanding, you can pursue a detailed, in-depth knowledge of green building methods and products.

How Being Green Works for **Al Maloney, Weatherization Specialist**

Al Maloney, 54, owns an insulation installation company in Wiscasset, Maine. Maloney has been working on green projects for the past two years. Here, Maloney uses an infrared camera to search for voids in a building's insulation.

Describe your job, including common daily tasks and long-term projects that you have worked on or are working on now. What, specifically, about your job makes it green?

My day largely consists of traveling to job sites to evaluate insulation needs and developing quotes to accomplish the work. I also do follow-up quality assurance for jobs that our crews have completed. Our goal is to improve the energy efficiency of new and existing homes in MidCoast Maine. Our product of choice is cellulose, which is a very green product. We also install two-part spray foam and some fiberglass insulation.

Why/how did you decide to work in a green industry?

Two years ago, my wife and I went to an energy trade show. We were very impressed with the solar hot-water systems that are available today, and we decided to have one installed in our fiber-processing mill. That got me interested in energy conservation, so I enrolled in a class to become an energy auditor.

How did you prepare for your current position?

I have thirty years of prior experience in the engineering side of shipbuilding. I was an electrical apprentice and a graduate of the Bath Ironworks apprenticeship program. Bath Ironworks is a shipyard that builds naval combatants. Insulation installation is a new career for me. Training for this job consisted of an energy auditor class and weatherization technician training offered by the Maine State Housing Authority (MSHA). I purchased a blower door and infrared camera and performed audits on low-income housing for a year. I also took several weeks of other related training during that time. Most of that training was in building science or house-as-a-system concepts, and the classes were offered by the Maine Indoor Air Quality Council.

Which aspect of your education and/or training do you think has been the most helpful and/or useful to you? Why?

The MSHA energy auditor training and the other building science classes that I have taken have been very helpful. I plan to get my Building Performance Institute (BPI) certification as an envelope specialist sometime this year. I do not have a LEED credential because I have no business need for that certification. Everything here requires BPI certification.

Do you find that the skills and/or knowledge required for your job continue to evolve? If so, what have you done to keep up-to-date?

Yes, I attend several building science seminars each year.

How have continuing education and/or training impacted the way you do your job?

My training allows me to evaluate the existing condition of a structure and guide the client toward solutions that are cost-effective and will improve the durability of the structure.

What is the most rewarding part of your work, and what do you find to be the most challenging?

I like the problem solving. Every job is different. It is like solving a puzzle each time I go to a new job site. If you succeed, it's rewarding. In either case, it's challenging.

What advice would you give to people interested in pursuing your career?

Just do it.

How Being Green Works for
Matt Dunham, HVAC Technician

Matt Dunham, 24, works as a heating, ventilation, and air-conditioning (HVAC) controls service technician for a mechanical contractor with a large service base in Lansing, Michigan. Dunham has worked in this green industry for two years. Here, Dunham verifies the operation of the floor heat in a building to ensure that the pump is operating correctly.

Describe your job, including common daily tasks and long-term projects that you have worked on or are working on now. What, specifically, about your job makes it green?

On a day-to-day basis, I work with energy management systems in buildings to ensure that equipment is operating correctly and as efficiently as possible to meet each building's heating and cooling requirements. On a long-term basis, I work with customers to put together plans to increase the operational efficiency of their buildings' heating and cooling equipment. This could include replacement of equipment or controlling the existing equipment better. . . . By applying

the best strategy for a given building, energy consumption can be reduced significantly.

Why/how did you decide to work in a green industry?

I was looking for a field that would provide a stable source of work as well as a challenging environment.

How did you prepare for your current position?

I have a bachelor of science in HVAC/R Engineering Technologies from Ferris State University. Since graduation, I have passed the Mechanical Service Contractors of America (MSCA) STAR test. I also have received my LEED AP from the U.S. Green Building Council (USGBC).

Which aspect of your education and/or training do you think has been the most helpful and/or useful to you? Why?

My education at Ferris State has been the most helpful. The HVAC/R Engineering Technologies program focuses intensively on building analysis and designing for mechanical systems. ·

Do you find that the skills and/or knowledge required for your job continue to evolve? If so, what have you done to keep up-to-date?

Manufacturers are continually changing their products, so I must stay up-to-date on the latest software and programs for programming energy management systems.

How have continuing education and/or training impacted the way you do your job?

Attending different training seminars has helped me to see ways that others would look at a problem or approach a situation to improve the efficiency of a building.

What is the most rewarding part of your work, and what do you find to be the most challenging?

The most rewarding part of my job is finding a problem that is causing a building to use excessive energy, which equates to high costs, and then coming up with a solution that not only improves the comfort for the building's occupants, but also lowers the operating expenses of the building.

The challenging part is that each day you are working on some type of system that is typically not functioning properly, and people in a facility are uncomfortable. Finding the problems and correcting them can be a challenge.

What advice would you give to people interested in pursuing your career?

Gain as much education as possible, and do not be afraid to think out of the box when it comes to solving a problem.

How Being Green Works for
James Baker, Facilities Manager

James Baker, 56, is the director of facilities for the Lancaster, Pennsylvania, headquarters of a worldwide corporation that designs and manufactures floors, ceilings, and cabinets with an emphasis on environmental stability. Baker has worked in this green industry for the past 12 years. As part of his job, Baker reviews blueprints to check square footages for glazing replacements in an office building.

Describe your job, including common daily tasks and long-term projects that you have worked on or are working on now. What, specifically, about your job makes it green?

My responsibilities include managing and supporting a talented group of facilities professionals. This includes managers, craftspeople, engineers, housekeepers, mail/copy personnel, and shipping/receiving employees, as well as hospitality/customer visitation center teams. In addition to my personnel management responsibilities, I also create and manage the expense and capital budgets for operating 26 office buildings that occupy roughly 1 million square feet of interior space on 225 acres of property.

Several key projects that I have worked on include the construction of our new corporate headquarters building in 1998 along with 425,000 square feet of interior building renovations that involved several buildings on our campus. I have also worked on the creation of a customer visitation center, the renovation of our hospitality facility, and the LEED EB application process for achieving a Platinum rating for our corporate headquarters facility.

What associates my job with green or sustainable work is that everything required to operate and manage our campus . . . requires following the sustainable policies and procedures that our company has developed over the past four years. These include, but are not limited to, energy and water conservation and a recycling program.

Why/how did you decide to work in a green industry?

My background is in mechanical engineering, and I have had positions that led me into the facilities management field. Practicing sustainable procedures is what the facilities management industry is all about. These practices save building owners money while improving the environment we live and work in everyday. My job is about emphasizing the values of following sustainable practices in a commercial office setting.

How did you prepare for your current position?

Any engineering degree would prepare you for a facilities management position. However, many colleges, universities, and technical schools do offer specific facilities management courses that focus on the criteria necessary to work in that environment. Additionally, these facilities management classes now include activities related to practicing sustainability in managing a facility.

As I mentioned before, my degree is a BSME (mechanical engineering) and I have worked as a project engineer on a number of manufacturing projects. I accepted a position change into facilities management after reviewing my options. Some organizations that I belong to that have assisted my facilities management career and networking include the International Facilities Management Association (IFMA) and the Association for Facilities Engineering (AFE).

Which aspect of your education and/or training do you think has been the most helpful and/or useful to you? Why?

What has been the most useful for me, in addition to my background in mechanical engineering, is the practical job experience I gained in a facilities management organization. The facilities organization is a well-versed professional team whose members support one another to add value to their customers. The relationships that have developed, and the working knowledge and experience that I have gained, have been excellent.

Do you have a LEED credential? Why or why not?

I am a LEED AP. I was actively involved in pursuing a LEED EB application for our corporate headquarters building, which achieved a Platinum rating. I took the LEED EB test to become more knowledgeable of the criteria that I use every day in my position. We utilize those criteria on every aspect of managing facilities in order to make them more sustainable.

Do you find that the skills and/or knowledge required for your job continue to evolve? If so, what have you done to keep up-to-date?

The skills and knowledge required in the facilities management field continue to evolve every year. As noted, I have become

a LEED AP along with joining IFMA and AFE to stay current in my area of responsibility. Also, networking is very beneficial to staying current in your area of expertise.

How have continuing education and/or training impacted the way you do your job?

Continuing education classes and training make me aware of the latest changes in my profession. They assist me in keeping best practices in place to make sure that I am adding value in my job and to my customers.

What is the most rewarding part of your work, and what do you find to be the most challenging?

One of the most rewarding activities in my work is getting employees or staff to change their ways of thinking and to show them the benefits of the change. In the facilities management field, change is constant and it's an ongoing challenge. You cannot be complacent in your job. Your job is never completed. It's continuous.

What advice would you give to people interested in pursuing your career?

If you have an interest in the facilities management field, I would recommend spending at least one day with an experienced facilities manager to better understand what his or her daily challenges include. Additionally, review what curriculum local colleges or technical schools have to offer in the facilities management, facilities management technology, or sustainable practices areas. Finally, join IFMA to network with others in the field and improve your skills and knowledge as a facilities manager.

CHAPTER 3

COMMERCIAL, INDUSTRIAL, AND RESIDENTIAL DESIGN JOBS

Trends for interior design jobs, like those in architecture and landscaping, are related to trends in the overall construction industry. Even though construction of new residential and commercial buildings slowed as a result of the recession that began in 2007, experts expect that it will bounce back over time. In the meantime, remodeling and retrofitting of existing structures picked up, thus creating demand for interior designers and decorators and other skills related to creating interior environments.

JOBS PROFILED HERE

The following occupations are profiled in this chapter:

- Bath Designer
- Flooring Installer
- Furniture Designer
- Interior Decorator
- Interior Designer
- Painter
- Kitchen Designer
- Product Designer

KEY TO UNDERSTANDING THE JOB PROFILES

The job profiles are classified according to one or more of the following categories:

- ✿ Bright Outlook
- 🌱 Green Occupation

The classifications "Bright Outlook" and "Green Occupation" are taken from the National Center for O*NET Development's O*NET OnLine job site. O*NET, which is sponsored by the U.S. Department of Labor/Employment and Training Administration (USDOL/ETA), has broken green jobs into three categories

- Green Increased-Demand occupations
  - o These are occupations that are likely to see job growth, but the work and worker requirements are unlikely to experience significant changes.
- Green Enhanced-Skills occupations
  - o These occupations are likely to experience significant changes in work and worker requirements. Workers may find themselves doing new tasks requiring new knowledge, skills, and credentials. Current projections do not anticipate increased demand for workers in these occupations, but O*NET notes that an increase is possible.

- Green New and Emerging occupations
  - These are new occupations—not growth in existing jobs—that are created as a result of activity and technology in green sectors of the economy.

Video Links

We've provided easy-to-use links that will take you directly to a particular career video from the One-Stop Career System Multimedia Career Video Library at CareerOneStop.org. The links will look like this:

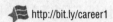 http://bit.ly/career1

Note that videos are not available for all jobs listed here. The videos come in QuickTime and Mpeg formats, with and without captions; download times may vary. CareerOneStop.org is sponsored by the U.S. Department of Labor/Employment and Training Administration.

Bath Designer

Alternate Titles and Related Careers
- Associate Bath Designer
- Bath Dealer/Distributor
- Bath Design and Sales Consultant
- Builder or Remodeler
- Display Designer (bath furnishings)
- Industrial Designer
- Junior Designer
- Project Manager

Bathroom designer is a specialty within the subcategory of interior design, and while not a specifically "green" occupation, bathroom designers have the opportunity to introduce green concepts and green materials into their work with clients.

About Green Kitchen and Bath Design
For information on suppliers of green kitchen and bath furnishings and materials, visit www.nkba.org/green/companies.aspx

Job Trends

The National Kitchen and Bath Association (NKBA) estimated in 2007 that 9.9 million bathrooms were remodeled. This doesn't include the several million new homes that were built that year and the number of bathrooms in each new home. While the recession of 2007 through 2009 decreased the number of new housing starts, the construction industry is expected to regain its lost momentum over the next few years. In addition, concern over the environment and increasing attention on sustainable green design are driving some of the interest in remodeling and retrofitting bathrooms in order to install water-efficient toilets, eco-friendly cabinets and flooring, and energy-efficient lighting.

The Bureau of Labor Statistics estimates that the interior designer occupation will have a faster-than-average growth rate of 19 percent. A design specialty such as bathroom designer will participate in the anticipated growth. Competition for jobs in the entire category of interior design is expected to be high because many people enter this profession.

Nature of the Work

Bathroom designers plan spaces that are functional, safe, and attractive, and meld client's aesthetics with the latest in technology and design innovation. Bath designers work with contractors, architects, engineers, electricians, and plumbers and must be able to read blueprints and use computer-aided design (CAD) software. According to O*NET, designers may perform the following tasks:

- Confer with clients to determine the factors that affect design planning such as budget, architectural and aesthetic preferences, and functionality of the space

- Advise clients on design factors such as space planning, layout, products, and color coordination
- Plan the overall space design
- Plan architectural details such as moldings, built-in components, and sometimes positions of walls or other features
- Prepare plans using CAD software
- Estimate material requirements and costs
- Present designs to clients for approval
- Review and detail shop drawings for construction plans
- Coordinate with other professionals
- Supervise the construction work for some clients
- Stay up-to-date on building and fire and safety codes and construction requirements of the locality
- Stay up-to-date on the trends, color, and materials as well as products in bath design

Bathroom designers who go into business for themselves as designers or owners of bath furnishing stores will need to have business and management skills in order to:

- Hire, direct, and train workers
- Maintain records and files
- Oversee the accounting aspects of the business including payroll
- Order supplies and equipment
- Advertise for clients
- Build relationships with contractors and suppliers

Career Path

Entry-level bath designers spend one to three years in on-the-job training under the supervision of an experienced designer. After they gain experience, bath designers are given responsibility for independent projects and may eventually become supervisors or chief designers. Some open their own design businesses.

Having a portfolio of work is necessary when applying for a job.

Earning Potential

Median hourly wage (2009): $22.20

Median annual wage (2009): $46,180

(Based on the Bureau of Labor Statistics' "Interior Designer" category)

A 2009 survey by the National Kitchen and Bath Association (NKBA) found that an NKBA-certified kitchen and bath designer earned on average $87,000.

Education/Licensure

Postsecondary education is necessary for interior designers. An associate degree is the minimum. Some design schools offer programs that last two or three years and grant a certificate or associate degree. This generally qualifies a person to work as a design assistant. A bachelor's degree in kitchen and bath design, interior design, or an art-related field is considered the standard qualification and enables a person to enroll in an apprenticeship program leading to a license.

About Wasting Water

It's not just installing water-saving showerheads that can save you water and money. Replacing older toilets with new high-efficiency or dual-flush models can save an average household at least 2,000 gallons of water per toilet per year.

The National Kitchen and Bath Association (NKBA), which began originally as the American Institute of Kitchen Dealers, accredits kitchen and bath design programs. Its Web site provides information on the more than fifty such accredited college and university programs. NKBA also offers three relevant certifications for bath designers: Associate Kitchen and Bath Designer (AKBD), Certified Bath Designer (CBD), and Certified Master Kitchen and Bath Designer (CMKBD).

NKBA provides more than 200 professional development courses each year, some of which focus specifically on green design topics.

The Council for Interior Design Accreditation (CIDA) accredits interior design programs that grant bachelor's degrees. Its Web site and the Web site of the American Society of Interior Designers (ASID) provide lists with links to accredited interior design programs. The National Association of Schools of Art and Design (NASAD) accredits schools of art and design, and its Web site provides a list of accredited programs. There is also a recognized apprenticeship program for interior designers.

Twenty-three states, Puerto Rico, and the District of Columbia require registration, certification, or licensing for interior designers. In all cases, a combination of education, experience, and passing an exam is necessary. The National Council for Interior Design Qualification (NCIDQ) administers the nationally recognized licensing exam for interior designers. To qualify to take the exam, a designer must have a combination of six years of education and experience, at least two years of which must be formal education. The exam consists of six sections that cover all areas of interior design. The NCIDQ Web site contains links to the states requiring this exam.

The Green Building Certification Institute offers LEED Professional Accreditation for interior designers.

For More Information

American Society of Interior Designers
608 Massachusetts Avenue, NE
Washington, DC 20002-6006
202-546-3480
www.asid.org

Council for Interior Design Accreditation
206 Grandville Avenue
Suite 350
Grand Rapids, Michigan 49503
616-458-0400
www.accredit-id.org

National Association of Schools of Art and Design
11250 Roger Bacon Drive
Suite 21
Reston, Virginia 20190-5248
703-437-0700
http://nasad.arts-accredit.org

National Council for Interior Design Qualification
1602 L Street, NW
Suite 200
Washington, DC 20036-5681
202-721-0220
www.ncidq.org

National Kitchen and Bath Association (NKBA)
687 Willow Grove Street
Hackettstown, New Jersey 07840
800-843-6522 (toll-free)
www.nkba.org

U.S. Green Building Council (USGBC)
2101 L Street, NW
Suite 500
Washington, DC 20037
800-795-1747 (toll-free)
www.usgbc.org

Flooring Installer

Alternate Titles and Related Careers

- Carpet Installer
- Carpet Journeyman
- Carpet Layer
- Flooring Installation Mechanic
- Flooring Mechanic

While not a "green" job in itself, installing flooring benefits the environment when the flooring is such "eco-friendly" coverings as linoleum, bamboo, and low-VOC (volatile organic compounds) carpet.

 http://bit.ly/career32

Job Trends

According to the Bureau of Labor Statistics, the carpet and flooring installation occupations will see little or no change in their rates of growth. However, installing flooring is hard physical labor, so there is high turnover and a consequent large number of workers to replace. Because of home remodeling, green retrofitting, and the need to replace worn carpet and wood flooring in existing structures, employment as carpet and flooring installers is less sensitive to changes in the construction industry. About 35 percent of carpet, floor, and tile installers and finishers are self-employed.

About Green Floor Solutions

According to the World Floor Covering Association (WFCA), evaluating the "greenness" of flooring includes the amount of the yield from raw materials, recyclability, and the energy consumed in transporting, processing, and selling the finished product. Stone, for example, would appear to be eco-friendly flooring, but WFCA states that there is "no generally accepted data on the environmental impact of using stone."

Nature of the Work

Carpet and flooring installers and finishers lay floor coverings in a variety of structures from homes and offices to schools, hotels, and stores—wherever there is flooring over concrete. Even factories with concrete shop floors have some type of floor covering in their offices. Floor installers lay a variety of materials, including linoleum, cork, and bamboo, all of which are eco-friendly. A hardwood floor may also be "green," if it comes from a certified sustainably managed forest. Generally, carpenters install new hardwood floors, although flooring installers may install wood floors.

According to O*NET, carpet and floor installers may perform the following similar tasks:

- Take measurements and study sketches to calculate the area for flooring and the amount of materials needed
- Sweep, scrape, sand, or chip dirt and irregularities to clean base surfaces, correcting imperfections that may show through the covering
- Inspect surface to be covered to ensure that it is firm and dry
- Form a smooth foundation by stapling plywood or Masonite over the floor or by brushing waterproof compound onto the surface and filling cracks with plaster, putty, or grout to seal pores
- Measure and mark guidelines on surfaces or foundations
- Cut covering according to blueprints and sketches, cutting material to fit around obstructions
- Determine traffic areas and decide location of seams
- Lay out, position, and apply shock-absorbing, sound-deadening, or decorative coverings following guidelines to keep courses straight and create patterns
- Prepare cost and labor estimates based on calculations of time and materials needed for project
- Supervise workers
- Coordinate with contractors, architects, designers, and other professionals and craftworkers

Carpet installers may also:

- Cut carpet padding to size and install padding, following a prescribed method
- Join edges of carpet and seam edges where necessary, by sewing or by using tape with glue and heated carpet iron
- Stretch carpet to align with walls and ensure a smooth surface and press carpet in place over tack strips or use staples, tape, tacks, or glue to hold carpet in place
- Install carpet on some floors using adhesive, following prescribed method
- Measure, cut, and install tackless strips along the baseboard or wall, or use old strips to attach edges of new carpet
- Fasten metal treads across door openings or where carpet meets flooring to hold carpet in place
- Cut and bind carpet material

Career Path

Entry-level employees typically begin as helpers and learn through on-the-job training under the supervision of experienced installers. Entry-level employees begin with simple tasks like installing padding under carpet and advance over time to more difficult assignments, such as cutting, fitting, and measuring. Over time, installers may become supervisors, salespeople, or cost estimators. Some set up their own flooring contracting businesses.

For those interested in advancement, knowledge of Spanish is increasingly important because of the large number of Spanish-speaking workers in the building trades.

Earning Potential

Median hourly wage (2009): $17.90

Median annual wage (2009): $37,230

(Based on carpet installers' information from the Bureau of Labor Statistics)

Education/Licensure

Typically, carpet and floor installers learn their trade on the job. A high school diploma or GED may not be required for entry-level positions, but to advance very far, a high school diploma will be useful. A cost estimator, for example, needs to be able to take measurements and compute time, materials, and cost estimates accurately. Knowledge of Spanish is also increasingly helpful.

For More Information

Finishing Trades Institute International (FTII)
7230 Parkway Drive
Hanover, Maryland 21076
www.finishingtradesinstitute.org

Forest Stewardship Council—United States
212 Third Avenue North
Suite 280
Minneapolis, Minnesota 555401
612-353-4511
www.fscus.org

World Floor Covering Association (WFCA)
2211 East Howell Avenue
Anaheim, California 92806
800-276-7289 (toll-free)
www.wfca.org

Furniture Designer

Alternate Titles and Related Careers

- Cabinet Maker
- Furniture Maker
- Furniture Showroom Sales Representative
- Interior Furniture Systems Designer
- Office Furniture CAD Designer
- Office Furniture Designer
- Retail Furniture Sales/Design Consultant

While not a "green" occupation in itself, designing furniture benefits the environment when the furniture is made of "eco-friendly" materials such as bamboo, reclaimed lumber and other materials, and coconut palm wood.

Job Trends

Furniture designer is a subcategory of "Commercial and Industrial Designer." The combined occupations are projected to have a growth rate of 7 to 13 percent, which is considered average growth according to the Bureau of Labor Statistics.

The interest in ergonomics and green design are major factors in the demand for all types of designers. Ergonomic design is an increasingly popular field because of the aging of the nation's population and workplace safety regulations. Furniture that is ergonomically sound emphasizes good posture and minimizes muscle strain. Ergonomically designed office furniture and work spaces can be important in reducing employee injuries and absenteeism.

Nature of the Work

Furniture designers create furniture—either one-of-a-kind art pieces or furniture that is mass-produced. They design residential furnishings like couches and dining room sets as well as office furnishings. Furniture designers need drawing skills and the ability to use computer-aided design (CAD) software to sketch their designs. Furniture designers must also have good math skills in order to develop the specifications for the manufacture of their pieces. A sense of what the marketplace wants in furniture and the ability to turn the ideas generated through market research into saleable merchandise are key skills.

Among the tasks that furniture designers may perform are the following:

- Prepare sketches of design concepts
- Evaluate feasibility of design ideas, based on factors such as appearance, safety, function, serviceability, budget, production costs/methods, and market characteristics
- Direct and coordinate the fabrication of models or samples and the drafting of working drawings and specification sheets from sketches
- Present designs and reports to customers or design committees for approval and discuss need for modification
- Modify and refine designs, using working models, to conform to customer specifications, production limitations, or changes in design trends
- Research production specifications, costs, production materials, and manufacturing methods and provide cost estimates and itemized production requirements
- Confer with engineering, marketing, production, or sales departments, or with customers, to establish and evaluate design concepts for manufactured products
- Investigate product characteristics such as the product's safety, market appeal, efficiency of production, distribution, and maintenance
- Develop manufacturing procedures and monitor the manufacture of designs to improve operations and product quality

- Participate in new product planning or market research, including studying the potential need for new products
- Coordinate the look and function of product lines
- Supervise assistants' work throughout the design process
- Read publications, attend showings, and study competing products and design styles and motifs to obtain perspective and generate design concepts

Career Path

Some furniture designers begin as interior designers and then specialize in designing furniture. Others may begin as textile designers or woodworkers and then take additional courses to learn the skills and knowledge required to design furniture. With experience, a furniture designer may advance to chief designer or design department head. Some designers may take responsibility for an entire product line or ultimately become the director of design for a company.

Earning Potential

Median hourly wage (2009): $27.92

Median annual wage (2009): $58,060

(Based on "Commercial and Industrial Designer")

Education/Licensure

Most entry-level jobs require a bachelor's degree in interior design, architecture, industrial design, product design, or design management. Some employers may prefer entry-level candidates with a degree in furniture design. Many designers earn master's degrees to improve their opportunities. An undergraduate degree in marketing, engineering, or information technology combined with a master's degree in industrial design is one possibility. Another is a master's degree in business administration (MBA) combined with an industrial design degree. A portfolio of design samples is also helpful.

The National Association of Schools of Art and Design provides a list and links to accredited art and design programs. These include colleges, universities, and other educational institutions. The Industrial Designers Society of America provides a specific list of schools with design programs. Many programs include internships.

About Furniture Made with Renewable Resources

The following renewable resources are turning up as furniture: bamboo, cork, beech wood, reclaimed lumber, recycled wood scraps, hemp, wool, jute, bent plywood, stainless steel, and coconut palm trees. Some artisans also make interesting furniture from rolled newspapers and recycled metal and wood.

For More Information

American Society of Furniture Designers (ASFD)
144 Woodland Drive
New London, North Carolina 28127
910-576-1273
www.asfd.com

Industrial Designers Society of America
45195 Business Court
Suite 250
Dulles, Virginia 20166-6717
703-707-6000
www.idsa.org

National Association of Schools of Art and Design
11250 Roger Bacon Drive
Suite 21
Reston, Virginia 20190-5248
703-437-0700
http://nasad.arts-accredit.org

Interior Decorator

Alternate Titles and Related Careers

- Commercial Interior Decorator
- Interior Decorating Consultant
- Interior Decorating Director
- Interior Decorating Sales Consultant
- Interior Decorating Supervisor
- Retail Store Decorator

While not specifically a "green" occupation, interior decorator can be a green occupation because of the proliferation of green materials such as flooring, paints, and fabrics available to interior decorators, which is reflected in design schools' course work.

Job Trends

The Bureau of Labor Statistics estimates that the interior design occupation will have a faster-than-average growth rate of 19 percent. While competition for jobs is expected to be high, candidates who have formal training or experience in green or energy-efficient design should be most attractive to employers and potential clients.

Environmental and health concerns as well the increasing interest in sustainable green design are driving some of the growth in this occupation. Green design involves choosing materials that are energy-efficient or are made from renewable resources. Green design also emphasizes the use of chemical-free and hypoallergenic materials, which are especially important in a time when there is a growing number of people with allergies and asthma.

The health-care industry as related to elder care and the hospitality sector of the economy are two areas where interior decoration will see an increase in demand.

Nature of the Work

An interior decorator is not the same as an interior designer. There are two differences between the two professions. An interior decorator plans and executes the decoration of a home, office, store, or other space. An interior designer designs the space, not just the decoration of that space. In addition, many states require that interior designers be licensed, whereas an interior decorator is not a licensed profession.

Interior decorators work with design teams or directly with clients to select a design scheme, including colors, fabrics, and furnishings, for a space. Interior decorators consult on the total look of a space from lighting to furniture layout to paint and/or wallpaper.

Among the tasks that interior decorators perform are the following:

- Meet with clients to determine the factors that affect the decoration plan such as budget, the purpose and function of the space, and color and textile preferences
- Advise clients on factors affecting the space such as layout and color coordination
- Render design ideas in the form of paste-ups or drawings using computer-aided design (CAD) and related software
- Estimate costs and prepare quotes for clients
- Select, or design, and purchase furnishings, art works, and accessories
- Subcontract fabrication, installation, and arrangement of carpeting, fixtures, accessories, draperies, paint and wall coverings, art work, furniture, and related items
- Supervise the installation and arrangement of carpeting, fixtures, accessories, draperies, paint and wall coverings, art work, furniture, and related items
- Direct and train workers
- Maintain records and files, prepare reports, and order supplies and equipment

Career Path

Typically, the first job for an interior decorator is assistant in an interior design firm or working for an interior decorator. With experience, an assistant in a design or decorator firm advances to junior interior decorator and then interior decorator. Some decorators who stay with large firms may become the director of interior decoration. Other interior decorators open their own consulting businesses working directly with clients.

Earning Potential

Median hourly wage (2009): $22.20

Median annual wage (2009): $46,180

(Based on the "Interior Designer" category)

Education/Licensure

Entry-level positions require an associate or bachelor's degree. Coursework in colors and color theory, textiles, ergonomics, lighting, and design trends as well as CAD software are desirable. Most training, however, is on-the-job. Apprenticeships and internships can be useful in landing the first job. Keeping a portfolio of work is also important.

For More Information

American Society of Interior Designers
608 Massachusetts Avenue, NE
Washington, DC 20002-6006
202-546-3480
www.asid.org

Council for Interior Design Accreditation
206 Grandville Avenue
Suite 350
Grand Rapids, Michigan 49503
616-458-0400
www.accredit-id.org

Interior Design Society
164 South Main Street
Floor 8
High Point, North Carolina 27260
888-884-4469 (toll-free)
www.interiordesignsociety.org

International Interior Design Association
222 Merchandise Mart
Suite 567
Chicago, Illinois 60654
888-799-4432 (toll-free)
www.iida.org

National Association of Schools of Art and Design
11250 Roger Bacon Drive
Suite 21
Reston, Virginia 20190-5248
703-437-0700
http://nasad.arts-accredit.org

Interior Designer

Alternate Titles and Related Careers

- Color and Materials Designer
- Commercial Interior Designer
- Design Assistant Director of Interiors
- Director of Interiors
- Interior Design Coordinator
- Interior Design Consultant
- Interior Design Director
- Senior Designer

While not specifically a "green" occupation, interior design can be a green occupation because of the proliferation of green materials such as flooring, paints, and fabrics available to interior designers, which is reflected in design schools' course work.

 http://bit.ly/career35

Job Trends

The Bureau of Labor Statistics estimates that this occupation will have a faster-than-average growth rate of 19 percent. Projected job openings between 2009 and 2018 are estimated to number 35,900. About 44 percent of interior designers work for professional design or architectural firms, 27 percent are self-employed, and 9 percent work in retail as in-store designers in furniture, home, and garden stores. Competition for jobs is expected to be strong because many people enter this profession. However, prospects are expected to be particularly good for designers with formal training or experience in green or energy-efficient design.

The increased interest in the environment and health concerns and the increasing interest in sustainable green design are driving some of the growth in this occupation. Green design involves choosing construction materials that are energy-efficient or are made from renewable resources. Green design also emphasizes the use of chemical-free and hypoallergenic materials, which is especially important in a time when there are a growing number of people with allergies and asthma.

The hospitality industry is expected to create additional demand for design services for hotels and restaurants as it expands along with tourism. The health-care sector will also generate demand for new facilities for the aging population. With new facilities comes the need to provide bright, airy environments and interior spaces that aid the movement of people who are elderly and with disabilities; this is a specialty known as elder design.

Nature of the Work

Interior designers design the interiors of homes, office buildings, hotels, restaurants, stores, schools, and hospitals. They also design outdoor living spaces such as patios and outdoor kitchens. Their objective is to plan spaces that are functional, safe, and attractive for the people who live and work in them. The goal of the design may be to raise worker productivity, sell merchandise, or improve a family's lifestyle. Some designers specialize in residential or commercial interiors, and others specialize in kitchens and baths. Interior designers work with contractors, architects, engineers, electricians, and plumbers and must be able to read blueprints.

According to O*NET, interior designers may perform the following tasks:

- Confer with clients to determine the factors that affect design planning such as budget, architectural preferences, and purpose and function of the space

- Advise clients on design factors such as space planning, layout and utilization of furnishings or equipment, and color coordination
- Plan the overall space design
- Plan architectural details such as moldings, built-in components, and sometimes positions of walls or other features
- Prepare plans using computer-aided design (CAD) software
- Estimate material requirements and costs
- Present designs to clients for approval
- Review and detail shop drawings for construction plans
- Coordinate with other professionals
- Supervise the work for some clients
- Stay up-to-date on building and fire and safety codes and construction requirements of the locality

Career Path

Entry-level interior designers spend one to three years in on-the-job training under the supervision of an experienced designer. After they gain experience, interior designers are given responsibility for independent projects and may eventually become supervisors or chief designers. Some open their own design businesses.

Having a portfolio of work is necessary when applying for a job.

Earning Potential

Median hourly wage (2009): $22.20

Median annual wage (2009): $46,180

Education/Licensure

Postsecondary education is necessary for interior designers. An associate degree is the minimum. Some design schools offer programs that last two or three years and grant a certificate or associate degree. This generally qualifies a person to work as a design assistant. A bachelor's degree is considered the standard qualification and enables a person to enroll in an apprenticeship program leading to a license.

The Council for Interior Design Accreditation (CIDA) accredits interior design programs that grant bachelor's degrees. Its Web site and the Web site of the American Society of Interior Designers (ASID) provide lists with links to accredited interior design programs. The National Association of Schools of Art and Design (NASAD) accredits schools of art and design, and its Web site provides a list of accredited programs. There is also a recognized apprenticeship program for interior designers.

Twenty-three states, Puerto Rico, and the District of Columbia require registration, certification, or licensing for interior designers. In all cases, a combination of education, experience, and passing an exam is necessary. The National Council for Interior Design Qualification (NCIDQ) administers the nationally recognized licensing exam for interior designers. To qualify to take the exam, a designer must have a combination of six years of education and experience, at least two years of which must be formal education. The exam consists of six sections that cover all areas of interior design. The NCIDQ Web site contains links to the states requiring this exam.

The Council for Qualification of Residential Interior Designers (CQRID), affiliated with the Interior Design Society, offers a certification for interior designers of residential properties. The CQRID site also contains information on the states requiring certification of interior designers.

The Green Building Certification Institute offers LEED Professional Accreditation for interior designers.

For More Information

American Society of Interior Designers
608 Massachusetts Avenue, NE
Washington, DC 20002-6006
202-546-3480
www.asid.org

Council for Interior Design Accreditation
206 Grandville Avenue
Suite 350
Grand Rapids, Michigan 49503
616-458-0400
www.accredit-id.org

Council for Qualification of Residential Interior
    Designers (CQRID)
164 South Main Street
Floor 8
High Point, North Carolina 27260
888-884-4469 (toll-free)
www.cqrid.org

Interior Design Society (IDS)
164 South Main Street
Floor 8
High Point, North Carolina 27260
888-884-4469 (toll-free)
www.interiordesignsociety.org

International Interior Design Association
222 Merchandise Mart
Suite 567
Chicago, Illinois 60654
888-799-4432 (toll-free)
www.iida.org

National Association of Schools of Art and Design
11250 Roger Bacon Drive
Suite 21
Reston, Virginia 20190-5248
703-437-0700
http://nasad.arts-accredit.org

National Council for Interior Design Qualification
1602 L Street, NW
Suite 200
Washington, DC 20036-5681
202-721-0220
www.ncidq.org

U.S. Green Building Council (USGBC)
2101 L Street, NW
Suite 500
Washington, DC 20037
800-795-1747 (toll-free)
www.usgbc.org

Painter ☼🌎

Alternate Titles and Related Careers

- Facilities Painter
- Maintenance Painter
- Industrial Painter

This is a "Bright Outlook" occupation in the construction sector of the economy. It is also a "Green" occupation in that painters can choose to use paints with low or no VOC (volatile organic compounds) that release gases into the air and can create short- and long-term adverse health effects.

 http://bit.ly/career33

About Volatile Organic Compounds

VOCs are found in a variety of household and paint products, including lacquers, paint strippers, wood preservatives, cleaning supplies, pesticides, building materials and furnishings, glues, adhesives, permanent markers, moth repellents, air fresheners, stored fuels and automotive products, and dry-cleaned clothing. The U.S. Environmental Protection Agency lists the following adverse health effects from exposure to VOCs: eye, nose, and throat irritation; headaches; loss of coordination; nausea; and damages to the liver, kidney, and central nervous system.

Job Trends

The Bureau of Labor Statistics projects that the occupation of painter will have an average growth rate of 7 to 13 percent between 2008 and 2018. Projected job openings are estimated to be about 106,000, about 25 percent more openings than currently available. About 45 percent of current painters are self-employed, and about 44 percent are employed directly by firms involved in construction, such as a painting contractor or a home builder. The remaining 11 percent are employed in a variety of industries not related to construction.

Nature of the Work

Using brushes, rollers, and spray guns, painters apply paint, stain, varnish, enamel, and other finishes to walls, equipment, buildings, bridges, and other structural surfaces. Painters may also use caulking guns and putty knives to fill cracks and sandpaper, scrapers, brushes, steel wool, and/or sanding machines to smooth the painting surface.

According to O*NET, painters may perform the following tasks:

- Cover surfaces with dropcloths or masking tape and paper to protect surfaces during painting
- Calculate amounts of required materials and estimate costs, based on surface measurements and/or work orders
- Read work orders or receive instructions from supervisors or homeowners in order to determine work requirements
- Erect scaffolding and swing gates, or set up ladders, to work above ground level
- Remove fixtures such as pictures, door knobs, lamps, and electric switch covers prior to painting
- Fill cracks, holes, and joints with caulk, putty, plaster, or other fillers
- Apply primers or sealers to prepare new surfaces, such as bare wood or metal, for finish coats
- Wash and treat surfaces with oil, turpentine, mildew remover, or other preparations, and sand rough spots to ensure that finishes will adhere properly
- Remove old finishes by stripping, sanding, wire brushing, burning, or using water and/or abrasive blasting
- Smooth surfaces
- Select and purchase tools and finishes for surfaces to be covered, considering durability, ease of handling, methods of application, and customers' wishes
- Mix and match colors of paint, stain, or varnish with oil and thinning and drying additives in order to obtain desired colors and consistencies
- Use special finishing techniques such as sponging, ragging, layering, or faux finishing to polish final coats to specified finishes
- Cut stencils and brush and spray lettering and decorations on surfaces
- Spray or brush hot plastics or pitch onto surfaces
- Direct and train workers
- Maintain records and files, prepare reports, and order supplies and equipment

About Environmentally Friendly Paint

Painting a room doesn't have to result in releasing clouds of toxic VOC fumes into the atmosphere. Check VOC levels in the Natura brand from Benjamin Moore; Glidden™, This Old House Paint™, and other brands from ICI paints; and Harmony®, Progreen™, and other brands from Sherwin Williams.

Career Path

Most painters begin as helpers for experienced painters. However, the *Occupational Outlook Handbook* notes that formal and informal training programs exist and provide a better foundation for a career as a painter. Beginning salaries are generally higher for individuals who have successfully completed an apprentice program.

Over time, an experienced painter may become a supervisor of a painting crew and then several crews. Experienced painters may also become cost estimators working with customers to evaluate jobs and prepare job quotes. Some painters go into business for themselves as painting contractors. Knowledge of Spanish can be helpful in order to advance because of the large number of Hispanics working in the construction industry.

Earning Potential

Median hourly wage (2009): $16.21

Median annual wage (2009): $33,720

Education/Licensure

Most training occurs on the job, but painter is a recognized apprenticeship. Typically, acceptance into an apprenticeship program requires a high school diploma or equivalent. The typical apprenticeship lasts two to four years and is a combination of classroom instruction and work experience. Topics include color harmony, surface preparation, blueprint reading, and safety. Some vocational schools also offer formal training programs for painters.

The National Association of Corrosion Engineers offers the Protective Coating Specialist certification for those interested in specializing in industrial painting. The Society for Protective Coatings offers Painting Contractor Certification Programs and the Protective Coatings Specialist Certification. Some specialties related to corrosive technology require an associate or even a bachelor's degree.

The Painting and Decorating Contractors of America (PDCA) operates the Contractor College to teach contractors "to save time or make more money."

For More Information

International Union of Painters and Allied Trades (IUPAT)
1750 New York Avenue, NW
Washington, DC 20006
202-637-0707
www.iupat.org

National Association of Corrosion Engineers (NACE)
1440 South Creek Drive
Houston, Texas 77084-4906
800-797-6223 (toll-free)
www.nace.org

National Center for Construction Education and Research (NCCER)
3600 NW 43rd Street
Building G
Gainesville, Florida 32606
888-622-3720 (toll-free)
www.nccer.org

Painting and Decorating Contractors of America (PDCA)
1801 Park 270 Drive
Suite 220
St. Louis, Missouri 63146
800-332-7322 (toll-free)
www.pdca.org

The Society for Protective Coatings (SSPC)
40 24th Street
6th Floor
Pittsburgh, Pennsylvania 15222-4656
877-281-7772 (toll-free)
www.sspc.org

Kitchen Designer

Alternate Titles and Related Careers

- Associate Industrial Designer
- Builder or Remodeler
- Cabinet Designer
- Display Designer (kitchen furnishings)
- Industrial Designer
- Junior Designer
- Kitchen Dealer/Distributor
- Kitchen Design and Sales Consultant
- Project Manager
- Senior Creative Designer

This is a specialty within the subcategory of interior design, and while not a specifically "green" occupation, kitchen designers have the opportunity to introduce green concepts and green materials into their work with clients.

Job Trends

The Bureau of Labor Statistics estimates that the interior designer occupation, of which kitchen designer is a subset, will have a faster-than-average growth rate of 19 percent between 2008 and 2018. Competition for jobs in the overall interior design category is expected to be high because many people enter this profession, but knowledge of and experience with green design will make candidates more attractive to employers and clients.

The National Kitchen and Bath Association (NKBA) cites a HomeSight survey that indicates that 36 percent of empty-nesters and 43 percent of families will probably remodel their kitchens. This doesn't include the kitchen designs needed for the several million new homes and apartments that are built each year. NKBA notes that the bath and kitchen industry was worth $200 billion in 2007, the latest year for which statistics are available.

While the recession of 2007 through 2009 decreased the number of new housing starts, the construction industry is expected to regain its lost momentum over the next few years. In addition, concern over the environment and increasing attention to sustainable green design are driving some of the interest in remodeling and retrofitting kitchens to be more water- and energy-efficient. The NKBA notes that many homeowners remodel "to reduce electricity and water use."

Nature of the Work

Kitchen designers plan new or renovated kitchens to achieve spaces that are functional, safe, and attractive and that combine their clients' aesthetics with the latest in technology and design innovation. Kitchen designers work with contractors, architects, engineers, electricians, and plumbers and must be able to read blueprints and use computer-aided design (CAD) software.

According to O*NET, designers may perform the following tasks:

- Confer with clients to determine the factors that affect the design planning such as budget, architectural and aesthetic preferences, and functionality
- Advise clients on design factors such as space planning, layout, products, cabinet design, and color coordination
- Plan the overall space including placement of appliances and built-in components, and positions of walls and other features as well as lighting, floor covering, finishes, and work surfaces
- Prepare plans using CAD software
- Estimate material requirements and costs
- Present designs to clients for approval
- Review and detail shop drawings for construction plans
- Supervise the construction work for some clients
- Keep up-to-date on building and fire and safety codes and construction requirements of the locality
- Keep up-to-date on trends, colors, and materials as well as products in kitchen design

Kitchen designers who go into business for themselves as designers or owners of kitchen furnishing stores will need to have business and management skills in order to:

- Hire, direct, and train workers
- Maintain records and files
- Oversee the accounting aspects of the business including payroll
- Order supplies and equipment
- Advertise for clients
- Build relationships with contractors and suppliers

Career Path

Entry-level kitchen designers spend one to three years in on-the-job training under the supervision of an experienced designer. As they gain experience, kitchen designers are given more responsibility for independent projects and may eventually become supervisors or chief designers. Some designers open their own businesses.

Some kitchen designers specialize. Some prefer to work only on new kitchen design and others concentrate on kitchen remodeling projects. Kitchen designers may also choose to specialize in either commercial or residential design. Some designers work on both kitchen and bath design.

Having a portfolio of work is necessary when applying for a job.

Earning Potential

Median hourly wage (2009): $22.20

Median annual wage (2009): $46,180

(Based on the Bureau of Labor Statistics' "Interior Designer" category)

A 2009 survey by NKBA found that an NKBA-certified kitchen and bath designer earned on average $87,000.

Education/Licensure

Postsecondary education is necessary for interior designers. An associate degree is the minimum. Some design schools offer programs that last two or three years and grant a certificate or associate degree. This generally qualifies a person to work as a design assistant. A bachelor's degree in kitchen and bath design, interior design, or an art-related field is considered the standard qualification and enables a person to enroll in an apprenticeship program leading to a license.

The National Kitchen and Bath Association (NKBA), which began originally as the American Institute of Kitchen Dealers, is the accrediting agency for kitchen and bath design programs. Its Web site provides information on the more then fifty such accredited college and university programs. NKBA also offers three relevant certifications for kitchen designers: Associate Kitchen and Bath Designer (AKBD), Certified Kitchen Designer (CKD), and Certified Master Kitchen and Bath Designer (CMKBD). NKBA provides more than 200 professional development courses each year, some of which focus specifically on green design topics.

The Council for Interior Design Accreditation (CIDA) accredits interior design programs that grant bachelor's degrees. Its Web site and the Web site of the American Society of Interior Designers (ASID) provide lists with links to accredited interior design programs. The National Association of Schools of Art and Design (NASAD) accredits schools of art and design, and its Web site provides a list of accredited programs. There is also a recognized apprenticeship program for interior designers.

Twenty-three states, Puerto Rico, and the District of Columbia require registration, certification, or licensing for interior designers. In all cases, a combination of education, experience, and passing an exam is necessary. The National Council for Interior Design Qualification (NCIDQ) administers the nationally recognized licensing exam for interior designers. To qualify to take the exam, a designer must have a combination of six years of education and experience, at least two years of which must be formal education. The exam consists of six sections that cover all areas of interior design. The NCIDQ Web site contains links to the states requiring this exam.

The Green Building Certification Institute offers LEED Professional Accreditation for interior designers.

For More Information

American Society of Interior Designers
608 Massachusetts Avenue, NE
Washington, DC 20002-6006
202-546-3480
www.asid.org

Council for Interior Design Accreditation
206 Grandville Avenue
Suite 350
Grand Rapids, Michigan 49503
616-458-0400
www.accredit-id.org

National Association of Schools of Art and Design
11250 Roger Bacon Drive
Suite 21
Reston, Virginia 20190-5248
703-437-0700
http://nasad.arts-accredit.org

National Council for Interior Design Qualification
1602 L Street, NW
Suite 200
Washington, DC 20036-5681
202-721-0220
www.ncidq.org

National Kitchen and Bath Association (NKBA)
687 Willow Grove Street
Hackettstown, New Jersey 07840
800-843-6522 (toll-free)
www.nkba.org

U.S. Green Building Council (USGBC)
2101 L Street, NW
Suite 500
Washington, DC 20037
800-795-1747 (toll-free)
www.usgbc.org

Product Designer 🌏

Alternate Titles and Related Careers
- Commercial Designer
- Industrial Designer

Commercial and industrial design occupations are considered a "Green Increased-Demand" occupation in the manufacturing and research, design, and consulting sectors of the economy.

 http://bit.ly/career36

Job Trends

The combined occupations are projected to have a growth rate of 7 to 13 percent, which is considered average according to the Bureau of Labor Statistics. Job openings are projected to number 17,600.

The increase of jobs is fueled by the growing demand for new and upgraded consumer products that are environmentally safe and produced in an environmentally friendly way. Most design jobs are contracted out to design firms, rather than staying in manufacturing companies. A trend toward using design firms in other countries causes some decrease in domestic jobs. However, because industrial designers are needed in so many industries, job opportunities and pay are generally good overall.

Nature of the Work

Sustainable design is becoming more important in product development. Sustainable products incorporate energy efficiency and materials that have been recycled and are capable of being recycled. This includes everything from hybrid vehicles to packaging made of biodegradable plastic and clothing made from organic fibers as well as energy-efficient household appliances and eco-friendly furniture and other interior design products.

About New "Green" Products

With Americans' increasing interest in going green, a number of large and small manufacturers are producing "green" products. Check your supermarket shelf for everything from "organic" cookies to recycled paper products and "natural" cleaning products. You'll find clothing lines that use recycled materials and specialty catalogues that sell everything from floor mats made from recycled flip-flops to bamboo shower stools.

Commercial and industrial designers design the products that people use every day—automobiles, furniture, appliances, toys, and computers. Designers are concerned with the function, style, and safety of products. They participate in market research to determine the features that consumers want and then use their artistic talent to create functional and appealing products using drafting instruments, paints, and computer-aided design (CAD) equipment.

Product designers may perform the following tasks according to O*NET:

- Prepare sketches of ideas, detailed drawings, illustrations, artwork, or blueprints
- Evaluate feasibility of design ideas, based on factors such as appearance, safety, function, serviceability, budget, production costs/methods, and market characteristics
- Direct and coordinate the fabrication of models or samples and the drafting of working drawings and specification sheets from sketches
- Present designs and reports to customers or design committees for approval and discuss need for modification
- Modify and refine designs, using working models, to conform to customer specifications, production limitations, or changes in design trends
- Research production specifications, costs, production materials, and manufacturing methods and provide cost estimates and itemized production requirements
- Confer with engineering, marketing, production, or sales departments, or with customers, to establish and evaluate design concepts for manufactured products
- Investigate product characteristics such as the product's safety and handling qualities, its market appeal, how efficiently it can be produced, and ways of distributing, using, and maintaining it
- Develop manufacturing procedures and monitor the manufacture of designs to improve operations and product quality
- Design graphic material for use as ornamentation, illustration, or advertising on manufactured materials and packaging or containers
- Participate in new product planning or market research, including studying the potential need for new products
- Coordinate the look and function of product lines
- Advise corporations on issues involving corporate image projects or problems
- Supervise assistants' work throughout the design process
- Read publications, attend showings, and study competing products and design styles and motifs to obtain perspective and generate design concepts

Career Path

Beginning designers usually receive up to three years of on-the-job training. With more experience, they may become supervisors or chief designers. Some open their own studio for consulting, start a design firm, or teach in colleges and universities.

Earning Potential

Median hourly wage (2009): $27.92

Median annual wage (2009): $58,060

Education/Licensure

Most entry-level jobs require a bachelor's degree in industrial design, product design, or design management. Many designers earn master's degrees to improve their opportunities. An undergraduate degree in marketing, engineering, or information technology combined with a master's degree in industrial design is one possibility. Another is a master's degree in business administration (MBA) combined with an industrial design degree. A portfolio of design samples is also helpful.

The National Association of Schools of Art and Design provides a list and links to accredited art and design programs. These include colleges, universities, and other educational institutions. The Industrial Designers Society of America provides a specific list of schools with design programs. Many programs include internships.

For More Information

Industrial Designers Society of America
45195 Business Court
Suite 250
Dulles, Virginia 20166-6717
703-707-6000
www.idsa.org

National Association of Schools of Art and Design
11250 Roger Bacon Drive
Suite 21
Reston, Virginia 20190-5248
703-437-0700
http://nasad.arts-accredit.org

Tips for Retrofitting a Bathroom for Green Design

There are a variety of ways to retrofit bathrooms to make them "green"—and save water and money at the same time.

1. **Choose high-tech toilets.** Almost 30 percent of indoor water use can be traced to toilets. In 1992, the Energy Policy Act called for more efficient-use toilets. Older toilets use between 3 and 7 gallons per flush. Replacing them with low-flow toilets cuts water use to 1.6 gallons for each flush. The Environmental Protection Agency estimates a savings of 11 gallons of water daily, or more than $90.00 a year saved in water utility bills, for a family of 4.

   Dual-flush toilets are another retrofit option. They were first developed in Australia, where water shortages are common. The technology allows users to select for liquid or solid waste, requiring less or more water per flush.

2. **Go with the low-flow.** Almost 17 percent of indoor water use goes down the drain with showers. Standard showerheads use about 2.5 gallons of water each minute. Installing low-flow showerheads can cut both water use and heating bills by 30 to 50 percent.

   Faucets in sinks and tubs can also be replaced or modified to decrease water usage. At the very least, consider replacing the aerator in older faucets with more efficient ones.

3. **Check components when choosing cabinets.** Many commercial wood products, especially those made of particle board, contain formaldehyde in the adhesive. Formaldehyde is one example of Volatile Organic Compounds (VOCs), harmful chemicals that create indoor pollution and smog. Alternative cabinetry such as wheatboard or solid wood cabinets is a better choice. Choose finishes carefully because they, too, may contain VOCs.

4. **Look for different options for countertops.** For a good low-emission countertop, choose recycled glass tile, poured concrete, or engineered stone, a quartz composite. Recycled paper and hemp also make attractive countertops. One countertop that looks like granite is actually a composite of soy flour and recycled newspaper.

5. **Consider cork or linoleum flooring.** Water-resistant cork is an attractive, noise-reducing look in a bathroom. It's also a great choice for allergy sufferers because it's hypo-allergenic. Linoleum, made of linseed oil and sawdust, is less toxic than vinyl flooring, which uses toxic and hazardous substances during production. Recycled materials can also make attractive flooring. Ceramic tile made completely from recycled materials is durable and low maintenance.

   Bamboo, while a renewable resource and attractive as flooring, is not a good choice for a bathroom because of the moisture factor. When exposed to moisture over a long period of time, it swells and warps.

6. **Replace your hot water heater with a tankless heater.** A tankless hot water heater heats water at the source. Standard hot water heaters use 10 to 20 percent more energy than tankless heaters because they are larger and use more water.

   If you can't replace the existing system, wrap the tank with a special insulating blanket to keep the standing water hotter.

7. **Choose eco-friendly paints and finishes.** Many paints, stains, and finishes include VOCs. At room temperature, they evaporate, causing asthma and allergy flare-ups. Look for eco-friendly, water-based brands that are labeled "No VOCs." Low- and no-VOC wallpapers, adhesives, sealers, and caulks are also available.

8. **Buy organic soft goods for a finishing touch.** When you're investing in new towels, select ones that are made of cotton that was grown organically. In addition to helping the environment, you'll find that cotton grown without chemical pesticides is softer.

   If you're replacing the shower curtain, select either one made of a fabric such as heavy cotton duck or of plastic that contains no or low VOCs.

How Being Green Works for **Sandra Gaylord, Kitchen/Bath Designer**

Sandra Gaylord, 59, works as a kitchen and bath interior designer in Charleston, South Carolina. Gaylord has worked in various facets of green industry for the past 28 years. Here, Gaylord measures cabinet doors for accuracy in a kitchen that she is redesigning. Some "green" aspects of the project include utilizing previously used plastic, using water-based lacquer paint, and retaining the existing kitchen cabinets.

Describe your job, including common daily tasks and long-term projects that you have worked on or are working on now. What, specifically, about your job makes it green?

I design kitchens and baths to meet functional and aesthetic requirements. This involves consulting with clients to determine exactly what they want and need. This is a very intimate interview that allows me to find out exactly what I need to know to complete the job. For example, how tall are the clients? Do they have any type of restraints or restrictions? What is their budget? How "green" do they want to go? Once I know these things, I can apply my skills and training to meet the National Kitchen and Bath Association (NKBA) guidelines, as well as individual client needs that may go beyond standard.

Once I have the initial parameters established, I look at the functional and safety requirements of the project. What type of cabinets are needed? How and in which direction should they open? I analyze the landing space, travel space, and hallway space. These are very detailed parts of the project, and sometimes even one eighth of an inch is critical.

Once I have the general plan, the aesthetic part of the design begins. This addresses things such as colors, finishes, and all of the other things that we need to do to make this space work. We've identified all of the points that meet NKBA guidelines, so it's time to look at the products we need to fill in the blanks. What kind of cabinets? Should we reuse the existing cabinets? If so, this falls into the area of green design. If we choose to incorporate new cabinets and we want them to be "green," we decide what to use based on a cabinet company's meeting the environmental stewardship certification and/or if possible cabinet choices are formaldehyde-free.

Then, we look at the countertop. What are our options? Recycled paper? Concrete? Quartz? We also have to look at the lighting. Natural lighting should be a part of the design.

We then make our determinations based on how green the client wants to be. Some people are greener than others. The final design is based on meeting all of the environmental parameters, working within the budget, and finding the products that meet the specific shade of green the client may be.

Why/how did you decide to work in a green industry?

I spent twenty-eight years working as an environmental protection specialist with the Department of the Navy. I was in the environmental restoration program when it began after Love Canal [toxic waste burial site in New York State]. That's when we discovered that what we did on top [of the ground] seeped into the ground. We had to determine what happened, what chemicals had been used, the migration pattern, and the overall impact so we knew how to clean it up. I think that's what sets me apart from other designers. Until you know the impact of what is going into the ground and how it will come back to get you—because it will—you're missing something. I really felt I needed to take that knowledge and attitude with me into my second career as a designer.

How did you prepare for your current position?

After working for years designing kitchens and baths for family and friends and collaborating with a local cabinet builder, I decided to pursue design full-time. I went to Marymount University in Arlington, Virginia, and obtained my degree as an interior designer. I worked in Washington, DC, with several interior designers and eventually found a very experienced kitchen designer who mentored me in the field.

After that, I studied and took the Certified Kitchen Designer exam and the Associate Certified Bath Designer exam through the NKBA. I am an allied member of the American Society of Interior Designers, a member of the National Kitchen and Bath Association (NKBA), Green Drinks of Charleston, Charleston's Green Committee, Architecture for Humanity, and the U.S. Green Building Council (USGBC). Everything I have done is an education. Going to events, meeting people, and sharing knowledge helps make me a better green designer. It also gives me the opportunity to educate someone else.

Which aspect of your education and/or training do you think has been the most helpful and/or useful to you? Why?

The on-the-job training and classes I received working as an environmental protection specialist have been the most beneficial. It's not that the knowledge I gained from these is specific to green design, but it gives me an understanding of the life cycle of bad environmental decisions. In addition, with that knowledge I gained an appreciation for the impact of chemicals in our products, groundwater, food, and so on.

Do you have a LEED credential? Why or why not?

I do not have a LEED credential at this time. I took many courses offered by the USGBC for certification for New Construction and Commercial Interiors, but . . . the USGBC was in the process of establishing the Home certification at the time. I am taking those classes and preparing for that certification. My goal is to complete that by the end of 2010.

Do you find that the skills and/or knowledge required for your job continue to evolve? If so, what have you done to keep up-to-date?

I have found in the past three years that there are more products available and so much more information that I am constantly reading periodicals. Each day, something has changed. Take, for example, the vinyl shower curtain. They are so dangerous in our lives. When you open that vinyl shower curtain, it releases so many volatile chemicals. Seven of those chemicals have been identified as hazardous air pollutants by the EPA. We open them, breathe them in, and the chemicals released can potentially damage the liver and the central nervous, respiratory, and reproductive systems. The heat from the shower causes these chemicals to release many times. Yet without that knowledge, we continue to purchase vinyl shower curtains.

The constant change within the industry makes research very interesting, and I have found several Internet sites to assist me with that. InformeDesign.com and BuildingGreen.com are both great sites.

How have continuing education and/or training impacted the way you do your job?

Continuing education and training help me learn about products that are better for my clients.

What is the most rewarding part of your work, and what do you find to be the most challenging?

The most rewarding part of my work is to prove that "green" can be beautiful. It is also rewarding to prove to clients that you do not have to do "all or nothing." The most challenging aspect of my work is getting the client to understand and accept that you can have a kitchen that meets green requirements without sacrificing your budget or the kitchen that you want.

What advice would you give to people interested in pursuing your career?

I think that reading about the history of environmental issues is very important. Things like the Love Canal catastrophe and the impact of DDT, as proved by Rachel Carson, are important. If you understand the impact of health of chemicals and hazardous wastes, you will be a better green designer. You will not just be a designer who has read that a certain product is good, but you will have an understanding of the life cycle of that decision.

How Being Green Works for **Michael D. Byun, Interior Designer**

Michael D. Byun, 46, is the design director for the corporate, commercial, and civic practice of a multi-disciplinary architecture and design firm in Chicago, Illinois. Byun, who specializes in commercial interiors, has spent 20 years in green design. Here, Byun reviews a rendering prepared for a design competition for a LEED Platinum building in Abu Dhabi.

Describe your job, including common daily tasks and long-term projects that you have worked on or are working on now. What, specifically, about your job makes it environmentally green work?

My daily tasks include the oversight of design development for many of the projects within our office and project-specific work including programming, schematic design, and design development. I work closely with the design teams within our office in developing concepts, the refinement of design

solutions (including material specifications), and the development of construction details.

Throughout my career, I have worked on many projects that primarily focused on the design of offices for professional service organizations, such as management consulting firms, law firms, financial institutions, and corporate headquarters. In addition to these opportunities, I have been involved with the design of an airport, a television studio, several residences, and a restaurant.

My position affords me the opportunity to design spaces that impact the quality of the work environment. [It's green in that] what I do can directly affect user comfort through improved ergonomics, indoor air quality, and access to natural light. Additionally, our work impacts resource conservation and energy consumption.

Why/how did you decide to work in a green industry?

My specific industry, interior design, has led the charge in terms of environmental conservation through the implementation of many sustainable initiatives, including Green-Guard certification, Green Label, Forestry Stewardship Council (FSC), ENERGY STAR, etc. When I entered this industry, many of these green initiatives did not exist.

How did you prepare for your current position?

I prepared for my career by attending Arizona State University, which is a Council for Interior Design (FIDER/CIDA) accredited university. I received a bachelor of science in design. Beyond my education, I sat for the National Council for Interior Design Qualification (NCIDQ) examination when my professional development requirements were met. Upon the successful completion of that examination, I received my NCIDQ certificate, which then made me eligible to apply to the State of Illinois to become a registered interior designer.

The company I work for is a leader in the architecture and design (A&D) industry and has a focus on environmentally sustainable buildings and environments. Our firm currently has more LEED-accredited professionals than any other firm in our field. As a part of our firm's own commitment to sustainability, every employee is required to receive LEED accreditation. We conduct bi-monthly, in-house workshops so that professionals within our office may stay current on new developments within the realm of green initiatives.

Which aspect of your education and/or training do you think has been the most helpful and/or useful to you? Why?

Certainly my education plays an important role. The strong background I received in concept development can be directly attributed to my education. In addition, I was fortunate to receive extensive coursework that was directly applicable to the professional practice of interior design.

Beyond my education, identifying a strong mentor through my various positions as a project designer, project manager, and project director has given me a well-rounded perspective on the field of interior design. This includes everything from the design aspects to implementation to the business end of this profession.

Do you have a LEED credential? Why or why not?

Yes, I am a LEED AP (without specialty). However, I will be changing my status to LEED AP ID+C (Interior Design + Construction). Why? Because our clients demand it, and we want to build a place that is better for future generations.

Do you find that the skills and/or knowledge required for your job continue to evolve? If so, what have you done to keep up-to-date?

Our world is ever changing. New developments in theory, strategies, construction (materials and methods), hardware, and software constantly require any profession to stay current or be left behind.

Continuing education is the key to staying current. I often try to attend seminars offered by professional organizations such as the American Institute of Architects (AIA) or the International Interior Design Association (IIDA) or those offered by material or furniture vendors. There are so many opportunities to keep current that it's difficult to fall behind in our industry.

I have also taught a senior-level design studio at my university and have juried several student studios at local design schools. Keeping an eye on what's coming out of our universities serves as an inspiration for what we may be seeing in the future.

How have continuing education and/or training impacted the way you do your job?

Continuing education keeps my mind sharp and open to new ways of thinking as well as ways to approach challenges.

What is the most rewarding part of your work, and what do you find to be the most challenging?

I really enjoy developing a good and thoughtful design that impacts a large audience. People spend a good portion of their lives at their workplace. It's nice to hear from clients and occupants that what we've done has a positive impact on their daily lives.

The greatest challenge is getting the larger population of an organization to embrace change, even when it's for the better. It's human nature to stick to what you know.

What advice would you give to people interested in pursuing your career?

In my opinion, my education was the most important aspect in the development of my career. I know I may sound like my father, but my education established a strong base of knowledge from which to build my career. Someone interested in pursuing a career in design should carefully evaluate the curriculum of a program to ensure a good balance of design and practice. They should also seek a faculty at a design school that balances education with professional practice.

After your education and when you begin your career, do not hesitate to reach out to co-workers senior to you who may serve as mentors or advocates in identifying professional growth opportunities for you.

CHAPTER 4

LANDSCAPING, GROUNDSKEEPING, AND TURF CARE JOBS

The American Nursery and Landscape Association (ANLA) notes that the core business of its members is "protecting and improving green spaces, and the environmental services they perform." This chapter looks at some of the occupations that directly impact the environment in which people live, work, and recreate daily.

The move to a plant protection, also called plant health care, and integrated pest management (IPM) approach to treating plant and tree diseases is one example of how the landscaping industry is responding to the need to be more eco-friendly. Educating the public about using more native plants and newer grass strains that require less watering are two other examples of environmentally responsible landscaping.

According to Hoover's, an industry analyst group, the U.S. landscaping services industry—lawn care, tree services, irrigation, pest control, landscape construction, and line clearing—had revenues of $50 billion in 2008, the latest year for which statistics were available. About 90,000 companies competed for this business. About 50 percent of the companies provided commercial landscaping services. They were contracted to plant and maintain landscaping for corporate campuses, shopping centers, educational institutions, and similar facilities. About 30 percent of landscaping companies had residential customers.

Landscape and groundskeeping encompass a wide range of activities. Landscape architects and designers develop attractive green spaces. Then, groundskeepers and landscapers implement these plans by preparing the soil; building terraces, retaining walls, pathways, patios, and irrigation systems; planting flowers, shrubs, and trees; seeding lawns; and then caring for and maintaining the lawns, plantings, and trees. Specialists like pesticide handlers and arborists play roles in making sure that flowers, shrubs, and trees don't fall victim to diseases, pests, and insects.

Turfgrass is a separate category that deals specifically with planting and maintaining athletic fields and golf courses.

JOBS PROFILED HERE

The following occupations are profiled in this chapter:

- Arborist
- First-Line Supervisor/Manager of Agricultural Crop and Horticultural Workers
- First-Line Supervisor/Manager of Landscaping, Lawn Service, and Groundskeeping Workers
- Landscape Architect
- Landscape Designer
- Landscaping and Groundskeeping Worker
- Lawn Care Specialist

- Nursery and Greenhouse Manager
- Pesticide Handler, Sprayer, and Applicator
- Turfgrass Manager

KEY TO UNDERSTANDING THE JOB PROFILES

The job profiles are classified according to one or more of the following categories:

☼ Bright Outlook
🌎 Green Occupation

The classifications "Bright Outlook" and "Green Occupation" are taken from the National Center for O*NET Development's O*NET OnLine job site. O*NET, which is sponsored by the U.S. Department of Labor/Employment and Training Administration (USDOL/ETA), has broken green jobs into three categories:

- Green Increased-Demand occupations
  - o These are occupations that are likely to see job growth, but the work and worker requirements are unlikely to experience significant changes.
- Green Enhanced-Skills occupations
  - o These occupations are likely to experience significant changes in work and worker requirements. Workers may find themselves doing new tasks requiring new knowledge, skills, and credentials. Current projections do not anticipate increased demand for workers in these occupations, but O*NET notes that an increase is possible.
- Green New and Emerging occupations
  - o These are new occupations—not growth in existing jobs—that are created as a result of activity and technology in green sectors of the economy.

Arborist

Alternate Titles and Related Careers

- Aerial Lift Operator
- Arboretum/Parks/Botanical Garden Arborist
- Arboriculture Consultant
- Climber
- Crew Leader
- Ground Worker
- Line Clearance Foreman
- Manager, Tree Care Company
- Municipal Arborist/Forester
- Plant Health Care Integrated Pest Management (PHC IPM) Monitor
- Plant Health Care Integrated Pest Management (PHC IPM) Technician
- Product/Equipment Manufacturer Salesperson
- Tree Care Foreman
- Tree Care Salesperson
- Tree Trimmer and Pruner ☼
- Urban Forester
- Utility Forestry Manager

This list of jobs is adapted from the International Society of Arboriculture and O*NET and shows the variety of jobs available to those interested in tree care.

Job Trends

The Bureau of Labor Statistics projects a much faster than average growth rate of 20 percent or higher for the category of tree trimmer and pruner between 2008 and 2018. The need for workers to plant and maintain attractive outdoor spaces for homeowners, educational institutions, government facilities, and businesses is driving demand for workers in this occupational category as it is in other landscaping and groundskeeping occupations.

Nature of the Work

Arborists work for commercial tree care companies, public utilities, and government agencies. They may begin as ground workers pruning and trimming trees and shrubs and move on to specialize in climbing trees and clearing power lines of overhanging branches. The purpose is to maintain right-of-way for roads, sidewalks, or utilities and to improve the appearance, health, and value of the trees. Some arborists become plant health care technicians using integrated pest management methods to treat tree diseases.

Tree trimmers and pruners may use climbing equipment such as hooks and belts or buckets of extended truck booms and ladders to reach their work area and chainsaws, hooks, handsaws, shears, and clippers to trim and prune trees. In the course of their work, they may operate boom trucks, loaders, stump chippers, brush chippers, tractors, power saws, trucks, and other equipment and tools. Depending on their jobs, arborists may also use sprayers and other forms of pesticide applicators.

Among the tasks that tree trimmers and pruners may perform are the following, based on O*NET surveys:

- Cut away dead and excess branches from trees, or clear branches around power lines
- Trim, top, and reshape trees to achieve attractive shapes or to remove low-hanging branches
- Prune, cut down, fertilize, and spray trees as directed by tree surgeons
- Inspect trees to determine if they have diseases or pest problems
- Spray trees to treat diseased or unhealthy trees, including mixing chemicals and calibrating spray equipment
- Cable, brace, tie, bolt, stake, and guy trees and branches to provide support
- Clear sites, streets, and grounds of woody and herbaceous materials, such as tree stumps and fallen trees and limbs
- Trim jagged stumps, using saws or pruning shears
- Transplant and remove trees and shrubs, and prepare trees for moving
- Water, root-feed, and fertilize trees

- Apply tar or other protective substances to cut surfaces to seal surfaces, and to protect them from fungi and insects
- Scrape decayed matter from cavities in trees and fill holes with cement to promote healing and to prevent further deterioration
- Install lightning protection on trees
- Operate shredding and chipping equipment, and feed limbs and brush into the machines
- Collect and load debris and refuse from tree trimming and removal operations onto trucks and haul it away for disposal
- Supervise others engaged in tree trimming work and train lower-level employees
- Provide information to the public regarding trees, such as advice on tree care
- Plan and develop budgets for tree work, and estimate the monetary value of trees
- Present and explain tree care plans to clients

Tree trimmers and pruners may also be called after storms to clean up fallen trees and assist in utility line clearance work.

About Polluting Stormwater

States and municipalities typically have programs that protect the quality of water including stormwater. Some things that foul water are fertilizers, pesticides, lawn and garden care products, and grass clippings. Limiting the use of fertilizers, pesticides, and lawn care products and trying nonchemical alternatives such as composting food wastes and grass clippings can help protect the sources of groundwater.

Career Path

The ISA provides several career paths in arboriculture. Each begins with entry-level positions as ground workers working under experienced crew leaders. Over time, as workers gain experience and on-the-job training, they may advance to higher positions such as crew leader and manager. Some choose to specialize as aerial lift operators or plant health-care technicians. Some open their own tree care businesses.

Earning Potential

Median hourly wage (2009): $14.57

Median annual wage (2009): $30,310

(Based on "Tree Trimmer and Pruner")

Education/Licensure

For jobs as arborists, a degree in aboriculture or a related science such as horticulture, forestry, or landscaping is necessary. For some jobs, an associate degree may be sufficient, but other jobs may require a bachelor's degree.

The International Society of Arboriculture (ISA) offers six certifications: ISA Certified Arborist, ISA Certified Arborist/Utility Specialist, ISA Certified Arborist/Municipal Specialist, ISA Certified Tree Worker/Climber Specialist, ISA Certified Tree Worker/Aerial Lift Specialist, and ISA Board-Certified Master Arborist. ISA also offers a variety of continuing education units. Certification requires an associate degree and a certain number of years of experience for each level.

The Tree Care Industry Association offers the Certified Treecare Safety Professional (CTSP) Certification. This is a train-the-trainer program. TCIA trains tree care professionals to become safety trainers who can then set up safety programs for their employers and train other company members in safety measures.

Most states require that workers who apply pesticides must be licensed or certified. States have different requirements, but typically a person must take and pass a test on the use and disposal of insecticides, fungicides, and herbicides.

For More Information

International Society of Arboriculture (ISA)
P.O. Box 3129
Champaign, Illinois 61826-3129
217-355-9411
www.isa-arbor.com

Tree Care Industry Association
136 Harvey Road
Suite 101
Londonderry, New Hampshire 03053
603-314-5380
www.treecareindustry.org

Utility Arborist Association (UAA)
P.O. Box 3129
Champaign, Illinois 61826-3129
217-355-9411
www.utilityarborist.org

First-Line Supervisor/Manager of Agricultural Crop and Horticultural Workers 🌐

Alternate Titles and Related Careers

- Farm Manager
- Farm Owner Operator
- Field Operations Farm Manager
- Grove Manager
- Grower
- Pest Management Supervisor
- Supervisor Grower

This is considered a "Green Increased-Demand" occupation in the agricultural and forestry green sector of the economy.

Job Trends

Using the category of First-Line Supervisors/Managers of Farming, Fishing, and Forestry Workers as the basis, the Bureau of Labor Statistics projects an average growth rate of 7 to 13 percent for workers in this category between 2008 and 2018. Whereas the consolidation of farms and the increasing productivity of large-scale agriculture are reducing the number of small-scale self-employed farmers, the same trends are resulting in increasing opportunities for managers.

Nature of the Work

The supervisor/manager of agricultural crop and horticultural workers directly supervises and coordinates the activities of agricultural crop or horticultural workers. Agricultural and horticultural managers manage the day-to-day operations of farms, nurseries, timber tracts, and greenhouses for farmers, absentee landowners, or corporations. Managers who specialize in horticulture oversee the production of fruits, vegetables, flowers, ornamental plants, and turf used in landscaping.

According to O*NET, supervisors of agricultural crop and horticultural workers may perform the following tasks:

- Inspect crops, fields, and plant stock to determine conditions and need for cultivating, spraying, weeding, or harvesting
- Read inventory records, customer orders, and shipping schedules to determine required activities
- Estimate labor requirements for jobs, and plan work schedules accordingly
- Assign duties such as cultivation, irrigation and harvesting of crops or plants, product packaging and grading, and equipment maintenance
- Observe workers to detect inefficient and unsafe work procedures or to identify problems, initiating corrective action as necessary
- Review employees' work to evaluate quality and quantity
- Plan and supervise infrastructure and collections maintenance functions such as planting, fertilizing, pest and weed control, and landscaping
- Requisition and purchase supplies such as insecticides, machine parts or lubricants, and tools
- Direct or assist with the adjustment and repair of farm equipment and machinery
- Train workers in techniques such as planting, harvesting, weeding, and insect identification, and in the use of safety measures
- Drive and operate farm machinery such as trucks, tractors, or self-propelled harvesters

in order to transport workers and supplies, or to cultivate and harvest fields

- Issue equipment such as farm implements, machinery, ladders, or containers to workers, and collect equipment when work is complete
- Confer with managers to evaluate weather and soil conditions, to develop plans and procedures, and to discuss issues such as changes in fertilizers, herbicides, or cultivating techniques
- Inspect facilities to determine maintenance needs
- Calculate and monitor budgets for maintenance and development of collections, grounds, and infrastructure
- Monitor and oversee construction projects such as horticultural buildings and irrigation systems
- Perform hardscape activities including installation and repair of irrigation systems, resurfacing and grading of paths, rockwork, or erosion control
- Recruit, hire, and discharge workers, contracting with seasonal workers and farmers to provide employment
- Investigate grievances and settle disputes to maintain harmony among workers
- Arrange for transportation, equipment, and living quarters for seasonal workers
- Prepare and maintain time and payroll reports, as well as details of personnel actions such as performance evaluations, hires, promotions, and disciplinary actions
- Prepare reports regarding farm conditions, crop yields, machinery breakdowns, or labor problems

Career Path

New managers often begin their careers working under experienced farmers. As they gain experience, they work more independently and in time may advance to positions where they oversee a single activity or the entire operation of a farm, nursery, or orchard.

Earning Potential

Median hourly wage (2009): $19.47

Median annual wage (2009): $40,500

(Based on First-Line Supervisors/Managers of Farming, Fishing, and Forestry Workers)

Education/Licensure

Some managers begin their training on the family farm. However, with the increasing complexity of agricultural operations, an associate or bachelor's degree has become important. O*NET notes that this occupation may require a background in agriculture, agriculture operations, and related sciences; agronomy and crop science; or plant sciences. In addition, courses in agricultural economics and business and farm management are useful.

The American Society of Farm Managers and Rural Appraisers offers the voluntary Accredited Farm Manager (AFM) certification. In addition to several years of experience, those qualifying for this certification must have a bachelor's, and preferably a master's, degree.

Most states require that workers who apply pesticides must be licensed or certified. States have different requirements, but typically a person must take and pass a test on the use and disposal of insecticides, fungicides, and herbicides.

About On-the-Job Health and Safety

The National Institute for Occupational Safety and Health (NIOSH) offers workplace health and safety tips for a number of industries, including construction, highway work zones, and other outdoor workers. Check out the information at www.cdc.gov/niosh/topics/industries.html.

For More Information

American Society of Farm Managers and Rural Appraisers (ASFMRA)
950 Cherry Street
Suite 508
Denver, Colorado 80246-2664
303-758-3513
www.asfram.org

ATTRA, National Sustainable Agriculture Information Service
P.O. Box 3657
Fayetteville, Arkansas 72702-3657
800-346-9140 (toll-free)
www.attra.ncat.org

First-Line Supervisor/Manager of Landscaping, Lawn Service, and Groundskeeping Workers

Alternate Titles and Related Careers

- Athletic Fields Superintendent
- Buildings and Grounds Supervisor
- Golf Course Superintendent
- Grounds Crew Supervisor
- Grounds Foreman
- Grounds Maintenance Supervisor
- Grounds Supervisor
- Groundskeeper Supervisor
- Landscape Manager
- Landscape Supervisor

While not currently categorized as a "green" job, this occupation impacts water and energy resource use.

Job Trends

The Bureau of Labor Statistics projects that the number of workers needed to keep up with the demand for lawn care and landscaping services will be among the largest for all occupations between 2008 and 2018. The Bureau estimates approximately 269,200 new workers will be needed. The demand is being driven by corporations, universities, and office complexes with large campuses and also by individual homeowners. As the population ages, elderly homeowners will need lawn care services to help maintain their yards.

A corresponding number of managers will be needed to keep up with the increase in workers. The Bureau of Labor Statistics projects a faster than average growth rate of 14 to 19 percent for this occupation. This means an increase of 56,000 workers between 2008 and 2018.

About the PLANET Alliance with OSHA

The Professional Landcare Network (PLANET) and the U.S. Occupational Safety and Health Administration formed an alliance in 2008 to provide information and access to training resources to protect workers from on-the-job injuries. Visit www.osha.gov/dcsp/alliances/planet/planet.html for more information.

Nature of the Work

First-line supervisors/managers of landscaping, lawn service, and groundskeeping workers plan, organize, direct, or coordinate the activities of workers engaged in landscaping or groundskeeping activities. These may include planting and maintaining ornamental trees, shrubs, flowers, and lawns. In following a landscape design, managers may also direct workers in terracing hillsides, building retaining walls, constructing pathways, installing patios, and similar activities. Managers must be able to review contracts in order to determine the work, machines, and labor needs of a job and to prepare estimates. Managers must have good communication skills in order to answer questions about work methods, materials, and costs from potential clients.

According to O*NET, first-line supervisors/managers of landscaping, lawn service, and groundskeeping workers may perform the following:

- Review contracts or work assignments to determine service, machine, and workforce requirements for jobs

- Establish and enforce operating procedures and work standards that will ensure adequate performance and personnel safety

- Schedule work for crews depending on work priorities, crew and equipment availability, and weather conditions

- Direct activities of workers who perform duties such as landscaping, cultivating lawns, or pruning trees and shrubs

- Monitor project activities to ensure that instructions are followed, deadlines are met, and schedules are maintained

- Train workers in tasks such as transplanting and pruning trees and shrubs, finishing cement, using equipment, and caring for turf

- Provide workers with assistance in performing duties as necessary to meet deadlines

- Inspect completed work to ensure conformance to specifications, standards, and contract requirements

- Inventory supplies of tools, equipment, and materials to ensure that sufficient supplies are available and items are in usable condition

- Confer with other supervisors to coordinate work activities with those of other departments or units

- Direct or perform mixing and application of fertilizers, insecticides, herbicides, and fungicides

- Identify diseases and pests affecting landscaping, and order appropriate treatments

- Order the performance of corrective work when problems occur, and recommend procedural changes to avoid such problems.

- Investigate work-related complaints in order to verify problems, and to determine responses

- Direct and assist workers engaged in the maintenance and repair of equipment such as power tools and motorized equipment

- Install and maintain landscaped areas, performing tasks such as removing snow, pouring cement curbs, and repairing sidewalks
- Confer with managers and landscape architects to develop plans and schedules for landscaping maintenance and improvement
- Tour grounds such as parks, botanical gardens, cemeteries, or golf courses to inspect conditions of plants and soil
- Design and supervise the installation of sprinkler systems, calculating water pressure, and valve and pipe coverage needs
- Answer inquiries from current or prospective customers regarding methods, materials, and price ranges
- Negotiate with customers regarding fees for landscaping, lawn service, or groundskeeping work
- Prepare service estimates based on labor, material, and machine costs, and maintain budgets for individual projects
- Perform personnel-related activities such as hiring workers, evaluating staff performance, and taking disciplinary actions when performance problems occur
- Prepare and maintain required records such as personnel information, project records, and work activity reports
- Perform administrative duties such as authorizing leaves and processing time sheets
- Recommend changes in working conditions or equipment use, in order to increase crew efficiency

Career Path

Entry-level workers may begin as laborers on grounds maintenance crews and learn their trade through on-the-job training under an experienced supervisor. Some may advance to crew leader or other supervisory positions. Supervisors may receive several months of on-the-job training.

Becoming a grounds manager or landscape contractor may require some formal education beyond high school plus several years' experience. Some managers choose to start their own landscaping businesses.

Earning Potential

Median hourly wage (2009): $19.69

Median annual wage (2009): $40,950

Education/Licensure

The majority of currently employed managers in this occupation have a high school diploma or equivalent. However, 31 percent have some college, which may include an associate degree, and 15 percent have a bachelor's degree or higher. Formal training in landscape design, horticulture, arboriculture, or business may improve a person's chances for employment, according to the *Occupational Outlook Handbook*.

The Professional Grounds Management Society offers the Certified Grounds Manager Certification for managers who have either a bachelor of science in a recognized green industry field or a two-year degree. To qualify, candidates must also have a certain number of years of experience in groundskeeping including supervisory experience.

The Professional Landcare Network offers Landscape Industry Certified Manager and Landscape Industry Certified Lawn Care Manager. The latter program was developed by the University of Georgia's Center for Continuing Education and includes turfgrass problems and Integrated Pest Management concepts.

Most states require that workers who apply pesticides must be licensed or certified. States have different requirements, but typically a person must take and pass a test on the use and disposal of insecticides, fungicides, and herbicides.

For More Information

Landscape Contractors Association—Maryland, District of Columbia, and Virginia
9707 Key West Avenue
Suite 100
Rockville, Maryland 20850
301-948-0810
www.lcamddcava.org

Professional Grounds Management Society
720 Light Street
Baltimore, Maryland 21230
410-223-2861
www.pgms.org

Professional Landcare Network (PLANET)
950 Herndon Parkway
Suite 450
Herndon, Virginia 20170
800-395-2522 (toll-free)
www.landcarenetwork.org

Landscape Architect ✿ 🌐

Alternate Titles and Related Careers

- Environmental Landscape Architect
- Golf Course Architect
- Land Planner
- Project Manager

This is considered a "Bright Outlook" and "Green Enhanced-Skills" occupation in the green construction, agricultural and forestry, and environment protection sector of the economy.

 http://bit.ly/career31

Job Trends

The Bureau of Labor Statistics projects a growth rate of 20 percent or higher, which is much faster than average for all occupations. Job openings are estimated to be 9,800 between 2008 and 2018. One factor increasing the demand for landscape architects is new construction to meet the needs of the growing population. Increasingly, landscape architects are also needed in planning the remediation and restoration of environmentally sensitive sites, such as wetlands and forests, and in preserving and restoring historic sites. Even the planning of safe bike trails and walkways involves landscape architects.

More than half of all landscape architects work for architectural, engineering, and related services. Almost 21 percent are self-employed. About 6 percent work for state and local governments. Most work in urban and suburban areas, but some who work for the federal government design recreation areas and parks in rural areas.

Nature of the Work

Landscape architects plan and design land areas for a variety of projects including residential developments, hospitals, college campuses, parks, recreation areas, golf courses, shopping centers, parkways, and airports.

Environmental landscape architects are involved in many types of environmental projects. They design plans for remediating and restoring natural sites such as forested areas, mining sites, stream corridors, and wetlands. They also work in national parks and recreation areas and preserve and restore historic sites and cultural landscapes. In their work, they consult with hydrologists, environmental scientists, and foresters.

About Organic Gardening

The National Gardening Association's 2008 Environmental Lawn and Garden survey estimated that 12 million U.S. households were using only all-natural fertilizers, insecticides, and weed control agents. This is up from 5 million in 2004. The National Gardening Association projected that if all the households that responded to the survey that they would use all-natural methods in the future actually did, 17 million households would be helping to reduce the risk of harmful chemicals in the nation's air, soil, and groundwater.

Green building and sustainable design also require the expertise of landscape architects. They design green roofs and plan tree coverage. These designs save energy, reduce runoff, and improve water and air quality. The U.S. Green Building Council LEED (Leadership in Energy and Environmental Design) building certification includes credit for a sustainable site that minimizes water use, erosion, light pollution, and other environmental impact.

Among the tasks that landscape architects perform according to O*NET are the following:

- Confer with clients, engineering personnel, and architects on overall program
- Consider the natural elements of the site, such as land contours, drainage, sunlight, and climate
- Consider how the site should function and where to place walkways, roads, gardens, and even buildings
- Prepare site plans, specifications, and cost estimates for land development, coordinating arrangement of existing and proposed land features and structures
- Prepare graphic representations and drawings of proposed plans and designs
- Compile and analyze data on conditions such as location, drainage, and location of structures for environmental reports and landscaping plans
- Inspect landscape work to ensure compliance with specifications, approve quality of materials and work, and advise client and construction personnel
- Seek new work opportunities through marketing, writing proposals or giving presentations
- Stay up to date on federal, state, and local environmental regulations and zoning laws

Much of the work of landscape architects is done using computer-aided design (CAD) programs and, for larger projects, geographic information systems (GIS).

Career Path

Generally, beginning landscape architects are apprentices or interns for about three years, working under the supervision of a licensed landscape architect. During this time, they do research and prepare drawings, but they are not responsible for the entire project. After becoming licensed, they take on responsibility for their own projects. With more experience, they may become managers or partners in a firm. Some may work as consultants or environmental planners. Many are self-employed.

Earning Potential

Median hourly wage (2009): $29.12

Median annual wage (2009): $60,650

Education/Licensure

A bachelor's degree in landscape architecture from an accredited school is the minimum requirement for a job. The Landscape Architectural Accreditation Board (LAAB), under the auspices of the American Society of Landscape Architects (ASLA), accredits educational programs. Some programs are in specialized schools, such as Boston Architectural College. Most programs include a design-studio experience. Employers also recommend that undergraduates participate in internships.

A master's degree is an advantage. Master's degree programs require two years for students entering with a bachelor's degree in landscape architecture and three years for those entering with a degree in another area. Training in urban planning is an advantage in finding a job in firms that do site planning and landscape design.

According to the ASLA, forty-nine states require licensing because landscape architecture has an impact on the safety, health, and welfare of the public. The Council of Landscape Architectural Registration Boards sponsors the national licensing exam. Before taking the exam, a candidate must have a degree from an accredited school and one to four years' experience (three years' apprenticeship is typical) under a licensed landscape architect, depending on state laws. In addition, fifteen states require passing a state exam. Continuing education is required in most states to maintain one's license.

The U.S. Green Building Council offers LEED (Leadership in Energy and Environmental Design) Professional Accreditation.

For More Information

American Society of Landscape Architects
636 Eye Street, NW
Washington, DC 20001-3736
888-999-2752 (toll-free)
www.asla.org

Council of Landscape Architectural Registration
    Boards
3949 Pender Drive
Suite 120
Fairfax, Virginia 22030
571-432-0332
www.clarb.org

U.S. Green Building Council (USGBC)
2101 L Street, NW
Suite 500
Washington, DC 20037
800-795-1747 (toll-free)
www.usgbc.org

Landscape Designer

Alternate Titles and Related Careers

- Head Horticulturist
- Landscape Design Estimator
- Landscape Design Project Director

A landscape designer typically has a different educational background from that of a landscape architect. The latter is a "Bright Outlook" and "Green Enhanced-Skills" occupation in the green construction, environment protection, and agriculture and forestry sectors of the economy.

Job Trends

Using the category of landscape architects as a basis, the projected growth for landscape designers would be 20 percent, or much faster than average between 2008 and 2018. The demand is driven by the increasing interest of individuals, institutions, and businesses to improve the appearance of their properties.

Nature of the Work

Landscape designers create designs for outdoor spaces such as around building exteriors, and along driveways, steps, and walkways. They may also design public and private gardens. Knowledge of basic design, color theory, balance, and proportion is important as well as a knowledge of horticulture. A designer needs to know what plants, shrubs, and trees grow well in a particular region based on soil, temperature, and moisture levels.

Among the tasks that landscape designers may perform are the following:

- Meet with clients including private individuals, facility managers, engineers, and architects to confer on an overall plan or program
- Prepare site plans, specifications, and cost estimates
- Prepare drawing of proposed plan
- Maintain records of work activities
- Supervise contractors implementing design plan
- Inspect completed work to ensure conformity with design plan
- Stay up to date on trends in landscape design

If self-employed, a landscape designer may:

- Market and advertise services to attract new business
- Hire, train, and manage employees.
- Maintain personnel records
- Pay bills including payroll

Career Path

Landscape designers may begin their careers working for landscape contractors, landscape design firms, and plant nurseries and garden supply stores that provide design services. In time, some designers open their own consulting businesses.

Earning Potential

Median hourly wage (2009): $29.12

Median annual wage (2009): $60,560

(Based on "Landscape Architect" category)

Education/Licensure

Landscape designers may have a two-year certificate in landscape design, or an associate or bachelor's degrees in landscape design or an allied field such as horticulture or ornamental horticulture. In addition to coursework in landscape design, students take courses in plant materials, site analysis, trends in landscape design, and construction materials and methods. Some universities also offer a master's degree or certificate in landscape design.

The Association of Professional Landscape Designers (APLD) offers a certification for landscape designers after a minimum of four years of job experience. Candidates must submit a design project for initial certification. Like most certification programs, APLD requires a certain number of hours of continuing education to retain certification.

For More Information

American Society for Horticultural Science (ASHS)
1018 Duke Street
Alexandria, Virginia 22314
703-836-4606
www.ashs.org

Association of Professional Landscape Designers (APLD)
4305 North Sixth Street
Suite A
Harrisburg, Pennsylvania 17110
717-238-9780
www.apld.org

Landscaping and Groundskeeping Worker ☼

Alternate Titles and Related Careers

- Gardener
- Greenskeeper
- Groundskeeper
- Grounds/Maintenance Specialist
- Grounds Maintenance Worker
- Grounds Supervisor
- Grounds Technician
- Grounds Worker
- Landscape Technician
- Lawn Care Technician
- Outside Maintenance Worker

This is considered a "Bright Outlook" occupation, and it has impact on the use of energy and water as well as the environment.

Job Trends

The Bureau of Labor Statistics projects that this occupation will require 362,200 new workers between 2008 and 2018. The occupation is expected to grow much faster than average at 14 to 19 percent. More workers are needed to keep up with increasing demand for lawn care and landscaping services.

The aging population of homeowners will require help in maintaining their properties, and corporate parks, college and university campuses, hospitals, shopping centers, and similar institutions and businesses use landscaping and groundskeeping personnel to plant and maintain attractive environments for employees and the public. Another source of employment is golf courses where greens and fairways require constant maintenance.

Nature of the Work

Landscaping and groundskeeping workers typically perform a variety of tasks that may include laying sod, mowing, trimming, planting, watering, fertilizing, digging, raking, and installing sprinklers. These workers may also install mortarless segmental concrete masonry wall units. Among the tools they may use are hand tools such as shovels, rakes, pruning saws, saws, shears, hedge and brush trimmers, axes, tillers, fertilizer spreaders, box blades, soil probes, and flexible chain-link harrows. They may also operate powered equipment such as mowers, tractors, twin-axle vehicles, snow blowers, chain-saws, electric clippers, sod cutters, and pruning saws.

According to O*NET, landscaping and groundskeeping workers may perform the following tasks:

- Mow and edge lawns
- Care for established lawns by mulching, aerating, weeding, grubbing and removing thatch, and trimming and edging around flower beds, walks, and walls
- Prune and trim trees, shrubs, and hedges
- Maintain and repair tools, equipment, and structures such as buildings, greenhouses, fences, and benches, using hand and power tools
- Mix and spray or spread fertilizers, herbicides, or insecticides onto grass, shrubs, and trees
- Provide proper upkeep of sidewalks, driveways, parking lots, fountains, planters, burial sites, and other grounds features
- Water lawns, trees, and plants
- Trim and pick flowers, and clean flower beds
- Rake, mulch, and compost leaves
- Gather and remove litter
- Follow planned landscaping designs to determine where to lay sod, sow grass, or plant flowers and foliage
- Plant seeds, bulbs, foliage, flowering plants, grass, ground covers, trees, and shrubs, and apply mulch for protection, using gardening tools
- Haul or spread topsoil, and spread straw over seeded soil to hold soil in place decorate gardens with stones and plants
- Maintain irrigation systems, including winterizing the systems and starting them up in spring
- Use irrigation methods to adjust the amount of water consumption and to prevent waste
- Attach wires from planted trees to support stakes
- Install rock gardens, ponds, decks, drainage systems, irrigation systems, retaining walls, fences, planters, and/or playground equipment
- Build forms, and mix and pour cement to form garden borders
- Plan and cultivate lawns and gardens
- Advise customers on plant selection and care
- Shovel snow from walks, driveways, and parking lots, and spread salt in those areas

Groundskeepers who work with both natural and artificial turf may perform the following tasks:

- Care for natural turf fields, making sure the underlying soil has the required composition to allow proper drainage and to support the grasses used on the fields
- Care for artificial turf fields, periodically removing the turf and replacing cushioning pads, and vacuuming and disinfecting the turf after use to prevent the growth of harmful bacteria
- Mark design boundaries, and paint natural and artificial turf fields with team logos and names before events

Career Path

Most entry-level grounds maintenance workers have a high school diploma or equivalent. Workers who show competency in their work as well as an interest in advancing and who possess good communication and interpersonal relations skills may be promoted to supervisor or crew chief. Some additional training may be required.

In time, groundskeepers may become landscape, lawn care, or groundskeeping managers. Some may decide to go into business for themselves. About 22 percent of currently employed landscaping and groundskeeping workers are self-employed.

Earning Potential

Median hourly wage (2009): $11.29

Median annual wage (2009): $23,480

Education/Licensure

Most entry-level landscaping and groundskeeping workers learn their trade on the job. Basic information includes how to plant and maintain plantings, how to operate equipment, and how to create a safe work environment. According to the *Occupational Outlook Handbook,* groundskeepers who work for institutional employers such as golf courses and municipalities may be offered courses in subjects such as horticulture and small engine repair. Coursework in landscape design, horticulture, and arboriculture can be an advantage for advancement.

Also, obtaining voluntary certification from a professional organization can be an advantage in seeking promotions. The Professional Grounds Management Society (PGMS) offers the Certified Grounds Technician (CGT) Certification for landscaping and groundskeeping workers with a high school diploma or GED and at least two years' experience.

The Professional Landcare Network offers the following certifications: Landscape Industry Certified Technician\-Exterior, Landscape Industry Certified Horticultural Technician, and the Landscape Industry Certified Lawn Care Technician.

The Landscape Contractors Association offers a Certified Landscape Technician Certification. Specialties include turf and ornamental maintenance, softscape installation, and softscape and hardscape installation.

Most states require that workers who apply pesticides must be licensed or certified. States have different requirements, but typically a person must take and pass a test on the use and disposal of insecticides, fungicides, and herbicides.

For More Information

Landscape Contractors Association of Maryland, District of Columbia, and Virginia
9707 Key West Avenue
Suite 100
Rockville, Maryland 20850
301-948-0810
www.lcamddcava.org

Professional Grounds Management Society (PGMS)
720 Light Street
Baltimore, Maryland 21230
410-223-2861
www.pgms.org

Professional Landcare Network (PLANET)
950 Herndon Parkway
Suite 450
Herndon, Virginia 20170
800-395-2522 (toll-free)
www.landcarenetwork.org

Lawn Care Specialist

Alternate Titles and Related Careers

- Lawn Care Crew Leader
- Lawn Care Technician

Like other occupations related to landscaping and groundskeeping, this occupation impacts water and energy resources as well as the environment.

Job Trends

Using the "Grounds Maintenance Workers" category as the basis for comparison, the projected growth rate for lawn care specialists would be faster than average at 14 to 19 percent. The total projected number of new openings in this category is 362,200. As more housing developments, corporate parks, and educational campuses are built and expanded, the more grass there is to plant, mow, and maintain.

About Grass Tennis Courts

Perhaps the most famous grass tennis courts in the world are at the All England Club in England where the two-week international Wimbledon tennis championships are held annually. The grasses used on the courts are first tested by the Sports Turf Research Institute to see if they can withstand the kind of abuse that two weeks of tennis can inflict on the courts.

Nature of the Work

Lawn care specialists take care of lawns. They may work for lawn care companies that contract with homeowners and businesses or directly for homeowners, government facilities, health-care facilities, corporate parks, and colleges and universities. According to the lawn care specialist program at the University of Texas at Dallas, among the tasks that lawn care specialists may perform are the following:

- Seed lawns
- Mow the grass
- Apply fertilizer, pesticides, herbicides, and fungicides
- Prevent disease and pest invasions by using environmentally friendly methods of plant protection and integrated pest management
- Trim hedges, shrubs, and trees
- Consult with clients on a maintenance program for lawn care
- Perform routine follow-up when required
- Document activities and procedures
- Offer tips and guidance on lawn and garden care to clients

Lawn care specialists who work for themselves may also:

- Market and advertise services to attract new business
- Hire, train, and manage employees
- Maintain personnel records
- Pay bills including payroll

Career Path

Entry-level employees work under an experienced lawn care specialist. In time, they take on more responsibility and work more independently. They advance to crew leader or supervisor. Some lawn care specialists may go to work for nurseries or garden centers. Others start their own businesses.

Every state requires licensing for professional lawn care companies and most states also require certification of commercial lawn care companies. Anyone starting his or her own lawn care company must become familiar with the rules and regulations governing lawn care businesses in the state.

Earning Potential

Median hourly wage (2009): $11.29

Median annual wage (2009): $23,480

(Based on "Grounds Maintenance Workers")

Education/Licensure

Most training is on-the-job, but a high school diploma or equivalent is typically required. However, formal courses in landscaping, environmental studies, horticulture, and forestry are an advantage for entry-level candidates and for promotion. Most states require that workers who apply pesticides be licensed or certified. States have different requirements, but typically a person must take and pass a test on the use and disposal of insecticides, fungicides, and herbicides. Having this license when applying for a job can be a plus.

The Professional Landcare Network offers a Landscape Industry Certified Lawn Care Technician Certificate appropriate for lawn care professionals in the northern United States.

For More Information

Professional Landcare Network (PLANET)
950 Herndon Parkway
Suite 450
Herndon, Virginia 20170
800-395-2522 (toll-free)
www.landcarenetwork.org

Nursery and Greenhouse Manager

Alternate Titles and Related Careers

- Farm Manager
- Garden Center Manager
- Garden Supply Store Manager
- Greenhouse Manager
- Grower
- Horticulturist
- Lawn and Garden Center Manager
- Nursery Manager
- Perennial House Manager
- Production Manager
- Propagation Manager

This occupation impacts energy and water use as well as the environment.

Job Trends

The Bureau of Labor Statistics lists nursery and greenhouse managers as a slower-than-average growth occupation. The rate of growth is projected to be 3 to 6 percent. However, the *Occupational Outlook Handbook* notes the increased interest in landscaping by homeowners and businesses with a resulting increase in spending on shrubs, trees, turf, and ornamental plantings.

Nature of the Work

Nursery and greenhouse manages plan, organize, direct, control, and coordinate the activities of workers engaged in propagating, cultivating, and harvesting horticultural specialties including shrubs, trees, flowers, and other plants.

O*NET lists the following as tasks that nursery and greenhouse managers may perform:

- Manage nurseries that grow horticultural plants for sale to trade or retail customers, for display or exhibition, or for research
- Determine types and quantities of horticultural plants to be grown, based on budgets, projected sales volumes, and/or executive directives
- Assign work schedules and duties to nursery or greenhouse staff, and supervise their work
- Determine plant growing conditions, such as greenhouses, hydroponics, or natural settings, and set planting and care schedules
- Tour work areas to observe work being done, to inspect crops, and to evaluate plant and soil conditions
- Apply pesticides and fertilizers to plants
- Select and purchase seeds, plant nutrients, disease control chemicals, and garden and lawn care equipment
- Prepare soil for planting, and plant or transplant seeds, bulbs, and cuttings
- Cut and prune trees, shrubs, flowers, and plants
- Graft plants
- Position and regulate plant irrigation systems, and program environmental and irrigation control computer
- Identify plants as well as problems such as diseases, weeds, and insect pests
- Provide information to customers on the care of trees, shrubs, flowers, plants, and lawns
- Construct structures and accessories such as greenhouses and benches
- Negotiate contracts such as those for land leases or tree purchases
- Confer with horticultural personnel in order to plan facility renovations or additions
- Inspect facilities and equipment for signs of disrepair, and perform necessary maintenance work

- Coordinate clerical, recordkeeping, inventory, requisitioning, and marketing activities
- Hire employees, and train them in gardening techniques
- Explain and enforce safety regulations and policies

About Biodegradable Nursery Pots

The Horticulture Research Institute in partnership with the U.S. Department of Agriculture's Agricultural Research Institute has developed a biodegradable plant container made from keratin, a substance extracted from poultry feathers.

Career Path

Some entry-level nursery and greenhouse workers may begin their careers as workers in nurseries and greenhouses and then advance after years of experience and formal training to become managers. However, more employers are preferring candidates with formal education such as an associate or bachelor's degree.

Earning Potential

Median hourly wage (2009): $28.58

Median annual wage (2009): $59,450

(Based on "Farm, Ranch, and Other Agricultural Managers")

Education/Licensure

About 26 percent of currently employed nursery and greenhouse managers have a bachelor's degree or higher. Another 29 percent have some college, typically an associate degree. A background in horticultural science or a related life science field such as agriculture studies or botany is typical.

For More Information

American Nursery and Landscape Association
1000 Vermont Avenue, NW
Suite 300
Washington, DC 20005-4914
202-789-2900
www.anla.org

Horticulture Research Institute (HTI)
1000 Vermont Avenue, NW
Suite 300
Washington, DC 20005-4914
202-789-2900
www.hriresearch.org

Pesticide Handler, Sprayer, and Applicator

Alternate Titles and Related Careers

- Applicator
- Chemical Applicator
- Integrated Pest Management Technician (IPM)
- Lawn Technician
- Lawn Specialist
- Pest Control Technician
- Pesticides Applicator
- Spray Applicator
- Spray Technician
- Tree and Shrub Technician
- Turf and Ornamental Spray Technician

The new trend in this field is integrated pest management, or IPM, which promotes "a science-based approach to managing pests in ways that generate economic, environmental, and human health benefits," according to the mission statement of the Southern Region IPM Center. IPM seeks to limit the use of pesticides and similar products to control pests.

About IPM

As a first line of pest control, IPM programs work to manage the crop, lawn, or indoor space to prevent pests from becoming a threat. For agricultural crops, this may mean using cultural methods, such as rotating between different crops, selecting pest-resistant varieties, and planting pest-free rootstock. These control methods can be very effective and cost-efficient and present little to no risk to people or the environment. For more information on integrated pest management, visit www.epa.gov/opp00001/factsheets/ipm.htm.

Job Trends

The Bureau of Labor Statistics projects a faster-than-average growth rate of 14 to 19 percent for this occupation between 2008 and 2018. This translates into 9,100 jobs in this period. The demand is being driven by the same forces driving the demand for lawn care and landscaping services: an aging population of homeowners and an increasing number of housing developments, shopping centers, office complexes, educational institutions, government facilities, and similar areas that require landscaping. Keeping these lawns and plantings disease- and pest-free necessitates maintenance.

Nature of the Work

Pesticide handlers, sprayers, and applicators for vegetation work with pesticides, herbicides, fungicides, and insecticides. They mix and apply these compounds through sprays, dusts, vapors, soil incorporation, and/or chemical application on trees, shrubs, lawns, or botanical crops. Pesticide handlers must be familiar with various products and how to handle them safely including storing, using, and transporting them. The work usually requires specific training and licensing.

Among the tasks that pesticide handlers, sprayers, and applicators may perform are the following, according to O*NET:

- Fill sprayer tanks with water and chemicals, according to formulas
- Mix pesticides, herbicides, and fungicides for application to trees, shrubs, lawns, or botanical crops
- Cover areas to specified depths with pesticides, applying knowledge of weather conditions, droplet sizes, elevation-to-distance ratios, and obstructions
- Lift, push, and swing nozzles, hoses, and tubes in order to direct spray over designated areas
- Start motors and engage machinery, such as sprayer agitators and pumps or portable spray equipment
- Connect hoses and nozzles selected according to terrain, distribution pattern requirements, types of infestations, and velocities
- Clean and service machinery to ensure operating efficiency, using water, gasoline, lubricants, and/or hand tools
- Provide driving instructions to truck drivers to ensure complete coverage of designated areas, using hand and horn signals

Pesticide handlers who work for chemical lawn care companies are more specialized. They inspect lawns for problems and apply fertilizers, pesticides, and other chemicals to stimulate growth and prevent or control weeds, diseases, or insect infestation. Many use IPM methods. They may also seed problem lawns and cover them with hay to protect the new plants.

Career Path

Entry-level pesticide handlers begin working under experienced supervisors or crew chiefs. In time, some become supervisors themselves. Some pesticide handlers may decide to go into business for themselves. About 23 percent of currently employed pesticide handlers are self-employed.

About Pesticide Safety Education

Check the National Institute of Food and Agriculture at www.csrees.usda.gov/pesticides.cfm to find out more about pesticides and the Institute's Pesticide Safety Education Program (PSEP).

Earning Potential

Median hourly wage (2009): $14.39

Median annual wage (2009): $29,930

Education/Licensure

Most entry-level grounds maintenance workers have a high school diploma or equivalent and learn their trade on the job. However, some formal training may be needed because most states require that workers who apply pesticides be licensed or certified. States have different requirements, but typically a person must take and pass a test on the use and disposal of insecticides, fungicides, and herbicides. Having this license when applying for a job can be a plus.

Undergraduate and graduate programs are now available from some universities in IPM or Plant Protection and IPM if an individual wishes to specialize in this field. Programs typically include courses in plant pathology, entomology, weed science, crop science, and environmental toxicology.

For More Information

Association of American Pesticide Control Officials (AAPCO)
P.O. Box 466
Milford, Delaware 19963
302-422-8152
http://aapco.ceris.purdue.edu

Association of Applied IPM Ecologists (AAIE) [Integrated Pest Management]
P.O. Box 1119
Coarsegold, California 93614
559-761-1064
www.aaie.net

International Association for the Plant Protection Sciences (IAPPS)
Department of Entomology
University of Nebraska
Lincoln, Nebraska 68583-0816
402-472-6011
www.plantprotection.org

National Pest Management Association (NPMA)
10460 North Street
Fairfax, Virginia 22030
703-352-6762
www.pestworld.org

Southern Region Integrated Pest Management Center (SRIPMC)
North Carolina State University
1730 Varsity Drive
Suite 110
Raleigh, North Carolina 27606
www.sripmc.org

Turfgrass Manager

Alternate Titles and Related Careers

- Assistant Golf Course Superintendent
- Athletic Fields Superintendent
- Buildings and Grounds Supervisor
- Golf Course Superintendent
- Grounds Crew Supervisor
- Grounds Foreman
- Groundskeeper Supervisor
- Grounds Maintenance Supervisor
- Grounds Supervisor
- Landscape Manager
- Landscape Supervisor
- Sod Farm Manager
- Sports Turf Manager
- Turf Technician

While not currently categorized as a "green" job, this occupation impacts water and energy resource use. It is an interesting field for someone who has a commitment to the environment and likes sports and working outdoors.

Job Trends

Using First-Line Supervisors/Managers of Landscaping, Lawn Service, and Groundskeeping Workers as the overall category, turfgrass managers would see employment grow by 14 to 19 percent between 2008 and 2018, which is much faster than the average for all occupations.

About Turfgrass

The Michigan Turfgrass Stewardship Initiative of the Michigan Turfgrass Foundation has information on how turfgrass can mitigate environmental problems and create good jobs in urban areas. For more information, go to www.michiganturfgrass.org.

According to the Department of Plant Sciences at North Dakota State University, there is a demand nationwide for turfgrass managers. The University's Sports and Urban Turfgrass Management program reports that between 200 and 300 new golf courses are built in this country each year, and the cost for lawn care in this country totals more than $17 billion annually. The School of Environmental and Biological Sciences at Rutgers University notes that the industry has grown steadily and continues to generate a need for turfgrass professionals.

Turfgrass provides numerous benefits to people and the environment. In addition to providing an aesthetically pleasing surface for sports and recreation, it improves air quality and reduces effects of global warming by absorbing carbon dioxide from the atmosphere and releasing oxygen. It also reduces erosion and conserves soil. Like other green plants, turfgrass has a cooling effect in urban areas. Care of turfgrass, however, can be detrimental to the environment when pesticides and chemical fertilizers are used and when excessive watering is needed. The challenge for turfgrass managers is to use natural fertilizers and grass varieties that require less water and are resistant to pests.

Nature of the Work

Turfgrass managers are responsible for the maintenance of golf courses, football fields, baseball fields, soccer fields, college and university athletic fields, fields for professional sports, parks, corporate parks, and home lawns. Turfgrass managers may also work in sales, research, or consulting for environmental groups. Some manage turf farms where turf for playing fields, etc., is grown for sale.

Based on the O*NET list of activities for mangers of groundskeepers, turfgrass managers may perform the following:

- Establish and enforce operating procedures and work standards that will ensure adequate performance and personnel safety
- Schedule work for crews depending on work priorities, crew and equipment availability, and weather conditions
- Plant and maintain turf through activities such as mulching, fertilizing, watering, and mowing
- Design and supervise the installation of sprinkler systems, calculating water pressure, and valve and pipe coverage needs
- Identify diseases and pests affecting turf, and order appropriate treatments
- Direct mixing and application of fertilizers, insecticides, herbicides, and fungicides
- Confer with other supervisors to coordinate work activities with those of other departments or units
- Perform personnel-related activities such as hiring workers, evaluating staff performance, and taking disciplinary actions when performance problems occur
- Review work assignments to determine service, machine, and workforce requirements for jobs
- Maintain required records such as personnel information and project records
- Prepare and maintain required records such as work activity and personnel reports

- Order the performance of corrective work when problems occur, and recommend procedural changes to avoid such problems
- Investigate work-related complaints in order to verify problems, and to determine responses
- Direct and assist workers engaged in the maintenance and repair of equipment such as power tools and motorized equipment
- Inventory supplies of tools, equipment, and materials to ensure that sufficient supplies are available and items are in usable condition
- Recommend changes in working conditions or equipment use, in order to increase crew efficiency
- Train workers in tasks such as using equipment and caring for turf
- Monitor project activities to ensure that instructions are followed, deadlines are met, and schedules are maintained
- Inspect completed work to ensure conformance to specifications and standards

Golf course superintendents also:

- Must be able to measure and interpret the speed of greens
- Oversee relocation of holes in greens
- Direct the seeding and conditioning of the grass in fairways, greens, and tee boxes
- Replace worn and damaged turf

Career Path

Turfgrass graduates usually begin as assistants. After several years, they may become superintendents of a golf course or an athletic field. Moving to larger courses or private courses or a larger sports complex is one form of advancement. Some golf course superintendents may eventually become managers of an entire resort facility.

Earning Potential

Median hourly wage (2009): $19.69

Median annual wage (2009): $40,950

(Based on "First-Line Supervisors/Managers of Landscaping, Lawn Service, and Groundskeeping Workers")

Golf Course Superintendent:

Average annual salary: $57,000–$105,000

Starting salary (assistant with no experience): $28,000–$35,000

Education/Licensure

A bachelor's degree is required for jobs such as golf course superintendent or sports turf manager. A number of colleges and universities now offer specific degree programs or certificate programs in turfgrass management. A degree in agronomy or horticulture also qualifies a person to work in this area. Those with bachelor's degrees in other subjects may be able to enter the field by obtaining a certificate or associate degree in turfgrass management. Internship programs are good preparation. Some jobs may be available to those with an associate degree or other postsecondary training, but the best opportunities are for those who hold at least a bachelor's degree. Those with master's degrees may work in research or as agricultural extension agents.

Certification is voluntary. The Golf Course Superintendents Association offers the Certified Golf Course Superintendent (CGCS) certification. The Professional Grounds Management Society offers the Certified Grounds Manager (CGM) certification, which requires a combination of education, experience, and passing an exam. The Professional Landcare Network offers the Certified Turfgrass Professional (CTP) certification program through the University of Georgia. Completion of the self-study program and passing two exams are required.

For More Information

Golf Course Superintendents Association of
    America
1421 Research Park Drive
Lawrence, Kansas 66049
800-472-7878 (toll-free)
www.gcsaa.org

Michigan Turfgrass Foundation
3225 West St. Joseph
Lansing, Michigan 48917
517-327-9207
www.michiganturfgrass.org

Professional Grounds Management Society
720 Light Street
Baltimore, Maryland 21230
410-223-2861
www.pgms.org

Professional Landcare Network
950 Herndon Parkway, Suite 450
Herndon, Virginia 20170-5528
703-736-9666
www.landcarenetwork.org

Sports Turf Managers Association
805 New Hampshire
Suite E
Lawrence, Kansas 66044
800-323-3875 (toll-free)
www.stma.org

Turf Equipment Technicians Association of the
    Carolinas (TETAC)
P.O. Box 210
Liberty, South Carolina 29657-0210
800-476-4272 (toll-free)
http://www.tetac.org/

Turfgrass Producers International
2 East Main Street
East Dundee, Illinois 60118
847-649-5555
www.turfgrasssod.org

Greenscaping With Native Plants

You may know people who moved from one part of the country to another and tried to reproduce their garden or lawn. They found the task to be nearly impossible, requiring large amounts of water, fertilizer, or both. In addition, allergy sufferers who changed climates found no relief after planting sources of the pollen they were trying to leave behind!

Had these would-be gardeners stayed with plants native to their new regions, they might have had more success with less effort—and fewer allergy problems. Native plants are those that were growing in a region before Europeans arrived. Some 20,000 native plants have been identified; almost 25 percent of them are at risk of becoming extinct.

About a fourth of the plants now growing in North America are nonnative species. Plants that are not indigenous to the area can become invasive, choking out native plants and requiring more water to survive. An example is the saltmarsh cordgrass that is native to coastal salt marshes in the Gulf and Atlantic Coast regions. When it was transplanted to the West Coast to restore marshes there, it became invasive, killing off native plants.

Native species offer several advantages to gardeners:

1. Native plants have long adapted to local conditions and will thrive with a minimum of care, fertilizer, and water. Once established, they don't require much maintenance.

2. Native plants produce long root systems that can reduce soil erosion and cut down the need for irrigation or extra watering.

3. Native species also tend to be resistant to disease, drought, freezing, and pests.

4. By planting native species, you are helping to sustain birds, mammals, and other animals that rely on those native plants for shelter or food.

5. Using native species can help preserve the genetic diversity of those species, which can vary a great deal based on environmental conditions.

6. Because native plants stay greener for a longer period of time, they slow the spread of fire.

Some Native Trees and Flowers by Region

- Northeast — Eastern red cedar, cardinal flower (bellflower)
- Midwest — black oak, wild columbine
- Southeast — Sweetbay magnolia, climbing aster
- Rocky Mountains — quaking aspen, scarlet gilia (skyrocket)
- Pacific Northwest — Douglas fir, red columbine
- Southwest — Rocky Mountain juniper, blackfoot daisy
- Alaska — western hemlock, heartleaf arnica
- Hawaii — diversity changes from island to island; check with local garden centers

When choosing native plants, consider factors such as soil, amount of rain, drainage, and sunlight. In buying native species, look for the designation "nursery propagated," meaning that they came from cuttings or seeds rather than being removed from the wild. Native plants should not be dug up from natural areas. The only exception might be a site that is about to be developed. You may also obtain permission in some natural areas to collect seeds. If so, collect from multiple plants and don't take all the seeds from any one plant.

How Being Green Works for **Margaret (Meg) Gaffney, Landscape Architect**

Meg Gaffney, 38, is a landscape architect in Jacksonville, Florida, with her own practice. Gaffney jokes that she has worked in this green industry "since birth," but "in a paid capacity since 1988." Here, Gaffney designed the master plan and signage for Jacksonville's new arboretum.

Describe your job, including common daily tasks and long-term projects that you have worked on or are working on now. What, specifically, about your job makes it green?

As a landscape architect, I provide consultation, planning, and design of residential and commercial landscapes. This includes planting design; hardscape design; construction detailing; code conformance analysis; architectural, civil, and electrical coordination; creation of project narratives; specifications editing; construction administration; cost estimating; irrigation design; site furnishings selection; and site sculpture/art selection.

During a typical day, I am working on layout and design in my office, while answering e-mail and taking phone calls. In preparation for design, there are client meetings on site as well as communications over the phone or by e-mail. Following the initial meeting, there is a good deal of preparation in the way of securing a survey or performing on-site measurements and checking on county, historic, or neighborhood codes and requirements.

As I am in business for myself, I get to wear all the hats. There is plenty of administration to worry about, but the fun part is working with clients to create an outdoor environment that suits their needs and is in harmony with the location.

Anyone trained in the field of landscape architecture is highly aware of the environmental impacts of the human use of land. We are trained in both the undergraduate (five-year program) and graduate level (three-year program) in understanding local ecology and sustainability trends. I have always had a love of plants and so first studied horticulture as an undergraduate and then acquired a graduate degree in landscape architecture.

Every individual or practice interprets or creates its own particular philosophy. For my part, I work to find innovative and accessible ways for my clients to reduce their footprint, so to speak. For example, in a commercial parking lot I recommended two locally made paving surfaces that percolate stormwater. One was created with recycled tires and was produced within 300 miles of the site. The other was made locally with local materials.

Ensuring that my landscapes are efficient and beautiful is very important to me.

I strive to ensure that trees are placed to cool adjacent structures and understudy plantings are grouped for the most efficient irrigation. When possible, I work with a local irrigation supplier to design and install low-volume irrigation systems that utilize water harvested from rain.

Why/how did you decide to work in a green industry?

I have been a gardener since childhood. My second love was architecture. I originally went to college to study architecture and historic preservation. It simply clicked one day that landscape architecture fulfilled both pulls. It seems like I have been working towards this profession all of my life.

How did you prepare for your current position?

For one and a half years, I attended the Savannah College of Art and Design in the pursuit of an architecture degree. When I "buckled down," it was to secure a bachelor of science in ornamental horticulture and later a master's in landscape architecture, both through the University of Georgia. I am certified as a "legacy" LEED Accredited Professional.

Personal research into sustainable materials and practices has been very important. Extra training in computer rendering and hand-drawing arts has been indispensable. Most recently, I have spent a great deal of time helping to get a new arboretum off the ground here in Jacksonville. It has been very challenging and rewarding—and has added immensely to my understanding of my community.

Which aspect of your education and/or training do you think has been the most helpful and/or useful to you? Why?

All of it. Plus every minute I spent working in the green industry, gardening, volunteering, and visiting botanical institutions all over the world.

Do you find that the skills and/or knowledge required for your job continue to evolve? If so, what have you done to keep up-to-date?

You must always be learning. In this profession, it is important to stay up-to-date with trends in best practices, materials, and design.

How have continuing education and/or training impacted the way you do your job?

Continuing education and training must be managed and come at an expense that must be figured into your overhead. Being licensed is a huge endeavor that takes many people years to achieve. This particular part of our training directs the first years of our career, as landscape architects must work under a licensed professional before they can sit for their exams. That individual or office may well shape the track of your future work.

After you have your license, you must continue to take additional training to keep your license. This covers everything from current practice and theory to knowing what materials and suppliers are available.

What is the most rewarding part of your work, and what do you find to be the most challenging?

The most rewarding part of being a landscape architect is merging the practical with the creative to design beautiful spaces for people to enjoy. The most challenging is that it's multi-faceted. I think it's to deliver a space that performs for the client that is environmentally sensitive and responds to local city and regional environmental requirements.

What advice would you give to people interested in pursuing your career?

I would suggest that you visit a number of landscape architectural offices before entering a program and intern as soon as possible during your college career. This will really open your eyes to the spectrum of work performed in an office and help you choose where to apply for a job when the time comes.

How Being Green Works for
James Michael (Mike) Goatley, Jr., Turfgrass Specialist

Mike Goatley, 48, is an extension turfgrass specialist and associate professor in the Crop and Soil Environmental Sciences Department at Virginia Polytechnic Institute and State University (Virginia Tech) in Blacksburg, Virginia. Goatley has worked in this green industry for the past 27 years. Here, Goatley seeds research plots at the Raleigh County Solid Waste Management Authority in Beckley, West Virginia. The project, a joint study with the USDA-ARS laboratory in Beaver, West Virginia, is an investigation of soil compaction and topsoil depth.

Describe your job, including common daily tasks and long-term projects that you have worked on or are working on now.

As Virginia's extension turfgrass specialist, I have statewide responsibilities in the development and implementation of educational outreach programs for all areas of turfgrass management in the state. I organize and conduct field days, short courses, workshops, and conferences both on campus and around the state. My research program focuses on applied strategies in environmental stewardship in turfgrass management by way of cultivar selection, improved establishment and maintenance methods, and nutrient management.

I spend approximately 30 percent of my time traveling through the state for site visits and training with professional turfgrass managers (golf turf managers, sports turf managers, sod producers, professional lawn care operators, and parks and recreation supervisors) and the general public through Master Gardener training. At the office and in and around campus, I spend a great deal of time writing and leading field research trials at our Turfgrass Research Center. On a daily/ weekly basis, I am regularly in the development and publication phase of numerous scientific and popular press articles.

On a long-term scale, I am regularly involved in the development of books and/or book chapters. For instance, I was co-author on the second edition of *Sports Fields: Design, Construction and Maintenance,* which was published by John Wiley and Sons, Inc., in April 2010. I am currently serving as the editor and author of specific chapters on a book entitled *Urban Nutrient Management Handbook,* which is being written with peers in my college. I maintain a weblog podcast site detailing best management practices in lawn care for homeowners entitled "Turf and Garden Tips" (http://www.anr.ext.vt.edu/lawnandgarden/turfandgardentips/). On a national scale, I serve as the secretary-treasurer of the Sports Turf Managers Association of America and as a technical editor for our professional society's e-Journal "Applied Turfgrass Science."

What, specifically, about your job makes it green?

A large portion of my research and outreach efforts focus on best management practices in turfgrass maintenance, regardless of the management situation (golf, sports turf, lawns, sod, etc.). Each situation has its own unique challenges regarding user needs and expectations for what makes "acceptable" turf, and there are an unlimited number of ways to achieve that goal. There also are an unlimited number of wrong ways to manage turf.

My job provides me daily opportunities to educate—and in some cases, simply "remind"—turfgrass managers on the ways to achieve their goals in an environmentally responsible manner. . . . The largest block of my time is spent working with professionals who desire the best-looking, best-playing turfgrass surface possible. However, the often overlooked "true value" of turf is its functional use. This includes its ability to rapidly and efficiently stabilize soil, its filtration ability in capturing potentially damaging chemicals and sediments that can move into our water resources, its capacity as a carbon sequestration agent, and its ability to buffer extreme temperatures and noise. A turfed area has the potential to be one of the most environmentally responsible components of a landscape if it is managed properly, and that is something I regularly focus on in my research and outreach efforts.

Why/how did you decide to work in a green industry?

I was raised on a farm in Kentucky, and while I enjoyed watching things grow, I did not have the passion and patience that is required to succeed in farming. While majoring in agricultural economics at the University of Kentucky, I enrolled by chance in a turfgrass management class to complete a schedule during my junior year. By the end of the first week, I knew that this segment of the green industry was what I wanted to study and where I wanted to work.

This profession combines my interest in growing plants and being outdoors with my love of all outdoor sports played on grass. . . . I decided to pursue graduate school and study turfgrass science in greater depth, and I have not looked back since.

How did you prepare for your current position?

I attended St. Catherine Junior College in Springfield, Kentucky, as a general studies student for my freshman year of college. . . . I transferred to the University of Kentucky as a computer science major (lasted one semester), then an agricultural economics major (lasted two semesters), before stumbling into turfgrass management class.

Everyone can recall the "best" and "worst" teachers, and the turfgrass science professor at UK, Dr. A. J. Powell, Jr., was simply one of the best teachers. He wore his passion for the industry on his sleeve, and his class was both challenging and engaging.

[Dr. Powell] told me that I did not have enough experience in the business to get a good job and said that his experience several years earlier as a Ph.D. student at Virginia Tech was exceptional. I took his advice, studied under another outstanding turfgrass scientist, Dr. Richard (Dick) Schmidt, and graduated from Virginia Tech in 1988. I took my first job out of college as an assistant professor at Mississippi State University, where I once again had the pleasure of being mentored by one of the best scientists/people in my industry, Dr. Jeff Krans. He taught me that "people skills" in academia were every bit as important as the science.

Combining everything I learned through my professional and personal relationships with these three scientists, I embarked upon 16 wonderful years as a faculty member at Mississippi State. My job was predominantly a teaching and advising position, and I worked with more than 230 turfgrass management majors during my tenure. Many of these students have now gone on to become some of the leading turfgrass managers in their areas of expertise, and it is through my contacts with them that I stay abreast of what is happening in the industry. In 2004, I had the chance to return to Virginia Tech in my current position as extension turfgrass specialist, and another chapter of my professional career was opened.

I am an active member in the Crop Science Society of America (the professional society of agronomists) and am a member of the Golf Course Superintendent's Association of America (GCSAA), and the Sports Turf Managers Association (STMA). I particularly enjoy working with sports turf managers of all levels of facilities. I served as the STMA education director in 2009–2010, and I was elected secretary-treasurer in 2010. I also serve my state's professional organization, the Virginia Turfgrass Council, and our state's chapters of the STMA and GCSAA.

Which aspect of your education and/or training do you think has been the most helpful and/or useful to you? Why?

Without a doubt the extensive training in plant and soil sciences that I received during all my years of study provides me the opportunity to go into much greater detail in diagnosing (and hopefully) solving problems of my clientele. That is simply a requirement in a job as specific as mine. However, the most critical education and training lessons didn't come from all the hours of study in and out of the classroom, but instead came from my parents. . . . I always tell my students that it is a given that you have to know your profession inside and out. However, that what will ultimately determine success is how you manage and work with people and money.

Do you find that the skills and/or knowledge required for your job continue to evolve? If so, what have you done to keep up-to-date?

Something new comes along seemingly every day. It has taken a long time to come to the realization that I can't know everything, so my goal is to at least be aware of things and know that there are experts on a particular subject that I can likely contact if I need further information.

I keep up-to-date by scanning the popular press and scientific literature in both written and electronic formats, and I regularly attend professional and industry meetings where science colleagues and turf professionals present their research and field observations. I subscribe to a host of "free" industry publications knowing that I cannot read them all, but that I can at least skim through them to keep up with the current topics. I encourage all of my clientele to do the same and to make these publications available to their employees.

How have continuing education and/or training impacted the way you do your job?

The speed with which new management strategies, equipment, grasses, and technology evolve is not going to slow down, and I find it somewhat frustrating that I simply cannot be an expert in all areas. Therefore, I try to at least stay abreast of changes by attending and leading meetings of my peers and clientele.

When I don't have an answer, it no longer bothers me to say, "I don't know, but I will ask someone who does and get back to you." I expect to see a continuing evolution of digital training opportunities on the web as well as training and outreach opportunities on social networks such as YouTube and Facebook. I'm afraid that I am likely a generation too early to fully realize the potential for social networking as an educational tool, but I am convinced that green industry education will continue to grow in these areas.

What is the most rewarding part of your work, and what do you find to be the most challenging?

Rewarding? These three things: Meeting people, helping them solve problems, and establishing life-long working relationships. Challenging? 1) Time management: one skill/trait that I woefully lack is organization, and this is compounded regularly by my saying "yes" far too often. 2) The misconceptions/perceptions of environmentalists and the general public who believe that all turfgrass management is "bad" for the environment.

What advice would you give to people interested in pursuing your career?

At the high school level, pursue job opportunities and experience in turfgrass management as much as possible. Summer jobs working at golf courses, sports complexes, lawn care companies, etc., are often possible if contacts are made before the busy season starts. Also, because most schools have athletic fields, there is a chance to volunteer to work on the athletic fields and gain some experience in this aspect of turf management. Similar opportunities exist at the college or university level.

I had very few internship or cooperative education opportunities in my career because I arrived in my major so late. However, these experiences are absolutely critical to student success. . . . The professional and personal experiences gained during cooperative education periods is invaluable, and every student—regardless of major—should spend at least a summer on the job, as much as anything to find out if they really like this area as a profession or not.

Most majors in the green industry will require extensive study in the plant and soil sciences, but pursue as many classes as possible in business, personnel management, communication, and finance to supplement your education. While most degree programs involve somewhere from 120 to 128 hours of college credit for graduation (with many of those hours being required courses), there is an opportunity to increase the value of an education by enrolling in additional hours of study as a full-time student.

If you have even a remote interest in graduate school, get involved in an undergraduate research project with one of your favorite professors or investigate different areas of study in your academic department. This will give you a sense of what is involved in designing and conducting research and likely can even count as academic credit.

Finally, if you decide to pursue graduate education, your academic advisor is a logical first resource to consult regarding programs and people that are noteworthy in specific areas of research. There might even be an opportunity for graduate education in the program at your undergraduate university. At the very least, an academic advisor will be able to point you toward programs known to be both academically challenging and rewarding. One thing to keep in mind regarding post-graduate study toward master's and Ph.D. degrees: Don't pursue the degrees assuming they guarantee a lot of money! Turfgrass faculty make good livings, but few are what an average person would call rich, and most people stay in this profession because of job satisfaction far beyond salary.

CHAPTER 5

JOBS IN POLICY, ANALYSIS, ADVOCACY, AND REGULATORY AFFAIRS

OVERVIEW

The area of public policy, administration, analysis, and advocacy is not an industry in itself, but a broad and diverse collection of jobs. The purpose of these jobs is to examine various aspects of the environment—social, economic, judicial, and political—and propose and implement solutions. The people employed in these jobs develop and execute policies, regulations, laws, standards, procedures, and guidelines. They study industries and technology and propose modifications that will be sustainable, create jobs, stimulate the economy, conserve resources, and protect the environment.

Many of the jobs in this area are in federal, state, and local government agencies. Others are in advocacy organizations or special interest groups that influence government and the public. Some jobs are in private companies, consulting firms, unions, and industry organizations whose work impacts the environment.

A number of these occupations do not require a background in engineering, science, or math. Individuals with majors in English, communications, economics, human resources, political science, and similar "soft-side" degrees are good candidates for jobs such as compliance manager and training specialist. Job opportunities abound in the green economy for people with diverse interests and backgrounds.

JOBS PROFILED HERE

The following sectors and occupations are profiled in this chapter:

- Chief Sustainability Officer
- City and Regional Planning Aide
- Compliance Manager
- Construction and Building Inspector
- Environmental Compliance Inspector
- Regulatory Affairs Specialist
- Training and Development Specialist
- Urban and Regional Planner
- Water Resource Specialist
- Water/Wastewater Engineer

KEY TO UNDERSTANDING THE JOB PROFILES

The job profiles are classified according to one or more of the following categories:

☼ Bright Outlook
🌐 Green Occupation

The classifications "Bright Outlook" and "Green Occupation" are taken from the National Center for O*NET Development's O*NET OnLine job site. O*NET, which is sponsored by the U.S. Department of Labor/Employment and Training Administration (USDOL/ETA), has broken green jobs into three categories:

- Green Increased-Demand occupations
  - These are occupations that are likely to see job growth, but the work and worker requirements are unlikely to experience significant changes.
- Green Enhanced-Skills occupations
  - These occupations are likely to experience significant changes in work and worker requirements. Workers may find themselves doing new tasks requiring new knowledge, skills, and credentials. Current projections do not anticipate increased demand for workers in these occupations, but O*NET notes that an increase is possible.
- Green New and Emerging occupations
  - These are new occupations—not growth in existing jobs—that are created as a result of activity and technology in green sectors of the economy.

Chief Sustainability Officer ✿ⓢ

Alternate Titles and Related Careers
- Campus Sustainability Coordinator
- Chief Green Officer
- Director of Social and Environmental Responsibility
- Director of Sustainability
- Director, Sustainability Integration Office
- Environmental Policy Manager
- Environmental Sustainability Manager
- Sustainability Coordinator
- Sustainability Manager
- Vice President, Corporate Social Responsibility

This is considered a "Bright Outlook" and "Green New and Emerging" occupation in governmental and regulatory administration.

Job Trends
The Bureau of Labor Statistics and O*NET are still gathering information on this occupation. Within the last decade or so, corporations have begun to take seriously their social responsibility in regard to the environment. In part this is because of the rise in energy and water costs and in part because executives, their employees, and shareholders have come to realize the damaging impacts on the environment that business as usual has caused. The result is a growing number of companies have either charged existing management positions with "greening" their businesses or created sustainability jobs to develop and execute environmentally responsible policies. Many of these jobs so far have been in the chemical and buildings industries.

Another area of growth for sustainability professionals is higher education. In the last few years, sustainability issues have gained prominence on many of the nation's college and university campuses as the damage to the environment has become clearer through research, much of it conducted by these same institutions. As a result, many colleges and universities have created offices of sustainability and initiated programs to engage faculty, staff, and students in environmentally responsible policies.

Public utilities are another field in which sustainability officers are beginning to play a role.

Nature of the Work
Sustainability officers communicate and coordinate with a variety of interests depending on their employers. In corporate settings, they interact with management, shareholders, customers, and employees to address sustainability issues. In educational settings, the stakeholders are the administration, faculty, staff, students, and on occasion the larger community outside the campus. Sustainability offers enact or oversee sustainability policies. These may include strategies to address issues such as energy use, resource conservation, recycling, pollution reduction, waste elimination, transportation, education, and building design.

Among the tasks that sustainability officers perform according to O*NET are the following:

- Direct sustainability program operations to ensure compliance with environmental or governmental regulations
- Monitor and evaluate effectiveness of sustainability programs
- Develop methodologies to assess the viability or success of sustainability initiatives
- Develop, or oversee the development of, marketing or outreach media for sustainability projects or events
- Develop, or oversee the development of, sustainability evaluation or monitoring systems
- Develop sustainability reports, presentations, or proposals for supplier, employee, academia, media, government, public interest, or other groups
- Evaluate and approve proposals for sustainability projects, considering factors such as cost effectiveness, technical feasibility, and integration with other initiatives
- Formulate or implement sustainability campaign or marketing strategies
- Research environmental sustainability issues, concerns, or stakeholder interests
- Review sustainability program objectives, progress, or status to ensure compliance with policies, standards, regulations, or laws
- Supervise employees or volunteers working on sustainability projects
- Conduct sustainability- or environment-related risk assessments
- Create and maintain sustainability program documents, such as schedules and budgets
- Identify and evaluate pilot projects or programs to enhance the sustainability research agenda
- Identify educational, training, or other development opportunities for sustainability employees or volunteers
- Write and distribute financial or environmental impact reports
- Write project proposals, grant applications, or other documents to pursue funding for environmental initiatives

Career Path

Depending on the industry, a sustainability officer may begin as a facility manager because many sustainability strategies are related to building and campus operations. If a manufacturing company is looking for a sustainability officer, its executives may want a person who has product development and manufacturing experience. A sustainability officer for this type of employer may have responsibility for product innovation and supply chain partnerships to reduce the environmental impacts of the company's manufacturing processes.

To advance to the highest level of management, a person must have a number of years of experience in sustainability and environmental stewardship as well as management experience.

Earning Potential

Median hourly wage (2009): $77.27

Median annual wage (2009): $160,720

(Based on the "Chief Executive" category)

Education/Licensure

A bachelor's degree is the minimum for entry-level positions in sustainability. Preferred majors are marketing, finance, business, public administration, environmental management, environmental science, and environmental engineering. For advancement, having a master's, especially in business administration (MBA), is an advantage. Some management experience may also be required.

For More Information

Association for the Advancement of Sustainability in Higher Education (AASHE)
213½ North Limestone
Lexington, Kentucky 40507
859-258-2551
www.aashe.org

Association for Facilities Engineering (AFE)
12801 Worldgate Drive
Suite 500
Herndon, Virginia 20170
571-203-7171
www.afe.org

International Facility Management Association
  (IFMA)
1 E. Greenway Plaza
Suite 1100
Houston, Texas 77046-0104
713-623-4362
www.ifma.org

National Association of State Facilities
  Administrators (NASFA)
c/o The Council of State Governments
P.O. Box 11910
Lexington, Kentucky 40578-1910
859-244-8181
www.nasfa.net

City and Regional Planning Aide

Alternate Titles and Related Careers
- Community Planner
- Development Technician
- GIS (Geographic Information Systems) Technician
- Planning Aide
- Planning Assistant
- Planning Technician
- Transportation Planning Assistant
- Zoning Technician

Aides work with urban and regional planners, which is a "Green Enhanced-Skills" occupation, so planning aides/technicians will require up-to-date skills and knowledge.

Job Trends
According to the U.S. Bureau of Labor Statistics, the rate of job growth for the category that includes city and regional planning aides is expected to be 14 to 19 percent, or faster than average for all occupations. Job opportunities will arise from meeting the housing and infrastructure needs of the increasing population, particularly in rapidly expanding communities that need streets and other services.

According to the *Occupational Outlook Handbook,* currently 68 percent of planners are employed in local governments. Only 21 percent are employed in private companies that provide architectural, engineering, and related services. However, employment in the private sector is expected to increase faster than government openings, especially in firms that provide technical services. Planning aides with good computer skills, including competence with geographic information systems (GIS), should have many opportunities.

Nature of the Work
City and regional planning aides assist urban and regional planners by compiling information used to create short- and long-term plans for the use of land and resources. Depending on the job, planning technicians

- Compile data from field investigations, reports, maps, and other sources
- Conduct interviews, site inspections, and surveys to collect data
- Analyze the data and prepare reports that include graphs and charts of statistics on population, zoning, land use, traffic flow, and other factors
- Develop and maintain databases of information, tracking systems, and records
- Review zoning permit applications or building plans
- Investigate violations of regulations

Some technicians specialize. For example, some will be GIS (geographic information system) technicians who provide support to planners by creating specialized maps that could show a variety of features, such as land use, population distribution, location of natural resources, and air pollution sources.

About New Urbanism

A current movement in urban and regional planning is called "New Urbanism." It promotes walkable neighborhoods that include a variety of occupations and different types of housing; for example, single-family homes, duplexes, and garden-style apartments. The emphasis is on reducing the use of cars and energy.

Career Paths

Planning technicians work under the supervision of planners. As they gain experience, they move to positions with greater responsibility and more independence. Some may continue their education to become planners.

Earning Potential

Median hourly wage (2009): $18.03

Median annual wage (2009): $37,500

Education/Licensure

Generally, an associate degree in urban planning, construction management, architecture, or a related field, plus two years of experience in building codes, zoning, or plans review, are required. However, many employers prefer a bachelor's degree, which may be substituted for experience.

A few schools offer a bachelor's degree in urban and regional planning. Graduates of these programs qualify for some entry-level jobs, but they may have limited opportunities for advancement. The Association of Collegiate Schools of Planning Web site (www.acsp.org) provides a list of accredited programs, starting at the bachelor's degree level.

Even though most states do not have requirements for certification, many communities do. The preferred certification is from the American Institute of Certified Planners (AICP), the professional institute of the American Planning Association (www.planning.org/aicp). The AICP certification is based on education, experience, and passing an exam. For those who do not have at least a bachelor's degree, eight years of experience is required.

Maintaining certification requires professional development on a two-year cycle.

For More Information

American Planning Association (APA)
1776 Massachusetts Avenue, NW
Suite 400
Washington, DC 20036-1904
202-872-0611
www.planning.org

Association of Collegiate Schools of Planning (ACS)
6311 Mallard Trace
Tallahassee, Florida 32312
850-385-2054
www.acsp.org

Compliance Manager ☼🌑

Alternate Titles and Related Careers

- Chief Compliance Officer
- Compliance Administrator
- Compliance Analyst
- Compliance Associate
- Compliance Director
- Compliance Engineer
- Compliance Inspector
- Compliance Officer
- Compliance Program Manager
- Compliance Team Manager
- Regulatory Compliance Manager

This is a "Bright Outlook" and "Green New and Emerging" occupation in government and regulatory affairs. Compliance managers work for public and private organizations in the areas of conservation and pollution control, regulation enforcement, and policy analysis and advocacy.

Job Trends

According to the U.S. Bureau of Labor Statistics, the compliance manager occupation is expected to have a growth rate that is about average of all occupations—7 to 13 percent. Compliance managers are employed in many industries from energy to banking and securities, and a large number of new compliance jobs will be in the financial field as the federal government moves to tighten regulations in this area. However, as state and local governments write new, more stringent energy regulations, and new federal rules and regulations related to energy take effect, parts of the green sector of the economy should see an increase in the need for compliance officers.

Nature of the Work

Compliance managers plan, direct, and coordinate the activities of an organization to ensure compliance with ethical or regulatory standards. They are the point of contact for a company's management, employees, and suppliers for information on government rules and regulations affecting the business. They work with corporate attorneys, internal and external auditors, and regulatory agencies on compliance issues.

Government regulations affect not just the products that a company manufactures, such as gasoline or environmentally friendly sneakers but also how the company operates internally. Compliance officers are needed to assess how well a company abides by government financial reporting regulations such as Sarbanes-Oxley and nondiscrimination laws. This is an occupation for which non-technically trained individuals with an interest in "green employment" can contribute.

According to O*NET, the following are some of the tasks that compliance managers perform:

- Direct the development or implementation of compliance-related policies and procedures
- Disseminate written policies and procedures and provide employee training
- Verify that all company and regulatory policies and procedures have been documented, implemented, and communicated
- Maintain the documentation

- Design or implement improvements in communication, monitoring, or enforcement of compliance standards
- Conduct periodic internal reviews or audits to ensure that compliance procedures are being followed
- Conduct or direct the internal investigation of compliance issues
- File appropriate compliance reports with regulatory agencies
- Prepare management reports regarding compliance operations and progress
- Report violations of compliance or regulatory standards to duly authorized enforcement agencies as appropriate or required
- Keep informed regarding pending industry changes, trends, and best practices and assess the potential impact of these changes on organizational processes
- Discuss emerging compliance issues and regulations with management or employees

About the Irish Plastic Bag Tax

In 2002, the Irish legislature passed a tax on plastic bags. As a result of the tax, Irish use of plastic bags dropped 94 percent in a few weeks. Now about the only shopping bags you see are cloth, reusable bags. The tax is $0.33 a bag.

Career Path

Typically, an individual interested in a compliance position begins as an associate or assistant working under a compliance manager. Over a period of time, the individual will gain greater responsibilities and take on projects with decreasing supervision. Depending on the area of expertise, a compliance officer may become a consultant, be self-employed, or work for a large company specializing in compliance and risk management issues.

Earning Potential

Median hourly wage (2009): $44.52

Median annual wage (2009): $92,600

Education/Licensure

Entry-level jobs in compliance need at least a bachelor's degree. Typical majors are business administration, human resources, accounting, or finance. In addition to their academic backgrounds, compliance officers must be familiar with applicable rules and regulations and any inspection or testing methods for their particular field. Promotion to a manager's position may require as much as seven years of experience. Additional graduate work or certifications are also useful in advancing to higher positions.

Most states require certification of accountants. The exam is administered under the authority of the American Institute of Certified Public Accountants (AICPA), the National Association of State Boards of Accountancy (NASBA), and the state boards of accountancy.

The Society for Human Resources Management through its Human Resources Certification Institute offers four HR certifications:

Professional in Human Resources (PHR®)

Senior Professional in Human Resources (SPHR®)

Global Professional in Human Resources (GPHR®)

California certification (PHR-CA® and SPHR-CA®)

For More Information

American Institute of Certified Public Accountants (AICPA)
1211 Avenue of the Americas
New York, New York 10036
888-777-7077 (toll-free)
www.aicpa.org

National Association of State Boards of Accountancy (NASBA)
866-696-2722 (toll-free)
www.nasba.org

Society for Human Resources Management (SHRM)
1800 Duke Street
Alexandria, Virginia 22314
800-283-7476 (toll-free)
www.shrm.org

Construction and Building Inspector 🌐

Alternate Titles and Related Careers

- Electrical Inspector
- Green Building Inspector
- Home Inspector
- Mechanical Inspector
- Plan Examiner
- Plumbing Inspector
- Public Works Inspector
- Specification Inspector
- Structural Inspector

This is a "Green Enhanced-Skills" occupation found in green construction and governmental and regulatory administration. The job of construction and building inspector, like so many others, is being affected by new technologies. In this case, new modeling technology is increasing the resources available to construction and building inspectors to do their work. Think of construction and building inspectors as ground-level compliance officers.

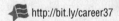 http://bit.ly/career37

Job Trends

The U.S. Bureau of Labor Statistics predicts that employment for construction and building inspectors will grow by 14 to 19 percent by 2018, which is faster than average for all occupations. According to the *Occupational Outlook Handbook,* local governments employed about 44 percent of inspectors in 2008. Architectural and engineering services companies employed another 27 percent who conducted audits for fee, mostly home inspections for potential buyers. Approximately 8 percent of building inspectors were self-employed, many of these as home inspectors.

Concerns for public safety in light of potential disasters arising from natural or human causes and increasing emphasis on high-quality construction are driving the demand for this occupation. Emerging emphasis on sustainable and green building will also stimulate employment opportunities for building inspectors. First, buildings may now be certified as green. The U.S. Green Building Council (USGBC) offers several levels of certification called Leadership in Energy and Environmental Design (LEED). Inspectors who are trained to conduct LEED audits will have new job opportunities. Second, new opportunities exist in local government to develop Green Building Programs and local codes for sustainable building. Once codes are in place, inspecting for compliance will continue to provide jobs.

About Paperless in Hawaii

In 2008, the state senate in Hawaii went paperless—no more stacks of bills on lawmakers' desks, and no more lines of assistants standing at copy machines. By 2010, the senate could boast that it had saved $1.2 million, nearly 8 million sheets of paper, and more than 800 trees.

Home inspection also is an area with potential for good job opportunities. This is partly because of economic conditions but also because of environmental concerns. The market for home remodeling is currently strong, and retrofitting and remodeling work to improve energy efficiency is on the rise. In addition, retrofitting industrial plants, office buildings, government buildings, and schools for energy efficiency will also create job opportunities. New residential construction, commercial construction, and building and repair of bridges and roads all contribute to employment for construction and building inspectors.

Nature of the Work

Building inspectors must know the federal, state, and local codes that regulate construction. The International Code Council (ICC) publishes national construction and building codes, but there are also many local codes. Many localities also have new green building codes that may be voluntary or mandatory. A new specialty called green building inspector evaluates buildings for energy efficiency, indoor air quality, and use of natural materials.

Construction and building inspectors are responsible for monitoring work during all phases of construction. They make necessary measurements and observations to ensure that the work follows plans, meets specifications, and complies with all construction and safety codes. In addition to monitoring new construction, inspectors also oversee repairs, remodeling, and maintenance work.

Career Paths

Certification improves job opportunities and opportunities for advancement. A degree in engineering or architecture may be required in order to advance to a supervisory position.

Earning Potential

Mean hourly wage (2009): $24.77

Mean annual wage (2009): $51,530

Education/Licensure

A high school diploma or GED is generally the minimum educational requirement. Currently, 30 percent of building and construction inspectors have no more than that. About 46 percent have some postsecondary training or an associate degree. Only 23 percent have a bachelor's degree or higher. Substantial construction experience qualifies a person for many jobs in this field. However, employers are increasingly hiring those who have experience and an associate degree from a community college or who have at least studied engineering, architecture, construction technology, building inspection, or home inspection. There are also apprenticeship programs for a variety of inspection specialties.

Many states and municipalities require certification, and individuals who hold certifications have the best job opportunities. Certification generally requires passing an exam, but may also include a specified amount of experience or a minimum level of training and education. There are many ways to become certified. Some states have licensing programs, whereas other states require specialized certification from an association such as the National Fire Protection Association (NFPA). Community colleges often offer certificate programs. The Green Building Certification Institute, affiliated with the U.S. Green Building Council (USGBC), offers green credentials.

The International Code Council (ICC) offers several certifications, including Code Safety Professional; Certified Class A or Class B Underground Storage Tank System to install, retrofit, or decommission petroleum storage tanks; and Code Safety Professional. ICC also provides testing services for a number of state certifications.

Continuing education to stay up-to-date on new materials, construction practices, and techniques, as well as codes, is an important part of an inspector's job.

For More Information

American Society of Home Inspectors (ASHI)
932 Lee Street
Suite 101
Des Plaines, Illinois 60016
800-743-2744 (toll-free)
www.ashi.org

Green Building Certification Institute (GBCI)
2101 L Street, NW
Suite 650
Washington, DC 20037
800-795-1746 (toll-free)
www.gbci.org

International Code Council (ICC)
500 New Jersey Avenue, NW
6th Floor
Washington, DC 20001-2070
888-422-7233 (toll-free)
www.iccsafe.org

National Association of Home Inspectors (NAHI)
4248 Park Glen Road
Minneapolis, Minnesota 55416
800-448-3942 (toll-free)
www.nahi.org

National Fire Protection Association (NFPA)
1 Batterymarch Park
Quincy, Massachusetts 02169-7471
617-770-3000
www.nfpa.org

U.S. Green Building Council (USGBC)
2101 L Street, NW
Suite 500
Washington, DC 20037
800-795-1747 (toll-free)
www.usgbc.org

About Washington, DC's Energy-Efficiency Program

The District of Columbia is an example of a city that takes reducing energy seriously. It has a four-pronged program to help its residents become energy savvy: Education/Outreach, Weatherization, Utility and Operations, and Energy Affordability. Among its services, the program provides knowledge and skill training to residents, promotes renewable energy sources, assists in weatherizing homes, and provides affordable and positive alternatives for energy sources for low-income residents.

Environmental Compliance Inspector ☼

Alternate Titles and Related Careers

- Compliance Investigator
- Enforcement Officer
- Environmental Compliance Technician
- Environmental Protection Specialist
- Environmental Quality Analyst
- Environmental Specialist
- Resource Conservation and Recovery Act Enforcement Officer (RCRA Enforcement Officer)
- Toxic Program Officer
- Waste Management Specialist

This is considered a "Bright Outlook" occupation. It has impacts on construction because of the potential harm to the environment that both commercial and residential building as well as civil engineering projects such as highways and bridges may have.

Job Trends

Job growth for compliance officers, those not employed in agriculture, construction, health and safety, or transportation, is expected to be much faster than average at 20 percent or higher. Projected job openings number 108,500 between 2008 and 2018.

Job opportunities are expected to be especially favorable in state and local government. About 64 percent of current compliance officers, not including those employed in agriculture, construction, health and safety, or transportation, work for a government agency—federal, state, or municipal. The remaining environmental compliance inspectors work across a variety of industries.

Nature of the Work

Environmental compliance inspectors inspect and investigate sources of pollution to protect the public and environment. Their job is to ensure compliance with federal, state, and local regulations and ordinances.

According to O*NET, environmental compliance inspectors may perform the following tasks:

- Determine the nature of code violations and actions to be taken, and issue written notices of violation; participate in enforcement hearings as necessary
- Examine permits, licenses, applications, and records to ensure compliance with licensing requirements
- Prepare, organize, and maintain inspection records
- Interview individuals to determine the nature of suspected violations and to obtain evidence of violations
- Prepare written, oral, tabular, and graphic reports summarizing requirements and regulations, including enforcement and chain of custody documentation
- Monitor follow-up actions in cases where violations were found, and review compliance monitoring reports
- Investigate complaints and suspected violations regarding illegal dumping, pollution, pesticides, product quality, or labeling laws
- Inspect waste pretreatment, treatment, and disposal facilities and systems for conformance to federal, state, or local regulations
- Inform individuals and groups of pollution control regulations and inspection findings, and explain how problems can be corrected
- Determine sampling locations and methods, and collect water or wastewater samples for analysis, preserving samples with appropriate containers and preservation methods
- Verify that hazardous chemicals are handled, stored, and disposed of in accordance with regulations
- Research and keep informed of pertinent information and developments in areas such as EPA laws and regulations

- Determine which sites and violation reports to investigate, and coordinate compliance and enforcement activities with other government agencies
- Learn and observe proper safety precautions, rules, regulations, and practices so that unsafe conditions can be recognized and proper safety protocols implemented
- Inform health professionals, property owners, and the public about harmful properties and related problems of water pollution and contaminated wastewater
- Analyze and implement state, federal or local requirements as necessary to maintain approved pretreatment, pollution prevention, and storm water runoff programs
- Observe and record field conditions, gathering, interpreting, and reporting data such as flow meter readings and chemical levels
- Perform laboratory tests on samples collected, such as analyzing the content of contaminated wastewater
- Review and evaluate applications for pollution control discharge permits
- Research and perform calculations related to landscape allowances, discharge volumes, production-based and alternative limits, and wastewater strength classifications, then make recommendations and complete documentation
- Participate in the development of spill prevention programs and hazardous waste rules and regulations, and recommend corrective actions for hazardous waste problems
- Conduct research on hazardous waste management projects in order to determine the magnitude of problems, and treatment or disposal alternatives and costs
- Respond to questions and inquiries, such as those concerning service charges and capacity fees, or refer them to supervisors

Career Path

Entry-level employees work as trainees under experienced inspectors. As they gain experience, they are given more responsibility.

If employed by a government entity, the environmental compliance inspector position is covered by civil service and candidates must take and pass a civil service examination. Advancement is through the civil service grades.

Earning Potential

Median hourly wage (2009): $23.92

Median annual wage (2009): $49,750

Education/Licensure

The majority of currently employed compliance inspectors hold bachelor's degrees, typically in the natural or applied sciences, engineering, or occupational safety and health. About 28 percent hold an associate's degree or have some postsecondary training.

Any engineering degree should be from a school accredited by the Accreditation Board for Engineering and Technology (ABET). As noted in the *Occupation Outlook Handbook,* some colleges and universities offer five-year programs that culminate in a master's degree in engineering. Some offer five- or six-year programs that include cooperative experience. Some four-year schools have arrangements with community colleges or liberal arts colleges that allow students to spend two or three years at the initial school and transfer for the last two years to complete their engineering degree.

All fifty states and the District of Columbia require engineers to be licensed as professional engineers (PE) if they serve the public directly. In most states, licensure requires graduation from a four-year engineering program accredited by ABET, four years of experience, and passing the state exam. Many engineers take the Fundamentals of Engineering portion of the exam upon graduation. They are then engineers in training (EIT). After obtaining appropriate work experience, they take the Principles and Practice of Engineering exam to complete their professional license. Most states recognize licenses from other states, as long as the requirements are the same or more stringent. Some states have continuing education requirements.

Some states such as California have their own certification process for environmental compliance inspectors. The federal Environmental Protection Agency has developed a training manual for this occupation.

For More Information

Accreditation Board for Engineering and
    Technology (ABET)
111 Market Place
Suite 1050
Baltimore, Maryland 21202
410-347-7700
www.abet.org

International Network for Environmental
    Compliance and Enforcement
USEPA Headquarters 2254A
Ariel Rios Building
1200 Pennsylvania Avenue, NW
Washington, DC 20460
202-564-6035
http://inece.org

Regulatory Affairs Specialist ✿ ⑤

Alternate Titles and Related Careers
- Compliance Manager
- Compliance Officer

This is a "Bright Outlook" and "Green New and Emerging" occupation in government and regulatory administration. Regulatory affairs specialists work for public and private organizations in the areas of conservation and pollution control, regulation enforcement, and policy analysis and advocacy.

Job Trends

The Bureau of Labor Statistics projects that the category of compliance officer, which includes regulatory affairs specialist, will grow at a rate of more than 20 percent between 2008 and 2018. This is much faster than average for all occupations.

About 64 percent of regulatory affairs specialists are employed in the government sector working with private industry on compliance with government regulations. About 11 percent work in the finance and insurance industries, and the remaining 25 percent are employed in other industries, such as energy and pharmaceuticals.

The trend toward additional government regulations in a variety of fields from banking and the financial industry to greater fuel efficiency for motor vehicles and better monitoring of agricultural products will result in the need for more regulatory affairs specialists to work with organizations to see that they know and comply with the regulations.

Nature of the Work

Regulatory affairs specialists coordinate and document regulatory processes within organizations. These include internal audits of practices, government inspections, and license renewals and registrations. Regulatory affairs specialists may compile and prepare materials for submission to regulatory agencies. This is an occupation for which individuals who may not have technical training but do have an interest in "green employment" can contribute.

According to O*NET, among the tasks that regulatory affairs specialists perform are the following:
- Coordinate, prepare, or review regulatory submissions for domestic or international projects
- Provide technical review of data or reports that will be incorporated into regulatory submissions to assure scientific rigor, accuracy, and clarity of presentation
- Review product promotional materials, labeling, batch records, specification

sheets, or test methods for compliance with applicable regulations and policies

- Interpret regulatory rules or rule changes and ensure that they are communicated through corporate policies and procedures
- Determine the types of regulatory submissions or internal documentation that are required in situations such as proposed device changes and labeling changes
- Advise project teams on subjects such as premarket regulatory requirements, export and labeling requirements, and clinical study compliance issues
- Prepare or maintain technical files as necessary to obtain and sustain product approval
- Coordinate efforts associated with the preparation of regulatory documents or submissions
- Prepare or direct the preparation of additional information or responses as requested by regulatory agencies
- Analyze product complaints and make recommendations regarding their reportability
- Escort government inspectors during inspections and provide post-inspection follow-up information as requested
- Participate in internal or external audits
- Communicate with regulatory agencies regarding presubmission strategies, potential regulatory pathways, compliance test requirements, or clarification and follow-up of submissions under review
- Identify relevant guidance documents, international standards, or consensus standards and provide interpretive assistance
- Review protocols to ensure collection of data needed for regulatory submissions
- Compile and maintain regulatory documentation databases and systems
- Prepare responses to customer requests for information such as product data, written regulatory affairs statements, surveys, and questionnaires
- Coordinate recall or market withdrawal activities as necessary
- Direct the collection and preparation of laboratory samples as requested by regulatory agencies
- Develop and track quality metrics
- Maintain current knowledge base of existing and emerging regulations, standards, or guidance documents
- Recommend changes to company procedures in response to changes in regulations or standards
- Obtain and distribute updated information regarding domestic or international laws, guidelines, or standards
- Write or update standard operating procedures, work instructions, or policies
- Develop or conduct employee regulatory training

Regulatory affairs specialists who work in federal, state, and municipal government agencies see the regulatory process from the other side of the desk, reviewing regulatory filings by private industry, inspecting facilities, and investigating complaints and problems.

Career Path

Entry-level regulatory affairs specialists begin under experienced regulatory affairs specialists or compliance officers. Over time, new hires gain greater responsibility and take on projects with decreasing supervision. After a number of years, a regulatory affairs specialist may advance to become a compliance officer in charge of a regulatory affairs or compliance department.

Regulatory affairs specialists employed by a government agency must pass a civil service exam. Advancement is based on moving up the grades.

Earning Potential

Median hourly wage (2009): $23.92

Median annual wage (2009): $49,750

(Based on figures for Compliance Officers)

Education/Licensure

Typically, entry-level employees require a bachelor's degree. Typical majors are business administration, human resources, accounting, and finance. Regulatory affairs specialists must also be familiar with all applicable rules and regulations for their particular field and any inspection or testing methods. Specialists must also keep up-to-date on regulatory trends. Additional graduate work or certifications, depending on the field, are useful in advancing to higher positions.

Most states require certification of accountants. The exam is administered under the authority of the American Institute of Certified Public Accountants (AICPA), the National Association of State Boards of Accountancy (NASBA), and the state boards of accountancy.

The Society for Human Resources Management through its Human Resources Certificate Institute offers four certifications:

Professional in Human Resources (PHR)

Senior Professional in Human Resources (SPHR)

Global Professional in Human Resources (GPHM)

California certificate for those working in
  California

For More Information

American Institute of Certified Public
  Accountants (AICPA)
1211 Avenue of the Americas
New York, New York 10036
888-777-7077 (toll-free)
www.aicpa.org

National Association of State Boards of
  Accountancy (NASBA)
866-696-2722 (toll-free)
www.nasba.org

Society for Human Resources Management
  (SHRM)
1800 Duke Street
Alexandria, Virginia 22314
800-283-7476 (toll-free)
www.shrm.org

Training and Development Specialist ✿ ⊕

Alternate Titles and Related Careers

- Computer Training Specialist
- Corporate Trainer
- E-Learning Developer
- Job Training Specialist
- Management Development Specialist
- Technical Trainer
- Training Coordinator
- Training Specialist

This is considered a "Bright Outlook" and "Green Enhanced-Skills" occupation in the energy efficiency, green construction, and research, design, and consulting services sectors of the economy.

Job Trends

The Bureau of Labor Statistics projects that the training and development specialist will grow at a much faster than average rate—20 percent or higher—between 2008 and 2018. Projected job openings are about 107,100. About 35 percent of currently employed trainers work in health care and social assistance, finance and insurance, and professional, scientific, and technical services. The remainder work across all variety of industries, including union training programs.

According to the *Occupational Outlook Handbook,* employers in coming years will devote greater resources to job-specific training programs because of the increasing complexity of many jobs and technological advances that can leave employees with obsolete skills—a problem in the slow recovery after the recession of 2007–2009. Also, highly trained and skilled baby boomers will retire in growing numbers this decade that will spark demand for training and development specialists to train their replacements. Retirements among trainers will also add to the demand for new employees.

Nature of the Work

Training and development specialists conduct training and development programs for employees. The programs are designed to help workers maintain or improve their job skills. Enhancing employees' skills benefits both the individual and the organization.

Trainers must be comfortable using computers and LCD (liquid crystal display) projectors, as well as software programs for charting, computer-based training, video-conferencing, presentations, and graphics. The ability to speak in front of an audience is a basic job requirement. Trainers must also be able to deliver instructional strategies effectively and accurately monitor the performance of trainees.

According to O*NET, training and development specialists may perform the following tasks:

- Monitor, evaluate and record training activities and program effectiveness
- Assess training needs through surveys, interviews with employees, focus groups, or consultation with managers, instructors or customer representatives
- Develop alternative training methods if expected improvements are not seen
- Organize and develop, or obtain, training procedure manuals and guides and course materials such as handouts and visual materials
- Present information, using a variety of instructional techniques and formats such as role playing, simulations, team exercises, group discussions, videos and lectures
- Evaluate training materials prepared by instructors, such as outlines, text, and handouts
- Design, plan, organize and direct orientation and training for employees or customers of industrial or commercial establishment

- Devise programs to develop executive potential among employees in lower-level positions
- Select and assign instructors to conduct training
- Schedule classes based on availability of space, equipment, and instructors
- Supervise instructors, evaluate instructor performance, and refer instructors to classes for skill development
- Coordinate recruitment and placement of training program participants
- Monitor training costs to ensure budget is not exceeded, and prepare budget reports to justify expenditures
- Negotiate contracts with clients, including desired training outcomes, fees and expenses
- Refer trainees to employer relations representatives, to locations offering job placement assistance, or to appropriate social services agencies if warranted
- Attend meetings and seminars to obtain information for use in training programs, or to inform management of training program status
- Keep up with developments in area of expertise by reading current journals, books and magazine articles

Career Path

Entry-level positions in human resources offices typically include administrative duties such as data entry, answering phones, and compiling employee handbooks and training materials. Over time, with specific on-the-job training, additional coursework, and several years of experience, human resources employees may advance to supervisory positions. Some become trainers, developing and giving training programs to the company's employees. Some will advance to training and development manager and then director. The ultimate HR position is vice president.

Individuals with specialties may be hired initially as trainers.

Some trainers who learn their skills in corporate settings open their own businesses and offer training and development services to businesses. For companies, this is a cost-effective method of training employees without having trainers on their payrolls.

Earning Potential

Median hourly wage (2009): $25.06

Median annual wage (2009): $52,120

Education/Licensure

Typically, training specialists have a college degree, often in the social sciences, business administration, or the behavioral sciences. Some training specialties such as computers require specialization in that field.

The American Society for Training and Development (ASTD) Certification Institute offers the Certified Professional in Learning and Performance Certification for trainers. ASTD also offers certificate and workshop programs, many of them online, covering a broad range of professional and development topics such as designing synchronous learning, e-learning instructional design, and facilitating synchronous learning.

For More Information

American Society for Training and Development (ASTD)
1640 King Street
Box 1443
Alexandria, Virginia 22313-2043
800-628-2783
www.astd.org

Urban and Regional Planner ⓢ

Alternate Titles and Related Careers

- Airport Planner
- Building, Planning, and Zoning Director
- City Planner
- Community Development Planner
- Community Development Director
- Community Planning and Development Representative
- Neighborhood Planner
- Planning Director
- Regional Planner

This is considered a "Green Enhanced-Skill" occupation.

 http://bit.ly/career25

Job Trends

The Bureau of Labor Statistics projects that between 2008 and 2018 the need for urban and regional planners will grow at a rate of 14 to 19 percent, which is faster than average for all occupations. This translates into 14,700 new job openings.

Nature of the Work

Urban and regional planners develop long- and short-term plans for land use and the growth and revitalization of urban, suburban, and rural communities and the regions in which they are located. These plans include transportation systems, conservation policies, utilities, and commercial, industrial, residential, and recreational use of land, facilities, and infrastructure. Urban and regional planners recommend locations for roads, schools, and other infrastructure and suggest zoning regulations. They promote the best use of land and resources. Their recommendations about such elements as transportation networks and public utilities, and noting residential and commercial areas in relation to mass transit and highways may indeed affect an area's energy use.

As part of their job, urban and regional planners project the future population needs of the location. In the course of their work, urban and regional planners hold public meetings, so all the stakeholders—the public, government officials, social scientists, lawyers, land developers, and special interest groups—can address the issues, for example, infrastructure involved in developing land use or community plans.

Among the duties that urban and regional planners may perform are the following, according to O*NET:

- Conduct field investigations, surveys, impact studies, and other research to compile and analyze data on economic, social, regulatory, and physical factors affecting land use

- Design, promote, and administer government plans and policies affecting land use, zoning, public utilities, community facilities, housing, and transportation

- Create, prepare, or requisition graphic or narrative reports on land use data, including land area maps

- Review and evaluate environmental impact reports pertaining to private and public planning projects and programs

- Recommend approval, denial, or conditional approval of planning proposals, identifying necessary changes

- Coordinate work with economic consultants and architects during the formulation of plans and designs of large pieces of infrastructure

- Keep informed about economic and legal issues involved in zoning codes, building codes, and environmental regulations

- Determine the effects of regulatory limitations on projects

- Advise planning officials on project feasibility, cost-effectiveness, regulatory conformance, and possible alternatives

- Mediate community disputes and assist in developing alternative plans and recommendations for programs or projects

Career Path

As planners gain experience, they advance to more independent assignments and gain greater responsibility in areas such as policy and budgeting. They may become senior planners or community-planning directors and meet with officials and supervise a staff. Often, advancement is to a larger jurisdiction with greater responsibilities and more difficult problems. In larger jurisdictions, an urban and regional planner may advance to community development director. About two thirds of all planners work for local governments. Students who have experience with planning software, especially GIS software, will have an advantage in the job market.

About Smart Growth

Learn more about how the smart growth movement is working to counteract sprawl at www.epa.gov/smartgrowth and www.smartgrowth.org.

Earning Potential

Median hourly wage (2009): $29.72
Median annual wage (2009): $61,820

Education/Licensure

Generally, a master's degree in urban and regional planning from an accredited program is required. The Planning Accreditation Board accredits college and university programs. Its Web site (www.planningaccreditationboard.org) includes links to schools with accredited planning programs. Master's degrees in related fields, such as geography, urban design, urban studies, economics, or business, may be acceptable for many planning jobs. Most planning departments offer specializations in areas such as urban design, environmental and natural resources planning, land-use or code enforcement, and urban design.

There were fifteen schools that offered a bachelor's degree in urban and regional planning in 2009. Graduates of these programs qualify for some entry-level jobs, but they may have limited opportunities for advancement.

Even though most states do not have requirements for certification, many communities do. The preferred certification is from the American Institute of Certified Planners (AICP), the professional institute of the American Planning Association (www.planning.org/aicp). The AICP-certified planner designation is based on education, experience, and passing an exam. Maintaining certification requires professional development on a two-year cycle.

Only two states currently have requirements for licensing planners. New Jersey requires that planners pass two exams to qualify for a license. One exam tests general planning knowledge, and the other tests knowledge of New Jersey laws. Michigan requires community planners to register in order to use that designation, and the registration is based on passing state and national exams and on professional experience.

For More Information

American Planning Association
1776 Massachusetts Avenue, NW
Suite 400
Washington, DC 20036-1904
202-872-0611
www.planning.org

Association of Collegiate Schools of Planning
6311 Mallard Trace
Tallahassee, Florida 32312
850-385-2054
www.acsp.org

Water Resource Specialist ☼⑨

Alternate Titles and Related Careers

- Natural Resource Specialist
- Resource Management Specialist
- Water Resource Management Specialist
- Water Technology Specialist

This is considered a "Bright Outlook" and "Green New and Emerging" occupation in the environmental protection sector of the economy. It also relates to the regulatory aspect of government administration as well as the impacts that construction may have on water resources.

About Healthy Communities

Check out Keep America Beautiful's Web site for "20 Tips for Maintaining Safe, Clean, Healthy Communities." These tips will help you improve your community's environment year-round, not just from March to May.

Job Trends

The Bureau of Labor Statistics estimates that the overall category of natural sciences managers will see a faster than average growth rate of 14 to 19 percent between 2008 and 2018. Currently, 36 percent of natural sciences managers work in professional, scientific, and technical services, whereas 31 percent work for some level of government. About 15 percent work in manufacturing and the remainder across all industries.

Nature of the Work

Water resource specialists design or implement programs and strategies related to water resource issues such as supply, quantity, and regulatory compliance. Among the technology that they must be able to use is geographic information systems (GIS) or global position systems (GPS) software

The following are tasks that water resource specialists may perform based on O*NET surveys:

- Conduct, or oversee the conduct of, chemical, physical, and biological water quality monitoring or sampling to ensure compliance with water quality standards
- Develop strategies for watershed operations to meet water supply and conservation goals or to ensure regulatory compliance with clean water laws or regulations
- Analyze storm water systems to identify opportunities for water resource improvements
- Conduct cost-benefit studies for watershed improvement projects or water management alternatives
- Conduct, or oversee the conduct of, investigations on matters such as water storage, wastewater discharge, pollutants, permits, or other compliance and regulatory issues
- Conduct technical studies for water resources on topics such as pollutants and water treatment options
- Develop or implement standardized water monitoring and assessment methods
- Develop plans to protect watershed health or rehabilitate watersheds
- Identify and characterize specific causes or sources of water pollution
- Identify methods for distributing purified wastewater into rivers, streams, or oceans
- Monitor water use, demand, or quality in a particular geographic area
- Present water resource proposals to government, public interest groups, or community groups
- Provide technical expertise to assist communities in the development or implementation of storm water monitoring or other water programs
- Recommend new or revised policies, procedures, or regulations to support water resource or conservation goals

- Negotiate for water rights with communities or water facilities to meet water supply demands
- Perform hydrologic, hydraulic, or water quality modeling
- Review or evaluate designs for water detention facilities, storm drains, flood control facilities, or other hydraulic structures
- Supervise teams of workers who capture water from wells and rivers
- Write proposals, project reports, informational brochures, or other documents on wastewater purification, water supply and demand, or other water resource subjects
- Compile and maintain documentation on the health of a body of water

Career Path

Entry-level employees begin work under experienced managers or engineers. Over time, they take on more complex work with less supervision and may become team leaders and supervisors in time. With more experience and possibly additional degrees, they may advance into upper-level management.

If water resource specialists work for a government agency, they typically will be part of the civil service system where advancement is by grade level.

Earning Potential

Median hourly wage (2009): $55.08

Median annual wage (2009): $114,560

(Based on "Natural Science Managers")

Education/Licensure

A bachelor's degree or higher is required in water resources engineering or a related science or engineering field such as agriculture, environmental sciences, or civil engineering. Any engineering degree should be from a school accredited by the Accreditation Board for Engineering and Technology (ABET).

As noted in the *Occupation Outlook Handbook,* some colleges and universities offer five-year programs that culminate in a master's degree in engineering. Some offer five- or six-year programs that include cooperative experience. Some four-year schools have arrangements with community colleges or liberal arts colleges that allow students to spend two or three years at the initial school and transfer for the last two years to complete their engineering degree.

All fifty states and the District of Columbia require engineers to be licensed as professional engineers (PE) if they serve the public directly. In most states, licensure requires graduation from a four-year engineering program accredited by ABET, four years of experience, and passing the state exam. Many engineers take the Fundamentals of Engineering portion of the exam upon graduation. They are then engineers in training (EIT). After obtaining appropriate work experience, they take the Principles and Practice of Engineering exam to complete their professional license. Most states recognize licenses from other states, as long as the requirements are the same or more stringent. Some states have continuing education requirements.

The American Academy of Water Resources Engineers (AAWRE) offers the Diplomate/Water Resources Engineer (D.WRE) certification as well as a number of seminars for continuing education credits.

For More Information

Accreditation Board for Engineering and
   Technology (ABET)
111 Market Place
Suite 1050
Baltimore, Maryland 21202
410-347-7700
www.abet.org

American Academy of Water Resources Engineers
   (AAWRE)
1801 Alexander Bell Drive
Reston, Virginia 20191
703-295-6414
www.aawre.org

American Water Resources Association (AWRA)
P.O. Box 1626
Middleburg, Virginia 20118
540-687-8390
www.awra.org

Association of Water Technologies (AWT)
9707 Key West Avenue
Suite 100
Rockville, Maryland 20850
www.awt.org

International Water Association (IWA)
E-mail: water@iwahq.org
www.iwahq.org

National Society of Professional Engineers
   (NSPE)
1420 King Street
Alexandria, Virginia 22314
(703) 684–2800
www.nspe.org

About Labels

When checking labels, look for third-party certifications such as Certified Humane-Raised and Handled, Fair Trade Certified, Energy Star, USDA Organic, and Forest Stewardship Council. Government agencies and private certifying organizations set standards for products and regulate the use of their labels.

Water/Wastewater Engineer ✿❀

Alternate Titles and Related Careers

- Civil Engineer, Water/Wastewater
- Civil Water-Wastewater Engineer
- Engineer, Water/Wastewater Resources
- Senior Civil Engineer

- Senior Water/Wastewater Engineer
- Waste/Water Environmental Engineer
- Water Treatment Specialist
- Water Quality Specialist

This is considered a "Bright Outlook" and "Green New and Emerging" occupation in the environmental protection sector of the green economy. It also has a role in regulatory affairs.

Job Trends

Water/wastewater engineer is a subset of the civil engineering occupation, which is expected to grow at a much faster than average rate of 20 percent or higher between 2008 and 2018. In addition to openings that result from job growth, openings will be created by the need to replace current engineers who retire or who transfer to management and sales positions or to other occupational categories.

About 51 percent of currently employed civil engineers work in professional, scientific, and technical services, and about 27 percent are currently working for government agencies. Another 11 percent are employed in construction. The remainder works across a number of industries.

General population growth and the related need to improve the nation's infrastructure will drive demand for civil engineers. Their expertise is needed to design and construct or expand transportation, water supply, and pollution control systems as well as buildings and building complexes. They will also be needed to repair or replace existing roads, bridges, and other public structures. Because construction industries and architectural, engineering, and relates services employ many civil engineers, employment opportunities will vary by region and typically are affected by economic downturns in the economy. The last may also affect jobs with government agencies.

Nature of the Work

Water/wastewater engineers design or oversee projects involving the provision of fresh water, the disposal of wastewater and sewage, or the prevention of flood-related damage. They prepare environmental documentation for regulatory program compliance, as well as water resources, data management and analysis, and field work. They also perform hydraulic modeling and pipeline design.

According to O*NET, water/wastewater engineers may design the following:

- Domestic or industrial water or wastewater treatment plants, including advanced facilities with sequencing batch reactors (SBR), membranes, lift stations, headworks, surge overflow basins, ultraviolet disinfection systems, aerobic digesters, sludge lagoons, or control buildings
- Pumping systems, pumping stations, pipelines, force mains, or sewers for the collection of wastewater
- Sludge treatment plants
- Water distribution systems for potable and nonpotable water
- Water or wastewater lift stations, including water wells
- Water run-off collection networks, water supply channels, or water supply system networks
- Water storage tanks or other water storage facilities

About Water Quality

Water is an important resource that we often take for granted. Under the federal Clean Air Act, states and municipalities as well as colleges and military bases are required to pass laws that prohibit a variety of activities that pollute stormwater. Violators can be fined.

The following are additional tasks that water/wastewater engineers may perform based on O*NET surveys:

- Analyze and recommend chemical, biological, or other wastewater treatment methods to prepare water for industrial or domestic use

- Analyze and recommend sludge treatment or disposal methods
- Assess storm water or floodplain drainage systems to control erosion, stabilize river banks, repair channel streams, or design bridges
- Analyze the efficiency of water delivery structures, such as dams, tainter gates, canals, pipes, penstocks, and cofferdams
- Conduct cost-benefit analyses for the construction of water supply systems, run-off collection networks, water and wastewater treatment plants, or wastewater collection systems
- Carry out environmental impact studies related to water and wastewater collection, treatment, or distribution
- Perform feasibility studies for the construction of facilities, such as water supply systems, run-off collection networks, water and wastewater treatment plants, or wastewater collection systems
- Gather and analyze water use data to forecast water demand
- Oversee the construction of decentralized and on-site wastewater treatment systems, including reclaimed water facilities
- Perform hydraulic analyses of water supply systems or water distribution networks to model flow characteristics, test for pressure losses, or to identify opportunities to mitigate risks and improve operational efficiency
- Conduct hydrological analyses, using three-dimensional simulation software, to model the movement of water or forecast the dispersion of chemical pollutants in the water supply
- Carry out mathematical modeling of underground or surface water resources, such as floodplains, ocean coastlines, streams, rivers, and wetlands
- Conduct water quality studies to identify and characterize water pollutant sources

- Design or select equipment for use in wastewater processing to ensure compliance with government standards
- Develop plans for new water resources or water efficiency programs
- Identify design alternatives for the development of new water resources
- Provide technical direction or supervision to junior engineers, engineering or computer-aided design (CAD) technicians, or other technical personnel
- Provide technical support on water resource or treatment issues to government agencies
- Review and critique proposals, plans, or designs related to water and wastewater treatment systems
- Write technical reports or publications related to water resources development or water use efficiency

Knowledge of regulations such as the U.S. Environmental Protection Agency's (EPA) Spill Prevention Control and Countermeasures (SPCC) rules and the U.S. Resource Conservation and Recovery Act (RCRA), as well as state rules and regulations is necessary.

Career Path

As water/wastewater engineers gain experience, they advance into positions where they supervise a team of engineers and other staff members. Some eventually become managers. Some go on to earn an MBA degree to prepare them for high-level managerial and executive positions.

Earning Potential

Median hourly wage (2009): $36.82

Median annual wage (2009): $76,590

(Based on "Civil Engineers")

Education/Licensure

For entry-level positions, a bachelor's degree in engineering from a college or university program that is accredited by the Accreditation Board for

Engineering and Technology (ABET) is required. Specialties that employers look for are water resources, civil, sanitary, and environmental engineering, although in some cases, engineers with degrees in one type of engineering may qualify for jobs in other areas of engineering. A master's is an advantage for advancement to upper-level positions.

As noted in the *Occupation Outlook Handbook,* some colleges and universities offer five-year programs that culminate in a master's degree in engineering. Some offer five- or six-year programs that include cooperative experience. Some four-year schools have arrangements with community colleges or liberal arts colleges that allow students to spend two or three years at the initial school and transfer for the last two years to complete their engineering degree.

All fifty states and the District of Columbia require engineers to be licensed as professional engineers (PE) if they serve the public directly. In most states, licensure requires graduation from a four-year engineering program accredited by ABET, four years of experience, and passing the state exam. Many engineers take the Fundamentals of Engineering portion of the exam upon graduation. They are then engineers in training (EIT). After obtaining appropriate work experience, they take the Principles and Practice of Engineering exam to complete their professional license. Most states recognize licenses from other states, as long as the requirements are the same or more stringent. Some states have continuing education requirements.

The American Water Resources Association (AWRA) offers the Certified Water Technologist (CWT) certification for those working in the industrial and commercial water treatment fields.

For More Information

Accreditation Board for Engineering and
  Technology (ABET)
111 Market Place
Suite 1050
Baltimore, Maryland 21202
410-347-7700
www.abet.org

American Academy of Water Resources Engineers
  (AAWRE)
1801 Alexander Bell Drive
Reston, Virginia 20191
703-295-6414
www.aawre.org

American Society of Civil Engineers
Transportation and Development Institute
1801 Alexander Bell Drive
Reston, Virginia 20191-4400
800-548-2723 (toll-free)
www.asce.org

American Water Resources Association (AWRA)
P.O. Box 1626
Middleburg, Virginia 20118
540-687-8390
www.awra.org

Association of Water Technologies (AWT)
9707 Key West Avenue
Suite 100
Rockville, Maryland 20850
www.awt.org

International Water Association (IWA)
E-mail: water@iwahq.org
www.iwahq.org

National Society of Professional Engineers
  (NSPE)
1420 King Street
Alexandria, Virginia 22314
703-684-2800 (toll-free)
www.nspe.org

Keep America Beautiful: Great American Cleanup™

Every year from March 1 through May 31, more than 3 million people from almost 1,000 organizations participate in Keep America Beautiful: Great American Cleanup™. In 2009, Americans gave more than 5.2 million hours in 32,000 communities to work on 30,000 specific events. Communities in all fifty states took part.

Projects ranged from cleaning up parks, playgrounds, and recreation centers to conducting educational workshops and hosting community beautification events. Participants removed litter from waterways, beaches, and nature trails; planted trees and flowers and removed graffiti to enhance urban areas; and collected clothing, paper, batteries, and electronics for reuse and recycling.

National sponsors, including The Dow Chemical Company, The Glad Products Company, Pepsi-Cola Company, The Scotts Miracle-Gro Company, Solo Cup Company, and Waste Management, Inc., provided a variety of support, including in-kind donations for local initiatives and employee volunteers.

To see how you can become involved, visit www.kab.org.

How Being Green Works for Kimberly A. Cameron, Weatherization Program Manager

Kimberly Cameron, 42, is the senior weatherization program manager for the Georgia Environmental Facilities Authority in Atlanta, Georgia. Cameron has been working in green projects for close to two decades. Here, Cameron and a colleague work on Georgia's statewide $125-million weatherization program.

Describe your job, including common daily tasks and long-term projects that you have worked on or are working on now. What, specifically, about your job makes it green?

I provide entrepreneurial leadership in implementing projects that result in the development of the state of Georgia's Weatherization Program. I oversee the program's performance and work with various community partners and weatherization agencies across the state. I communicate the results of the program's performance to the U.S. Department of Energy and to state officials.

In this position, I serve as a liaison with a variety of contacts both inside and outside of the organization. It is my responsibility to keep abreast of trends in the construction and energy industries. I manage the budget of the program, and I also look for opportunities to create innovative ways of implementing weatherization, which will ultimately reduce gashouse gas emissions created by low-income households.

My job is green work because we are installing energy conservation methods in the homes of low-income individuals and families where the energy burden can be up to 17 percent higher than households with higher incomes.

Why/how did you decide to work in a green industry?

I first worked in weatherization in 1994, when I ran a local program in Milwaukee, Wisconsin. At that time, "green" was not a buzzword, but the goal was still to decrease the energy burden of low-income individuals and families. When I was 26, I took over what, at the time, was the largest weatherization program in Wisconsin. I ran a department of 55 staff, including energy auditors, intake specialists, warehouse staff, and field staff. We weatherized over 1,100 units a year and renovated 50 homes a year. About this same time, I received a Rental Weatherization Certification from the State of Wisconsin. About five years ago, I reacquainted myself with "green building" through my involvement with Habitat for Humanity. Again, in the interest of serving low-income families in the United States, I became the leader to encourage urban-based Habitat for Humanity affiliates across the U.S. to build "green" homes. By building "green," Habitat is helping its homeowners reduce their energy burden. This helps the environment, while also increasing the disposable income of these families.

How did you prepare for your current position?

I received my bachelor of science in construction management from the University of Wisconsin–Madison. This prepared me for the basic construction side of "green" building. I was the first African American woman to receive a degree in construction management from the University of Wisconsin. Right after college, I became licensed in asbestos abatement and lead-based paint abatement. My first job was for an asbestos and lead-based paint abatement contractor. Looking back, this job, in which I safely removed and stored materials that are hazardous to the environment, was my entrée into the green industry. About three years after college, I was recruited by the Milwaukee-based nonprofit to run the weatherization and home rehabilitation programs.

Six years after college, I decided to go back to school to obtain an MBA in finance from Concordia University Wisconsin. I wanted to expand my knowledge base for management and number crunching, so I could go into the field of real estate development. Receiving my MBA opened doors for me to go into higher executive levels of management. My MBA really gave me the knowledge to think strategically. I have held several vice president positions at large construction and real estate companies. These positions and the networking involved with them gave me the background and preparation for my current job, running the statewide weatherization program.

Which aspect of your education and/or training do you think has been the most helpful and/or useful to you? Why?

My basic undergraduate degree gave me a start to have construction management knowledge, and my MBA opened doors. However, the training I received from my parents growing up has been the most useful to me in my adult years. They taught me to be an independent thinker, a self-starter, and a high achiever. Being a conceptual thinker is what any employer and/or client values the most. Allowing yourself to see the big picture by considering all aspects of a situation, making quick sound decisions, and then executing those decision and making them reality are invaluable abilities.

Do you find that the skills and/or knowledge required for your job continue to evolve? If so, what have you done to keep up-to-date?

Keeping up with the trends is great, but you have to have a basic knowledge, or skill set, as a foundation to build upon. That foundation will always stay the same no matter what new trends come about. Having conceptual skills is a must—you have to be able to filter a great deal of information in a short amount of time and create solutions.

To expand my knowledge base, I have always taken classes and taken advantage of certifications and licensing. I received a certificate in rental weatherization from the state of Wisconsin in 1993. I have attended various seminars offered through the Southface Energy Institute[1]. I have also completed the Green Community program offered through Enterprise Community Partners, Inc.[2] I recently received a certificate for a Healthy Home Professional through the National Environmental Health Association, and I am now preparing to study to sit for the LEED AP exam.

How have continuing education and/or training impacted the way you do your job?

You never know when you will need a skill or the knowledge you picked up at some training. Again, I have taken advantage of every opportunity I've been given to learn, take a class, or receive a certification because I never know when I'll need to reach back for knowledge to help with a current situation.

What is the most rewarding part of your work, and what do you find to be the most challenging?

The most rewarding part of my work is when I read thank-you letters from families that tell how much of an impact we've had on their living situations. The most challenging part is working with people who don't want to change or try new, creative, and innovative ways of getting a job done.

What advice would you give to people interested in pursuing your career?

Education, education, education! Never stop learning. After that, never half-way do anything, whether it be work, school, or volunteering. Your reputation follows you everywhere! Get the basic construction and management knowledge, and build yourself up from there by following your passion. If "green" building is your passion, then go for it.

---

[1]The Southface Energy Institute promotes sustainable energy and environmental technologies and is based in Atlanta, Georgia.

[2]Enterprise Community Partners, Inc., founded in 1982, is a "leading provider of capital and expertise for affordable housing and community development."

How Being Green Works for
Tom Chiu, Plan Check Engineer

Tom Chiu, 52, is a plan check engineer for Santa Clara County, California, also known as Silicon Valley. Although Chiu has worked in the county building department for 15 years, new state-mandated regulations made his position "green" in 2007. Conducting ceiling inspections, as shown here, is just one part of the job for Tom Chiu.

Describe your job, including common daily tasks and long-term projects that you have worked on or are working on now. What, specifically, about your job makes it green?

Effective January 1, 2010, the County of Santa Clara began requiring permit issuing for residential construction to comply with its green building ordinance. My primary job function is to review building permit construction plans to ensure that they are complying with the adopted codes, which include structural, fire and life safety, flood, energy efficiency, and CalGreen [state] rules and regulations. Occasionally, I inspect complicated large-scale projects (over $1 million in valuation). I am part of the green building committee for the County Development Services Office that establishes the green building standards for building owners to make energy efficiency and green improvements to their properties.

Why/how did you decide to work in a green industry?

There isn't any choice. It is a state-mandated green building code that local agencies must adopt and enforce. Therefore, plan checkers must learn about the green building business.

How did you prepare for your current position?

I have a master's degree in civil engineering from San Jose State University. I am a licensed professional engineer (PE) and a licensed general building contractor by the state of California. I am also an International Code Council (ICC) certified building plan examiner. I worked in private engineering companies and had my own design-build business for more than 10 years before I joined the county building department in 1995. Overall, I have 25 years of experience in the construction business and have been on both sides as a builder applicant and as a code enforcement officer.

Which aspect of your education and/or training do you think has been the most helpful and/or useful to you? Why?

A civil engineering degree is the minimum requirement in order to be a plan check engineer. It gives you the basic knowledge of how a building is constructed. However, all of the training sessions that I have gone to during my employment period with the county have been the most valuable and helpful to me. This training validates what I have learned and keeps my knowledge updated. The 2007 building code is very different from the 1994 building code. Both state law and license renewal require continuous education. I attend seminars, trade shows, conventions, field trips, and round-table discussion meetings with stakeholders—homeowners, architects, and contractors who have a direct interest in a project—once a month on average.

Do you have a LEED credential? Why or why not?

I do not have a LEED credential at this moment. I understand that a lot of private design professionals have gotten LEED-certified during the past few years. Santa Clara County started paying attention to the green building industry about three years ago when California began pushing going green (green building, water conservation, wind power, etc.). Educational funds from the government have been tight the past two years. However, the county did receive some stimulus funds from the federal government, and I expect to get LEED- or Build-It-Green–certified in the coming year.

Do you find that the skills and/or knowledge required for your job continue to evolve? If so, what have you done to keep up-to-date?

Finally, the three major building code governing bodies of the United States decided to join together and produce one building code, the International Building Code (IBC). The first IBC was published in the year 2000. Every three years, there will be an update to the IBC to incorporate new skills and knowledge. California energy efficiency standards and green building codes are also revised every three years following

the IBC. Changes in every code cycle are approximately 10 to 15 percent.

In order to keep up, I became a member of a tri-chapter committee (formed by the building departments of local government agencies), nonprofit professional associations like the Structural Engineers Association of California, Build It Green, the ICC, and online forums. Attending monthly meetings and participating in forums and newsletter discussions are ways to stay up-to-date and gain trade information.

How have continuing education and/or training impacted the way you do your job?

Continuing education and training are the best ways to gain knowledge on what is new out there and what other jurisdictions are doing.

What is the most rewarding part of your work, and what do you find to be the most challenging?

When homeowners, architects, engineers, and contractors show their appreciation for my knowledge in helping them to finish a project, and the feeling I have when I walk through the building during the final signing off are most satisfactory parts of my job.

The most challenging? Nothing compared to a violation. Some owners do not want to spend money to bring the building into compliance with the code and ordinance. Sometimes, there is absolutely no other way, but to tear down the illegal structure.

What advice would you give to people interested in pursuing your career?

To become a plan check engineer, obtain a four-year engineering degree. . . . During one's career, continue taking classes from local community colleges. These classes are often taught by working professionals who have the most current knowledge. Also attend training provided by specialty organizations. Examples of this include Build It Green for green building business information and a utilities provider for information on how to save energy.

PART II

COLLEGES AND UNION ORGANIZATIONS WITH GREAT GREEN PROGRAMS

CHAPTER 6

25 FOUR-YEAR SCHOOLS WITH GREAT GREEN PROGRAMS

The twenty-five colleges and universities profiled in this chapter support innovative programs in construction, interior design, and horticulture and landscaping. These institutions also have vibrant on-campus sustainability programs and organizations. Each of the schools listed here includes inventive programs in its curricula, and all have made a commitment to making their campus communities sustainable.

Many of the undergraduate programs listed here are interdisciplinary and draw on the strengths of the faculty in several areas. Some of the programs include research opportunities or internships for undergraduates. Many of the universities on this list also have graduate programs that lead to advanced degrees or certificates. The information presented here has been culled not only from college Web sites, but also from *Peterson's Survey of Sustainability Efforts in Higher Education,* sent to two-year and four-year schools in the United States and Canada and completed by representatives of the schools themselves.

In addition to strong academics, each college or university on this list has a strong commitment to sustainability. Approximately 40 percent have signed the American College and University Presidents Climate Commitment, pledging to eliminate global-warming emissions through policy and curriculum. These schools have sustainability policy committees and active student groups promoting the environment through advocacy, action, awareness, and activities. Some offer green residence halls and are either building or have already built buildings certified by LEED (Leadership in Energy and Environmental Design).

The colleges and universities in this chapter represent a broad cross-section of schools in the United States: public and private institutions, large and small schools, schools in urban and rural settings, state universities, liberal arts colleges, and schools specializing in a single discipline.

Keep in mind that this is a list of highlights: Many other colleges and universities not listed here also offer energy studies programs. Check out *Peterson's Four-Year Colleges* and look for any of the majors listed below in the "Majors" index to find other schools offering similar programs.

ABOUT THE LISTINGS

Here's what you need to know to navigate this chapter.

Contact Information

The school profile lists the school name, address, phone number, e-mail address, and Web site.

College Videos

Virtual college tours are available for some of the colleges and universities listed here on YOUniversityTV.com. You'll find easy-to-use links to campus videos that look like this:

 http://bit.ly/collvid1

YOUniversityTV.com assists students with the college selection process by providing access to videos and educational resources for colleges across the United States. YOUniversityTV.com is free-of-charge and does not receive compensation from any of the universities it features.

Undergraduate Degrees and Certificates

This section includes majors and minors in building and landscaping–related subjects and other degree programs that have a building and landscaping–related focus. Inclusion of majors depends on how the college or university describes its program—so a certain program, for example, the environment and natural resources, may be included for one school, but not for another, even if the second school also offers the degree.

Many schools offer a number of options, concentrations, or specializations within a degree program. Information relevant to construction, interior design, and landscaping has been included to show the wide variety of possible study areas.

Undergraduate Distance Learning

A number of schools offer courses online, some of which may meet requirements of the degrees listed in this guide. Some schools offer online degrees, but few are at the undergraduate level. They are more often at the master's level. However, many offer certificates online at both the undergraduate and graduate levels.

Undergraduate Costs

The information on the costs for an undergraduate is the latest available at the time that this publication went to press.

Undergraduate Financial Aid

Scholarships are generally based on merit rather than need. For most schools, scholarships for students majoring in certain fields are awarded through the individual academic departments, so you are advised to visit departmental Web sites for details.

Undergraduate Admissions Requirements

General admissions requirements to undergraduate programs are listed in this section. Where appropriate, any special prerequisites for science majors are listed.

Undergraduate Application Information

This section includes the type of application that is required by each school, application fees, and deadlines for applying and for notification.

Green Campus Organizations and Projects

This section gives a sampling of green extracurricular activities, not limited to those with a building and landscaping focus, that students may participate in. The colleges and universities included in this guide have substantial sustainability efforts and thus offer a variety of ways in which students may become involved and take leadership roles.

Fast Facts

The section "Fast Facts" provides insight into a school's commitment to sustainability and the environment, as well as to areas related to construction, interior design, and landscaping.

Graduate Degrees and Certificates

This guide focuses on undergraduate programs, but graduate programs are listed here for several reasons. First, graduate programs combined with the undergraduate degree offerings show the depth and breadth of the programs available at these colleges and universities in the fields of construction, interior design, and landscaping and related concerns.

Second, many of the schools included in this guide encourage or require undergraduates to participate in research projects or internships during their upper-class years. By listing the graduate programs, you can get an idea of the possibilities for junior or senior research projects. Even though as a prospective freshman, you may not be thinking about graduate school, these programs show you possibilities and give you additional information to consider as you choose your school and major and map your education.

Third, if you already hold a bachelor's degree, you may be interested in becoming "green" by pursuing an advanced degree, certificate, or training. The graduate programs and certificates listed in this guide show you the myriad possibilities.

Graduate Distance Learning

A number of schools offer courses online, some of which may meet requirements of the degrees listed in this guide at the master's level. Some distance learning programs are geared toward certificate programs at the graduate level.

Schools Profiled Here

The following four-year colleges and universities are profiled in this chapter:
- Arizona State University
- Auburn University

- Ball State University
- Boston Architectural College
- California Polytechnic State University, San Luis Obispo
- Colorado State University
- Cornell University
- Drexel University
- Kansas State University
- Louisiana State University Agricultural and Mechanical College
- Massachusetts Institute of Technology
- New York School of Interior Design
- Parsons The New School for Design
- Pennsylvania State University
- Pratt Institute
- Purdue University
- Rhode Island School of Design
- Syracuse University
- Texas A&M University
- The University of Texas at Austin
- University of Cincinnati
- University of Georgia
- University of Oregon, Eugene
- University of Virginia
- Virginia Polytechnic Institute and State University

ARIZONA STATE UNIVERSITY (ASU)

University Drive and Mill Avenue
Tempe, Arizona 85287
480-965-9011
E-mail: campus.asu.edu/tempe
www.asu.edu

 http://bit.ly/collvid1

About ASU's Conservation Initiatives

Check out the Campus Metabolism site at http://cm.asu.edu. It shows in real time the campus's energy use. You can download a variety of information about ASU's energy conservation initiatives at http://sustainability.asu.edu/campus/energy.php.

Undergraduate Degrees

All degrees are offered at the Tempe campus.

Architectural Studies (major or minor)
Civil Engineering (Construction Engineering concentration)
Construction (Concrete Industry Management, General Building Construction, Heavy Construction, Residential Construction, and Specialty Construction concentrations)
Design Studies (major or minor)
Industrial Design
Interior Design
Interior Design History (minor)
Landscape Architecture
Landscape Architecture Studies (minor)
Mechanical Engineering
Urban Planning

Undergraduate Costs

Academic year 2010–11 (estimate): $7793 resident, $20,257 nonresident (tuition); $10,996 books, room and board

Undergraduate Financial Aid

FAFSA required.

Undergraduate Admissions Requirements

Required: High school diploma or GED. One of the following: 3.0 GPA in competency courses, top 25 percent of class, ACT 22 (24 nonresidents) or SAT 1040 (1110 nonresidents). Competency requirement: 4 years English, 4 years math, 3 years laboratory science, 2 years social science, 2 years same foreign language, 1 year fine arts. Some exceptions may be considered, and some programs have higher requirements.

Undergraduate Application Information

Option: Online application

Application fee: $25 (residents), $55 (nonresidents)

Required: Application, high school transcript

Application deadlines: March 1 (freshmen), June 1 (fall transfers), December 26 (winter transfers), December 1 (spring transfers)

Notification: Continuous

Green Campus Organizations

Society of Automotive Engineers (SAE): Student chapter of this international organization; works on projects related to automotive and aerospace technology, including Mini Baja car competition.

Recycling Club of ASU: Promotes recycling on and off campus by collecting and disposing of recyclable items and holding activities to raise awareness.

Sustainability Jedi: Enhances students' educational experience through involvement in real-world sustainability projects that improve rural and underprivileged communities worldwide.

ASU Emerging Green Builders (EGB): For students interested in the green building movement. Offers opportunities for involvement with the U.S. Green Building Council (USGBC) and similar organizations to create a network of green building leaders.

EcoAid on Campus: Provides scholarship and internship opportunities, mentoring, and training to students in green industries.

Students of Arizona Network for Sustainability: A network of student organizations and community groups dedicated to promoting sustainability in Arizona. Activities include education, outreach, and action. Web site: http://azsans.com/.

Fast Facts

The Phoenix Urban Research Laboratory (PURL), an extension of ASU's Herberger Institute School of Architecture and Landscape Design, serves many purposes, including think tank, project center, design and research, and link to the city of Phoenix. PURL researchers address and search for answers to the complex urban challenges of the twenty-first century.

The Global Institute of Sustainability, which includes the School of Sustainability, conducts research, problem solving, and education with an emphasis on urban sustainability. The institute grew out of the Arizona State University Center for Environmental Studies that conducted research for more than 30 years. Phoenix, because it is among the fastest growing urban areas in the country, is a prime laboratory for the institute's studies. For more information, visit sustainability.asu.edu.

ASU's School of Sustainability is the first such school in the nation.

ASU's W.P. Carey School of Business began offering a BA in sustainability in 2008. Students can combine their traditional coursework with specializations in sustainability, urban policy, communication, or tourism management.

Graduate Degrees

Architecture (MArch)
Built Environment (Energy Performance/Climate Responsive Architecture) (MS)
Civil/Environmental Engineering (Hydrology and Water Resources Engineering, Structural Engineering, and Transportation Engineering specialties) (MS, MSE, PhD)
Construction (MS, PhD)
Environmental Design/Planning (PhD)

Environmental Design/Planning (Healthcare and Healing Environments) (PhD)
Industrial Design (MSD)
Interior Design (MSD)
Landscape Architecture (MLA)
Mechanical Engineering (MS, MSE, PhD)
Real Estate Development (MRED)
Urban and Environmental Planning (MUEP)
Urban Design (MUD)

Graduate Certificates

Transportation Systems

Graduate Distance Learning

Construction (MS)

AUBURN UNIVERSITY

Auburn, Alabama 36849
334-844-4000
E-mail: www.auburn.edu/main/auweb_campus_directory.html
www.auburn.edu

http://bit.ly/collvid45

About Auburn Online

Auburn Sustainability Online at www.auburn.edu/projects/sustainability/website includes links to lectures addressing sustainability issues presented through the TED (Technology, Entertainment, Design) talk series, student-made videos about sustainability, Green Lunch Series Webcasts, and information about a variety of university sustainability initiatives.

Undergraduate Degrees

Agronomy and Soils (Turfgrass Management track)
Architecture

Building Science
Civil Engineering
Environmental Design (Post Baccalaureate
    program)
Horticulture (Landscape Horticulture emphasis)
Industrial Design
Interior Architecture/Architecture
Interior Design
Mechanical Engineering

Undergraduate Costs

Academic year 2009–10: $15,896 resident, $28,376 nonresident (tuition, fees, room and board)

Undergraduate Financial Aid

FAFSA required. Scholarships: General Spirit of Auburn Scholarships and Spirit of Auburn Presidential Scholarships; four-year, renewable Freshman Resident and Non-Resident Scholarships; one-year General Scholarships for new and current students. One-year and four-year Departmental Scholarships awarded annually; go to www.auburn.edu/scholarship for more information.

Undergraduate Admissions Requirements

Required: ACT and/or SAT scores (including the Writing score from at least one test date). High school preparation: 4 years English, 3 years math (must include 1 year each algebra I and II, geometry, trigonometry, calculus, or analysis), 2 years science (must include 1 year each biology and physical science), 3 years social studies.

Undergraduate Application Information

Options: Early Action, rolling admission

Application fee: $40

Required: Online application, official high school transcript, activities and interest form, official ACT/SAT scores

Application deadline: November 1 (first round), December 1 (second round), February 1 (third round), October 1 (Early Action)

Notification: November 15 (first round), December 15 (second round), February 15 (third round), October 15–February 15 (Early Action)

About the Talloires Declaration

In 1990, 35 university presidents met to discuss the university's role in environmental education and stewardship. The result was the Talloires Declaration, a commitment by higher educational institutions from around the world to promote awareness of environmental issues and to establish policies and programs to counter environmental problems.

Green Campus Organizations

Auburn Green Builders: Dedicated to sustainable practices in design, construction, and engineering.

Green Lunch Series: Monthly program hosted by Auburn's Office of Sustainability; invited speakers from campus and off-campus talk about a sustainability theme; open and free to all.

Sustain-A-Bowl: Annual competition among residence halls to see which hall can reduce its resource use the most; in conjunction with RecycleMania.

Res Life Eco-Rep Program: A cooperative effort between the Office of Sustainability and Housing and Residence Life; "eco-reps" organize sustainability-themed area events, encourage residents and other housing staff to live more sustainably, educate residents about sustainability, act as go-betweens with the Office of Sustainability, and lead participation in Sustain-A-Bowl.

Fast Facts

The Office of Sustainability is developing the Auburn Climate Action Plan, a blueprint for significantly reducing the university's carbon footprint.

The university joined this national project in 2008. Campus working groups are addressing areas including energy, buildings, transportation, and grounds (landscaping).

The goal of Auburn University's Center for Bioenergy and Bioproducts, part of its Natural Resources Management and Development Institute, is to advance economic development in Alabama by reinvigorating natural resource-based industries and by establishing new industries based on energy and value-added renewable biomass products. The Center has created a comprehensive Bioenergy and Bioproducts Laboratory that provides a single location for research and education activities—from feedstock production and processing through biofuel conversion and testing. The campus lab has attracted faculty, staff, and students from around the world, as well as regional entrepreneurs who are interested in partnering with the university to create sustainable products and solve energy problems.

Graduate Degrees and Certificates

Agronomy and Soils (Turfgrass Management) (MAg, MS, PhD)
Architecture (MLA, MCP, MDB, MRED)
Building Construction (MBC, MDB)
Civil Engineering (MCE, MS, PhD)
Community Planning (MCP)
Design Build (Design or Construction tracks) (MS)
Horticulture (MAg, MS, PhD)
Industrial and Systems Engineering (MS, MISE, PhD)
Industrial Design (MID)
Landscape Architecture (MLA)
Mechanical Engineering (MME, MS, PhD)

Graduate Distance Learning

Civil Engineering (MCE)
Mechanical Engineering (MME)

Professional and Continuing Education

Auburn's Office of Professional and Continuing Education offers online courses for building professionals that address sustainable practices, green job training, and LEED test-prep courses. Representative courses include Building Energy Efficiency level I, Energy Efficient Design for Architects, Energy Auditing Software Training, Fundamentals of Solar Water Heating, Green Building Sales Professional, and Weatherization Energy Auditor.

Certificates

Indoor Air Quality Manager
Indoor Environmentalist
Microbial Investigator
Senior Certified Sustainability Professional
Sustainability Professional

BALL STATE UNIVERSITY

2000 W. University Avenue
Muncie, Indiana 47306
765-289-1241
800-382-8540 (toll-free)
http://cms.bsu.edu/

About Going Geothermal

Ball State is in the process of creating the nation's largest closed geothermal energy system. Once complete, the system will heat and cool more than forty-five buildings over the university's 660-acre campus. It will save the university nearly $2 million a year in operating costs and will cut the university's carbon footprint roughly in half.

Undergraduate Degrees

Architecture
Business Administration for Construction
    Management (minor)
Construction Management (minor)
Design Technology (minor)
Environmental Design, Architecture
Historic Preservation (minor)
Industrial Technology (Construction Management
    option)
Interior Design (minor)
Landscape Architecture (major or minor)
Real Estate Development (minor)
Urban Planning (minor)
Urban Planning and Development

Undergraduate Costs

Academic year 2010–11 (estimate): $16,290 resident, $29,742 nonresident (tuition, fees, room and board)

Undergraduate Financial Aid

FAFSA required.

Undergraduate Admissions Requirements

Required: SAT or ACT. High school preparation: 4 years English; 3 years college preparatory mathematics (algebra I, algebra II, geometry); 3 years science, 2 with lab; and 3 years social studies. Foreign language study strongly recommended, but not required.

Also considered: Strength of high school curriculum (including senior year); curricular patterns or grade trends in academic courses; participation in extracurricular activities.

Undergraduate Application Information

Options: Online application

Application fee: $25

Required: Application, official high school transcript or GED score report; SAT or ACT scores; guidance counselor form

Also required: Supplemental applications for students enrolling in architecture, interior design, landscape architecture, or urban planning and development programs. For more information, go to http://cms.bsu.edu/AdmissionsLanding/UndergraduateAdmissions/AdmissionRequirements/SpecialPrograms.aspx.

Optional: One-page applicant statement

Application deadline: March 1 (fall semester); December 1 (spring semester); April 1 (summer and first summer session); May 1 (second summer session

Notification: Rolling basis

Green Campus Organizations

American Society of Landscape Architects: Ball State chapter of the national organization; provides educational and social activities for members to learn more about the profession.

Emerging Green Builders: Integrates students and professionals into the green building movement by creating a network of emerging green building leaders.

Council on the Environment: University-wide clearinghouse for sustainability initiatives; representatives from each of the university's academic colleges and vice presidential areas, the student body, and the greater Muncie community. The Council, which provides an open forum for the discussion of environmental issues, works to protect the environment by, for example, promoting the sustainable use of natural resources.

Fast Facts

CapAsia is a unique field study semester offered to Ball State juniors, seniors, or graduate students studying architecture, urbanism, and planning. Participants spend eleven weeks in South Asia studying the social and cultural aspects of urban spaces and built environments. In 2010, the program consisted of a seven-week "Planning to Learn" project in India and a three-week "Building to Learn" component in Nepal.

Students from the College of Architecture and Planning constructed the Eco Center, the first load-bearing straw building in the Midwest. The students used straw bales for support and insulation in the walls, and they incorporated into the roof and floors other sustainable materials, such as laminated veneer lumber and fly ash concrete. They also installed solar collectors and a wind turbine to generate energy for lights and heat.

The Building Futures Institute, a research unit of the College of Architecture and Planning, investigates ideas and concepts in areas including open building, integrated practice, nanotechnology, learning environments, and architectural structures/digital heritage. Recent projects include an international environmental design conference that focused on the design of open-ended, but sustainable physical environments in education.

Ball State and the Association for the Advancement of Sustainability host the biennial Greening of the Campus conference, which is a forum for university personnel to share "green" ideas ranging from practical day-to-day operational issues to creating "green" curriculum.

At the Center for Energy Research/Education/Service (CERES), researchers focus on issues related to energy and resource use, alternatives, and conservation. Their projects range from issues as broad as community planning to topics as specific as materials technology.

Graduate Degrees

Architecture (MArch)
Architecture II (MArch II)
Historic Preservation (MSHP)
Landscape Architecture (MLA)
Urban and Regional Planning (MURP)
Urban Design (MUD)

Graduate Distance Learning

Interior Design (MS, MA)
Urban Design (MUD)

BOSTON ARCHITECTURAL COLLEGE (BAC)

320 Newbury Street
Boston, Massachusetts 02115
617-262-5000
www.the-bac.edu
See Ad on Inside Front Cover

About the Degree Program at BAC

Most students work during the day in the design profession and take classes at night. Students may also take courses at any of the five art and design schools in the Boston area. During the last two semesters of the program, students are required to complete a capstone project that synthesizes their general and professional education. Through the program, students are able to meet most, if not all, of the intern requirements for licensing by the National Council of Architectural Registration Boards or certification by the National Council for Interior Design Qualification.

Undergraduate Degrees

Architecture
Design Studies (Architectural Technology, Design
    Computing, Historic Preservation, Sustainable
    Design concentrations)
Interior Design
Landscape Architecture

Undergraduate Distance Learning

Certificates:

Sustainable Building Design and Construction
Sustainable Design
Sustainable Community Planning and Design
Sustainable Residential Design

Continuing Education

Certificates:

Advanced Rendering
Design Computing
Historic Preservation
Kitchen and Bath Design
Landscape Design
Landscape Design History
Landscape Preservation
Planting Design
Residential Interiors

About Online Firsts at BAC

Boston Architectural College is the only accredited college in the United States to offer the Sustainable Design Certification program, both undergraduate and graduate, completely online.

Undergraduate Costs

Academic year 2010–11: $8064 per semester (tuition, 6–10 credits, full-time academic study); $10,725 per semester (tuition, 12–18 credits, Academic Only Program)

Undergraduate Financial Aid

FAFSA required.

Undergraduate Admission Requirements

Required: Completion of a high school program or its equivalent.

Undergraduate Application Information

Options: Online application

Application fee: $50

Required: Application, official high school transcript or GED scores, current resume or statement of academic and/or work experience

Application deadline: Rolling admissions; applications accepted up until the start of each semester (September or January)

Green Campus Organizations

American Institute of Architecture Students: BAC chapter of national organization; offers lectures, field trips, social and networking events, and conferences. Members also carry out community service projects such as Freedom by Design, in which they modify the homes of low-income elderly people and people with disabilities to address safety and comfort issues.

American Society of Interior Designers: Promotes and networks for career opportunities in the interior design industry.

National Organization of Minority Architecture Students: Promotes diversity in architecture through educational and recreational activities such as participating in national design competitions and mentoring local high school students.

Student American Society of Landscape Architects: Student group that explores the field of landscape architecture and related skills.

Fast Facts

In 2009, students from BAC and neighboring Tufts University joined forces to compete in the U.S. Department of Energy's biennial Solar Decathlon as Team Boston. The competition is an educational project in which twenty selected college and university teams attempt to design, build, and operate the most attractive and energy-efficient solar-powered house.

BAC's online Sustainable Design courses are offered in partnership with BuildingGreen. Many of the courses are endorsed by and included in the U.S. Green Building Council's Education Providers Program. Many have also been reviewed and approved by the Royal Institute of British Architects Continuing Professional Development Program. The courses are taught by practicing design professionals and green building experts.

Graduate Degrees

Architecture (MArch)
Interior Design (MID)
Landscape Architecture (MLA)

Graduate Distance Learning

Architecture (MArch)

CALIFORNIA POLYTECHNIC STATE UNIVERSITY (CAL POLY), SAN LUIS OBISPO

San Luis Obispo, California 93407
805-756-1111
www.calpoly.edu

About Green Certificate Programs Online

Cal Poly's Continuing Education and University Outreach program offers six-month online courses for certificates for Home Inspection, HVAC Technician, and Interior Design, as well as Building Analyst, Certified Indoor Air Quality Manager Training, Indoor Environmentalist Training, Principles of Designing Green Buildings, and Performing Comprehensive Building Assessments. The university also offers an online five-course professional certificate in Green Building Construction.

Undergraduate Degrees

Architectural Engineering (major or minor)
Architecture
City and Regional Planning (major or minor)
Civil Engineering
Construction Management (major or minor)
Environmental Horticultural Science
Integrated Project Delivery (minor)
Landscape Architecture
Landscape Horticulture (minor)
Mechanical Engineering (HVAC concentration)
Plant Protection and Integrated Pest Management
Real Property Development (minor)
Sustainable Environments (minor)

Undergraduate Costs

Academic year 2010–11: $16,569 resident (tuition, room and board); nonresident, the same plus an additional $248 per unit

Undergraduate Financial Aid

FAFSA required.

Departmental scholarships: www.ess.calpoly.edu/_finaid/types_aid/scholarships.htm.

Undergraduate Admissions Requirements

General admissions requirements for the California State University System; check the Cal Poly admissions site for individual Cal Poly college requirements.

Required: SAT or ACT (Writing Test not included).

High school preparation: 4 years English, 3 years math (algebra I and II, geometry), 2 years history and social science (including 1 year U.S. History or U.S. History/Government), 2 years science with lab (one biological and one physical), 2 years the same foreign language, 1 year visual and performing arts (single year-long course), and 1 year college prep elective, all with C grade or higher.

Undergraduate Application Information

Options: Online application preferred; Early Assessment Program for California residents who attend or attended public high schools

Application fee: $55

Required: CSU application, SAT or ACT scores, official high school transcript

Application deadline: November 30 (freshmen and transfers)

Green Campus Organizations

Design Build Institute of America: Professional organization of students from all disciplines (the College of Architecture and Design, College of Engineering, College of Business) that deal with designing and building the environment we live in.

The Construction Specifications Institute Student Club: Diverse student organization in which members exchange knowledge in an effort to help advance the process of creating and sustaining the built environment.

Green Campus Program: Part of the Alliance to Save Energy's Green Campus Program; participants on thirteen University of California, California State University, and private campuses in the state; campaigns and competitions to improve campuswide energy efficiency.

Engineers Without Borders: Cal Poly chapter of the international nonprofit organization that partners with communities to improve their quality of life through environmentally and economically sustainable engineering projects.

Student Chapter of the American Society of Landscape Architects: Student chapter of national organization that promotes education, wise planning, and artful design of cultural and natural environments.

Fast Facts

In 2009, Cal Poly expanded its student learning objectives to include four related to sustainability. According to the institute, "graduating seniors should be able to define and apply sustainability principles within their academic programs; explain how natural, economic, and social systems interact to foster or prevent sustainability; analyze and explain local, national, and global sustainability using a multidisciplinary approach; and consider sustainability principles while developing personal and professional values."

The College of Architecture and Design is one of thirteen U.S. universities that now offer both architecture and construction programs in the same college. The Architecture + Construction Alliance (A+CA) has three key initiatives: "teaching combined architecture and construction students; undertaking combined faculty research efforts;

and responding to collaborative project initiatives generated by professional and industry partners."

Poly Canyon, which is located next to the main Cal Poly campus, is a nine-acre experimental construction laboratory. CAED students have used the site for more than four decades. Each spring, students from across the United States travel to Poly Canyon to compete in the university's Design Village Competition. The rules: the structure's parts must be carried by hand up a mile-long trail into the canyon; the structure must be assembled in 12 hours without the use of plugged electricity; and team members must live in their structure throughout the weekend. Winners are selected based upon craftsmanship, sustainability, excellence in design, suitability to the theme, and public response.

The Renewable Energy Institute promotes research and development of solar and renewable energy technologies and sustainable community infrastructure.

Graduate Degrees

Agriculture (Environmental Horticulture specialization) (MS)
Architecture (MS)
Architecture (Architectural Engineering specialization) (MS)
City and Regional Planning (MCRP)
Civil and Environmental Engineering (MS)
Mechanical Engineering (MS)

About Used Ink/Toner Cartridges

Staples® accepts used printer cartridges and gives you a certificate worth $6 off on a future purchase of anything Staples sells. Not near a Staples store? Check www.recycleplace.com for other ways to recycle used cartridges.

COLORADO STATE UNIVERSITY (CSU)

Fort Collins, Colorado 80523
970-491-6444
www.colostate.edu

About CSU's History of Being Green

Colorado State University began researching alternative energy solutions in the 1960s and is well known for its clean-energy research and sustainability efforts both on campus and abroad. CSU scientists constructed the world's first engineered building to be heated and cooled using solar energy. The university was also one of the first in the country to give students living on campus the option of using green power. For a complete list of CSU's green "firsts," go to http://www.green.colostate.edu/greenfirsts.aspx.

Undergraduate Degrees

Civil Engineering
Construction Management (major or minor)
Horticulture (Horticultural Therapy concentration available) (major or minor)
Interior Design
Landscape Architecture (Landscape Design and Contracting concentration)
Landscape Horticulture (Turf Management concentration) (major or minor)

Undergraduate Certificate

Horticultural Therapy

Undergraduate Costs

Academic year 2010–11 (estimate): $6318 resident, $22,240 nonresident (tuition and fees), $11,788 (Western Undergraduate Exchange student); $9472 (books, supplies, room and board)

Additional tuition is assessed on a per-credit-hour basis for undergraduate students enrolled in upper division courses, high-cost/high-demand programs, and/or programs that require supplemental tuition. For more information, go to http://registrar.colostate.edu/pdf/Additional-Tuition-Charges.pdf.

Undergraduate Financial Aid

FAFSA required.

Undergraduate Admissions Requirements

Required: High school diploma or GED; ACT or SAT (written sections not required); priority consideration given to freshman applicants with a minimum 3.25 GPA. Recommended high school preparation: 4 years English (can include speech, grammar, literature, writing); 4 years math (must include algebra I, algebra II, and geometry); 3 years natural science (two years must be lab-based); 3 years social studies (1 year must be U.S. history or world civilization); 2 years same foreign language; 2 years academic electives including art, music, drama/theater, computer science, career-technical education programs, or any of the core subjects listed above.

Undergraduate Application Information

Options: Online application (preferred)

Application fee: $50

Required: Colorado State University Application for Admission or Common Application; personal statement; official high school transcript; ACT or SAT results; letters of recommendation (one is required; more are optional; letters from teacher or school-based counselor preferred)

Application deadline: February 1 (priority fall freshmen); June 1 (priority fall transfers); July 1 (final fall deadline); November 1 (spring semester)

Notification: Rolling basis beginning in September

Green Campus Organizations

Engineers Without Borders: Campus chapter of this international organization that works to aid communities in developing nations.

Coalition for Campus Sustainability: Promotes awareness among student peers by educating them about sustainability and how to integrate it into their lives.

Environmental Action Collective: Raises awareness of environmental issues through volunteer and outreach programs within the community.

The Student Environmental Leadership Network (SELN): Serves as a conduit for various student organizations and individuals who are interested in environmental leadership and sustainability and share ideas and uncover areas of common interest.

Student Sustainability Center: Goal to "become a center of student activity surrounding sustainability, including efforts in curriculum, research, and environmental projects."

Fast Facts

CSU's horticulture program offers a concentration in horticultural therapy, which combines horticulture courses with the study of therapy/human sciences. Students learn to cultivate plants and gardens in ways that can improve people's mental and physical health. Graduates manage and work in programs at mental health, vocational, correctional, rehabilitative, wellness, educational, community-based, and long-term care facilities.

The Institute for the Built Environment (IBE) is a multidisciplinary research institute that gives professionals and students from the design and construction industries a place to solve problems through research related to the built environment. The IBE has completed many projects, including the university's New Academic Village, a "green" living/learning laboratory on campus. IBE also offers twelve-week programs in which professionals can earn a Green Building Certificate or a Green Home Certificate.

CSU's School of Global Environmental Sustainability is an umbrella organization that encompasses all environmental education and research at the university. Areas of emphasis include everything from sustainable engineering to water management strategies.

Students who choose to live on the Live Green Floor in Summit Hall live in a sustainable living community. Residents participate in sustainability initiatives and pilot recycling, composting, water conservation, energy reduction, and green power projects. The floor is co-sponsored by the Live Green Team and the Warner College of Natural Resources.

Graduate Degrees

Civil Engineering (MS, PhD)
Construction Management (MS)
Design and Merchandising (Interior Design) (MS)
Horticulture (MS, PhD)
Landscape Architecture (MLA)

CORNELL UNIVERSITY

Campus Information and Visitor Relations
Day Hall Lobby
Ithaca, New York 14853
607-254-4636
E-mail: info@cornell.edu
www.cornell.edu

 http://bit.ly/collvid47

Undergraduate Degrees

Architecture (major or minor)
Civil Engineering (Civil Infrastructure focus)
Civil Infrastructure (minor)
Facilities Planning and Management
Human Factors and Ergonomics
Interior Design
Landscape Architecture
Landscape Studies (minor)
Mechanical Engineering (major or minor)
Plant Sciences: Horticulture (major or minor)
Urban and Regional Studies (major or minor)

Undergraduate Costs

Academic year 2010–11 (estimate): $39,450 (Endowed College Units tuition); $23,310 (resident Contract College Units tuition); $39,450 (nonresident Contract College Units tuition); $216 (student activity fees); housing options vary from $3840 to $9050 per year; meal plans range from $2050 to $2990 per semester.

Undergraduate Financial Aid

FAFSA and CSS Profile required. Scholarship information may be found on the scholarship Web site: https://www.finaid.cornell.edu/types/scholarships/.

Undergraduate Admissions Requirements

Required: SAT Reasoning test or ACT with Writing. Admission requirements vary by college. Go to http://admissions.cornell.edu/forms/FreshmanRequirementsChart.pdf.

Undergraduate Application Information

Options: Online application

Application fee: $70

Required: Common Application (including pages AP1–AP5, secondary school report, teacher evaluations, mid-year report, and final report); Cornell Supplement to the Common Application; official high school transcript; formal interview required for students enrolling in architecture program and encouraged for those enrolling in art department.

Application deadline: November 1 (early decision); January 2 (regular decision)

Green Campus Organizations

Design, Education, Engineering and Development (DEED): Students discuss, design, plan, and act on sustainable and environmental solutions for developing communities.

Engineers for a Sustainable World: Engineering students working for global sustainability through engagement, education, and mobilization.

Environmental Law Society: Students interested in environmental legal issues.

Farm to Cornell: Students promoting sustainable agriculture by discussing the benefits of eating locally for the environment, the economy, and society.

Sustainability Hub: Carries on research; connects other organizations related to sustainability and environmental issues through events such as Earth Day and Campus Sustainability Day.

Fast Facts

The Center for Sustainable Global Enterprise manages sustainability through an approach that "frames social and environmental challenges as unmet needs that can be addressed with business solutions." This philosophy is the basis of the university's masters in business administration (MBA) and executive programs in business and sustainability.

The Cornell Center for a Sustainable Future was created in 2007 in response to the need for solutions to worldwide challenges related to energy, the environment, and economic development.

Weill Hall, home of the Department of Biomedical Engineering and the Weill Institute for Cell and Molecular Biology, was dedicated in 2008 as Cornell's first LEED-certified green building.

Graduate Degrees

Architecture (MS, MArch professional)
Architecture (Architecture & Urbanism, Architecture & Ecology, Architecture & Technology, Architecture & Discourse, Architecture & Media trajectories) (MArch post-professional)
City and Regional Planning (MRP, PhD)
Civil and Environmental Engineering (MEng, MS/PhD)
Design and Environmental Analysis (MArch)
Historic Preservation Planning (MA)
History of Architecture and Urban Development (PhD)
Horticulture (MLA, MS)
Landscape Architecture (MLA, MPS)
Mechanical Engineering (MEng)
Urban Studies (minor)

DREXEL UNIVERSITY

3141 Chestnut Street
Philadelphia, Pennsylvania 19104
215-895-2000
E-mail: www.drexel.edu/about/contact/general
    .aspx
www.drexel.edu

 http://bit.ly/collvid3

About Drexel Green

In 2008, students, faculty, and staff dedicated to transforming Drexel's campus into a sustainability leader created the Drexel Green initiative. The initiative covers all aspects of operations, buildings, academic initiatives, and student life and is responsible for creating and monitoring the strategic plan to further campus sustainable practices and policies.

Undergraduate Degrees

Architecture (major or minor)
Architectural Engineering (major or minor)
Civil Engineering
Construction Management (major or minor)
Human Factors and Ergonomics (minor)
Interior Design
Mechanical Engineering (minor)
Urban Environmental Studies (major or minor)

Undergraduate Certificate

Construction Management

Undergraduate Costs

Academic year 2010–11 (estimate): Four-year plan (one or no co-ops): $53,730 (tuition, fees, room and board); Five-year plan (three co-ops): $46,519 (tuition, fees, room and board). Travel tuition reduction program: Travel expenses up to $500 deducted from first tuition bill for full-time freshman or transfer student visiting campus from a distance of 150 miles or greater after enrollment confirmation. NOTE: Total cost varies depending on a student's course of study and whether a student chooses a co-op program or not.

Undergraduate Financial Aid

FAFSA required. Scholarship information may be found on the scholarship Web site: www.drexel.edu/financialaid/sg_ug.asp.

Undergraduate Admissions Requirements

Required: 2.0 GPA. SAT or ACT. Admission prerequisites vary with majors; see: www.drexel.edu/em/undergrad/apply/admissions-policies.aspx

Undergraduate Application Information

Options: Online application, VIP application, deferred entrance

Application fee: $75 (waived for online or on-campus application)

Required: Drexel's Online Application, The Common Application (online), Universal College Application (online), or Drexel's Undergraduate Admission Application (paper); high school transcripts, two letters of recommendation (one by high school counselor), 1–2 page essay online (not accepted on paper)

Recommended: Two letters of recommendation, interview

Application deadline: Mar 1 (freshmen), Aug 15 (fall transfers), Feb 15 (spring transfers)

Notification: Continuous

Green Campus Organizations

Drexel Green: An initiative begun in 2008 by students, faculty, and staff dedicated to transforming Drexel's campus into a sustainability leader. The initiative covers all aspects of operations, buildings, academic initiatives, and student life and is responsible for the strategic plan to further campus sustainability practices and policies.

Drexel Smart House: A student-led, multidisciplinary project to design an urban home that serves as a "living laboratory" for exploring cutting-edge design and technology. Participants conduct research and develop designs for the environment, energy, interaction, health, and lifestyle of potential users, with the ultimate goal of improving the quality of life in an urban residential setting.

Drexel Student Sustainability Committee (DSSC): A subgroup of the Undergraduate Student Government Association and Drexel Green program; goal is to reduce campus energy waste and pollution.

Energy Club: For students interested in energy conservation technologies on campus and in the community; goals are to promote environmental and societal awareness, and to support professional development of members.

Engineers Without Borders: Drexel chapter of international organization; works on sustainable development projects worldwide.

Fast Facts

Among the first universities to purchase wind-generated energy, Drexel now derives 30 percent of its total annual electric use from wind energy. Computer control systems turn off lighting after hours or when unnecessary, and stand-alone occupancy sensors are being used in newer construction and in renovations to conserve lighting.

Drexel University's first green dorm features concrete walls that do not need to be painted, windows that reflect heat, but allow light to enter, and a lobby floor made of recycled tires.

In 2009, *Sierra* magazine, a publication of the Sierra Club, named Drexel one of its "Cool Schools" for its "eco-enlightened" policies.

Graduate Degrees

Civil Engineering (Structural; Sustainable Engineering; Building Systems/Energy concentrations) (MS, PhD)
Construction Management (Sustainability and Green Construction concentration) (MS)
Interior Architecture and Design (MS)

Graduate Certificates

Construction Management
Sustainability and Green Construction

KANSAS STATE UNIVERSITY (K-State)

Manhattan, Kansas 66506
785-532-6011
E-mail: kstate@k-state.edu
www.k-state.edu/

 http://bit.ly/collvid48

About Academics at K-State

K-State ranks first nationally among state universities in its total of Rhodes, Marshall, Truman, Goldwater, and Udall scholars since 1986. Its students have won more than $2 million in those five competitions, earning K-State a place among the nation's elite universities.

Undergraduate Degrees

Architectural Engineering
Civil Engineering (Construction Engineering or Structural Engineering options)
Community Planning (minor)
Construction Science and Management
Horticulture (Horticultural Science, Horticultural Therapy, Landscape Design, Landscape Management, Public Horticulture, and Sports Turf Operations Management options) (major or minor)

Interior Architecture
Mechanical Engineering

Undergraduate Costs

Academic year 2009–10 (estimated costs for Manhattan campus): $5773 resident, $15,766 non-resident (tuition); $683 (fees); $6604 (residence hall, 10-meal plan); $6752 (residence hall, 20-meal plan). Other housing options are available. Go to http://consider.k-state.edu/tuitionandcosts/.

Undergraduate Financial Aid

FAFSA required. To apply for K-State scholarships, complete the K-State Scholarship application. Scholarship information may be found on the scholarship Web site: www.k-state.edu/sfa/scholarships/.

Undergraduate Admissions Requirements

Required: Applicants must meet any one of three criteria: (1) achieve a 21 or higher composite score on ACT assessment or a minimum score of 980 on the SAT (Critical Reading and Math sections); (2) rank in top third of graduating class; (3) complete the Kansas precollege curriculum with a 2.0 GPA (residents) or 2.5 or higher GPA (nonresidents). To see precollege curriculum requirements, go to http://consider.k-state.edu/admissions/precollege.htm.

Undergraduate Application Information

Options: Online application

Application fee: $30

Required: ACT or SAT (writing components not required); official high school transcript

Application deadline: November 1 (priority freshmen); February 1 (applicants entering the College of Architecture, Planning, and Design or the interior design program in the College of Human Ecology)

Green Campus Organizations

Emerging Green Builders: Student organization affiliated with the U.S. Green Building Council; facilitates education and development of students interested in green building design.

Students for Environmental Action: Committed to ensuring a healthy natural environment and conserving the ecological community on campus and in the surrounding community; sponsors activities including Game Day Recycling, making recycled notebooks and other crafts, and hosting speakers on environmental topics.

Student Farm Club "Harvesters of Environmental Sustainability": Grows fresh produce and promotes knowledge of sustainable agriculture through the KSU vegetable farm at Willow Lake Farm.

Greeks Go Green: Student organization that sponsors events such as Greek Week and Ecolympics to promote environmental awareness and sustainability on campus and in the larger community. Each chapter house works to minimize its environmental impact by lowering waste production, consumption, and energy use.

KSU Green: Student organization created by Zeta Phi Beta sorority to promote recycling at K-State.

Fast Facts

The crew of the Kansas State grounds department has gone green by substituting trucks for bicycles for spring flower planting. Crew members attach large baskets, crates, and even trailers big enough to carry flowers, gardening tools, and push-type lawn mowers to a small fleet of bicycles. On average, the bikers cover 8 to 10 miles a day as they travel from site to site during spring planting season.

The K-State Sustainability Web site is an all-in-one spot for people to learn how to promote environmental, social, and economic sustainability on campus. The site addresses several key areas including students, curriculum, operations, research, engagement, and how to get involved. To view the site, go to: www.sustainability.k-state .edu.

Graduate Degrees

Architectural Engineering (MS)
Architecture (Ecological and Sustainable Design option) (MS)
Architecture (Environmental Design Studies curriculum) (MArch)
Civil Engineering (MS, PhD)
Community Development (MS)
Environmental Design and Planning (PhD)
Horticulture (MS, PhD)
Interior Architecture and Product Design (MIAPD)
Landscape Architecture (MLA)
Mechanical Engineering (MS)
Regional and Community Planning (MRCP)

Graduate Certificates

Community Planning and Development
Horticultural Therapy

Graduate Distance Learning

Civil Engineering (MS)
Community Development (MS)
Mechanical Engineering (MS)

LOUISIANA STATE UNIVERSITY AGRICULTURAL AND MECHANICAL COLLEGE (LSU)

Undergraduate Admissions
1146 Pleasant Hall
Baton Rouge, Louisiana 70803
225-578-1175
E-mail: www.lsu.edu/paurec/prospect_card.shtml
www.lsu.edu

About Sustainable Irrigation

LSU is always looking for ways to become a more sustainable campus, and thanks to three mechanical engineering students, it can add irrigating the LSU Golf Course to its list. The golf course was using 180,000 gallons of potable city water daily for irrigation. The students, working from a proposal created by LSU Facility Services, built an array of eight photovoltaic panels that power a submersible well pump. The pump moves groundwater through a piping system and into three reservoir ponds. The system is able to harvest up to 20 percent of the daily water required to irrigate the golf course.

 http://bit.ly/collvid49

Undergraduate Degrees

Architecture
Civil Engineering
Community Design (minor)
Construction Management (major or minor)
Heritage Conservation (minor)
Interior Design
Landscape Architecture
Mechanical Engineering (major or minor)
Structural Engineering (minor)

Undergraduate Costs

Academic year 2009–10 (estimate): $5241 resident, $14,391 nonresident (tuition and fees); housing costs vary from $4610 (3 student room in residence hall with hall bath) to $8310 (efficiency on-campus apartment); meal plans range from $1500 to $1675 per semester

Undergraduate Financial Aid

FAFSA required. For information on LSU scholarship qualifications and awards for entering freshmen, go to www.lsu.edu/financialaid/schl-qualifications.htm.

Undergraduate Admissions Requirements

Required: Minimum 3.0 GPA on 18 units of college-preparatory high school courses and a 1030 SAT (Critical Reading and Math)/22 Composite ACT; minimum SAT Critical Reading score of 450 (ACT English subscore of 18) and minimum SAT Math score of 460 (ACT Math subscore of 19).

Recommended high school preparation: 4 years English (composition and literature); 3 years math (algebra I, algebra II, and additional course); 3 years natural science (biology, chemistry, physics); 3 years social studies (U.S. history, world course, elective in civics, free enterprise, economics, or U.S. government); 2 years same foreign language; 1 math or science elective; half unit computer science or substitute; 1.5 units of academic electives including art, music, drama/theater, computer science, or any of the core subjects listed above.

Undergraduate Application Information

Options: Online application; early admission

Application fee: $40

Required: ACT or SAT scores; official high school transcript, essay (when applicable)

Application deadline: April 15 (summer and fall); November 15 (priority date for scholarships); December 1 (spring)

Green Campus Organizations

American Institute of Architecture Students: Serves as liaison between students and practicing professionals; represents student body on faculty committees, makes recommendations to the director, hosts visiting speakers, and organizes various social activities.

American Society of Landscape Architects: Provides members with access to practicing professionals, encourages community service, and prepares students for professional careers.

Environmental Conservation Organization: Dedicated to and instrumental in the advancement of sustainability, energy efficiency, and alternative transportation across the LSU campus and throughout the surrounding Baton Rouge community.

Fast Facts

The Office of Building Research in LSU's School of Architecture gives faculty and students alike the opportunity to focus on areas that have the potential to significantly enhance the quality of the built environment. Research areas include everything from energy conservation and solar design to facility planning and structure failure analysis.

The Green Tiger Project, a vision of the LSU Foundation, integrates campus beautification with campus sustainability. In 2010, the foundation held its first annual Spring Greening Day as a part of the project. Student volunteers worked with Landscape Services and Student Life staff members to plant flowers, lay sod, and spread mulch in prepared beds across the core of LSU's campus.

Graduate Degrees

Architecture (MS, MArch)
Civil Engineering (MS)
Mechanical Engineering (MS)
Landscape Architecture (MLA)

MASSACHUSETTS INSTITUTE OF TECHNOLOGY (MIT)

77 Massachusetts Avenue
Cambridge, Massachusetts 02139-4307
617-253-1000
web.mit.edu

About House_n

House_n is a research group in MIT's Department of Architecture that designs and builds real living environments into which they incorporate new technologies, materials, and strategies for design. They then study how people interact with and respond to these innovations. Their goal is to understand how the design of homes should evolve to better meet the opportunities and challenges of the future. For more information, see http://architecture.mit.edu/house_n/.

Undergraduate Degrees

Architecture
Art and Design (Architectural Design and Building Technology disciplines)
Civil Engineering
Mechanical Engineering
Planning
Urban Studies and Planning (minor)

Undergraduate Costs

Academic year 2010–11: $38,940 (tuition and fees), between $5820 and $7906 (housing)

Undergraduate Financial Aid

CSS PROFILE® and FAFSA required. Scholarships: Public Service Center Fellowships: Living expenses and stipend for one semester for students working on independent sustainable community projects; Morris K. Udall Scholarship; Department of Defense Science, Mathematics and Research for Transformation (SMART) Scholarship for Service Program. For more information, go to: http://www.asee.org/fellowships/smart/.

Undergraduate Admissions Requirements

Required: SAT (Critical Reading, Math, and Writing sections) or ACT with the writing test; SAT Math Subject Test (level 1 or 2); one SAT Science Subject Test (physics, chemistry, or biology).

High school preparation: 1 year physics; 1 year chemistry; 1 year biology; math, through calculus; 2 years foreign language; 4 years English; 2 years history and/or social sciences.

Undergraduate Application Information

Options: Online application

Application fee: $75

Required: Biographical information form; essays, activities, and tests form; self-reported coursework form; ACT/SAT scores; two teacher evaluation forms; secondary school report form; high school transcript; mid-year report; financial aid materials

Recommended: Interview

Application deadline: November 1 (early action); January 1 (regular action)

Notification: Mid-December (early action); mid- to late March (regular action)

Green Campus Organizations

American Institute of Architecture Students: Addresses issues affecting students including studio culture, internships, the accreditation process, and the advancement of architecture.

Share a Vital Earth (SAVE): Promotes environmental conservation and awareness at MIT and in the surrounding activities; campaigns to reduce paper consumption and electricity use on campus, and greening the MIT campus.

MIT Electric Vehicle Team: Students from various disciplines who research, design, build, and test electric vehicles.

Solar Electric Vehicle Team: Student group that designs, builds, and races solar electric vehicles; participates in environmental and ecological events where they promote vehicles powered by alternative energy

Fast Facts

The Smart Cities group at MIT's Media Lab conducts research that is focused on "intelligent, sustainable buildings, mobility systems, and cities. It explores the application of new technologies to enable urban energy efficiency and sustainability, enhanced opportunity and equity, and cultural creativity."

The Department of Civil and Environmental Engineering undertakes research projects on such diverse topics as smart grids, next generation utility systems, tunnel design and construction, enhanced oil recovery, energy flows between natural and built environments, and transforming Chicago's transit system.

Graduate Degrees

Architecture (MArch)
Architecture Studies (SMArchS)
Building Technology (SMBT, PhD)
City Planning (MCP)
Civil and Environmental Engineering (CE, MS,
    MEng, PhD, ScD)
Mechanical Engineering (MechE, MS, MEng,
    PhD, ScD)
Urban Studies and Planning (MS, PhD)

Graduate Certificate

Urban Design

NEW YORK SCHOOL OF INTERIOR DESIGN (NYSID)

170 East 70th Street
New York, New York 10021
212-472-1500
E-mail: info@nysid.edu
www.nysid.edu

About a Degree in Sustainable Interior Environments

NYSID offers a Master of Professional Studies in Sustainable Interior Environments. Students in this one-year post-professional program are exposed to a wide range of topics, research methods, integrated design development methodologies, and sustainable project management practices. The goal is to create interior designers who can develop and maintain sustainable interior spaces that will positively impact the world.

Undergraduate Degrees

Interior Design (BFA)
History of the Interior and Decorative Arts (BA)

Undergraduate Certificate

Basic Interior Design

Undergraduate Costs

Academic year 2010–11: $765 per credit (tuition); $280 per semester (fees); $14,200 to $20,750 (housing)

Undergraduate Financial Aid

FAFSA required. To view NYSID undergraduate scholarships, see www.nysid.edu/NetCommunity/Page.aspx?pid=428.

Undergraduate Admissions Requirements

Required: High school diploma or GED; SAT Reasoning or ACT

Undergraduate Application Information

Options: Online application, rolling basis

Application fee: $50 (U.S. residents)

Required: Application; personal essay; official high school transcript or GED official scores; at least two letters of recommendation; SAT or ACT scores; portfolio of work (not required for BA program)

Application deadline: March 1 (fall); October 1 (spring)

Notification: Continuous

Green Campus Organizations

American Society of Interior Designers: Provides education and resources and promotes professionalism in interior design.

Contract Club: Arranges visits to top interior design firms where members can view projects being designed, ask questions of senior designers/architects, and tour professional working offices.

Green Design Awards: NYSID presents Green Design Awards to acknowledge individuals and businesses who have made outstanding contributions toward advancing the cause of sustainable design.

Fast Facts

NYSID sponsors special lectures including the Sally Henderson Memorial Lecture on Green Design. In 2009, sustainable-design expert David Oakey provided an in-depth overview of how nature can become a mentor for design. In 2010, interior designer Stephanie Odegard lectured on "Weaving Together Sustainability and Design."

Graduate Degrees

Interior Design (MFA-1, MFA-2)
Sustainable Interior Environments (MPS)

Institute for Continuing and Professional Education

Prep Workshop for the LEED Green Associate Exam

PARSONS THE NEW SCHOOL FOR DESIGN

66 Fifth Avenue
New York, New York 10011
212-229-8900
E-mail: thinkparsons@newschool.edu
www.newschool.edu/parsons

About DESIS

Parsons is a member of Design for Social Innovation and Sustainability (DESIS), a network of schools of design and other schools, institutions, companies, and non-profit organizations that are interested in supporting and promoting design for social innovation and sustainability. At the DESIS Lab, researchers are proposing plans for new community gardens, cohousing, and other sustainability initiatives for the Lower East Side. For information, see www.desis-network.org.

Undergraduate Degrees

Architectural Design
Environmental Studies (Sustainable Design)
Interior Design
Urban Design

Undergraduate Certificate

Interior Design and Architecture Studies

Undergraduate Distance Learning

Parsons offers hundreds of nondegree courses, which can be taken on a for-credit or noncredit basis, each term.

Undergraduate Costs

Academic year 2009–10 (estimate): $17,610 BFA (tuition), $235 (fees); $16,905 (BA, BS Environmental Studies; tuition), $145 (fees); $15,260 (room and board); $920–$2050 (books)

Undergraduate Financial Aid

FAFSA required. For information on scholarships, see www.newschool.edu/studentservices/financialaid/subpage.aspx?id=32352.

Undergraduate Admissions Requirements

Required: High school diploma; SAT or ACT

Undergraduate Application Information

Options: Online application; deferred entrance

Application fee: $50

Required: Official high school transcript, SAT or ACT scores; TOEFL results (if English is not native language); Parsons Challenge (exercise that helps the Admission Committee understand how a potential student structures and conveys ideas); portfolio (BFA applicants); two letters of recommendation (BA/BS applicants); Statement of Purpose Essay (BA/BS applicants)

Optional: Personal interview

Application deadline: November 1 (fall early action freshmen; spring priority all applicants); February 1 (fall regular decision priority freshmen); April 1 (fall priority transfers)

Notification: End of December (fall early action freshmen; spring priority applicants); April 1 (fall regular decision priority freshmen); May 1 (fall priority transfers)

Green Campus Organizations

Student Sustainability Committee: Strives to have a sustainable campus by mitigating the negative environmental impacts that members observe and participate in on campus.

Sustainable Design Review: Seeks to foster and encourage awareness of social, artistic, and designed-based sustainable solutions to dynamic challenges presented to students inside and outside their classroom walls.

Fast Facts

The architecture, interior, lighting, and product design students in Parsons' School of Constructed Environments tackle challenges facing the modern world. These challenges include shifts in global and ecological flows, changes in living patterns, growing economic disparities, excessive consumption, and increasing ethnic diversity.

Parsons and Stevens Institute of Technology have teamed up to compete in the U.S. Department of Energy's 2011 Solar Decathlon. Their entry, Better Together, is designed to provide solar-powered Habitat for Humanity housing for residents of a low-income neighborhood in Washington, D.C. The structure consists of two symbiotic modules that unite to form a functioning solar duplex.

Graduate Degrees

Architecture (MArch)
Architecture/Lighting Design (MArch/MFA)
Interior Design (MFA)
Lighting Design (MFA)

PENNSYLVANIA STATE UNIVERSITY (Penn State)

201 Old Main
University Park, PA 16802
814-865-4700
E-mail: ask.psu.edu/psu.html
www.psu.edu

 http://bit.ly/collvid33

About Green Power

In 2010, the U.S. Environmental Protection Agency named Penn State number 43 of the top 50 purchasers of green power. It was purchasing 83 million kilowatt-hours of green power annually, which met 20 percent of the university's electric power needs. Biomass, small hydro, and wind were the alternate sources of energy that the university used. Penn State also ranks number 3 in the EPA's ranking of the top 20 colleges and universities using green power.

Undergraduate Degrees

Some degrees are completed at other campuses in the Penn State system.

Arboriculture (minor)
Architectural Engineering (Construction, Lighting/Electrical, Mechanical; and Structural options)
Architecture
Architecture Studies (minor)
Civil Engineering
Community, Environment and Development
Horticulture (major or minor)
Landscape Architecture
Landscape Contracting (Design/Build or Management options)
Mechanical Engineering

Structural Design and Construction Engineering Technology
Turfgrass Science

Undergraduate Certificates

Turfgrass Management
Turfgrass Management, Advanced

Undergraduate Distance Learning

Turfgrass Science

Undergraduate Costs

Academic year 2009–10: $23,236 residents, $34,766 nonresidents (tuition, room and board). Tuition rates vary by campus, student level, program, and residency.

Undergraduate Financial Aid

FAFSA required. Scholarships, grants, loans, and work study available. See www.psu.edu/studentaid.

Undergraduate Admissions Requirements

Required: SAT or ACT.

High school preparation: 4 years English, 3 years mathematics, 3 years science, 5 years total foreign language, social studies, art, and humanities

Recommended: High school preparation: 2 years same foreign language. Some programs have additional math and science requirements.

Undergraduate Application Information

Options: Online application

Application fee: $50

Required: Application, high school transcript, counselor form. Letters of recommendation and/or interview required for some programs

Application deadline: November 30 (fall freshmen), November 1 (spring freshmen), December 31 (fall transfers for Architecture and Landscape Architecture), February 1 (fall transfers), October 15 (spring transfers)

Notification: January 31 (fall freshmen), December 15 (spring freshmen, transfers), April 1 (fall transfers)

Green Campus Organizations

Mechanical Contractors Association of America, Penn State Student Chapter: Hosts an annual fall project in which participants create a proposal for the mechanical contract of a construction project aimed at acquiring a LEED rating; top four contestants present their proposal at the MCAA National Convention.

National Electrical Contracting Association (NECA) and ELECTRI International (EI) Student Chapter Competition: Competition in which student teams identify a community building needing energy efficiency improvements, conduct an energy audit, and create a preliminary design for an energy retrofit for power and/or lighting systems.

American Indian Housing Initiative: A collaborative effort to adapt and deploy sustainable building technologies on American Indian reservations.

Students Taking Action to Encourage Recycling (Staters): Promotes campus recycling.

Sustainability Coalition: Coordinates relationships among students, staff members, faculty members, clubs, and the community to provide outreach, education, and support regarding sustainability issues.

Fast Facts

In 2009, the Penn State Solar Decathlon Team participated in the competition sponsored by the U.S. Department of Energy to design, build, and operate an entirely solar-powered home. Penn State's team of more than 900 faculty members and students designed and built the MorningStar Solar Home; the project stimulated sustainability-related curriculum.

On April 22, 2009, Penn State became the first member of the Environmental Protection Agency's Sustainability Partnership Program (SPP) for the Mid-Atlantic region. The SPP, a pilot project of the EPA, enlists large organizations like Penn State to reduce energy and water use, waste generation, and climate impact.

Penn State received $5 million in funding under the American Recovery and Reinvestment Act in 2010 for the GridSTAR Center (Smart Grid Training Application Resource Center). The university will contribute another $5 million to the center that will provide a system-based continuing education and train-the-trainer program in advanced power systems design, energy economics, cyber security, distributed energy generation, and building-vehicle-grid systems.

Graduate Degrees

Architectural Engineering (MS, PhD)
Architecture (MArch)
Civil Engineering (MS, MEng, PhD)
Community and Economic Development (MPS)
Horticulture (MAgr, MS, PhD)
Landscape Architecture (Community and Urban
   Design option) (MLA, MSLA)
Mechanical Engineering (MS, PhD)

Graduate Certificate

Community and Economic Development

Distance Learning Certificate

Community and Economic Development (MPS)
Turfgrass Management (MPS-TM)

PRATT INSTITUTE

200 Willoughby Avenue
Brooklyn, New York 11205
718-636-3600
E-mail: info@pratt.edu
www.pratt.edu

About CSDS

Pratt's Center for Sustainable Design Studies (CSDS) serves as a physical and virtual hub for the Institute's commitment to educate environmentally responsible citizens. The Center encourages people to use Pratt's campus as a living laboratory that links what is happening in the classroom to campus initiatives. To learn more about CSDS and take a virtual tour of sustainability at Pratt, go to http://csds.pratt.edu/.

Undergraduate Degrees

Programs may be located on the Brooklyn or Manhattan campuses.

Architecture
Construction Management (major or minor)
Industrial Design
Interior Design

Undergraduate Costs

Academic year 2010–11 (estimate): $35,410 (tuition); $1,680 (fees); $10,020 (on-campus room and board); $3,000 (books/supplies); $3,500 (computer/software purchase for sophomore-level interior design majors)

Undergraduate Financial Aid

FAFSA required. For available scholarships, go to www.pratt.edu/admissions/financing_your_education/financial_aid_options/financial_undergrad/ug_financial_scholarships/.

Undergraduate Admissions Requirements

Required: Official high school transcript or GED scores; SAT or ACT (with Writing Test)

Undergraduate Application Information

Options: Online application (preferred)

Application fee: $50

Required: Application; official high school transcript; SAT/ACT with writing scores; letter of recommendation; portfolio; essay

Application deadline: November 1 (fall freshmen early action); January 5 (fall freshmen); February 1 (fall transfers); October 1 (spring)

Notification: April 1 (freshmen); April 15 (transfers)

Green Campus Organizations

Sustainable Pratt: Multidisciplinary group of faculty, administrators, students, and staff dedicated to identifying, interpreting, inspiring, incorporating, and instituting ecologically responsible practices into curricula, operations, and programs at Pratt Institute.

Interns for Change: Interns who serve as sustainability consultants for faculty and students working within the Center for Sustainable Design Studies.

Sift Journal: Pratt Institute's first renewable publication about sustainable design written by students. Go to http://siftjournal.wordpress.com/.

Envirolution: Student-led nonprofit organization that works to facilitate the expansion of the sustainability movement.

LEAP: Environmental advocacy group.

Fast Facts

Pratt's Green TV news crew produces weekly stories and highlights on people, places, and new materials. To view the latest videos, go to http://csds.pratt.edu/green_tv10.php.

The Green Dorm Project is a course in which interior and industrial design students collaborate to incorporate "green" ideas into an actual dorm room on campus. The design addresses furniture, lighting, and accessories for sustainable living. Participating students conduct field visits and consult with environmental engineers, alternative energy consultants, and local fabricators.

In 2009, the Pratt Design Incubator, which is a division of CSDS, partnered with the home furnishing company West Elm to design and produce a series of sustainable home-office furniture.

In 2009, TerraCycle created an "upcycling" competition exclusive to Pratt students. The company challenged the students to do what it does in its own business: take post-industrial waste materials (sponges, cookie wrappers, zip-loc bags, and toothbrushes) and post-consumer water materials (plastic bottle caps, wine corks, and plastic gift cards) and turn them into something new. To see photos of student creations, go to http://csds.pratt.edu/terracycle.html.

Graduate Degrees

Programs may be located on either the Brooklyn or Manhattan campuses.

Architecture (MArch, MS)
Architecture and Urban Design (MS)
City and Regional Planning (MS) (Community Development, Physical Planning, Environmental Planning, Preservation Planning, and Facilities Management concentrations) (MS/JD joint degree with Brooklyn Law School)
Design Management (MPS)
Facilities Management (MS)

Historic Preservation (MS)
Industrial Design (MID)
Interior Design (MS)
Urban Environmental Systems Management (MS)

Graduate Certificate

Sustainable Building, Infrastructure Design & Management

PURDUE UNIVERSITY

West Lafayette, Indiana 47907
765-494-4600
www.purdue.edu

 http://bit.ly/collvid35

About Purdue's Green Cleaning Program

Purdue's College of Agriculture joined forces with the university's Building Services department to identify and implement the latest innovations in low environmental impact—or green—cleaning in campus buildings. Major elements of the program include using environmentally friendly cleaning products, installing dispensing systems that accurately dilute chemicals with cold water, using recycled consumable products, and educating and training the campus workforce on green practices.

Undergraduate Degrees

Building Construction Management Technology
Civil Engineering
Construction Engineering
Horticulture (Horticulture Science, Landscape Horticulture and Design, Horticultural Production and Marketing, or Public Horticulture options)
Interior Design
Landscape Architecture
Mechanical Engineering
Turf Science

Undergraduate Costs

Academic Year 2010–11: Resident $18,190; non-resident $35,742 (tuition, fees, room and board). Some programs have additional fees: Technology ($526), Engineering ($1050), Management ($1,338)

Undergraduate Financial Aid

FAFSA required.

Undergraduate Admissions Requirements

Required: High school transcript; SAT or ACT (with Writing Test)

High School preparation: 8 years English; 4 years math; 2 or 3 years laboratory science (depends on program); 3 years social studies; 2 years foreign language

Undergraduate Application Information

Option: Online application, early admission, deferred entrance

Application fee: $50

Required: Application, ACT or SAT scores (including writing); official high school transcript

Application deadlines: November 15 (freshmen seeking scholarship consideration); March 1 (freshmen); July 1 (fall transfers); November 1 (spring transfers)

Notification: Continuous beginning early December (freshmen)

Green Campus Organizations

GreenBuild: A student/faculty/staff organization promoting green building practices; provides students with green career opportunities through industry partners and sponsors.

Boiler Green Initiative: Multidisciplinary student organization that raises awareness of sustainability issues at Purdue and in the community; particular focus on green building. The organization led the way in installing the first green roof on campus.

Carbon Neutrality at Purdue University: Student organization whose goals are to reduce energy consumption on campus and raise awareness of carbon neutrality in the community; part of Boiler Green Initiative.

Purdue Green Week: A week of campus activities to bring awareness to sustainability issues.

Purdue Sustainability Council: Members from various departments and offices; identifies issues and options, educates the campus community, and makes recommendations for sustainability improvements.

Fast Facts

Schleman Hall is the first building on the Purdue campus to have a green roof. The plant-covered rooftop was installed to provide building insulation, increase energy efficiency, and lengthen the life span of the roof. To determine how effective the new roof is, researchers are using soil moisture probes, rain gauges, and temperature probes powered by a solar pane to measure water levels to determine the plants' absorption of rainwater.

Purdue was chosen by the U.S. Department of Energy to participate in the 2011 Solar Decathlon. Teams from twenty colleges in the United States, Canada, Belgium, New Zealand, and China were chosen on the basis of competitive applications to create solar homes.

"Boiler Up, Power Down" was the message of Purdue's 2010 energy conservation awareness campaign. The campaign included an energy conservation competition between five residence halls. It also featured "Power Down Hour," 1 hour in which all students and faculty and staff members were asked to turn off lights, computers, and electrical equipment.

Graduate Degrees

Civil Engineering (MS, PhD)
Horticulture (MA, MS; PhD)
Mechanical Engineering (MSME, PhD)

Graduate Distance Learning

Building Construction Management (MS)
Mechanical Engineering (MSME)

RHODE ISLAND SCHOOL OF DESIGN (RISD)

Two College Street
Providence, Rhode Island 02903
401-454-6100
E-mail: admissions@risd.edu
www.risd.edu

> ### About Dining C.A.R.E.S.
>
> Dining C.A.R.E.S. (Community, Action, Responsibility, Environment, Sustainability) is RISD's Dining + Catering Services program that promotes recycling, energy efficiency, and local purchasing. As part of the program, RISD became one of the first schools in the Northeast to use an ecologic cleaning system, a move that increased the school's green rating for cleaning products by 80 percent.

Undergraduate Degrees

Architecture
Furniture Design
Industrial Design
Interior Architecture

Continuing Education Certificates

Historic Preservation
Interior Design

Undergraduate Costs

Academic year 2009–10: $36,364 (full-time degree candidate tuition); $295 (student activities fee); $6120 (double room); $4726 (19+ meal plan); $2000 (estimated supplies)

Undergraduate Financial Aid

FAFSA and CSS Profile required. (CSS Profile must be filed online.) Scholarships available. Freshmen who exhibit outstanding academic and artistic need can compete for $10,000 scholarships. Up to five $10,000 renewable Trustee Scholarships are also awarded to freshmen. For information, see www.risd.edu/apply_financial aid_scholarships.cfm.

Undergraduate Admissions Requirements

Required: High school transcript or GED; SAT or ACT (with Writing Test)

High School preparation: College-preparatory program with courses in studio art or art history. Candidates for Bachelor of Architecture must have 2 semesters algebra, 1 semester trigonometry; 1 year science (preferably physics).

Recommended: Studio drawing and courses that develop visual and design skills.

Undergraduate Application Information

Option: Online application

Application fee: $60

Required: Application, ACT or SAT scores (including writing); official high school transcript; three drawing samples; portfolio of work; two writing samples

Recommended: 1–3 letters of recommendation

Application deadlines: December 15 (early fall freshmen); February 15 (fall freshmen); November 1 (spring freshmen)

Notification: Last week of January (for those who apply by December 15); first week of April (for those who apply by February 15); late November (spring freshmen—only if openings occur)

Green Campus Organizations

eMotive: Collaboration between RISD and Brown University. Research and design innovative, responsible transportation for use in emerging economies.

Respond/Design: Interdisciplinary forum for RISD students and faculty interested in how design can respond to the critical issues of the day.

Fast Facts

The Passive Solar Studio is a graduate seminar in which students explore contemporary environmental concerns through a focus on energy-conscious architecture.

RISD students and faculty were invited to compete in the EPA's Solar Decathlon in 2005. As a result of that competition, project members were asked to present their energy innovations to the U.S. Subcommittee on Science and Technology. The team also participated in the Emerging Architecture Session on Technology, Architecture and Education at the American Solar Energy Society Conference. The team joined the U.S. Department of Energy in designing a 30,000-square-foot zero-energy kindergarten for the 2008 Beijing Olympic Village.

In 2008, RISD students traveled to Accra, Ghana, for a winter session course at the Kokrobitey Institute. The program featured artist demonstrations, lectures, field trips, workshops, and independent research. Students explored the history and culture of Ghana while concentrating on visual communication systems, traditional design, and the built environment.

Graduate Degrees

Architecture (MArch)
Furniture Design (MFA)
Industrial Design (MID)
Interior Architecture (MIA)
Landscape Architecture (MLA)

SYRACUSE UNIVERSITY (SU)

Syracuse, NY 13244-5040
315-443-1870
www.syr.edu

 http://bit.ly/collvid38

About the Green Data Center

Syracuse University teamed up with IBM and New York State to build and operate a new computer data center on campus. By incorporating an advanced infrastructure and smarter computing technologies, designers expect to cut energy usage by 50 percent, making this one of the greenest computer centers in existence.

Undergraduate Degrees

Architecture
Civil Engineering
Interior Design
Mechanical Engineering

Undergraduate Costs

Academic year 2010–11: $49,152 (tuition, fees, average room and board)

Undergraduate Financial Aid

CSS PROFILE® and FAFSA required.

The Office of Financial Aid and Scholarship Programs has detailed information on a variety of SU and external scholarship sources. Go to: http://financialaid.syr.edu/scholarships.htm.

Undergraduate Admissions Requirements

Required: High school graduation; SAT or ACT (with Writing Test). Some colleges have specific high school preparation requirements.

General preparation: 4 years English; 4 years science; 4 years social studies; 4 years mathematics (through geometry and intermediate algebra); at least 3 years foreign language

Undergraduate Application Information

Option: Online application; early decision; early admission; deferred entrance

Application fee: $70

Required: Common Application with Syracuse University Supplement or Syracuse University Application for Admission; high school transcript; senior year grade report; SAT or ACT (with Writing Test) scores; secondary school counselor evaluation; two academic recommendations

Recommended: Interview

Application deadlines: November 15 (early decision); January 1 (fall freshmen)

Notification: Mid-December (early decision); mid-March (fall freshmen)

Green Campus Organizations

Campus Sustainability Committee: Students, staff, and faculty committee; develops policies and guidelines for the university sustainability program.

Irish Today, Green Forever: Joint project between the Residence Hall Association, the university residence hall office, and the university sustainability program to increase recycling in residence halls and decrease consumption of bottled water.

SU Sustainability Showcase: Annual event held in conjunction with Earth Day that features student sustainable design projects.

University Sustainability Action Coalition: Committed to improving sustainability, energy use, and recycling on campus; sponsors campus events to educate and raise awareness.

Fast Facts

In September 2009, the Syracuse Center on Excellence in Environmental and Energy Innovations (SyracuseCoE) opened its new headquarters, a LEED Platinum-certified building—the highest LEED rating given by the U.S. Green Building Council. The building has many energy-conserving and environmental features, and houses research space for SyracuseCoE's three focus areas: clean and renewable energy, indoor environmental quality, and water resources.

The Department of Entrepreneurship and Emerging Enterprises (EEE) is one of the few formal academic departments in the nation devoted to entrepreneurship.

In 2010, the U.S. Environmental Protection Agency named Syracuse University number 15 of the top 20 college and university purchasers of green power. It was purchasing almost 23 million kilowatt-hours of green power annually, which met 20 percent of the university's electric power needs. Small hydro was the alternate source of energy that the university used.

Graduate Degrees

Architecture (MArch I, MArch II)
Civil Engineering (MS, PhD)
Mechanical Engineering (MS, PhD)

TEXAS A&M UNIVERSITY

College Station, Texas 77843
979-845-3211
E-mail: services.tamu.edu/directory-search
www.tamu.edu

 http://bit.ly/collvid39

About the P3 Competition

A "solar pipe" system designed by a Texas A&M College of Architecture team was among the winning entries in the 2010 P3 (People, Prosperity and the Planet) competition, which was sponsored by the U.S. Environmental Protection Agency. Using an outdoor light collector, the device "funnels sunlight from the collector through a pipe of highly reflective material into a simulated office space built within a rail car container." The team received $75,000 to further develop their design, implement it in the field, or move it to the marketplace.

Undergraduate Degrees

Architecture (Home Architecture Track)
Civil Engineering
Community Development
Construction Science
Environmental Design (Architecture)
Floriculture
Horticulture (major or minor)
Global Art, Design and Construction (minor)
Landscape Architecture
Mechanical Engineering
Plant Protection and Integrated Pest Management
Urban and Regional Planning (minor)
Urban and Regional Sciences

Undergraduate Distance Learning

Many courses are available online, through the TTVN interactive videoconferencing system, or a combination of formats. Some meet requirements of the degrees listed above. For complete listing of all E-Learning courses, degrees, certificates, and programs, check out http://distance.tamu.edu/futureaggies/distance-degrees.

Undergraduate Costs

Academic year 2010–11: $16,375 (residents), $30,925 (nonresidents) (tuition, fees, room and board)

Undergraduate Financial Aid

FAFSA, or TASFA for students ineligible for federal aid.

Scholarships, grants, and internships and co-ops are available. See http://financialaid.tamu.edu

Undergraduate Admissions Requirements

Required: SAT or ACT with Writing Test. High school preparation: 4 years English, 3.5 years mathematics (including algebra I and II, geometry, half a year advanced math), 3 years science (2 years must be biology, chemistry, or physics). For Engineering: minimum math score 550 SAT or 24 ACT.

Recommended: High school preparation: 2 years same foreign language. Meet the Texas State Distinguished Achievement Program requirements.

Undergraduate Application Information

Options: Online application

Application fee: $60

Required: Apply Texas Application, high school transcript, Essays A and B

Recommended: Essay C, interview, campus visit, or any Academic Association activity

Application deadline: January 21 (fall, summer freshmen), October 1 (spring freshmen), March 15

(fall, summer transfers), October 15 (spring transfers)

Notification: Continuous (by early April for fall and summer, by early December for spring)

Green Campus Organizations

Emerging Green Builders: Student chapter of the U.S. Green Building Council; for students and others getting started in the green building industry.

Aggies Cleaning the Environment: Promotes leadership and service regarding environmental issues.

Environmental Issues Committee: Committee of the Student Government Association providing environmental awareness and education and promoting environmental legislation.

Texas Environmental Action Coalition: Students and community members work to improve the environment and increase awareness of environmental issues.

Environmental Programs Involvement Committee: Promotes awareness of environmental departmental programs and encourages involvement in dealing with issues impacting the environment

Facility Management Student Chapter: Provides educational and networking opportunities.

Fast Facts

The Residence Hall Association ran a Compact Florescent Light (CFL) Program to replace all incandescent light bulbs with CFLs in the thirty residence halls.

The Center for Housing and Urban Development confers the Sustainable Urbanism Certificate. The program addresses the integration and interdependence of the various aspects of the urban environment, including energy, infrastructure, and transportation networks, and land use and urban design.

A team from the College of Architecture designed and built a solar-powered home for the 2007 U.S. Department of Energy's Solar Decathlon. Twenty teams from across the United States and Europe competed. The Aggie's Gro-Home took first place from the American Institute of Architecture Students and the American Institutes of Architects' Committee on the Environment.

In 2010, the U.S. Environmental Protection Agency named the Texas A&M system number 7 of the top 20 college and university purchasers of green power. The system was purchasing 43 million kilowatt-hours of green power annually, which met 15 percent of the university's electric power needs. Wind power was the alternate source of energy that the university uses.

Graduate Degrees

Architecture (MS, MArch, 4+2 BArch/MArch, PhD)
Civil Engineering (MS, MEng, PhD)
Construction Management (MS)
Floriculture (MS, MAgr)
Horticulture (MS, MAgr, PhD)
Land Development (MS)
Landscape Architecture (MLA)
Mechanical Engineering (MS, MEng, PhD, DEng)
Urban Planning (MUP)
Urban and Regional Science (PhD)

Graduate Certificates

Community Development
Environmental Hazard Management (Architecture)
Facility Management
Health Systems and Design
Historic Preservation
Historic Community Development
Sustainable Urbanism

THE UNIVERSITY OF TEXAS AT AUSTIN (UT AUSTIN)

2400 Inner Campus Drive
Austin, Texas 78712
512-475-7348
www.utexas.edu

About Tree Campus USA

In 2010, the Arbor Day Foundation recognized UT as a Tree Campus USA for its efforts to maintain a green and sustainable environment. The university received this same honor in 2009 and was one of the first three campuses in the nation to receive this honor.

Undergraduate Degrees

Architectural Engineering
Architectural Studies
Architecture
Civil Engineering
Interior Design
Mechanical Engineering

Undergraduate Certificate

Environment

Undergraduate Costs

Academic year 2010–11: Tuition flat rates vary by college. (Architecture: $9496/year for 12+ hours new freshman resident) $8184 to $14,232 (room and board).

Undergraduate Financial Aid

FAFSA required. Some colleges and departments administer their own scholarship programs through a separate application process. For information, go to www.texasscholarships.org/types/dept_links.html.

Undergraduate Admissions Requirements

Required: High school graduation; SAT or ACT (with Writing Test)

High school preparation: 4 years language arts; 4 years math; 4 years science; 3.5 years social studies; half a year economics; 1 year physical education; 1 year fine arts; 2 years same foreign language; half a year speech; 6 electives.

Undergraduate Application Information

Options: Online application (preferred)

Application fee: $60

Required: Application; two essays; official high school transcript; SAT or ACT (with writing) scores. Some programs have specific requirements. For information, go to http://bealonghorn.utexas.edu/freshmen/admission/majors/.

Recommended: Resumé; letters of recommendation; essay noting special circumstances

Application deadline: December 15 (summer/fall freshmen); October 1 (spring freshmen/transfers); March 1 (summer/fall transfers)

Notification: Late February (summer/fall freshmen); late May (summer/fall transfers); November (spring applicants)

Green Campus Organizations

Green 'Horns: Students with an interest in sustainability and environmental integrity who provide outreach and education to staff at UT Austin regarding environmental efficiency, minimization of pollution, and sustainable practices on campus.

Student Historic Preservation Association: Promotes the study of preservation and related areas of study through activities including volunteering, advocacy, and community outreach.

The University of Texas Campus Environmental Center: Empowers the campus community to reduce its negative environmental impact and foster a genuine culture of sustainability through activities such as the annual Trash to Treasure garage sale, the Orange Bike Project, and the campus plastic and aluminum recycling program.

Urban Sustainability Collective: Students who partner with the Austin community to find workable solutions to problems including economic growth and diversification and improving the recreational quality of parks and other public places.

UT Sustainability Network: Cross-departmental team of faculty, staff, and students who work on sustainability-related activities on campus.

Fast Facts

The Construction Industry Institute is a research consortium including leading owners and contractors working together to advance the delivery of capital facilities. Researchers work to improve the business effectiveness and sustainability of capital project delivery.

Most projects at the Phil M. Ferguson Structural Engineering Laboratory include large-scale testing. Research results are used to evaluate design, behavior, and durability of reinforced and prestressed concrete, structural steel, masonry, and composite structures.

GreenIT@UT is a campuswide initiative to promote sustainable IT products, services, and best practices on campus. The initiative is divided into three sections: reducing and recycling by using Blackboard, SharePoint, WebSpace, etc.; saving power and space (through custom web publishing and virtual servers); and saving on travel by teleconferencing, videoconferencing, and using a virtual private network, webcasts, and streaming media.

Graduate Degrees

Architectural Engineering (MSE)
Architectural History (MA, PhD)

Architectural Studies (MSArchSt)
Architecture (MArch, PhD)
Civil Engineering (MSE, PhD)
Community and Regional Planning (MSCRP, PhD)
Historic Preservation (MArch, MSCRP, MSHP, PhD)
Interior Design (MID)
Landscape Architecture (MLA)
Mechanical Engineering (MSE, PhD)
Sustainable Design (MSSD)
Urban Design (MSUD)

Graduate Dual-Degree Programs

Community and Regional Planning/Geography (MSCRP/PhD)
Community and Regional Planning/Sustainable Design (MSCRP/MSSD)
Community and Regional Planning/Urban Design (MSCRP/MSUD)
Law/Community and Regional Planning (JD/MSCRP)
Mechanical Engineering/Business Administration (MA/MBA)
Public Affairs/Community and Regional Planning (MPAff/MSCRP)
Public Affairs/Engineering (MPAff/MSE)

About Your Old Tech Equipment

Check your campus for a recycling drop-off location. Many local communities also run drop-off locations for recycling used computers, printers, DVD players, and similar equipment. Staples and Best Buy will take most electronics for free, but charge $10 for computers. For information on why responsible recycling of toxic wastes is important, check www.ban.org.

UNIVERSITY OF CINCINNATI (UC)

2600 Clifton Avenue
Cincinnati, Ohio 45221
513-556-6000
E-mail: www.uc.edu/contact/
www.uc.edu

About DesignIntelligence and UC

DesignIntelligence's 2010 list of "America's Best Architecture and Design Schools" ranked the undergraduate interior design program at UC number 1 in the nation, the undergraduate industrial design program number 4, the graduate industrial design program number 5, and the graduate architecture program number 6. *DesignIntelligence* is the publication of the Design Futures Council, an inter-disciplinary network of design, product, and construction practitioners.

Undergraduate Degrees

Architecture
Civil Engineering (Construction Engineering and Structural Engineering)
Construction Management
Interior Design
Sustaining the Urban Environment (minor)
Urban Planning
Urban Studies

Undergraduate Certificate

Computer-Aided Design

Undergraduate Costs

Academic year 2010–11: $10,065 resident, $24,688 nonresident (tuition and fees); $9510 to $10,767 (room and board)

Undergraduate Financial Aid

FAFSA required.

Undergraduate Admissions Requirements

Required: SAT or ACT (including Writing Test)

High school preparation: Requirements may vary by program; expect the following: 4 years English, 3 years math, 2 years social studies, 2 years science, 2 years same foreign language, 1 year fine art, 2 additional college prep subjects.

Recommended: Involvement in hobbies, community activities, theater or music groups, or sports; AP courses; postsecondary enrollment option programs.

Undergraduate Application Information

Options: Online application; rolling admission

Application fee: $50

Required: Application; official high school transcript; college prep form; supplemental information (personal statement and co-curricular activities form)

Application deadline: November 15 (fall freshmen in College of Design, Architecture, Art, and Planning); December 1 (fall freshmen in College of Engineering and Applied Science); February 1 (priority deadline other fall freshmen); June 1 (general deadline fall freshmen); August 1 (fall transfers)

Notification: Continuous

Green Campus Organizations

American Institute of Architectural Students: Promotes student development through lectures, discussion groups, conferences, and exhibitions.

American Planning Association: Provides activities and field trips for professional development.

American Society of Interior Designers: Promotes artistic and ethical concepts of the interior design profession on an apprentice level.

reUC: Educates about and advocates for the preservation of architecture, habitat, and cultural heritage at UC, its surrounding region, and beyond.

Student Society for the School of Architecture and Interior Design (SAID): Facilitates and promotes positive social interaction among students of SAID through social and academic events.

Students for Ecological Design: Created to bring together and transmit knowledge between people interested in the education, promotion, and implementation of environmentally focused design.

Engineers Without Borders: Student chapter of nonprofit, nongovernment organization that works with developing countries to improve the quality of life of their citizens through implementation of sustainable engineering projects, while developing internationally responsible students.

International Interior Design Association: Acts as a liaison between students and faculty of the School of Architecture and Design and the College of Design, Architecture, Art, and Planning.

Developing and Emerging Nations Society: Provides an academic network for students in interdisciplinary fields to discuss and promote awareness of contemporary issues and identify key challenges facing developing and emerging nations around the world.

Leaders for Environmental Awareness & Protection (LEAP): Hopes to foster an environmental movement, both on campus and in the community, by engaging the talents of students and faculty; focuses on networking with environmental organizations, volunteerism, promoting special events, increasing environmental education, and creating open discussion.

PACES (The Presidential Advisory Council on Environment & Sustainability): Committee that oversees UC's sustainability mission and serves as hub for information for all sustainability programs and projects at the university.

Fast Facts

The University of Cincinnati requires that all new construction, and, wherever possible, renovations, be certified LEED Silver or higher. During the past sixteen years, the university has committed more than $2 billion to new construction, building renovations, recreation facilities, improved residential environments, athletic and performance venues, and sculpted landscapes and plazas.

The Center for Sustaining the Urban Environment is a transdisciplinary education and research center at the University of Cincinnati. Students, faculty, and staff work with citizens of Cincinnati—and around to globe—to find ways to make "city living" more sustainable.

UC engineering, planning, architecture, and political science students are working with neighborhood groups on urban solutions and neighborhood development plans to capitalize on upcoming and potential changes to three area interstates: I-71, I-75, and I-74. Projects include a green hike/bike trail parallel to I-75; sustainable, green industry in nearby Avondale; and green infrastructure/wetlands along I-75 to control stormwater runoff.

In March 2009, UC became the first university in Ohio to implement a pioneering agreement to reuse "waste" methane gas produced by a landfill as a power-generation source. This saves the university $2.7 million over three years and reduces UC's carbon footprint by 10 percent.

UC's campus restaurants buy all of their produce from local restaurants and purchase sustainable seafood in conjunction with the Monterey Bay Aquarium Seafood Watch Program.

Graduate Degrees

Architecture (MArch, MSArch)
Civil Engineering (MS, MEng, PhD)
Community Planning (MCP)
Mechanical Engineering (MS, MEng, PhD)
Regional Development Planning (PhD)

UNIVERSITY OF GEORGIA (UGA)

Athens, Georgia 30602
(706) 542–3000
E-mail: www.uga.edu/inside/contact.html
www.uga.edu

 http://bit.ly/collvid50

About UGA's Student Sustainability Fee

In 2009, UGA students voted to impose a $3 fee on themselves to support the university's new Office of Sustainability. Sustainability is a priority in the university's 2010–2020 Strategic Plan. The fee, though small, is expected to generate about $120,000 a year for sustainability efforts on campus.

Undergraduate Degrees

Art (Interior Design concentration)
Furnishings and Interiors
Horticulture (major or minor)
Landscape Architecture
Turfgrass Management (major or minor)

Professional Development Online Courses

Building Analyst Quick Start Program
HVAC Technician
Interior Design
Performing Comprehensive Building
    Assessments
Principles of Green Buildings
Senior Certified Sustainability Professional

Undergraduate Costs

Academic year 2009–10: $15,576 (residents), $33,786 (nonresidents) (tuition, fees, average room and board)

Undergraduate Financial Aid

FAFSA required. Scholarships available; see www.admissions.uga.edu/article/scholarships_at_uga.html.

Undergraduate Admissions Requirements

Required: SAT or ACT with Writing Test. High school preparation: 4 years English; 4 years mathematics (algebra I and II, geometry, one higher level than algebra II); 3 years science (one life science with lab and one physical science with lab); 3 years social studies (including U.S. and World history); 2 years same foreign language

Recommended: SAT Subject Tests; Honors, AP, and International Baccalaureate courses

Undergraduate Application Information

Options: Online application; early action; early admission; deferred entrance

Application fee: $60

Required: Application Parts I and II; SAT/ACT scores with writing assessment; official high school transcript; counselor/school evaluation form; teacher recommendation

Recommended: Essay

Application deadline: January 15 (freshmen), October 15 (Early Action), April 1 (transfers)

Notification: April 1 (freshmen), December 15 (Early Action), continuous (transfers)

Green Campus Organizations

Student Historic Preservation Organization: Promotes awareness of historic preservation throughout the UGA and Athens communities; provides preservation advocacy opportunities for its members.

Clean Out Your Files Day: Recycling day for the entire campus held as part of RecycleMania.

Ecology Club: Environmental advocacy student organization that connects members with research and service opportunities; conducts campus and community outreach on sustainability initiatives.

Go Green Alliance: Educates the university and Athens communities on sustainability and environmental issues; promotes conservation of energy and other resources and recycling.

Sustainapalooza: A fair sponsored by the Physical Plant and the Go Green Alliance as part of the university's Go Green Initiative.

Students for Environmental Action: Promotes environmental responsibility on campus, in the community, and worldwide through programs and involvement in politics.

Fast Facts

The College of Environment and Design offers an interdisciplinary program of research, education, and outreach with a design vision for communities, cities, and global landscapes. Its activities focus on environmental and urban design, natural resources, land use, design for recreation, and historical landscapes.

In its effort to create the optimal, sustainable learning environment, UGA's Office of University Architects is focusing on resource conservation and quality of life improvement. Sustainability initiatives include: historic preservation, sustainable site design and greenspace creation, alternative transportation, high-performance buildings, water resource conservation, renewable energy and energy efficiency, and waste minimization.

Graduate Degrees

Art (Interior Design concentration) (MFA)
Environmental Planning and Design (MEPD)
Historic Preservation (MHP, MHP/JD)
Horticulture (MS, PhD)
Landscape Architecture (MLA)

Graduate Certificate

Historic Preservation

UNIVERSITY OF OREGON, EUGENE

Eugene, Oregon 97403
541-346-1000
E-mail: www.uoregon.edu/contact/
www.uoregon.edu

About CASL

The Center for the Advancement of Sustainable Living (CASL) is a student-driven organization that demonstrates and promotes sustainable living. The center itself is a low-impact house designed by University of Oregon architecture students and built near the campus. It has a solar panel and green room and is used to educate and interact with community members, faculty, and students.

Undergraduate Degrees

Architecture (major or minor)
Historic Preservation (minor)
Interior Architecture (major or minor)

Landscape Architecture (Planning and Design program; Landscape Architectural Technology, Plants in the Landscape, Landscape Analysis and Planning, History and theory of Landscape Architecture, and Landscape Architectural Media areas) (major or minor)

Planning, Public Policy, and Management (major or minor)

Undergraduate Costs

Academic year 2010–11 (estimate): $20,931 resident, $38,481 nonresident (tuition, fees, room and board, books and supplies, personal expenses)

Undergraduate Financial Aid

FAFSA required.

Undergraduate Academic Requirements

Required: Graduate from a standard or regionally accredited high school; at least 3.0 GPA; C– or higher in fourteen college preparatory courses; SAT or ACT scores

High school preparation: 4 years English (preparatory composition and literature with emphasis on writing expository prose); 3 years math (algebra I and II or higher); 2 years science (two separate college-preparatory fields); 3 years social studies; second-language proficiency (as evidenced by 2 years same foreign language or proficiency test)

Recommended: Advanced mathematics course in senior year; 1 year laboratory science

Option: If a student has not completed the required high school coursework, requirements may be fulfilled by taking SAT Subject Tests (Math I or II and a second test of the student's choice) or by taking high school or college courses to satisfy course deficiencies.

Undergraduate Application Information

Options: Online application, tentative admission, deferred admission

Application fee: $50

Required: Application; official high school diploma; SAT or ACT (Writing Test optional) scores; application essay

Optional: Essay explaining personal circumstances

Application deadline: November 1 (fall freshmen early notification); January 15 (fall freshmen regular notification); March 15 (fall transfers early notification); May 15 (fall transfers regular notification). Some departments have different application deadlines; see http://admissions.uoregon.edu/freshmen/deadlines/departmental.

Green Campus Organizations

Associated Students for Historic Preservation: Working to advance knowledge and understanding of historic preservation among students, professionals, and educators throughout the nation.

Coalition Against Environmental Racism: Students committed to bridging the gap between social and environmental equality; focuses on how pollution and resource depletion disproportionately affect communities of color.

Environmental Leadership Program: Interdisciplinary service-learning program within the University of Oregon's Environmental Studies Program that matches students with nonprofit organizations, governmental agencies, and businesses to address local environmental needs.

Summer Sustainability Trips: Fun, engaging program that provides incoming freshmen hands-on opportunities to reduce the environmental footprint of the university. In 2010, the Office of Sustainability and the Holden Leadership Center offered two four-day programs: Project Tomato, which focuses on local and organic agriculture, and H2Oregon, which explores water issues.

Fast Facts

The Ecological Design Center (EDC) believes that the relationship between the built and natural worlds must be sustainable and that it is the job of designers to pioneer this relationship. The EDC advocates for interdisciplinary ecological design curriculum as well as the implementation of ecological planning and design on campus and in the Eugene community. As part of its mission, the EDC has sponsored the HOPES (Holistic Options for Planet Earth Sustainability) conference since 1995. The conference is the nation's only ecological design conference developed and managed by students.

Design/Build is a course offered by the Departments of Architecture and Landscape Architecture that offers experience in all facets of the building process. Students spend three to six months on projects, taking them from predesign through final construction.

At the Oira Summer Field School, historic preservation students can work alongside master masons and craftspeople while learning about the traditional building methods found in the Ossola Valley in the Piedmont region of northern Italy. Students study, explore, and document cultural history, including Roman ruins, medieval villages, and castles.

The Institute for a Sustainable Environment conducts research into a variety of issues that fall into three general areas: ecological, economic, and social stability. One current project is the ISE Geographic Information Systems Lab, which analyzes patterns of landscape change to study issues such as healthy patterns of urbanization.

Graduate Degrees

Architecture (MArch)
Community and Regional Planning (MCRP)

Historic Preservation (MS)
Interior Architecture (MIarc)
Landscape Architecture (Graduate BLA, First Professional MLA, Post-professional MLA, PhD)

Graduate Certificate

Ecological Design

UNIVERSITY OF VIRGINIA (UVA)

Charlottesville, Virginia 22904
434-924-0311
www.virginia.edu

 http://bit.ly/collvid51

About the Learning Barge

Since 2006, UVA students, alumni, faculty, and consultants have been working on a floating classroom in Norfolk, dubbed the "Learning Barge." The project includes a classroom, bathrooms, demonstration wetland habitat, and breezeway on a solar-powered barge. Since the project's inception, more than 100 students have participated in the project through design studios, environmental seminars, engineering courses, competitions, fundraising efforts, and construction.

Undergraduate Degrees

Architectural History (major or minor)
Architecture (major or minor)
Civil Engineering
Historic Preservation (minor)
Landscape Architecture (minor)
Mechanical Engineering
Urban and Environmental Planning (major or minor)
Urban Studies (minor)

Undergraduate Costs

Academic year 2009–10 (estimate): $21,140 resident, $43,140 nonresident (tuition and fees, books and supplies, room, board, personal expenses)

Undergraduate Financial Aid

FAFSA and University Financial Aid application required.

Undergraduate Admissions Requirements

Required: SAT or ACT (with Writing Test).

High school preparation: 4 years English; 4 years college preparatory math; 2 years foreign language; 1 year social science; 2 years science (from among biology, chemistry, and physics). Engineering applicants must take 3 years science, including physics.

Recommended: Courses listed above are minimum requirements. Rigorous academic program, including at least 5 academic courses each year, AP, IB, and honors courses is recommended, as are 2 SAT II Subject tests of the student's choice.

Undergraduate Application Information

Options: Online applications (recommended)

Application fee: $60

Required: Common Application with UVA supplement; official SAT or ACT (with Writing Test) scores; secondary school report; official high school transcript; counselor and teacher recommendations; mid-year reports

Optional: Arts supplement

Application deadline: January 1 (fall freshmen); March 1 (fall transfers); November 1 (spring transfers)

Notification: April 1 (freshmen); May 1 (fall transfers); December 1 (spring transfers)

Green Campus Organizations

Global Architecture Brigades: Part of Global Brigades. Volunteers apply architectural design and construction skills to bring about socially responsible change to developing communities around the world.

Global Environmental Brigades: Part of Global Brigades. Students assess and deliver sustainable solutions to impoverished villages and areas with environmental degradation.

Greek Recycling Program: Students in the Greek system promote the reduction, reuse, and recycling of reclaimable materials from all fraternities and sororities at UVA.

Green Grounds Group: Students dedicated to educating and advocating for the implementation of sustainable planning, design, and community-based efforts at UVA.

Protect Our Planet Non-Profit Organization Worldwide: Aims to increase knowledge and recognition of global warming.

Fast Facts

UVA offers many undergraduate and graduate classes related to sustainability. Undergraduate offerings range from managing sustainable development to the ethics of sustainability. Graduate topics include new urban housing and green engineering and sustainability. For a complete list, go to www.virginia.edu/sustainability/classes.html.

In 2007, the university required that all new and renovated buildings be eligible for LEED certification. Three years later, the university celebrated the fruits of that mandate when it dedicated its first LEED-certified building, a 15,000-square-foot addition to the Printing and Copying Services building. The $3.3 million addition, which received a Silver ranking, was completed in May 2009.

The Institute for Environmental Negotiation promotes conflict resolution and consensus building as a way to ensure that communities are sustained ecologically, socially, and economically. Areas of focus include everything from land use and planning to sustainable development. For more information, go to www.virginia.edu/ien/.

A student-initiated food-composting program received a silver medal in the 2010 Governor's Environmental Excellence Awards. The university and students partnered with the food service company that operates UVA dining facilities to remove about 2.5 tons of food waste from the Observatory Hill Dining Hall each week. That waste is pulped and taken to a farm where it is composted.

Graduate Degrees

Architectural History (MArH)
Architecture (MAr)
Civil Engineering (ME, MS, PhD)
History of Art and Architecture (MA, PhD)
Landscape Architecture (MLAr)
Urban and Environmental Planning (MUEP)

Graduate Certificate

Historic Preservation

Graduate Distance Learning

Civil Engineering (ME)

VIRGINIA POLYTECHNIC INSTITUTE AND STATE UNIVERSITY (Virginia Tech)

Blacksburg, Virginia 24061-0002
540-231-6000
E-mail: www.vt.edu/contacts/
www.vt.edu

 http://bit.ly/collvid52

About National Rankings

DesignIntelligence, the only national college ranking focused exclusively on design, gave all of Virginia Tech's architecture and design programs high marks in 2010. Undergraduate programs and their rankings: landscape architecture ranked number 1, architecture ranked number 4, and industrial design ranked number 11. Graduate programs and their rankings: landscape architecture ranked number 2, architecture ranked number 8, and interior design ranked number 7. *DesignIntelligence* is the publication of the Design Futures Council, an interdisciplinary network of design, product, and construction practitioners.

Undergraduate Degrees

Architecture
Building Construction (major or minor)
Civil and Environmental Engineering
Construction Engineering and Management
Horticulture (major or minor)
Industrial Design
Interior Design
Landscape Architecture
Mechanical Engineering
Public and Urban Affairs

Undergraduate Costs

Academic year 2010–11 (estimate): $15,748 resident, $29,507 nonresident (tuition, fees, room and board)

Undergraduate Financial Aid

FAFSA and General Scholarship Application required.

Undergraduate Admissions Requirements

Required: SAT or ACT (with Writing Test); high school transcript

High school preparation: 4 years English; 3 years math (algebra I and II, geometry); 2 years laboratory science (biology, chemistry, or physics); 2 years social studies (1 must be history); 3 additional academic units (foreign language highly recommended); 4 elective units. Some majors, such as engineering and architecture, have additional requirements; see www.admiss.vt.edu/apply/freshman/what_do_we_look_for.php.

Undergraduate Application Information

Options: Online application; deferred enrollment

Application fee: $50

Required: SAT or ACT (with Writing) scores; high school transcript; high school counselor supplemental form; mid-year high school report; final grades/high school transcript.

Optional: Letter of recommendation; personal essay

Application deadline: November 1 (freshmen early decision); January 15 (freshmen regular decision); June 30 (fall transfers)

Notification: December 15 (freshmen early decision); April 1 (freshmen regular decision); May 1 (fall transfers)

Green Campus Organizations

Eco-Olympics: Student-planned campus-wide program focused on education, awareness, and impact reduction.

Environmental Coalition: Largest sustainability-focused student organization on campus; works directly with the Office of Sustainability on a variety of initiatives; organizes such projects as Earth Day.

Student Government Association's Sustainability Committee: Committee facilitated by the SGA Director of Sustainability and Director of Green Initiatives; works directly with the Environmental Coalition on various initiatives.

Sustainable Food Corps: Students focused on sustainable food and dining issues, including the development of a student-run farm off-campus.

The Coalition for Campus Sustainability: Coalition of eighteen different student organizations that work together on sustainability issues.

Virginia Tech Green Team: The Office of Sustainability's environmental education and awareness team.

YToss?: YMCA group that organizes a pick-up drive during move-out to save items from the landfill.

Fast Facts

Eco-City Alexandria is a strategic collaborative planning process designed by the City of Alexandria in partnership with Virginia Tech's Department of Urban Affairs and Planning. The partners have created the Environmental Action Plan 2030 that outlines Alexandria's path toward sustainability. Goals include leading the new green economy, addressing the challenges of climate change, and sustaining the city's high quality of life while decreasing its carbon and ecological footprints.

In 2010, Virginia Tech completed its tenth annual RecycleMania. This year, the university's overall recycling rate rose 6.6 percent to 18.62 percent. Total recyclable materials increased by 19,260 pounds (a 7.3 percent increase from 2009), and the amount of trash decreased by 60,880 pounds (a 4.7 percent reduction from 2009).

In its 2010 Campus Sustainability Report Card, the Sustainable Endowments Institute (SEI) awarded Virginia Tech an overall "B" rating. The rating, up from a "B−" last year, marks the second year in a row that the university's overall score has increased.

Graduate Degrees

Architecture (MArch, MS)
Architecture and Design Research (PhD)
Building Construction (MS)
Civil Engineering (MEng, MS, PhD)
Construction (PhD)
Environmental Design and Planning
    (Construction emphasis) (PhD)
Horticulture (MS, PhD)

Landscape Architecture (MLA, PhD)
Planning, Governance, and Globalization (Urban
    and Environmental Design and Planning track)
    (PhD)
Urban and Regional Planning (MURPL)

Graduate Certificate

Construction Engineering and Management

RecycleMania

RecycleMania began in 2001 with a competition between Miami University of Ohio and Ohio University to see which school could recycle more campus waste. By 2010, the ten-week competition had grown to 607 schools, more than 5 million students and 1.3 million staff and faculty members, and eight categories of awards. Participating colleges and universities in 49 states, the District of Columbia, Canada, and Qatar recycled or composted 84 million pounds of waste in 2010. RecycleMania is a joint project of the RecycleMania Steering Committee of the College and University Recycling Coalition, Keep America Beautiful, and the U.S. Environmental Protection Agency's WasteWise program.

The following list names the 2010 participating schools profiled in this book:

Arizona State University
Auburn University
Century Community and Technical College
Colorado State University
Drexel University
Fox Valley Technical College
Kansas State University
Los Angeles Trade-Technical College
Louisiana State University Agricultural and Mechanical College
Massachusetts Institute of Technology
Purdue University
Rhode Island School of Design
Texas A&M University
The University of Texas at Austin
University of Cincinnati
University of Georgia
University of Oregon
University of Virginia
Virginia Polytechnic Institute and State University

Are You Being Fashionably Green?

You can be fashionable and still be environmentally responsible. Here are a few ideas to get you started.

1. **Shop at second-hand stores and vintage clothing stores.** Remember that shirt your aunt gave you and you hated, but your friend loved? Your castoffs can be someone else's find, and vice versa. Also check out eBay for previously owned clothing and accessories.

2. **If you want new, look for items that are made from post-consumer waste materials.** The label or packaging will tell you. Bagallini® handbags, wallets, backpacks, and luggage are made from recycled plastic bottles. You can find them at www.travelsmith.com.

3. **If you want new clothes, look for items made from natural fibers.** But be a careful consumer. Look for items made with organic cotton like those from www.underthecanopy.com and www.truly-organic .com. Cotton uses 18–25 percent of the world's pesticides, depending on which expert you read, so be sure it's organic cotton. Other natural fibers to look for are hemp and bamboo. Bamboo makes really soft fabric.

4. **See how far your dollars can go.** Buy the Sak™ Shopper Tote made of bamboo and recycled cotton from www.travelsmith.com and your money will benefit the Nature Conservancy's Plant a Billion Trees Campaign. Other retailers are also supporting this project that was certified in 2010 for fighting climate change. Check out www.plantabillion.org.

5. **Eco-friendly is high style.** Banana Republic launched its Heritage Collection of organic cotton and soy silk clothing in 2009. Check out http://bananarepublic.gap.com/. On its Corporate Responsibility page, H&M lists the sustainable materials that its manufacturers use for H&M clothing: organic wool, organic linen, recycled cotton, recycled polyester (from recycled plastic bottles and textile waste), recycled polyamide (from fishing nets and textile waste), recycled wool, and tencel.

6. **Even your shoes can be eco-friendly.** The Simple® shoe company makes sneakers from organic cotton, hemp, and recycled car tires. Other eco-friendly shoe brands are Acorn, El Naturalista, Greenbees, Merrell, Nava, Patagonia, Terrasoles, Teva, and Timberland.

7. **Dry your hair and save energy at the same time.** Rusk manufactures the Go Green Blow Dryer. It uses 23 percent less energy than similar dryers. It is packaged in recycled corrugated with soy ink printing.

8. **Make your hair environmentally friendly.** A variety of hair-care products now boast natural ingredients, recycled packaging, and a commitment to preserving the environment. Check out www.paul-mitchell.com, http://telabeautyorganics.com/science, and www.pureology.com.

9. **Think globally and shop globally.** Shop for interesting and unusual clothing, accessories, and furniture at stores like Ten Thousand Villages (www.tenthousandvillages.com) and online at http://worldofgood .ebay.com/. You can help the environment by buying goods made from natural materials and at the same time help poor workers in this country and in developing nations support themselves and their families.

10. **Find repurposed garments to wear.** A repurposed garment was at one point another, or many other, articles of clothing. Fashion designers have become more and more involved in repurposed fashion. You may find a unique look by breathing new life into older fabric.

CHAPTER 7

25 TWO-YEAR COLLEGES WITH GREEN GREEN PROGRAMS

The twenty-five community colleges in this chapter were chosen to represent a cross-section of types of programs, areas of the country, settings, and innovative curricula. If you are interested in retraining for the new economy, degree and certificate programs at local community colleges are a good way to learn new skills. Community colleges welcome older students and career-changers. Some of the colleges offer online courses, and some also have research facilities or demonstration projects that involve students as part of their course work. Some also partner with local unions and businesses to run apprenticeship programs.

The colleges have strong commitments to sustainability and have campus sustainability programs. Many have student organizations that sponsor a variety of green educational and community service projects. More than half have signed the American College and University Presidents Climate Commitment.

The information presented here has been culled not only from college Web sites, but also from *Peterson's Survey of Sustainability Efforts in Higher Education,* sent to two-year and four-year schools in the United States and Canada and completed by representatives of the schools themselves.

Keep in mind that this is a list of highlights. Other community and junior colleges not listed here also offer programs related to careers in various aspects

of building, construction, and landscaping. Check out *Peterson's Two-Year Colleges* and read the "Majors" index to find other schools offering any of the majors listed in this chapter.

ABOUT THE LISTINGS

Here's what you need to know to navigate the two-year college profiles.

Contact Information

The first paragraph of each school profile lists the school name, address, phone number, e-mail address, and Web site info.

Degrees and Certificates

This section includes associate degrees and certificates in programs related to building and landscaping. Some degrees allow a student to concentrate in a particular aspect of a field such as an energy efficiency option in construction technologies or greenhouse concentration in agribusiness.

Costs

Costs are quoted for the most recent period available. In most cases, full-time as well as credit hour costs are given, as are in-state and out-of-state residency costs.

Financial Aid

All schools offering financial aid require the FAFSA forms be filled out. Usually, these forms can be found online. Any other requirements or special financial aid are detailed in this section.

Admission Requirements

Most schools require a high school diploma or GED. Any specific testing and/or requirements are detailed here.

Application Information

Most schools have online applications for admission. Fees for applications are noted.

Distance Learning

A number of two-year schools offer courses online, some of which may meet requirements of the degrees listed in this guide.

Green Campus Organizations

This section gives a sampling of green activities that students may participate in. The schools included in this guide have sustainability efforts and, thus, a variety of ways students may become involved and take leadership roles. This section also lists campus groups focused on construction issues and projects, as well as students' future careers in landscaping and turf management.

Fast Facts

The Fast Facts sections give insights into the school's commitment to sustainability and the environment. They also provide additional information on projects and awards related to a school's construction and landscaping degree programs.

Schools Profiled Here

The following two-year colleges are profiled in this chapter:

- Albany Technical College
- Anne Arundel Community College
- Cape Cod Community College
- Century Community and Technical College
- Cleveland State Community College
- Crowder College
- Cuyahoga Community College
- Edmonds Community College
- Fox Valley Technical College
- Hudson Valley Community College
- Iowa Lakes Community College
- Kankakee Community College
- Lane Community College
- Lansing Community College
- Los Angeles Trade-Technical College
- Macomb Community College
- Mercer County Community College
- Midlands Technical College
- Mount Wachusett Community College
- Red Rocks Community College
- Santa Fe Community College
- St. Petersburg College
- Tidewater Community College
- Tulsa Community College
- Wake Technical Community College

ALBANY TECHNICAL COLLEGE (ATC)

1704 South Slappey Boulevard
Albany, Georgia 31701
877-261-3113 (toll-free)
www.albanytech.edu

Degrees and Certificates

Associate Degrees:

Commercial Construction Management (A.A.S.)
Construction Management (A.A.S.)
Electrical Construction and Maintenance (A.A.S.)
Residential Construction Management (A.A.S.)

Certificates:

Air Conditioning Technician Assistant
General Maintenance Mechanic
Industrial/Commercial Air

Diplomas:

Air Conditioning Technology
Building Maintenance
Carpentry
Environmental Horticulture
Masonry
Plumbing
Welding and Joining Technology

Through the Carlton Construction Academy, students can earn the following technical certificates:

Basic Plumbing
Commercial Wiring

Costs

(Academic year 2010) Georgia residents: Full-time students (15 or more credit hours) $756 tuition and fees; part-time students (fewer than 15 credit hours) $45 per credit hour plus additional fees of $65. Nonresidents: Total tuition twice that charged Georgia residents. Alabama residents of Barbour, Henri, and Houston Counties pay Georgia resident fees.

For students who qualify for HOPE scholarships, tuition and books are free.

Financial Aid

FAFSA required.

Admission Requirements

Options: Online

Application fee: $15.00

Required: Official high school transcript or GED scores; official college or technical college transcript for prior credit. Entrance exam required unless a student has a "C" or higher grade in English and math from a college or technical college or 400 in math or 430 in verbal SAT, CPE of 77 in English, 77 reading, and 75 in math; composite score of 17 on the ACT.

Application deadline: Two terms per season; fall: September 7 and October 13; winter: September 7 and January 20; spring: December 16 and April 13; summer: June 5 and July 23

Fast Facts

Students in ATC's Carlton Construction Academy partner with Flint River Habitat for Humanity to build at least one home a year. The students manage and build the housing project.

ANNE ARUNDEL COMMUNITY COLLEGE (A.A.CC)

101 College Parkway
Arnold, Maryland 21012-1895
410-777-A.A.CC
www.A.A.cc.edu

Degrees and Certificates

Associate Degrees:

Architecture/Interior Design (A.A.S.)
Construction Management (A.A.S.)
Arts and Science Transfer: Environmental
    Science Option (A.S.)
Arts and Science Transfer: Horticulture Option
    (A.S.)

Certificates:

Architectural CAD
Architectural Illustration
Landscape Architecture Design
Interior Design Advanced Option
Construction Management
Construction Management Entrepreneurship
Alternative and Sustainable Energy Systems
Computer Aided Design

Costs

(Academic year 2009–10) County residents $88 per semester hour; residents of other Maryland counties: $169 per semester hour; out-of-state residents $299 per semester hour

Financial Aid

FASFA required. In FY 2009, the Anne Arundel Community College Foundation Inc. authorized $511,177 to 474 students. Scholarships range from $50 to $3,500. The foundation manages more than 200 funds supporting scholarships and college programs. A.A.CC students received a total of $21,792,886 in federal financial aid (grants, loans, and work study) in FY 2009. In addition, 1,610 students received $1,642,118 from Maryland state awards.

Admission Requirements

A.A.CC maintains an open-door policy to all high school graduates, those with a high school equivalency certificate, and anyone at least 16 years of age who demonstrates an ability to benefit from a college education.

Application Information

Options: Application for admission can be made online, in person, by fax, or by mail

Application fee: None

Required: Admission is available to all applicants, but some courses of study may have additional requirements. To demonstrate proficiency in English and Math, provide results from ACT, SAT, or A.A.CC Accuplacer Test and any proof of prerequisite or co-requisite requirements.

Application deadline: Rolling

Notification: Continuous

Distance Learning

A number of courses and degree programs use one or more of the A.A.CC Virtual Campus offerings. These include online courses via ANGEL learning management system, hybrid courses, telecourses, interactive courses, and Web-based courses.

Green Campus Organizations

AIAS@A.A.CC!: For architecture, interior design, and construction management majors; student chapter of the American Institute of Architectural Students.

Campus Activities Board: Coordinates Earth Day events.

Interior Design–ASID (American Society of Interior Designers): Provides students with the opportunity to expand their understanding and appreciation of interior design and network with other students and professionals in the field.

Institute for the Future: Partner with the World Future Society; publishes *futureportal*, an e-zine that "studies the future to build a better tomorrow."

Fast Facts

Interior design students won 12 first-place and honorable mention awards in the annual American Society of Interior Designers Maryland–Chesapeake home design competition in fall 2009.

Established in 1980, the Environmental Center at A.A.CC supports the college's mission through applied research projects designed to address local environmental necessities. In selecting solutions to a given problem, the center bases decisions on the idea that what makes good environmental sense also makes good economic sense. The Center's areas of specialty include the creation and restoration of wetlands, habitat creation, bioremediation, toxicity testing, and environmental monitoring.

CAPE COD COMMUNITY COLLEGE (CCCC)

2240 Iyannough Road
West Barnstable, Massachusetts 02668
877-846-3672 (toll-free)
E-mail: info@capecod.edu
www.capecod.edu

Degrees and Certificates

Associate Degrees:

Environmental Studies (A.A.)
Environmental Technology (A.S.)

Certificates:

Construction Technology
Horticulture
Landscape Construction
Landscape Maintenance
Horticulture Technician

The Environmental Technology certificates listed below are a collaborative partnership among CCCC, Massachusetts Maritime Academy, and University of Massachusetts Dartmouth. Students may need to travel to each of the institutions in order to complete all the courses in any of the following certificate programs:

Coastal Zone Management
Environmental Site Assessment
Geographic Information Systems
Photovoltaic Technology

Solar Thermal Technology
Wastewater Management
Water Supply Management

Costs

(Academic year 2009–10) Full-time tuition and fees per year: $4320 for Massachusetts residents; $10,500 for nonresidents. Part-time tuition and fees: $144 per credit hour for Massachusetts residents; $350 for nonresidents.

Financial Aid

Financial aid consists of scholarships, grants, loans, and employment opportunities to help students who lack sufficient financial resources to attend college. This aid is considered as a supplement to the contributions made by the student and family. Any student receiving financial aid must abide by the Satisfactory Academic Progress Policy as defined by College policy and stated in the Student Handbook.

Admissions Requirements

A high school diploma, GED, or passing grade on an "Ability to Benefit" test is required of applicants regardless of age or previous college experience. Students who graduated from a Massachusetts public high school after 2003 must have successfully completed all MCAS requirements.

Application Information

Options: Online application form or request for application via e-mail or phone; completed applications must be returned via fax or mail.

Application fee: None

Required: Transcript of any prior postsecondary course work; high school transcript or GED certificate required, if either have not yet been attained at time of application.

Application deadline: Applications reviewed on a rolling admissions basis until seats are filled; priority to candidates who apply by August 15 for fall semester and January 10 for spring semester.

Distance Learning

Some courses are available as e-courses. Class lectures are accessed via the Web; assignments are submitted by fax, mail, or over the Internet; and testing is scheduled on a flexible basis. Some materials for online courses or online components may be available from the Web via the college's Learning Management System. For more information, contact the Office of Distance Learning at 508-362-2131 Ext. 4040.

Green Campus Organizations

CCCC is a signatory of the American College & University Presidents' Climate Commitment (ACUPCC) and is actively planning ways to reduce the campus's carbon footprint under this initiative.

Students for Sustainability: Promotes awareness among students, faculty and staff members, and the Cape Cod community about sustainability issues; it encourages community involvement.

Fast Facts

The Lorusso Applied Technology Center, completed in 2006, was the first state-owned building in Massachusetts to receive Gold LEED certification. This "green" building uses alternative energy sources, such as solar panels; was built with recycled materials; was designed for water conservation; and has low-impact and environmentally appropriate landscaping.

Cape Cod Community College's Wilkens Library is powered by a 200-kilowatt fuel cell.

CENTURY COMMUNITY AND TECHNICAL COLLEGE

3300 Century Avenue North
White Bear Lake, Minnesota 55110
800-228-1978 (toll-free)
admissions@century.edu
www.century.edu

About New Environmentally Friendly Design Products

The National Kitchen and Bath Association (www.nkba.org) promotes sustainable kitchen and bath design by providing information and resources about energy efficient, water-efficient, and environmentally friendly products and methods.

Degrees and Certificates

Associate Degrees:

Engineering CAD Technology: Mechanical Design Drafting (A.A.S.)
Facilities System Technology (A.A.S.)
Heating, Ventilation, and Air Conditioning Technology (A.A.S.)
Horticulture (A.S.)
Horticulture Technology: Greenhouse, Landscape (A.A.S.)
Horticulture Technology: Greenhouse, Landscape (Associate Diplomas)
Interior Design (A.A.S.)
Interior Design (Associate Diploma)
Renewable Energy: Solar (A.A.S.)

Certificates:

Home Furnishing Sales
Horticulture Assistant
Horticulture: Greenhouse, Landscape
Interior Design Consultant
Kitchen and Bath Design
Solar Assessor
Advanced Solar Thermal Energy Systems

Century College also offers a number of courses to help students update skills or prepare for new careers. These include boiler operation, home inspection, introduction to gas heating, National Electrical Code Review, and plumbing (apprenticeship program).

Costs

(Academic year 2010–11) $145 tuition; $164.46 per credit; Wisconsin, North Dakota, and Manitoba residents pay on the same basis as Minnesota residents; fees for South Dakota residents are based on reciprocity agreements.

Financial Aid

FAFSA required. State residents may also be eligible for Minnesota State Grants.

Admission Requirements

Required: High school diploma or GED

Application Information

Options: Online application

Application fee: $20

Required: Placement testing using Accuplacer

Application deadline: Varies by semester and program

Notification: Six to eight weeks after application deadlines

Distance Learning

Home Inspection (in partnership with American Home Inspectors Training Institute)
Kitchen and Bath Design (certificate)

Green Campus Organization

Horticulture Club: Extends educational opportunities and community and campus service projects.

Fast Facts

Century's Kitchen and Bath Design Program is accredited by the National Kitchen and Bath Association (NKBA) and is the only stand-alone one-year program in the country. It was the first course at Century to be given online and is also given on-site at International Market Square, the major interior design center in Minneapolis.

Since 2005, kitchen and bath design students have participated in a service-learning project with St. Paul College. Century's students design kitchens for Homeward Bound as their final project. The winning selection is then built and installed by students in St. Paul's carpentry and cabinetry program.

CLEVELAND STATE COMMUNITY COLLEGE (CSCC)

P.O. Box 3570
Cleveland, Tennessee 37320
423-472-7141
800-604-2722 (toll-free)
E-mail: clscc_info@clevelandstatecc.edu
www.clscc.cc.tn.us

Degrees and Certificates

Associate Degrees:

Construction Technology (A.A.S.)
Drafting and Design (A.A.S.)
Public and Government Service (A.A.S.)

Certificates:

Climate Control Technology
Construction Surveying
Construction Technology
Zero Energy Housing

Costs

(Spring 2010) Residents: $111 per semester hour plus registration fee; nonresidents: $460 per semester hour plus registration fee

Financial Aid

FAFSA required. Scholarships and federal financial aid available; see http://www.clscc.cc.tn.us/departments/financial_aid/aid_types.asp

Admissions Requirements

Required: High school graduate or equivalent

Application Information

Options: Online application

Application fee: $10

Required: High school transcript or GED test scores plus ACT or SAT if under 21 years of age; if over 21 and seeking a degree, must take academic placement (COMPASS) test

Application deadline: Rolling (freshmen/transfers)

Notification: Continuous

Distance Learning

CSCC is expanding into online and hybrid class offerings. Field work/hands-on work will be addressed by using Habitat for Humanity building projects.

Green Campus Organizations

Sustainability Committee: Formed in Fall 2008; set up recycling program, print management, printer cartridge recycling.

It'$ All About the Green!: Annual one-day campus event celebrating environmental awareness on Earth Day; presentations and exhibits by local vendors and college departments on ways to improve the environment as well as own lives and the community.

Arbor Day Celebration: Held in March at the state-certified arboretum on campus; includes walk led by Cleveland's city forester.

Fast Facts

CSCC was the only community college in the state to receive an American Recovery and Reinvestment (ARRA) grant. The grant totaled approximately $328,000 and enabled the Technology Department to enhance its Energy Efficient Construction program.

A 1-kilowatt solar panel array is installed outside the Technology Building. The array, including its controlling electronics, is an educational aid for Cleveland State tech classes and ties directly to Cleveland Utilities' electric grid to help Cleveland Utility and the Tennessee Valley Authority (TVA) generate "green power."

CSCC was awarded $5,000 by the TVA to set up solar-powered sun-tracking equipment to monitor local weather conditions in order to record the energy production of the CSCC's solar panel. This innovative program teaches students how to install and maintain solar paneling on residential and commercial structures.

About Being Car-Less

Need a car for a couple of hours? Try Zipcar, the car-sharing company. More than 100 campuses now have Zipcars. You can rent a car for a couple of hours or a day. Check out www.zipcar.com.

CROWDER COLLEGE

601 Laclede
Neosho, Missouri 64850
417-451-3223
E-mail: admissions@crowder.edu
www.crowder.edu

Degrees and Certificates

Associate Degrees:

Alternative Energy: Solar (A.A. and A.A.S)
Agribusiness Technology: Horticulture Emphasis (A.A.S.)
Construction Technology: Energy Efficient Building Option (A.A.S.)
Environmental Science (A.A.)

Certificates:

Active Solar Technician
Water and Wastewater Management

Costs

(Academic year 2009–10) In-district resident: $68 per credit hour; in-state resident: $95 per credit hour; nonstate resident: $123 per credit hour.

Technology/facility use fee: $12 per credit hour; distance learning fee: $7 per credit hour.

Financial Aid

FAFSA required (www.fafsa.gov). Students are eligible for federal financial aid programs, work-study grants, and various scholarship programs. If a student has been designated an A+ student by his/her high school, the state of Missouri will pay tuition and common student fees at Crowder.

Crowder Connection Scholarship: Qualifying students who are residents of Kansas, Oklahoma, and Arkansas are granted the privilege of enrolling at in-state tuition rates. Initially, the total number of grantees is limited to 100.

Admission Requirements

Required: High school diploma or GED

Application Information

Options: Online application

Application fee: $25

Required: High school transcript or GED scores, placement exam (ACT or COMPASS)

Notification: Continuous

Distance Learning

Courses available online are indicated in the course catalog. Online courses are available through the Blackboard e-education platform.

Green Campus Organization

Solar Vehicle Club: Annual Solar Challenge solar car and bike races.

Fast Facts

Crowder's Solar House entry in the Solar Decathlon in Washington, D.C., in 2009 was selected as the "People's Choice" and placed sixth overall in the competition. Students used their solar trailer to power the tools used during the building process on the Mall.

Since 2006, Crowder has been the host of the annual E-conference that features local, regional, and national experts in the fields of energy, efficiency, and the environment. The mission of the E-conference is to provide a forum for discussing new energy sources, energy efficiency, and environmentally sound practices to create economic opportunity and a sustainable future for the region.

Crowder's soccer field has been equipped with solar power to run the scoreboard and sprinkler system.

CUYAHOGA COMMUNITY COLLEGE (TRI-C)

700 Carnegie Avenue
Cleveland, Ohio 44115
800-954-8742 (toll-free)
E-mail: CustomerService@tri-c.edu
www.tri-c.edu

Degrees and Certificates

Associate Degrees:

Applied Industrial Technology: Bricklaying, Carpentry, Cement Masonry, Drywall Finishing, Electrical Construction, Floorlaying, Glazing, Ironworking, Operating Engineer, Painting (A.A.S.)
Interior Design (A.A.B)
Plant Science and Landscaping Technology (A.A.S.)
Plant Science and Landscaping Technology: Design/Build, Garden Center Operations (A.A.S.)

Certificates:

Plant Science and Landscaping Technology: Landscape Technician, Landscape Contracting

Costs

(Academic year 2009–10) County residents: $80.54 per enrolled hour; Ohio residents: $106.48 per enrolled hour; nonresidents: $218.04 per enrolled hour

Financial Aid

FAFSA required. Federal financial aid programs and a number of scholarships are available.

Admission Requirements

Required: High school diploma, documentation of GED completion for non–high school graduates 18 years or older

Application Information

Options: Online application or in person at any Tri-C Admissions Office

Application fee: None

Required: High school transcript (if under 25 years old)

Application deadline: One week prior to registration

Notification: Continuous

Distance Learning

Cuyahoga Community College offers a variety of options for distance learning, including Web-based, hybrid (a combination of classroom and computer-based learning), cable college, and independent learning. Contact the Office of eLearning & Innovation at 216-987-4257 or by e-mail at elearning@tri-c.edu.

Green Campus Organization

Campus sustainability initiatives: CFL light bulb exchange, Eco-Lounge, waste audit, green newsletter, and green office audit.

Fast Facts

The Green Academy and Center for Sustainability (GACS) at Tri-C trains individuals in the principles of sustainability, green construction, green interior design, green business development, sustainable investing, and more. Classes, seminars, and certifications are offered.

About LEED Certification and Landscape Design

The U.S. Green Building Council LEED building certification includes credit for using regionally appropriate landscaping that minimizes water use, prevents erosion, and reduces energy use, for example, for outdoor lighting. For more information, check the Council's Web site, http://www.usgbc.org.

EDMONDS COMMUNITY COLLEGE

20000 68th Avenue West
Lynnwood, Washington 98036
425-640-1459
E-mail: info@edcc.edu
www.edcc.edu

Degrees and Certificates

Associate Degrees:

Environmental Science (A.S.)
Restoration Horticulture (ATA)
Energy Management (ATA)

Certificates:

Building Inspection Certificate
Civil Construction Management and Inspection
Commercial Lighting Auditor
Energy Accounting Specialist
Energy Efficiency Technician
Residential Energy Auditor

Costs

(Academic year 2009–10) State residents: $80.60 per credit hour; nonresidents: $252.60 per credit hour. Eligible veterans, National Guard, and dependents: $50.45 per credit hour.

Financial Aid

FAFSA required. Award offers attempt to meet financial need with 45 percent "gift" aid (grants, waivers, scholarships), and 55 percent "self-help" aid (work/study and loans). Funds are limited and awarded to eligible students based on date financial aid paperwork is completed: May 1 for early priority consideration for all terms and August 15 for secondary consideration for fall quarter.

Admission Requirements

Required: High school diploma, GED certificate, or qualifying under "ability to benefit"

Application Information

Options: Online application

Application fee: $28

Required: Accuplacer assessment test (can be taken online); meeting with academic adviser

Application deadline: Rolling

Notification: Continuous

Distance Learning

A number of courses and even complete degree and certificate programs are offered either online or as a hybrid, that is, part on campus and part online. Contact the Distance Learning Office by e-mail at its@edcc.edu or by phone at 425-640-1098.

Green Campus Organizations

The Energy Management Group: Enhances the energy management program by expanding available resources through mentorships, tutoring, networking, and extracurricular activities.

Sustainability Council: Composed of faculty members, administrators, staff members, and students. It is a major component of the college's sustainability initiative.

Recycling Program: Headed by grounds department with student assistance.

S.A.V.E. the Earth Club (Student Association for a Viable Environment): Participates in community and save-the-earth projects.

Fast Facts

Over seventy species of trees have been identified on the 50-acre campus, and the horticulture department has developed a map to help students and the community learn about and understand how trees benefit the environment and improve the quality of life. The Campus Tree Walk was developed with a Community Forestry Assistance Grant provided by the Washington State Department of Natural Resources with support from the U.S. Department of Agriculture Forest Service.

The Learn-and-Serve Environmental Anthropology Field (LEAF) School provides an opportunity for students to earn academic credit and an AmeriCorps scholarship while working collaboratively with local tribes, governments, nonprofits, and businesses to help make fishing, farming, and forestry more sustainable. Financial aid for this program is available through AmeriCorps awards or from the Edmonds Community College Foundation.

FOX VALLEY TECHNICAL COLLEGE (FVTC)

1825 N. Bluemound Drive
P.O. Box 2277
Appleton, Wisconsin 54912-2277
920-735-5600
www.fvtc.edu

Degrees and Certificates

Associate Degrees:

Construction Management Technology (A.A.S.)
Interior Design (A.A.S.)
Laboratory Science Technician (A.A.S.)
Natural Resources Technician (A.A.S.)

Certificates:

Construction Technician, Commercial
Electrical Code, National
Energy Auditor (Residential)
Exploring Agriculture, Horticulture, and Natural
    Resources
Greenhouse Grower/Plant Propagation Technician
Landscape Construction Technician
Landscape Maintenance Technician
Photovoltaic Installer Entry Level
Environmental Management Systems for
    Emerging Technologies

Technical Diploma:

Construction, Residential Building (TD)
Horticulture Technician (TD)

FVTC also offers the following apprenticeships:

Construction Electrician
Electrician
Operating Engineer
Plumbing
Sheet Metal Construction
Steamfitting/Steamfitting Service

Costs

(Academic year 2009–10) Wisconsin residents: $116.55 per credit; nonresidents: $556.15 per credit. Minnesota residents use Wisconsin resident fees.

Financial Aid

FAFSA required (www.fafsa.gov). Students should check the Wisconsin Higher Education Grant program for eligibility.

Admission Requirements

Optional: ACT, SAT, SAT Subject Tests; essay, interview, campus visit

Program/Plan admissions assessment

Application Information

Options: Online application

Application fee: $30

Required: Student orientation

Application deadline: None

Notification: Rolling

Distance Learning

All Fox Valley Technical College Internet courses are in the Blackboard course management system. There is a self-assessment test on the college's Web site to help prospective students evaluate if they are a good candidate for online learning.

Green Campus Organizations

Natural Resources Club: Provides educational experiences to Natural Resources majors and outreach to the community and local school district to promote the conservation ethic and the principles of ecology/natural resources.

Fast Facts

FVTC is a member of the Association for Advancement of Sustainability in Higher Education to promote the message of sustainability among its campus communities.

As part of the sixteen-member Wisconsin Technical College System, FVTC is part of the newly launched Regional Industry Skills Education (RISE) program, financed with American Recovery and Reinvestment Act (ARRA) funding. The program's goal is "to connect worker education to student and employer needs" in a career pathways model.

HUDSON VALLEY COMMUNITY COLLEGE (HVCC)

80 Vandenburgh Avenue
Troy, New York 12180
518-629-HVCC
877-325-HVCC (toll-free)
E-mail: admissions@hvcc.edu
www.hvcc.edu

Degrees and Certificates

Associate Degrees:

Architectural Technology (A.A.S.)
Civil Engineering Technology (A.A.S.)
Computer-Aided Drafting (A.A.S.)
Construction Technology-Building Construction (A.A.S.)
Environmental Science (A.S.)
Electrical Construction and Maintenance (A.O.S.*)
Heating/Air Conditioning/Refrigeration Technical Services (A.O.S.*)
Public Administration Studies (A.A.S.)

_____

Associate in Occupational Studies (A.O.S.)

Certificates:

Computer-Aided Drafting
Construction
Heating Systems
Photovoltaic Installation
Refrigeration and Air Conditioning

Costs

(Academic year 2009–10) Residents of New York State: Full-time: $1550; part-time: $129 per credit hour. Nonresidents: Full-time: $4650; part-time: $387 per credit hour

Financial Aid

FAFSA required (www.fafsa.gov).

Nonresidents of New York State who are enrolled exclusively in distance learning will receive a scholarship in the amount of the nonresident tuition charge, effectively reducing tuition to that of a New York State resident.

New York State residents may be eligible for a variety of Tuition Assistance Programs (TAP). The Express TAP Application (ETA) must be completed to apply for all TAP awards. There are also Tuition Awards for Gulf War and Vietnam Veterans who are New York State residents.

Other financial aid is available to qualified students in the form of Federal Aid or scholarships.

About NASCAR's Going Green

In 2008, NASCAR announced plans for a green initiative to reduce energy use at its stockcar racing venues and to encourage sponsors to develop their own initiatives related to the sport. It's even exploring replacing carburetors with fuel injection and possibly introducing alternative fuels.

Admission Requirements

Required: High school diploma or GED. Most fields of study also require a high school average of 70 or above. The Educational Opportunity Program (EOP) is provided for New York State residents meeting the requirements of the state-supported program.

Application Information

Options: Online application

Application fee: $30

Required: High school transcript or copy of GED score report

Application deadline: Rolling

Notification: Continuous

Distance Learning

A number of courses and some degree programs offer fully online programs through Blackboard or Hybrid, which is a combination of online and on-campus meetings. An online self-evaluation exercise is available to help determine if distance learning is a good option for you.

Green Campus Organizations

Air Conditioning Club: Student branch of the American Society of Heating, Refrigeration and Air Conditioning Engineers (ASHRAE).

American Society of Civil Engineers Student Club (ASCE): Promotes understanding of the work of civil engineers; holds steel bridge competition.

Associated General Contractors of America (AGGC) Student Chapter: Promotes interest in and understanding of the construction industry.

Hudson Valley Community College Builders Club: Student chapter of the National Association of Home Builders (NAHB).

Society of Refrigeration (Mechanics) Technicians: Students interested in the application of commercial refrigeration and air conditioning.

Fast Facts

Hudson Valley Community College's Workforce Development Institute was one of the hosts and led the educational sessions for the first Northeast

Green Building Conference, the leading green building educational event in upstate New York. New York State is the first state to register for LEED certification for the governor's residence as part of the "Greening the Executive Mansion" initiative.

HVCC's Workforce Development Institute includes the Center for Energy Efficiency & Building Science, which provides ongoing training on incorporating energy efficiency methods into the building trades. Check out https://www.hvcc.edu/ceebs/index.html.

HVCC's newest facility, TEC-SMART (Training and Education Center for Semiconductor Manufacturing and Alternative and Renewable Technologies), opened January 25, 2010. It features more than a dozen state-of-the-art classrooms and laboratories that will be used to train the workforce in green technologies, including semiconductor manufacturing, photovoltaic, home energy efficiency, geothermal, alternative fuels, and wind energy. See https://www.hvcc.edu/tecsmart/.

IOWA LAKES COMMUNITY COLLEGE (ILCC)

3200 College Drive
Emmetsburg, Iowa 50536
712-362-2604
800-521-5054 (toll-free)
E-mail: info@iowalakes.edu
www.iowalakes.edu

Degrees and Certificates

Associate Degrees:

Construction Technology (A.A.S.)
Landscape and Turfgrass Technician (A.A.S.)

Certificates:

Welding Technology

Diplomas:

Construction Technology
Landscape and Turfgrass Technology
Welding Technology

Costs

(Academic year 2009–10) Resident tuition: $128 per credit; nonresident tuition: $130 per credit. Minnesota residents receive waiver of nonresident tuition through a reciprocity agreement.

Financial Aid

FAFSA required (www.fafsa.gov). Online scholarship applications; scholarship deadlines vary, but April 1 is a typical deadline for full scholarships and October 1 for spring term scholarships. In addition to scholarships, various loans, grants, and work-study opportunities exist.

Admission Requirements

Required: High school diploma or GED

Recommended: ACT scores

Application Information

Options: Online application

Application fee: None

Required: High school transcript or GED certification

Application deadline: Rolling

Notification: Continuous

Distance Learning

Iowa Lakes offers a number of distance learning formats that include online Internet courses, alternative delivery formats, and TV formats. Iowa Lakes is part of the Iowa Community College Online Consortium (ICCOC), which consists of seven Iowa community colleges. For more information on taking online credit courses or obtaining an online degree from ILCC, visit the consortium Web site at www.iowacconline.org.

Green Campus Organizations

Conservation Club: Projects include an extensive prairie restoration project at Fort Defiance State Park, participation in the Iowa Adopt-A-Highway program, tree-planting project for the Estherville city park system, and various projects for local county conservation boards and the Iowa Department of Natural Resources.

Landscape and Turfgrass Club: Community projects to promote and educate; money-making projects such as aerating yards, laying sod, and landscaping.

Fast Facts

Students in the Landscape and Turfgrass Technology program get hands-on experience on the college's 330-yard fairway with a PGA (Professional Golf Association) specification green, a native green, and a 300-yard driving range.

The Wind Energy and Turbine Technology program is the first in Iowa and has been in existence since 2004. The college owns and operates a V-82 turbine located about a half-mile south of the campus in Estherville. Power generated there is sold to the city of Estherville with proceeds used to offset the energy consumed by the college. Students learn maintenance activities as well as equipment operation and safety practices. (See http://www.iowalakes.edu/programs_study/industrial/wind_energy_turbine/indes.htm)

KANKAKEE COMMUNITY COLLEGE (KCC)

100 College Drive
Kankakee, Illinois 60901
815-802-8100
E-mail: www.kcc.edu/Pages/ContactUs.aspx
www.kcc.edu

Degrees and Certificates

Associate Degrees:

Air Conditioning and Refrigeration (A.A.S.)
Computer-Aided Drafting (A.A.S.)
Construction Management (A.A.S.)
Electrical Technology (A.A.S.) (specialization in Renewable Energy Technology)
Fine Arts (AFA)
Horticulture Technology (A.A.S.)
Welding

Certificates:

Air Conditioning and Refrigeration
Construction Craft Laborer
Construction Management
Horticulture

Costs

(Academic year 2009–10) District residents: $84 per credit hour; out-of-district state residents: $172.26 per semester hour; out-of-state residents: $387.69 per semester hour.

Students from certain counties in Indiana are charged the Illinois out-of-district tuition and fees rather than the out-of-state rates. There is a charge-back program and a cooperative agreement with some other districts in Illinois.

Financial Aid

FAFSA required (www.fafsa.gov). Scholarships are awarded annually by the KCC Foundation to over 350 students. There are a number of other sources of federal and state aid, including loans, grants, and work-study programs.

About Recycling Clothes

In 2005, Patagonia launched Common Threads Garment Recycling for its used Capilene® Performance Baselayers, Patagonia® fleece clothing, Polartec® fleece clothing, Patagonia cotton T-shirts, and other Patagonia clothing with the Common Threads tag. The goal is to reduce the use of new polyester fabrics and, thus, use less petroleum each year. To learn more, check out www.patagonia.com.

Admission Requirements

Required: High school diploma or GED

Application Information

Options: An online application form is available and can be electronically submitted or printed and mailed to the Office of Admissions.

Application fee: None

Required: High school or GED and prior college transcript, assessment testing for some programs and courses, academic advisement appointment, orientation session

Application deadline: Rolling

Notification: Continuous

Distance Learning

Some courses are offered online through the college's ANGEL system. A self-assessment to determine if this type of learning will be beneficial to you is available at www.kcc.edu/students/onlinelearning/pages/isonlineforme.aspx.

Green Campus Organization

Campus Sustainability Committee: Projects include campus recycling, auditing energy consumption, curriculum and course development, annual Sustainability Week events, and dissemination of information about sustainability issues.

Fast Facts

The 2009 Sustainability Week featured the Solar Globe Art Project. The globe uses light and dark orange to depict energy use throughout the world. Solar panels mounted on the globe collect solar energy, which is stored and used at night to power the lights that represent the energy use of major cities.

The KCC Sustainability Center opened in January 2009. It is a one-stop-shop for information about energy incentives and grant opportunities, energy efficiency and conservation, renewable energy, career development, and employment referral.

As a result of the Kankakee Community College's Community Sustainability Initiative, community leaders in Kankakee created the Council for Community Sustainability with the goal of promoting sustainability in the Kankakee River Valley. Their four-pronged approach is based on developing a green community, green jobs and businesses, sustainable agriculture and local food, and energy efficiency.

LANE COMMUNITY COLLEGE

4000 East 30th Avenue
Eugene, Oregon 97405
541-463-3100
E-mail: enrollmentadvisors@lanecc.edu
www.lanecc.edu

Degrees and Certificates

Associate Degrees:

Construction Technology (A.A.S.)
Construction Trades, General Apprenticeship
  (A.A.S.)
Drafting (A.A.S.)
Electrician Apprenticeship Technologies (A.A.S.)
Energy Management Technician (A.A.S.)
Fabrication/Welding (A.A.S.)
Renewable Energy Technology (A.A.S.)
Sustainability Coordinator (A.A.S.)
Water Conservation Technician (A.A.S.)

Certificates:

Construction Technology
Construction Trades, General Apprenticeship
Drafting
Electrician Apprenticeship Technologies
Welding Processes

Sustainability Continuing Education Classes include:

Introduction to Permaculture and Gardening
Organic Gardening Principles and Practice
Sustainable Landscaping

Costs

(Academic year 2009–10) Residents: $81 per credit; nonresidents: $213 per credit. Residents of Idaho, Nevada, and Washington pay the Oregon in-state tuition rate.

Financial Aid

FAFSA must be filed as early as possible after January 1 for any need-based aid (www.fafsa.gov). Grants, work-study, and loans as well as a number of scholarships are available to eligible students. Visit the Financial Aid Web page for more information at www.lanecc.edu/finaid/index.htm.

Admission Requirements

Required: 18 years of age or older; high school diploma, or GED

Application Information

Options: Online application

Application fee: None

Required: Placement testing

Application deadline: None

Notification: Continuous

Distance Learning

Lane offers a variety of options for some courses. These include live interactive courses either via cable TV or IP video to off-campus locations; online courses via Moodle, the online course management system; or as telecourses.

Green Campus Organizations

Learning Garden Club: Oversees all aspects of Lane's organic learning garden; provides practical hands-on experience in sustainable local food production. Bulk of harvest goes to Culinary Arts Department as part of the national Farm to Cafeteria Program.

RecycleMania: Thirteenth place in the Waste Minimization Category in 2009; second year of competition and improved by 37 percent over previous year's cumulative waste-per-person figure.

Green Chemistry Club: Built a biodiesel processor that will be used to turn waste grease from the campus kitchen into fuel for campus boilers and vehicles.

Oregon Student Public Interest Research Group (OSPIRG): Chapter of the national organization.

Sustainability Group: Committee of Lane staff and student volunteers who work together on sustainability issues; initiatives include recycling, reuse, composting, using organic and local foods, energy conservation, and water conservation.

Fast Facts

The Northwest Energy Education Institute is located at Lane and provides energy and building-related continuing education training across the United States.

With a grant from the American Recovery and Reinvestment Act (ARRA), Worksource Lane offered a number of no-cost training classes that included Weatherization Auditor and Technician, Sustainable Building Practices, and Basic Manufacturing Certificate with Solar Emphasis.

In 2008, Lane hosted the first Conference on Sustainability for Community Colleges. Forty-seven colleges and organizations from sixteen states attended.

Lane has set a goal of becoming carbon-neutral by 2050 and has established benchmarks and mechanisms for tracking progress and impact of its efforts.

About Mowing the Lawn

Get some exercise while you mow the lawn. Instead of a riding mower with gas fumes trailing you across the lawn, try one of the battery-powered mowers or a reel mower that (gasp!) you push to power. There's even a solar-hybrid robot mower by automower.com.

LANSING COMMUNITY COLLEGE (LCC)

P.O. Box 40010
Lansing, Michigan 48901-7210
517-483-1957
800-644-4522 (toll-free)
www.lcc.edu

Degrees and Certificates

Associate Degrees:

Architectural Technology, Residential Design (A.A.S.)
Architecture Technology (A.A.S.)
Civil Technology (A.A.S.)
Energy Management Technology (A.A.S.)
Heating and Air Conditioning (A.A.S.)
Horticulture (A.A.S.)
HVAC/R Energy Management Engineering Technology (A.A.S.)
Inside Wireman Technician (A.A.S.)
Interior Environment Design Technology (A.A.S.)
Landscape Architecture (A.A.S.)
Residential Building (A.A.S.)
Residential Interior Design (A.A.S.)
Welding Technology (A.A.S.)

Certificates:

Architectural Technology, Residential Design
Building Maintenance
Electrical Technology, Construction
Electrical Wiring
Energy Efficiency Technician
Geothermal Technician
Interior Design Technology
Residential Building
Residential Interior Design
Solar Energy Technician
Surveying and Materials Technology
Sustainability
Welding Technology

Costs

(Academic year 2009–10) District residents: $73 per billing hour*; nondistrict residents: $134 per billing hour; nonresidents: $201 per billing hour.

(*Note: A billing hour is not the same as a credit hour. A billing hour represents an amount of time that a student spends in direct contact with an instructor or with laboratory equipment.)

Financial Aid

FAFSA required (www.fafsa.gov). Students wishing to receive financial aid must submit a FAFSA prior to March 1 for priority consideration, or six weeks prior to payment due date for other aid programs. This aid can be in the form of loans, grants, scholarships, or work-study. For more information, visit www.lcc.edu/finaid.

Various awards and scholarships are available to qualified students. Applications must be submitted at the appropriate deadline date, generally before the end of January. The LCC Foundation provides more than $780,000 in scholarships annually.

Admission Requirements

Required: Students must be 18 years of age or older, or they must have graduated from high school.

Application Information

Options: Online application, print and mail application, apply in person

Application fee: $25

Required: Many courses have minimum skill level requirements that must be met before enrollment. Skill prerequisites can be met either by taking a placement test or passing specific courses at LCC. Assessment testing should be completed prior to orientation. Academic advisers and counselors are available to provide information.

Application deadline: Rolling

Notification: Continuous

Distance Learning

Some courses are available online via the ANGEL Computer Management System, which is administered by LCC's eLearning Department.

Green Campus Organizations

Sustainability Advisory Committee: Made up of students and faculty members; supports sustainability initiatives on campus and with the wider community.

Annual "Spring Fling Goes Green": Sponsors a Dumpster-diving competition.

Fast Facts

A team from five academic programs at LCC won the BuildUP! Building a Brighter Michigan Competition in 2010. In addition to $10,000 in scholarship money, the team gets to build its 3,075-square foot Victorian-style home on Mackinac Island. The 16-member team represented Alternative Energy Engineering Technology; Architecture Technology; Digital Media, Audio, and Cinema; Landscape Architecture; and Residential Building programs and was led by the chair of the Environment Design and Building Technology Department.

LCC is one of the nation's first colleges to incorporate alternative energy into its curricula and its sustainable practices on campus.

LCC's West Campus is heated and cooled by a geothermal system, which is seeking LEED certification. The college also has a small solar array and wind turbine on campus.

LOS ANGELES TRADE-TECHNICAL COLLEGE (LATTC)

400 West Washington Boulevard
Los Angeles, California 90015
213-763-7000
http://college.lattc.edu

Degrees and Certificates

Associate Degrees:

Architectural Technology (A.A.)
Carpentry (A.A., AS)
Community Planning and Economic
    Development: Urban Real Estate Development
    (A.A.)
Construction Technologies: Plumbing (A.A.)
Electrical Construction and Maintenance (A.S.)
Electrical Construction Technologies (A.A.)
Plumbing Technologies (A.S.)
Refrigeration and Air-Conditioning Mechanics
    (A.A., AS)
Water Systems Technology (A.S.)
Welding (A.S.)

Certificates:

Carpentry
Community Planning and Economic
    Development: Urban Real Estate Development
    Computer-Aided Drafting
Construction Technologies: Plumbing
Digital Design
Electrical Construction and Maintenance
Electrical Construction Technologies
Home Remodeling and Repair Technician
Plumbing Technologies
Refrigeration and Air-Conditioning Mechanics
Water Systems Technology
Weatherization and Energy Efficiency
Welding

To find specific "green" courses, log on to http://college.lattc.edu/green./ The page lists the green disciplines at LATTC. Clicking on each discipline brings up course descriptions with the percentage of the content that is considered "green," as well as new courses such as Green Building Basics for Developers.

Costs

(Academic year 2009–10) Residents: $26 per unit (subject to change by the California state legislature); nonresidents: $213 per unit.

Financial Aid

FAFSA required (www.fafsa.gov). Scholarships are available, as well as Board of Governors fee waivers. Graduating high school seniors may also be eligible for CAL Grants. For full financial aid information, go online to http://college.lattc.edu/financialaid/financial-aid/.

Admission Requirements

Required: Must be a high school graduate or at least 18 years old and able to benefit from instruction.

Application Information

Options: Online application or paper application mailed or delivered to Admissions Office

Application fee: None

Required: High School diploma or assessment test, orientation, academic counseling

Application deadline: Continuous

Notification: Continuous

Distance Learning

LATTC is moving to offer all courses online. Monitor progress at http://college.lattc.edu/online/

Green Campus Organizations

Culinary Arts Department: Recycling of used vegetable oil for biodiesel fuel.

Electronics Department: Computer recycling program.

Building Green/Building Healthy: As part of the commitment to sustainable principles, four major building initiatives that are underway are seeking LEED certification.

RecycleMania: LATTC participated in the 2010 RecycleMania in the Benchmark Division.

Fast Facts

The Utilities and Construction Prep Program (UCPP) at LATTC prepares low-skilled youth and adults for entrance into utilities or the construction trades. UCPP is based on strong partnerships with the Los Angeles Department of Water and Power, the Southern California Gas Company, locals for the International Brotherhood of Electrical Workers (IBEW), and the UAW Labor Employment and Training Corp, among others. For more information, go online to http://www.lattc.edu/dept/lattc/WED/UtilityPrep.html.

The White House Office of Urban Affairs brought U.S. Secretary of Labor Hilda Solis to the LATTC campus in 2009 for an overview of the biofuel, weatherization, photovoltaic, and green construction programs that are a keystone of the education-industry-labor partnership at the College.

In May 2008, the College established the Sustainable Energy Center, a dedicated lab for courses, activities, and programs related to renewable energy and energy efficiency technologies. The Green College Initiative now offers numerous courses, degrees, and certificates in a variety of green disciplines. See http://www.lattc.edu/dept/lattc/WED/GCIPrograms.html for more information.

In 2010, the students and instructor in the Alternative Fuels course were featured in the ABC News feature story "Going Green to Make Green," which aired on the show *Focus Earth* with Bob Woodward.

The Natural Resources Defense Council (NRDC) recently released a video featuring students and faculty members in LATTC's Solar, Energy Efficiency (Weatherization), and Diesel-Technology Alternative Fuels courses. The video highlights companies and training and education programs that support California's clean energy sector, which is rapidly growing as a result of AB 32, the state's landmark global warming law. You can watch the video at http://college.lattc.edu/wed/2010/05/28/trade-tech-green-education-and-training-programs-featured-in-natural-resources-defense-council-video/.

LATTC is the only community college with a community development program.

Green Business Certification Project: LATTC is developing a green business certification program that consists of changing departments to operate within the standards of a green certified business. The Automotive and Diesel Technology programs are developing a pilot program to offer green business certification education modules.

MACOMB COMMUNITY COLLEGE

14500 E. 12 Mile Road
Warren, Michigan 48088
586-445-7999
866-Macomb (toll-free)
E-mail: answer@macomb.edu
www.macomb.edu

Degrees and Certificates

Associate Degrees:

Architectural Commercial Design (A.A.S.)
Building Construction Technology (A.A.S.)
Climate Control Technology (A.A.S.)
Civil Construction (A.A.S.)
Construction Technology (A.A.S.)
Construction Technology: Renewable Energy
  Specialist (A.A.S.)
Customer Energy Specialist (A.A.S.)
Land Surveying Technology: Field Technician,
  Office Technician (A.A.S.)

Certificates:

Air Conditioning
Air Conditioning, Heating, and Refrigeration
Architectural Commercial Design
Architectural Residential Drafting and Design
Civil Construction
Civil Technology
Construction Technology
Construction Technology: Renewable Energy
  Specialist
Customer Energy Specialist: Design
Heating
HVAC Installation & Service Technician
Refrigeration
Land Surveying Technology: Field Technician,
  Office Technician
Renewable Energy Technology

Macomb also offers Building Construction Apprenticeship and Certification programs in Bricklayer, Mason, Carpenter, and Electrical Construction and Maintenance.

Costs

(Academic year 2009–10) In-district: $72 per credit hour; out-of-district: $110 per credit hour; out-of-state/international: $143 per credit hour; affiliate: $91 per credit hour.

Financial Aid

FAFSA required (www.fafsa.gov). Macomb participates in a variety of financial aid programs, including scholarships, grants, loans, and employment opportunities.

Admission Requirements

Admission is open to any citizen or permanent resident of the United States whose high school class has graduated or is at least 18 years of age.

Application Information

Option: Apply online or submit a completed application to the Enrollment Office.

Application fee: None, but there is a $40 registration fee.

Distance Learning

More than 250 online and hybrid course sections are available each semester in virtual classrooms supported by ANGEL Learning software.

Green Campus Organization

Go Green Eco-Olympics: Series of monthly events designed to reduce the campus's carbon footprint with a reward system; for examples, turn in five incandescent bulbs to Student Activities and get an energy-saving CFL bulb; turn in twenty-five plastic bags and get a reusable tote bag.

Fast Facts

Macomb Community College has two nature areas preserved for the study of the environment, both of which are open to the public.

Macomb's renewable energy technology certificate program debuted in fall 2009 and focuses on five different emerging technologies: wind, solar, biomass, geo-thermal, and hydrogen fuel cell.

The Renewable Energy Technology certificate is designed to complement several existing program paths including, but not limited to associate degrees in Building Construction Technology, Architectural Technology, and Business.

Two Macomb classes have been certified by the Michigan Department of Energy, Labor, and Economic Growth to meet the educational requirements for those planning to take the Michigan Residential Builders License examination. The two courses, Blueprint and Math–Residential and Construction Law and Contract Administration, are given for fifteen weeks as part of the college's Applied Technology program. Students successfully completing both courses meet the 60-hour state educational requirement and are eligible to take the residential builders exam.

MERCER COUNTY COMMUNITY COLLEGE (MCCC)

1200 Old Trenton Road
West Windsor, New Jersey 08550
609-586-4800
E-mail: admiss@mccc.edu
www.mccc.edu

Degrees and Certificates

Associate Degrees:

Architecture (A.S.)
Architecture and Building Construction
    Technology (A.A.S.)
Civil Engineering Technology (A.A.S.)
Energy Utility Technology (A.A.S.)
Heating, Refrigeration and Air Conditioning
    (A.A.S.)
Ornamental Horticulture: Landscape Design
    Concentration (A.A.S.)
Plant Science (A.S.)
Technical Studies (A.A.S.)

Certificates

Architectural Technology
Heating, Refrigeration and Air Conditioning
Ornamental Horticulture
Solar/Energy Technology

Costs

(Summer and Fall 2010) County resident: $127 per credit hour; noncounty resident: $169.50 per credit hour; out-of-state or international student: $254.50 per credit hour.

About IKEA

Looking for a job with an environmentally responsible company? Check out IKEA. It buys wood products only from responsibly managed forests and bans harmful substances from its merchandise. Beginning in 2009, IKEA sells only solar-powered outdoor electric lights.

Financial Aid

To be considered for all federal, state, and MCCC financial aid, students must complete the FAFSA. Deadlines are May 1 for the full academic year or fall semester, and October 1 for spring semester. A range of financial aid opportunities exist. Details can be found on the college Web site.

Admission Requirements

Admission is open to all people who will benefit from a postsecondary education.

Application Information

Option: Application can be completed online or mailed in.

Required: High school transcripts or GED scores; immunization records for full-time students; college transcripts. The results of standardized tests are not required, but SAT scores may be used for placement and should be sent.

Distance Learning

MCCC offers The Virtual College. For full information, see http://mccc.edu/programs_tvc.shtml.

Green Campus Organization

Horticulture Club: Projects include planning and planting gardens on campus, participating in Earth Day celebrations, helping schools in the area build terrariums and start gardening projects on their own, participating in planting and clean-up projects for local organizations.

Fast Facts

The A.A.S. in Technical Studies program provides a means for students to earn an applied science degree based partly on credits received through technical training within their employing organization. The opportunity to earn college credit based on a certified apprenticeship in the construction and building trades is provided in cooperation with New Jersey PLACE and the U.S. Department of Labor.

MCCC offers a 70-hour Green Future Management Certificate Program for professionals in architecture, engineering, real estate, government, nonprofits, and sales who want information on the latest in sustainable practices and projects. Much of the content relates to LEED.

MIDLANDS TECHNICAL COLLEGE (MTC)

P.O. Box 2408
Columbia, South Carolina 29202
803-738-8324
800-922-8038 (toll-free)
E-mail: askmtc@midlandstech.edu
www.midlandstech.edu

Degrees and Certificates

Associate Degrees:

Architectural Engineering Technology (AET)
Building Construction Technology (AIT)
Civil Engineering Technology (AET)
Engineering Transfer: Civil and Environmental (A.S.)
Heating, Ventilation and Air Conditioning Technology (AIT)

Certificates:

Architectural Design
Architectural Systems and Codes
Building Systems
Construction Engineering Technology
Carpentry: Qualified Framer
Environmental and Economic Design
Heating, Ventilation, Air Conditioning and Refrigeration
Low Impact Land Development
Mechanical Systems Technician
Structural Technology
Welding Technologies

Diploma:

Air Conditioning/Refrigeration Mechanics

Costs

(Spring 2010) Richland and Lexington County residents: $131 per credit hour; Fairfield County residents: $131 per credit hour (tuition varies depending on county funding); residents of other South Carolina counties: $164 per credit hour; out-of-state students: $393 per credit hour.

Financial Aid

FAFSA required (www.fafsa.gov). Types of aid available include lottery-funded tuition assistance, Federal Pell Grants, Academic Competitive Grant, Federal Work Study, Stafford Loans, SC

Needs-Based Grants, LIFE Scholarships, MTC Foundation Scholarships, and Department of Energy Student Fellowship.

Admission Requirements

All applicants must possess a high school diploma or its equivalent or must be at least 18 years old.

Application Information

Option: Online

Fee: None

Required: High school transcript or proof of GED completion

Deadline: Three weeks prior to published application deadline

Notification: Continuous

Distance Learning

Midlands offers a variety of distance-based courses. Computer-based courses use instructional CDs and a computer to view lectures. Broadcast classes are transmitted from a studio to other classroom locations where students view the lecture on television. Internet courses are also offered.

Green Campus Organization

Habitat for Humanity: Supports this national organization by building homes with the Central South Carolina organization.

Fast Facts

Community College Week recognized Midlands Tech in 2010 as one of the nation's top 50 fastest growing public two-year colleges. It ranked number 35 nationally among colleges with enrollment of more than 10,000 students. It is South Carolina's largest source of transfer students to the University of South Carolina at Columbia and to Columbia College.

MOUNT WACHUSETT COMMUNITY COLLEGE (MWCC)

444 Green Street
Gardner, Massachusetts 01440
978-632-6600
E-mail: admissions@mwcc.mass.edu
www.mwcc.edu

Degrees and Certificates

Associate Degrees:

Art: Professional Track (RTP)
Energy Management (EGD)
Natural Resource (NRD)

Certificate:

Energy Management

Costs

(Academic year 2009–10) Residents: $165 per credit hour; New England Regional Student Program: $177.50 per credit hour; nonresidents: $370 per credit hour.

Financial Aid

FAFSA required (www.fafsa.gov). The MWCC scholarship application deadline is March 10 for the fall semester. An essay and two letters of recommendation must be submitted with the application. Final deadline for the MASSGrant program is May 1.

Admission Requirements

Required: High school diploma or GED preferred; otherwise, a placement test or waiver is required. Certain courses of study require a high school diploma.

Application Information

Options: Online application

Application fee: $10

Required: High school transcript or GED suggested; otherwise a placement test or waiver is required. Certain courses of study require a high school transcript.

Application deadline: Rolling

Notification: Continuous

Distance Learning

MWCC offers many courses online through Blackboard. See www.mwcc.edu/distance/default .html.

Green Campus Organizations

Green Society: Increase awareness through participation in education outside the classroom, to stimulate interest in the greenhouse and the Natural Resource program within the college and to the community, and to promote and develop ideas for the interest and welfare of the greenhouse and Natural Resource curriculum at the college.

Community Garden, Farmer's Market, and a composting program: Recycles food waste from the cafeteria and kitchen for use in an organic garden that produces food for the kitchen.

Fast Facts

Mount Wachusett converted its all-electric main campus to a biomass heating system, using wood chips as fuel. The system saves the college an estimated $300,000 a year. It was partially funded by a $1 million grant from the U.S. Department of Energy.

In 2008, Mount Wachusett Community College was named the winner of the National Wildlife Federation's Campus Ecology Chill-Out Contest. The competition recognizes institutions of higher education that are implementing innovative programs to reduce the impacts of global warming. The award was made based on the biomass heating system and solar and wind technology that reduce the college's dependence on fossil fuels and reduce greenhouse gas emissions.

In January 2010, MWCC released its Climate Action Plan that details the college's commitment to achieve carbon neutrality by 2020.

MWCC offers the perfect setting for its natural resources program with its hundreds of acres of undeveloped plant communities and forested areas, two pond ecosystems, and a life studies center consisting of a greenhouse, potting area, and lecture facility.

About Your Old Athletic Shoes

Don't trash your old athletic shoes. Recycle them for reuse. Check out these Web sites:

- www.oneworldrunning.com—sends wearable shoes to athletes in Africa, Latin America, and Haiti
- www.nikereuseashoe.com—recycles old shoes into playground and athletic flooring

RED ROCKS COMMUNITY COLLEGE (RRCC)

13300 West Sixth Avenue
Lakewood, Colorado 80228
303-914-6600
E-mail: admissions@rrcc.edu
www.rrcc.edu

Degrees and Certificates

Associate Degrees:

Electro-Mechanical Industrial Maintenance (A.A.S.)

Environmental Technology (A.A.S.)

Industrial Maintenance Technology: Electrical, Mechanical (A.A.S.)

Industrial Maintenance Technology, Mechanical (A.A.S.)

Interior Design (A.A.S.)

Renewable Energy Technology: Solar Photovoltaic Specialty (A.A.S.)

Renewable Energy Technology: Solar PV Business Owner Specialty (A.A.S.)

Renewable Energy Technology: Solar Thermal Business Owner Specialty (A.A.S.)

Renewable Energy Technology: Solar Thermal Specialty (A.A.S.)

Water Quality Management (A.A.S.)

Certificates:

Advanced PV Installation

Codes and Standards

Commercial and Industrial Heating and Cooling

Electro-Mechanical Technician

Energy Efficiency Weatherization

Energy Auditing

Environmental Compliance Operations

Industrial Electrical Technician

Industrial Maintenance Technology

Introduction to Air Compliance

Introduction to Water Compliance

Post EIC Degree Solar Photovoltaic

Post HVA Degree Solar Thermal

Solar Thermal Installer

Water Treatment

Wastewater Treatment

Costs

(Academic year 2009–10) Residents: $156.30 per credit hour; nonresident: $393.90 per credit hour. Colorado residents can apply for a College Opportunity Fund tuition rebate, which entitles them to a credit of $68 per credit hour on their tuition bill.

Financial Aid

FAFSA required (www.fafsa.gov). Types of aid available include grants, loans, and work study. A number of scholarships are also available. RRCC Foundation provides over $200,000 annually in scholarships. Contact www.finaid@rrcc.edu.

Admission Requirements

Required: High school graduate; nongraduate: must be 17 years or older.

Application Information

Options: Online application

Application fee: None

Required: Skills testing (exemption proof via ACT/SAT scores or previous college degree), must meet with adviser

Application deadline: Rolling

Notification: Continuous

Distance Learning

Many courses are available online and as hybrid/flex courses. Students may also take courses from other Colorado community colleges through the CCC Online network.

Green Campus Organization

Campus Green Initiative: Engages students, faculty and staff members, and community members in efforts to promote sustainable technologies and behaviors related to conserving energy; includes businesspeople as advisers for course additions.

Fast Facts

RRCC was honored with the 2008 Governor's Excellence in Renewable Energy Award. RRCC's Energy Technology Program grew from 10 students in fall 2007 to 231 students by spring 2009.

The Environmental Training Center at RRCC is one of only twelve centers in the country where students can acquire the knowledge and skills needed to develop a career in environmental technology. The center is also the home of the only Water Quality Management Technology degree program in Colorado. For more information, see http://www.rrcc.edu/rmec/cetc.html.

In 2009, RRCC became one of the first community colleges in Colorado to offer the state's new Green Advantage certification program. The program teaches the latest in green construction practices and technologies. For more information, go online to http://www.greenadvantage.org/greengov.php.

SANTA FE COMMUNITY COLLEGE (SFCC)

6401 Richards Avenue
Santa Fe, New Mexico 87508-4887
505-428-1000
E-mail: info@sfccnm.edu
www.sfccnm.edu

Degrees and Certificates

Associate Degrees:

Architectural Design (A.A.)
Drafting and Engineering Technologies (A.A.S.)
Environmental Technologies (A.A.S.)
Interior Design (A.A.S.)

Certificates:

Architectural Design
Computer-Aided Drafting
Drafting Technologies

Environmental Technology
Facilities Technology
Green Building Construction Skills
Green Building Systems
Interior Design
Solar Energy

Costs

(Spring 2010) In-state/in-district: $34 per credit hour, Early Bird* $30 per credit hour; in-state/out-of-district: $45 per credit hour, Early Bird $41 per credit hour; nonresident: $88 per credit hour, Early Bird $73 per credit hour.

*Dates for Early Bird registration vary, but generally end about a month prior to start of class.

About Your Unused Cell Phone

Donate old cell phones, batteries, chargers, and PDAs to help

- Protect victims of domestic violence: www.nnedv.org
- Soldiers call home: www.cellphonesforsoldiers.com
- Charities nationwide: www.collectivegood.com.

Financial Aid

Scholarships, loans, grants, and work study are available. Most require FAFSA. Scholarships have deadlines and require a separate application; see www.sfcnm.edu/financial_aid.

Admission Requirements

Required: High school diploma or GED

Application Information

Options: Online application

Application fee: None

Required: Placement testing (ACT/SAT scores or prior college transcripts can be used to determine appropriate placement), adviser/counselor session, orientation

Application deadline: Rolling

Notification: Continuous

Green Campus Organizations

Green Task Force: Composed of faculty and staff members, students, and members of the community to promote sustainability initiatives.

Student Environmental Education Development (SEED): Promotes campuswide recycling program, low-consumption lighting, recycling wastewater for campus irrigation, use of recycled copier paper; makes filtered water available to reduce plastic bottle usage.

Fast Facts

The SFCC Sustainable Technologies Center (STC) incorporates 21st-century trades with advanced technologies and "green" curricula to promote a sustainable economy. The new facility, completed in 2010, provides space for credit and noncredit courses as well as for workforce development programs. For more information, visit www.sfccnm .edu/sustainable_technologies_center.

New campus buildings, such as STC and the Health and Science building, are being constructed with a view to obtaining LEED green building certification at the highest levels.

Campus electricity is generated by a grid-tied solar photovoltaic system. Solar thermal collectors heat the campus swimming pool.

Students in the Principles of Accounting classes completed a campuswide survey and calculations for a profile of campus energy usage and carbon footprint as benchmarks for efforts at energy efficiency and reduction of carbon emissions.

SFCC is a signatory to the American College & University Presidents' Climate Commitment (ACUPCC).

SFCC was awarded over $500,000 in grant money for the 2009–10 academic year for its green initiatives. The money was targeted to scholarships, curriculum development, a biofuels program, and training at-risk youth in green technologies.

ST. PETERSBURG COLLEGE (SPC)

P.O. Box 13489
St. Petersburg, Florida 33733-3489
727-341-4772
E-mail: information@spcollege.edu
www.spcollege.edu

Degrees and Certificates

Associate Degrees:

Architectural Design and Construction
 Technology (A.S.)
Architectural Transfer (A.A.)
Construction Technology (A.S.)
Drafting and Design Technology (A.S.)
Environmental Science Technology (A.S.)
Sustainability (A.S.)

Certificates:

Building Construction Technology
Computer-Aided Design and Drafting
Drafting

For students looking to transfer to bachelor programs, SPC offers two new programs related to sustainability: Sustainability Management (BAS) and Management and Organizational Leadership (BAS).

About Buying Locally

Buying locally grown food is not the same as buying organically grown food. "Organic" indicates the way food is grown and is a process certified by the U.S. Department of Agriculture. Buying locally means buying food products that are raised within a 100-mile radius of your home. For more information on what locally grown means, check http://www.sustainabletable.org.

Costs

(Academic year 2009–10) In-state residents: $87.12 per credit hour; out-of-state residents: $316.35 per credit hour.

Financial Aid

FAFSA required (www.fafsa.gov). Federal and state grants, loans, and work study, as well as various scholarships, are available. See the financial aid Web site at www.spcollege.edu/central/SSFA/HomePage/prooff.htm.

Admission Requirements

Required: High school diploma or GED

Application Information

Options: Online application or by mail or in person

Application fee: $40

Required: High school transcript or GED scores; orientation; Computerized Placement Test (CPT) or ACT/SAT substituted; meet with academic adviser

Application deadline: Rolling

Notification: Continuous

Distance Learning

eCampus offers hundreds of accredited online college courses in dozens of majors, plus online student support services. A sample online course is available at www.spcollege.edu/ecampus to help students evaluate how online learning works. Online certification programs related to green subjects include Sustainability Professional, Indoor Environmentalist, Indoor Air Quality Manager, Green Building Sales Professional, Energy Management, Green Building Technical Professional, Green Purchasing Fundamentals, Green Supply Chain Professional, Senior Certified Sustainability Professional, Building Energy Efficiency Level I, Weatherization Energy Auditor, and Photovoltaic System Design and Installation.

Green Campus Organizations

Club Green: Based on the Clearwater Campus, initiatives include Earth Day participation, volunteer support for Pinellas Living Green Expo, coastal clean-ups, native tree planting, and invasive species removal.

Emerging Green Builders: Based at the Clearwater Campus, initiatives include volunteer support for the local chapter of the U.S. Green Building Council at the Pinellas Living Green Expo, bus tour of LEED-certified buildings in St. Petersburg, and presentation of a "Green Lecture Series" focusing on sustainability as related to architecture, solar installation, and building construction.

Environmental Science Club: Based on the Seminole Campus, initiatives include participating in community clean-ups, volunteering for environmental organizations, and sponsoring "Green Day" with the student government.

Friends of Florida Environmental Club: Based on the Gibbs Campus, initiatives include participating in annual Earth Day activities; volunteering at the Pinellas Living Green Expo; and participating in coastal clean-ups, native tree planting and invasive species removal, and environmental lecture series.

Sustainability Club: Based on the Tarpon Springs Campus. Coordinates the recycling program and participates in community events; plans and coordinates educational environmental activities on campus.

Fast Facts

SPC installed its first photovoltaic system on the roof of its LEED-Gold Natural Science, Mathematics, and College of Education building, one of Tampa's most environmentally friendly buildings. The 3.5-kilowatt thin-film solar blanket is the first commercial installation of the new generation of solar collection systems installed in the area. The system was chosen partly because of its tolerance to hurricane force winds and harsh environments.

SPC participated in the World Wildlife Fund's Annual Earth Hour Initiative, turning off all nonessential lighting to demonstrate its concern for climate change.

SPC is developing a Natural Habitat Park and Environmental Center on the Seminole Campus to serve as an educational, environmental, and passive recreational "green zone" for use by SPC students, faculty and staff members, and the larger community. All invasive species growing in the area were cleared and 1,000 native slash pines were planted around the perimeter of the wetlands. This planting was accomplished by students and other volunteers in a single day.

The Natural Science Department planted a Botanical Garden at the Clearwater Campus, which will be used as a teaching tool for upper and lower biology classes. The gardens consist of only native Florida plants.

SPC's Solar Source Institute provides training, both online and in a traditional educational setting, in the generation, installation, and inspection of solar photovoltaic power.

TIDEWATER COMMUNITY COLLEGE (TCC)

121 College Place
Norfolk, Virginia 23510-1938
757-822-1122
800-371-0898 (toll-free)
E-mail: info@tcc.edu
www.tcc.edu

Degrees and Certificates

Associate Degrees:

Civil Engineering Technology (A.A.S.)
Computer-Aided Drafting and Design Technology: Architectural Drafting and Design (A.A.S.)
Horticulture: Greenhouse Production and Garden Center Management, Landscape Design and Management (A.A.S.)
Interior Design (A.A.S.)

Certificates:

Air Conditioning and Refrigeration
Computer-Aided Drafting and Design Technology

Career Studies Certificates:

Associate Designer
Civil Engineering Technician
Green Design for Interiors
Greenhouse Production
Kitchen and Bath Design
Land Surveying
Landscape Design and Management
Turfgrass Management

Costs

(Spring semester 2010) Virginia resident: $94.50 per credit hour; out-of-state resident: $266.60 per credit hour; business contract rate*: $134.50 per credit hour.

*The Business Contract Rate applies to out-of-state students covered under a contract between the college and a Virginia employer.

Financial Aid

FAFSA required. Scholarships from private, external, and institutional sources and the TCC Educational Foundation may have academic requirements. A separate application is required. Other financial aid is available in form of grants, loans, and work-study.

Admission Requirements

Required: High school diploma or equivalent, GED; must be over 18 years old and able to benefit from a program of instruction

Application Information

Options: Online application, by mail or in person

Application fee: None

Required: Placement testing, unless appropriate ACT/SAT scores; orientation

Application deadline: Rolling

Notification: Continuous

Distance Learning

A number of courses are offered as online or hybrid courses. Most online courses use the Blackboard system for access. TCC's Workforce Development and Continuing Education division offers a range of "green" certification programs including Green Designer, Level 1; Green Specialist, Level 1; Commercial Energy Auditor, Level 1; Fundamentals of Mold Inspection, Level 1; Fundamentals of Solar Water Heating; Fundamentals of Sustainable Buildings; Home Energy Analyst, Level 1; Indoor Air Quality; LEED AP Building Design and Construction; LEED AP Operations and Maintenance; LEED Green Associate; Weatherization Energy Auditor; and Green Building Sales Professional. Send an e-mail to tcyingr@tcc.edu for more information.

Green Campus Organization

Engineering Club: Involved since 1997 in the CANstruction design/build competition with cans of food that are then contributed to food banks.

Fast Facts

The fifteenth highest producer of associate degrees in the nation, and the thirty-fifth largest community college, TCC is among the twenty fastest-growing, large, two-year institutions in the United States.

TCC celebrates Earth Day Week with its "Living Green Expo" to help educate the community on opportunities to incorporate "green" into daily work and life.

The Chesapeake Campus received status as an Audubon Sanctuary, the only school to hold that status in the state. The Sanctuary is used as an outdoor classroom for many disciplines at the college.

TULSA COMMUNITY COLLEGE

6411 East Skelly Drive
Tulsa, Oklahoma 74135
918-595-7000
www.tulsacc.edu

Degrees and Certificates

Associate Degrees:

Civil Engineering/Surveying Technology
 (A.A.S.)
Civil Engineering/Surveying Technology:
 Construction Option (A.A.S.)
Drafting and Design Engineering (A.A.S.)
Horticulture Technology (A.S.)
Horticulture Technology: General Horticulture
 Option (A.A.S.)
Horticulture Technology: Golf and Sports Turf
 Option (A.A.S.)
Horticulture Technology: Greenhouse and
 Nursery Production Option (A.A.S.)
Horticulture Technology: Floral Design and
 Interiorscape Option (A.A.S.)
Horticulture Technology: Landscape Design and
 Construction Option (A.A.S.)
Horticulture Technology: Landscape Maintenance
 Option (A.A.S.)
Interior Design (A.A.S.)

Certificates:

Civil Engineering/Surveying Technology
Drafting and Design Engineering
Interior Design
Interior Plant Care Specialist
Landscape Specialist

Costs

(Academic year 2009–10) In-state residents:
$62.20 per credit hour; nonresidents: $217.75 per
credit hour.

Financial Aid

Financial aid is available through grants, scholarships, loans, and part-time employment from federal, state, institutional, and private sources. The types and amounts of aid awarded are determined by financial need, availability of funds, student classification, and academic performance.

Among the requirements for financial aid, students must maintain a minimum cumulative 1.70 grade point average (GPA) for the first 30 credit hours attempted; and a minimum cumulative 2.0 GPA for all hours attempted thereafter.

Admission Requirements

The admission criteria set forth at Tulsa Community College are the minimum standards established by the Oklahoma State Regents for Higher Education. Although they provide for "open door" admission to the College, certain programs require additional standards to be met before a student is admitted. Selected workforce development programs require that a separate program application for admission be submitted prior to entry into specific courses.

Application Information

To apply for admissions at Tulsa Community College, contact the Enrollment Services Office located on each campus. The phone number for all campuses is 918-595-2010. An online application is also available, as well as a PDF version that can be mailed or faxed.

Application fee: $20

Required: Students seeking a degree or those seeking financial aid or veterans' benefits must provide official transcripts and test scores from ACT, SAT, or the TCC College Placement Test if age 20 years or younger.

Application deadline: Applications and transcripts should be submitted a minimum of ten working days in advance of registration for classes.

Notification: Continuous

Distance Learning

Internet courses, offered through partnerships, include a variety of disciplines and may require some on-campus orientations or exams. Many other courses are offered completely online and have no on-campus requirements. Some result in certification. Among the courses offered are Building Analyst Quick Start Program, Certified Green Supply Chain Professional, Certified Indoor Air Quality Manager, Principles of Green Buildings, and Senior Certified Sustainability Professional.

Green Campus Organization

EcoFest: Event to cultivate "Practical, Sustainable, Green Living."

Fast Fact

Tulsa Community College hosted a green living festival to celebrate the College's eco-friendly initiatives and to promote a new farmer's market opening in north Tulsa in spring 2010.

WAKE TECHNICAL COMMUNITY COLLEGE (Wake Tech)

9101 Fayetteville Road
Raleigh, North Carolina 27603
919-866-5500
www.waketech.edu

Degrees and Certificates

Associate Degrees:

Air Conditioning, Heating and Refrigeration Technology (A.A.S.)
Architectural Technology (A.A.S.)
Civil Engineering Technology (A.A.S.)
Construction Management (A.A.S.)
Electrical/Electronics Technology (A.A.S.)
Environmental Science Technology (A.A.S.)
Interior Design (A.A.S.)
Landscape Architecture Technology (A.A.S.)
Surveying Technology (A.A.S.)

Certificates:

Air Conditioning, Heating and Refrigeration Analyst for Home Safety and Energy Saving
Architectural Technology: Architectural CAD
Civil Engineering Technology: Civil Design
Construction Management Technology
Electrical/Electronics Technology Commercial/ Residential Wiring
Landscape Architecture Technology: Landscape Architecture
Plumbing: Applications and Diagrams
Plumbing: Modern Plumbing Codes and Blueprint Reading
Smart Home Technology
Welding Technology

Diplomas:

Air Conditioning, Heating and Refrigeration Technology
Electrical/Electronics Technology
Plumbing
Welding Technology

Costs

(Academic year 2009–10) Residents: $50 per credit hour; nonresidents: $241.30 per credit hour.

Financial Aid

FAFSA required (www.fafsa.gov). Scholarships, loans, grants, and work-study are available.

Admission Requirements

Required: High school diploma or GED

Application Information

Options: Online application

Application fee: None

Required: High school transcript or GED scores; COMPASS placement test in reading, writing and math; ACT/SAT scores can result in exemption from testing

Application deadline: Rolling

Notification: Continuous

Distance Learning

Wake Tech uses both Blackboard and Moodle as online course delivery tools for credit and non-credit courses.

Green Campus Organizations

Architecture Club: Promotes real-world exploration of the field of architecture.

Design and Garden Club: Exposure to profession of environmental design; opportunities for hands-on gardening.

Students for Environmental Education: Advance understanding of the environment on the college's campus and how the ecology affects humans and vice versa; focus on energy issues.

Fast Facts

Wake Tech's Northern Wake Campus, opened in 2007, is the first campus in North Carolina and one of the first in the nation to be completely LEED-certified.

The Energy Conservation and Awareness Committee was established in July 2006 to address the impact of rising energy costs and to develop a coordinated effort for an aggressive energy conservation program for Wake Tech. The Committee's focus is on awareness, sustainability, and continued improvements in energy conservation.

Top 10 Green Tips for Campus Life

1. **Don't buy anything in polystyrene.** This includes coffee and take-out food. Americans fuel their caffeine habits with 25 million polystyrene cups a year, and almost all of them end up in landfills, where they will sit for centuries without decomposing. Buy a metal mug that can be reused.

2. **Skip soda in cans and fancy water in plastic bottles.** First, buy a couple of refillable plastic-free bottles. Then mix 2 parts tap water to 1 part juice for flavored water, or 2 parts mineral water to 1 part juice as a replacement for soda.

3. **Recycle pizza boxes.** You can't recycle the bottom of boxes if they are greasy or food stained, but you can recycle the tops and sides if they haven't come in contact with the pizza. So tear off the bottom, toss it in the trash, and recycle the rest.

4. **Shut down your electronic equipment.** You probably already turn off the lights when you leave a room, but you can do more to save energy. Don't turn on the screen saver on your computer; put your computer in sleep mode when you are going to be gone for a while. Screen savers use more energy. Unplug your cell phone charger and your MP3 player when you're not using them. Anything that charges batteries or has an LCD light uses power even when it's not "on."

5. **Cut down on paper use.** Read your e-mails online and file them online or on your computer. When you need to print a document, use both sides of the paper. If you receive documents that are printed on one side only, use the blank side for scratch paper. If only half of a sheet is blank, fold the page in half, and use the blank part for scratch paper.

6. **Rethink your snacks.** Skip the chips and buy organically produced, locally grown fruits and vegetables. When you have ice cream to go, ask for a cone, not a plastic spoon and a cup—polystyrene or paper.

7. **Buy recycled products.** All kinds of things like toilet paper, umbrellas, and plates are now made from post-consumer waste. Look for labels that indicate recycled materials.

8. **Buy Fair Trade tea and coffee.** Look for the U.S. Fair Trade label on packages of coffee and tea. Ask where you buy cups of coffee or tea if it's Fair Trade. If it's not, lobby to get Fair Trade beverages.

9. **Join a green organization.** Join one of your campus's green organizations and support its efforts to make your campus sustainable. Join a national or international organization and spread the word to the larger community.

10. **RECYCLE. REUSE. REDUCE. RETHINK.**
    - Separate your trash. Toss recyclables into recycle bins on campus.
    - Buy ceramic mugs and dishes, glass drinking glasses, and metal cutlery for in-room eating.
    - Reduce the amount of plastic you use by taking your own reusable cloth bags when you shop. Look for dorm room furniture like a chair or a lamp at used-furniture stores.

CHAPTER 8

UNION TRAINING PROGRAMS FOR GREEN JOBS

This chapter contains profiles of labor unions that offer apprenticeship and training programs to upgrade members' skills for the new green energy economy. It also profiles the National Labor College that grants undergraduate degrees and certificates to AFL-CIO members.

Because of the move away from manufacturing to new green industries and the greening of older industries, unions are working aggressively to train current members and recruit new members for jobs in these industries. The goal is not only to provide a well-trained union membership to fill these "green jobs," but to gain new members for the labor movement and to ensure that all members have access to "family-sustaining careers" in the words of then president of the AFL-CIO John Sweeney.

APPRENTICESHIPS

Apprenticeship programs are available through union locals. To join a union, a person has to contact the local and see if there are any openings for apprentices. Unions try not to hire more apprentices than they think they will need in the foreseeable future, so there may be a wait, especially if the work is seasonal like construction. A potential union member must meet certain requirements and often has to pass an interview with a committee of the local. Training costs are negotiated as part of contracts with employers, and, as

a result, apprenticeships are earn-while-you-learn programs.

Local One-Stop Career Centers and state apprenticeship programs can also help with finding apprenticeship programs. Check out www.doleta.gov/OA/stateoffices.cfm and www.careeronestop.org for more information.

ABOUT THE UNION PROGRAM LISTINGS

Here's what you need to know to navigate the union training and apprentice program profiles.

Contact Info

The first paragraph of each union profile lists the union's name, address, phone number, e-mail address, and Web site information.

About the Union

This section details important information about the union. It may include union goals or the history of the organization, as well as any relevant data about available apprenticeships.

Programs and Training

The final paragraph of the profile includes a description of the program or apprenticeship. In some cases, more than one may be listed. This section will also explain the training process and the necessary program skills and requirements.

Unions and Union Activities Profiled Here

The following unions and union activities are profiled in this chapter:

- National Labor College
- International Association of Bridge, Structural, Ornamental and Reinforcing Iron Workers (Iron Workers)
- International Association of Heat and Frost Insulators and Allied Workers (AWIU)
- International Brotherhood of Electrical Workers (IBEW)
- International Union of Bricklayers and Allied Craftworkers (BAC)
- International Union of Operating Engineers (IUOE)
- International Union of Painters and Allied Trades, AFL-CIO (IUAPT)
- Laborers' International Union of North America (LIUNA)
- Operative Plasterers' and Cement Masons' International Association (OPCMIA)
- Service Employees International Union (SEIU)
- Sheet Metal Workers International Association (SMWIA)
- United Association of Journeymen and Apprentices of the Plumbing and Pipefitting Industry of the United States and Canada (UA)
- United Brotherhoods of Carpenters and Joiners
- United Steel, Paper and Forestry, Rubber, Manufacturing, Energy, Allied Industrial & Service Workers International Union (USW) (Steelworkers)

About the Center for Green Jobs

In February 2009, the AFL-CIO created the Center for Green Jobs to partner with affiliated unions to, according to then AFL-CIO President John Sweeney, "make progressive energy and climate change a first order priority" and ". . . to help our labor unions implement real green jobs initiatives—initiatives that retain and create good union jobs, provide pathways to those jobs, and assist with the design and implementation of training programs to prepare incumbent workers as well as job seekers for these family-sustaining careers."

NATIONAL LABOR COLLEGE (NLC)

10000 New Hampshire Avenue
Silver Spring, Maryland 20903
301-431-6400
800-462-4237 (toll-free)
www.nlc.edu

About the College

The National Labor College was originally founded in 1969 by the AFL-CIO as a labor studies center. In 1974, the center moved to its present site and began offering undergraduate degrees through a partnership with Antioch College. In 1997, the center was granted the authority to confer undergraduate degrees and was renamed the National Labor College. It offers certificate and degree programs and is "the nation's only accredited higher education institution devoted exclusively to educating union leaders, members, and activists."

Programs and Training

The NLC offers a Green Workplace Representative Certificate program, which is part of the AFL-CIO's Center for Green Jobs (CGJ) initiative.

Offered for the first time in spring 2010 in response to innovative work on sustainability and climate change by unions in the United States and Great Britain, this program provides union members and working people with the theoretical knowledge and practical training they need to conduct workplace sustainability audits. "This certificate program will provide education that empowers workers to become change agents, working to advance sustainability values and practices that meet the mutual interests of worker and managers, as well as enhance the competitiveness of American firms in the global economy," said Tom Kriger, NLC provost, when the program was announced.

The NLC offers degree and certificate programs online using the Blackboard online management system. In 2010, the AFL-CIO joined the National Labor College and the Princeton Review to create an online college for the Federation's 11.5 million members and their families. The purpose is to provide education and retraining for members in an affordable and accessible way. The new program builds on the NLC's existing distance learning curricula. One of the new degree programs under consideration is in the field of sustainability and green jobs.

About Green Initiatives

The Iron Workers are an affiliate of the Building and Construction Trades Department (BCTD) of the AFL-CIO. The BCTD is partnering with the Green Jobs Center of the AFL-CIO to help the more than 1,100 affiliate training programs incorporate the skills needed for the new green economy.

INTERNATIONAL ASSOCIATION OF BRIDGE, STRUCTURAL, ORNAMENTAL AND REINFORCING IRON WORKERS (IRON WORKERS)

1750 New York Avenue, NW
Suite 400
Washington, DC 20006
202-383-480
E-mail: iwmagazine@iwintl.org
www.ironworkers.org

About the Union

The union's Department of Apprenticeship and Training and the National Training Fund oversee, coordinate, and manage the education and training programs that range from the basic to the very advanced. The goal is to ensure that members receive comprehensive and effective education and training that will enable them to carry out their work safely and efficiently and with the highest standards of quality.

Programs and Training

Apprenticeship Programs

Apprentices are required to sign an indenture agreement with their Joint Apprenticeship Committee/Trade Improvement Committee that spells out the requirements and expectations of an apprentice ironworker. Most ironworker apprenticeships are three or four years in length, depending on the requirements of the local union. An ideal schedule provides equal training in structural, reinforcing, ornamental, welding, and rigging. The actual length of training for each subject may vary depending on the predominant type of work available in the local area.

Apprentices are required to receive at least 204 hours of classroom and shop instruction during each year of training. The subjects taken in the shop and classroom components complement the hands-on training received in the field. Subjects include blueprint reading, care and safe use of tools, mathematics, safety issues, welding, and oxy-acetylene flame cutting.

Apprentices receive an evaluation about every six months to determine if they are learning the craft. If the on-the-job or school work is not satisfactory, they may be dropped from the program or sent back to repeat that segment. If, however, their work is satisfactory, they will receive a pay raise.

Additional Training Options

Beyond the apprenticeship program, additional training options exist. Apprenticeship training in the ironworking trade can be applied toward college credit. A worker can earn as many as 65 credits toward a college degree. An associate degree can be completed online through Ivy Tech Community College of Indiana. A bachelor's degree can be completed online through the National Labor College.

Journeyman upgrade classes (available through the local union and contractors) provide opportunities to continually increase skills and keep up with the new technologies being introduced into the industry.

INTERNATIONAL ASSOCIATION OF HEAT AND FROST INSULATORS AND ALLIED WORKERS (AWIU)

9602 M.L. King Jr. Highway
Lanham, Maryland 20706
301-731-9101
http://www.insulators.org/pages/index.asp

About the Union

The insulation industry, which insulates mechanical systems and equipment, is a specialized craft within the framework of the building and construction trades. The Heat and Frost Insulators and Allied Workers Union is committed to providing an adequate supply of trained insulation mechanics with the competitive skills necessary to meet industry needs now and in the future.

Mechanical insulators work in the fields of industrial and commercial insulation, and cryogenics. Mechanical insulation encompasses all thermal, acoustical, personnel, and life safety requirements in industrial and commercial buildings and facilities. The latter includes buildings, building services, and refrigerated spaces. Cryogenics is the field of low-temperature services, generally below −100°. An example is liquefied gases.

As a result, the AWIU updated its apprenticeship program and added a course to train members to use the *3EPlus* computer program to analyze the effectiveness of insulation in reducing energy use and costs.

Programs and Training

Apprenticeship Programs

The goal of the apprentice program is to provide the highest level of training to apprentices, so they may assume positions as fully qualified journeymen ready to meet the professional challenges of the insulation industry. The program is structured for entry-level workers, as well as for insulation workers already employed within the industry who wish to upgrade their skills and to advance to journeyman status.

The apprenticeship program takes five years and integrates on-the-job training with classroom instruction to give participants a thorough knowledge of the trade. Apprentices are assigned to work for an insulation contractor, which enables the apprentice to work side by side with experienced journeymen who understand both the practical application and the theory. As apprentices progress through each year of the program, the tasks they are assigned become more complicated and the amount of supervision decreases. In addition, earnings are adjusted upward each year to reflect advancing skills and increasing knowledge of the trade. The average starting wage for first-year apprentices is 50 percent of the mechanics wage rate plus fringe benefits. During the five-year program, apprentices take about 160 hours of related classroom instruction each year, and the apprentice is indentured to the Joint Apprenticeship Committee of the Local Union.

To qualify to become an apprentice, a candidate must be at least 18 years of age, have a high school education or the equivalent, and be in good physical condition. To be admitted, the Joint Apprenticeship Committee requires completion of an application with picture; submission of a birth or baptismal certificate, high school diploma or GED scores, high school transcripts, and two letters of reference; and attaining a qualifying score on an aptitude test.

Additional Training Option

Insulators may also be certified for an asbestos abatement program that is approved by the Environmental Protection Agency (EPA). Certified insulators remove asbestos from schools, hospitals, power plants, and chemical and industrial facilities.

Green Initiatives

Because proper insulation can result in a significant drop in energy use, the AWIU in partnership with the National Insulation Association (NIA) compiled data for commercial buildings documenting the jobs potential of energy conservation and emission reductions through the use of mechanical insulation. According to the results, 89,000 new jobs would be generated if mechanical insulation is just repaired and replaced on piping and duct work in industrial facilities and on HVAC equipment in commercial buildings.

As a result, the AWIU updated its apprenticeship program and added a course to train members to use the *3EPlus* computer program to analyze the effectiveness of insulation in reducing energy use and costs.

INTERNATIONAL BROTHERHOOD OF ELECTRICAL WORKERS (IBEW)

900 Seventh Street, NW
Washington, DC 20001
202-833-7000
www.ibew.org

About the Union

The National Joint Apprenticeship and Training Committee (NJATC) of the National Electrical Contractors Association (NECA) and the International Brotherhood of Electrical Workers (IBEW) operate programs for apprentice and journeyman electricians. The programs are privately funded, and most apprenticeship programs last five years. The NJATC developed uniform standards that have been adopted and used nationwide to select and train thousands of qualified men and women annually.

About the IBEW's Commitment to Going Green

In May 2009, the IBEW's apprenticeship and training committee launched a new green jobs training curriculum. According to the IBEW, the program is being "woven into the . . . apprenticeship training and will serve as a resource of journeymen looking to upgrade their skills in the growing green market." The seventy-five program lessons include topics such as green building fundamentals and automated building operation.

Programs and Training

Through the NJATC, the IBEW and NECA sponsor hundreds of local programs offering apprenticeship and training in the following areas:

Residential Wireman: Specializes in installing the electrical systems in single-family and multi-family homes.

Outside Lineman: Installs the distribution and transmission lines that move power from power plants to buildings and homes.

Inside Wireman: Installs the power, lighting, controls, and other electrical equipment in commercial and industrial buildings.

Telecommunication VDV Installer-Technician: Installs circuits and equipment for telephones, computer networks, video distribution systems, security and access control systems, and other low-voltage systems.

Journeyman Tree Trimmer: Works outdoors year-round clearing trees from around powerlines.

INTERNATIONAL UNION OF BRICKLAYERS AND ALLIED CRAFTWORKERS (BAC)

620 F Street, NW
Washington, DC 20004
202-783-3788
E•mail: askbac@bacweb.org
www.bacweb.org

About the Union

BAC represents all skilled trowel trades workers, including bricklayers, tile setters, plasterers, cement masons, stone and marble masons, restoration workers, terrazzo and mosaic workers, and pointers/cleaners/caulkers.

Programs and Training

The International Union of Bricklayers and Allied Craftworkers' apprenticeship and training system is widely recognized for producing highly skilled craftworkers. Through local union programs and those offered through the International Masonry Institute (IMI), BAC members and contractors have access to training opportunities unmatched in the masonry industry. These training programs are jointly funded by labor and management through collectively bargained contributions.

About Green Masonry at Work

The challenge in building Kroon Hall at Yale University was to blend the classic architecture of the past with the green initiatives of the future. Stone masons from BAC Local 1 CT and Joe Capasso Enterprises, Inc., worked with IMI and the architects on the design and building of Yale's greenest campus building, which achieved Platinum LEED status. The building is now the home of the Yale School of Forestry and Environmental Studies.

BAC University @ WCC

With the creation of BAC University, U.S. and Canadian BAC members can now access affordable, advanced training—completely online —to broaden their career options. In partnership with Washtenaw Community College (WCC), BAC University @ WCC grants 25 college credits to BAC members for completion of a registered BAC apprenticeship program in conjunction with WCC's Construction Supervision program.

Degree Programs

Some members may decide to take the additional general education courses required to earn an associate degree, and ultimately, go on to earn a bachelor's degree at a four-year institution such as the National Labor College.

International Masonry Institute

The International Masonry Institute (IMI) is a labor-management cooperative of the BAC and the contractors who employ its members. IMI programs are funded by contributions collectively bargained by BAC members and their contractors. These funds are used to develop and conduct apprenticeship and training programs for BAC trowel trades craftworkers and provide safety training. IMI operates the John J. Flynn BAC/IMI International Training Center in Bowie, Maryland, regional training centers, and mobile training units that deliver quality training on an as-needed basis. IMI's team of engineers, architects, and certified instructors offer design and technical assistance and training to the unionized masonry industry.

Green Initiatives

One initiative of the IMI is the Sustainable Masonry Certification for contractors. Using masonry to meet the goals of energy efficiency, air quality, durability, and waste minimization, the Sustainable Masonry Certification program addresses energy efficiency through the building envelope. Contractors who have successfully completed this program can provide strong direction in constructing a building able to earn LEED certification. Masonry plays a role in four of the five LEED building categories: sustainable sites, energy and atmosphere, materials and resources, and indoor environmental quality. The IMI provides an easy-to-use LEED checklist that can help projects earn up to fifty-two LEED points.

INTERNATIONAL UNION OF OPERATING ENGINEERS (IUOE)

1125 17th Street, NW
Washington, DC 20036
202-429-9100
www.iuoe.org

About the Union

The union consists of two broad job classifications: operating engineers and stationary engineers. Operating engineers do the heavy lifting and are often referred to as hoisting and portable engineers, because the equipment they control lifts and/or moves. Stationary engineers operate, maintain, renovate, and repair mechanical systems in a facility. For example, in the wind-turbine industry, operating engineers run the cranes that put the turbines and towers in place. Stationary engineers are in charge of continuing operations, maintenance, and repair.

About Green Jobs for Operating Engineers

Operating Engineers are essential in the construction of wind farms. This is a major growth initiative, especially in the corridor of the Texas/Oklahoma Panhandle, western Oklahoma, and along the corridor north to the Canadian border.

Programs and Training

Operating Engineer

IUOE locals provide training programs nationwide, and most are registered with a state or federal apprenticeship agency. Apprentices are paid while they work and learn. Apprentices work with skilled journey-level operators on actual job sites as well as attend related classroom instruction and field training. The average length of an operating engineer apprenticeship is three to four years.

After completing an apprenticeship, many journey workers take additional classes offered by their locals. Continued training upgrades skills, making union members more employable, and also helps them move into management and supervisory jobs. Certification is conducted by outside groups. For example, crane operators are tested by the National Commission for the Certification of Crane Operators (NCCCO).

Stationary Engineer

IUOE stationary local unions provide skill-development training programs for apprentices and journey-level engineers. The programs are jointly sponsored by IUOE local unions and the employers who hire stationary engineers.

The average length of an apprenticeship is four years. During this period, apprentices learn their craft by working with skilled stationary engineers at an actual workplace and also attend related classroom instruction. Apprentice training may also be supplemented by course work at trade or technical schools. Training is critical for preparing apprentices to take the test for the stationary engineer license, which is required by most states.

Employers often encourage journey-level stationary engineers to continue their education. Many IUOE locals offer free training to members to help them broaden and update their skills and improve their employability. Because of the increasing complexity of the equipment, many stationary engineers also take college courses.

INTERNATIONAL UNION OF PAINTERS AND ALLIED TRADES, AFL-CIO (IUPAT)

1750 New York Avenue, NW
Washington, DC 20006
202-637-0707
E-mail: gmcdonald@uipat.org
www.iupat.org

About the Union

The IUPAT is a labor organization representing over 140,000 members in the construction industry, such as painters, drywall finishers, glaziers, glass workers, floor covering installers, sign makers, display workers, and convention and show decorators. These skills are commonly referred to as the finishing trades.

Programs and Training

Apprenticeship Program

Apprentices spend anywhere from two to four years learning the fine points of the trade. They master skills through instructor-led training at one of over 168 training centers across North America and through on-the-job experience and the advice and leadership of journey-level workers.

There is also a "pre-apprentice" program. Skill training in various crafts is available to youth through the Job Corps program at over 50 sites in the United States. This training program, developed during the Johnson administration, gives young people job and life skills. To finish the program, they must complete their GED, get a driver's license and show a certain level of proficiency in their trade.

Degree Program

Union members can earn credit towards a bachelor's degree in Labor Studies from the National Labor College while participating in any one of IUPAT's other educational programs.

Finishing Trades Institute (FTI)

The Finishing Trades Institute is IUPAT's innovative and exciting job training program. It is governed by a board of trustees consisting of members of the IUPAT and the union's signatory employers. Currently, the training program offers more than 157 classes for IUPAT apprentices and journey-level workers.

LABORERS' INTERNATIONAL UNION OF NORTH AMERICA (LIUNA)

905 16th Street, NW
Washington, DC 20006
202-737-8320
www.liuna.org

About the Union

LIUNA members build and repair roads, highways, bridges, and tunnels; construct residential and commercial buildings; clean up hazardous waste sites; drill and blast sites; build scaffolds; prepare and clean up job sites; lay pipe underground; pour concrete; flag and control traffic on highways; and remove asbestos and lead from buildings.

Programs and Training

LIUNA training is available in every state in the United States and every province in Canada. Among the fifty courses that are offered are hazardous materials remediation, remote tunneling, concrete work, and a variety of building construction skills. Apprenticeship training consists of a minimum of 288 hours of classroom training. These skills are practiced with a skilled journey worker for 4,000 hours of on-the-job training.

About a Green Jobs Pilot and LIUNA

A green-collar job initiative between LIUNA and the state of New Jersey was launched in January 2009. Its first training class of 22 graduated in April 2009 in Newark. They had previously been unemployed or underemployed. The program trained them to work in green construction and in retrofitting existing buildings. A similar program was launched in June 2009 in Trenton.

OPERATIVE PLASTERERS' AND CEMENT MASONS' INTERNATIONAL ASSOCIATION (OPCMIA)

11720 Beltsville Drive, Suite 700
Beltsville, Maryland 20702
301-623-1000
E-mail: opcmiaintl@opcmia.org
www.opcmia.org

About the Union

Dating back to the Civil War, the Plasterers' Union is the oldest union in the United States. The OPCMIA represents workers in two major segments of the construction industry: plaster and concrete. Both segments have multiple specialty fields and niche markets that are essential to maintaining the variety and quality of construction projects throughout the nation and North America.

The concrete specialties are the following:
- Commercial
- Concrete Repair
- Curb and Gutter
- Decorative Concrete
- Flatwork Concrete
- Heavy & Highway
- Industrial
- Residential

The plaster specialties are the following:
- Exterior Insulation Finish Systems
- Fireproofing
- Free Form & Theme Plastering
- Historical Restoration
- Interior Gypsum Plaster
- Motion Picture & Special Effects
- Portland Cement Plaster (Stucco)
- Specialty & Colored Finishes

Programs and Training

The OPCMIA offers training for every level within the industry. Job Corps training is available to those with no experience who need a helping hand before beginning a formal apprenticeship. Successful completion of an apprenticeship program leads to the journeyman stage. OPCMIA's journeyman programs keep members safe and up-to-date on the latest developments in the industry.

Apprenticeship Training

The apprenticeship training programs are managed by labor and management as equal partners and have evolved to meet the needs of the modern construction industry. An apprentice in the OPCMIA is taught the skills and knowledge of the trade through a combination of on-the-job training and related classroom instruction. The union apprenticeship programs offer a standardized curriculum and include the following important aspects of training:

- Introduction to the industry and trade history
- Identification and proper use of tools
- Material composition and mixes
- Repair and restoration
- Scaffolding and OSHA safety courses
- Blueprint reading
- First-aid and CPR certification

About Cement Work

Cement work is one of the major components of many of the projects funded by the American Recovery and Reinvestment Act (ARRA). It is the foundation of building bridges; industrial, commercial, and residential construction; and road work.

SERVICE EMPLOYEES INTERNATIONAL UNION (SEIU)

1800 Massachusetts Ave, NW
Washington, DC 20036
202-730-7000
800-424-8592 (toll-free)
www.seiu.org

About the Union

The Service Employees International Union is the largest and the fastest-growing union in the nation, reflecting the changing nature of the U.S. economy from manufacturing to service. The union represents workers in three key service sectors: health care, public service, and property services. Health-care union members include registered nurses, licensed practical nurses, doctors, lab technicians, nursing home workers, and home health-care workers. Union members in the public service sector include local and state government workers, public school employees, bus drivers, and child-care providers. Workers who protect and clean commercial and residential office buildings, private security officers, and public safety personnel make up the membership of the property services sector. Membership depends on whether a job site is organized.

Programs and Training

Environmental Labor-Management Committees are involved in many green initiatives. Green initiatives, which are part of contract negotiations, include the use of green cleaning products, healthier health-care practices, and recycling.

SEIU Green Training Initiative

The following summary is provided by James Barry, Manager of Program Development, Building Service 32BJ, Thomas Shortman Training Program (TSTP): SEIU Local 32BJ in New York City is the largest building service workers union in the country, representing more than 100,000 cleaners, doormen, porters, maintenance workers, superintendents, resident managers, window cleaners, and security guards. TSTP, founded in 1971, is a nonprofit education fund supported primarily by contributions from participating employers. Every year, the program provides industry, academic, and computer courses to thousands of Local 32BJ building service workers at over twenty locations in New York, New Jersey, Connecticut, Pennsylvania, the District of Columbia, and Maryland.

Since 2005, the Thomas Shortman Training Program has worked with the New York State Energy Research and Development Authority (NYSERDA) and other partners to offer a wide range of training focusing on existing buildings. The major program is an eleven-session green building review that includes basic instruction on green building concepts, energy and water efficiency, building controls, and green cleaning supplies, as well as two building tours: an energy audit of a typical residential building and a tour of a LEED-certified green building.

The Shortman program has also launched a lighting retrofitting workshop, provided a recycling seminar, hosted a LEED-Existing Building (EB) Technical Review and worked with The Center for Sustainable Energy to prepare several 32BJ instructors for the Building Performance Institute's (BPI) Building Analyst Certification.

Starting in 2009, the 32BJ expanded its training to give workers a deeper understanding of the connection between their jobs and the environment. The local offered a second green building course and a series of new trades-oriented U.S. Green Building Council certifications such as "Green Buildings Operations and Maintenance," "Green Buildings: Building Operator Certification," and "Green Buildings: New Technologies and Materials." The certification program offers an educational track for those who wish to work in green buildings or make improvements in the buildings where they currently work. Workers learn how to run a building efficiently, use cleaning supplies and materials that have a low impact on indoor air quality, reduce waste, and recycle effectively in their buildings.

"One Year, One Thousand Green Supers Program," which is approved by the U.S. Green Building Council and the Building Performance Institute, is part of the Thomas Shortman Training Fund. The program enrolls building service workers in 40 hours of classwork in which they will learn the latest, state-of-the-art practices in energy-efficient operations. The curriculum trains workers to identify and address wasted energy, create a green operating plan, and perform cost-benefit analysis for building owners and managers. The program, launched in late 2009, is a labor-management partnership.

In January 2010, the U.S. Department of Labor granted the 32BJ Thomas Shortman Training Fund nearly $3 million to expand green buildings training in New York City as part of the American Recovery and Reinvestment Act. This is expected to increase the number of trained workers by 2,000. This grant also provides training for 200 Local 32BJ workers to attend specialized building training through the City University of New York.

SHEET METAL WORKERS INTERNATIONAL ASSOCIATION (SMWIA)

1750 New York Avenue, NW
6th Floor
Washington, DC 20006
E-mail: info@smwia.org
www.smwia.org

About the Union

SMWIA members work in several industries. Sheet metal workers fabricate, install, and service heating, venting, and air conditioning systems; blowpipe and industrial systems; metal roofing;

coping and flashing; and stainless steel work for restaurants, kitchens, and hospitals. They prepare shop and field drawings manually and with computer programs. Members also provide HVAC/R service. Sheet metal workers are unique in the construction industry as the only trade that designs, manufactures, and installs its own products. These skilled craftworkers take ordinary types of flat metal and make them into specialized products for various duct and ventilation systems, as well as architectural and specialized metal fabrication.

Programs and Training

The training SMWIA members receive is done through a four-year apprentice program that combines on-the-job and extensive classroom training. Journeymen continue to advance their skills and certifications utilizing the union's world-class training centers to stay abreast of changes in technology and work practices. SMWIA has over 170 Joint Apprenticeship Training Centers in the United States, Canada, and Puerto Rico.

UNITED ASSOCIATION OF JOURNEYMEN AND APPRENTICES OF THE PLUMBING AND PIPEFITTING INDUSTRY OF THE UNITED STATES AND CANADA (UA)

Three Park Place
Annapolis, Maryland 21401
410-269-2000
E-mail: http://www.ua.org/contact.asp
www.ua.org

About the Union

The UA has a variety of apprenticeship and training programs, as well as delivery methods, which are coordinated through its Sustainable Technologies Department. This department is responsible for all the activities, training, and outreach for sustainable technologies in the plumbing and pipefitting industry.

Programs and Training

5-Star Service Training Program

This apprenticeship program teaches the core skills of plumbing, pipefitting, sprinkler fitting, or HVAC/R services, along with basic mathematics, safety, and customer service skills. On-the-job training is combined with classroom training in this five-year program. Apprentices earn while learning.

At the completion of the program, the apprentice has 32 college credits towards an Associate in Applied Science (AAS) degree and is a UA STAR certified technician. The college credits can be transferred to a local community college or the UA's College On Demand degree program in partnership with Washtenaw Community College in Ann Arbor, Michigan. College On Demand is a distance-learning program that delivers text, Web-based materials, and classroom lectures on DVD for self-paced study. Graduates earn an AAS degree in Sustainable Technology, with a choice of majoring in HVAC/R, plumbing, sprinkler fitting, or construction supervision.

Green Systems Awareness Certificate

The UA offers a Green Systems Awareness Certificate. It requires a 16- to 20-hour course and a written exam, administered by a third-party certification group. The U.S. Green Building Council recognizes the UA as a certified training provider.

Partnership in Environmental Leadership

The Partnership in Environmental Leadership provides less formal training in sustainable mechanical service and construction, and "new building system technologies that promote greater energy efficiency, use fewer natural resources, have minimal impact on the environment, and use materials that can be reused or recycled." The program is a collaboration of the UA, Mechanical Contractors Association of America (MCAA), Mechanical Service Contractors of America (MSCA), Plumbing Contractors of America (PCA), U.S. Green Building Council (USGBC), and Green Mechanical Council.

Training is delivered through the Green Trailer and the Sustainable Technology Demonstration Trailer. Both are mobile units that travel from local to local. The Green Trailer provides trainers and simulators. The trailer drives to a site, the sides go up, the chairs come out, and the training begins. Topics include the latest environmental systems: fuel cell technologies, wind power generation, solar heating system, solar photovoltaic system, gray water toilet flushing system, anaerobic treatment process, infiltration demonstrator, geothermal system trainer, gas-fired warm air heating demonstrator, 1/8 GPF urinal, high-efficiency toilet, and water-saving toilet.

The Sustainable Technology Demonstration Trailer is the newest mobile unit used for outreach and training. While the Green Trailer provides simulators, the Sustainable Technology Demonstration Trailer contains working systems in the latest green technologies, including, among other items, a geothermal heat pump that feeds the radiant heating and cooling systems used in the trailer.

UNITED BROTHERHOOD OF CARPENTERS AND JOINERS (UBC)

101 Constitution Ave NW
Washington, DC 20001
202-589-0520
http://carpenters.org/Home.aspx

About the Union

The skilled members of the United Brotherhood of Carpenters touch every aspect of a construction project. The union represents one trade with many crafts, including carpenters, cabinetmakers and millworkers, floor coverers, framers, interior systems carpenters, lathers, millwrights, and pile drivers. At the UBC's International Millwright Leadership Conference in 2010, a major topic was the union's role in the green economy. Speakers spoke of a future in which the power-generation business will be greener and command a greater share of construction dollars, creating opportunities for UBC millwrights and carpenters. Speakers noted that over the next twenty years, the demand for more efficient, environmentally sound, renewable energy sources is going to drive the demand for skilled workers who know how to build and service power plants. Bill Irwin, executive director of the Carpenters International Training Fund, which develops UBC training, said all instructional materials from now on will incorporate green elements.

Programs and Training

With a $175 million annual budget, 2,000 full-time instructors, and 250 centers across North America, the UBC's affiliated training programs offer a variety of skills-development courses in the construction industry. Apprenticeship programs are typically four-year programs, but can vary depending on the skill area.

The state-of-the-art Carpenters International Training Center (ITC) serves as a hub in a system that can rapidly get in-demand skills into the field. At the 12-acre campus in Las Vegas, new craft-skill training is developed for UBC members in areas like commercial door and hardware, concrete formwork, and gas- and steam-turbine installation and maintenance. The ITC's Curriculum Development Project has published nearly fifty training manuals.

Green Initiatives

In Missouri, after the American Recovery and Reinvestment Act (ARRA) was signed, the carpenters and joiners' union was first in the country to start a funded project: They broke ground on a new bridge over the Osage River in Tuscombia, Missouri, to replace the Depression-era span that was crumbling with age. It's one of about twenty stimulus-funded projects in Missouri that will put UBC members to work driving piles, setting forms, completing interior systems, constructing concrete forms, laying floors, and doing finish work at worksites such as bridges, schools, hospitals, and every kind of infrastructure improvement.

UNITED STEEL, PAPER AND FORESTRY, RUBBER, MANUFACTURING, ENERGY, ALLIED INDUSTRIAL & SERVICE WORKERS INTERNATIONAL UNION (USW) (STEELWORKERS)

Five Gateway Center
Pittsburgh, Pennsylvania 15222
412-562-2400
www.usw.org

About the Union

The Institute for Career Development (ICD), headquartered in Merrillville, Indiana, develops and offers workforce training programs for the United Steelworkers Union. The ICD was created in 1989 as a result of contract negotiations between the USW and major steel companies. Since then, ICD has expanded to include training programs for the employees of rubber companies.

Programs and Training

ICD is a joint initiative between labor and management. The emphasis is on teaching "portable" skills that workers can use in their current careers or take with them to new careers. Most classes are taught in learning centers in or near the plants or in the union halls and are offered before and after shift changes.

Union members may also take other courses, such as those offered by community colleges, through a tuition assistance program. Each worker may receive up to $1800 annually for tuition, books, and fees at accredited institutions. The program is paid for by a fund created as a result of contract negotiations in 1989 between the USW and participating companies. Companies pay a certain amount into the fund for each hour worked by a steelworker.

Partnerships for Green Jobs

In addition to providing training and apprenticeship programs, labor unions have been active in lobbying for and supporting the growth of green jobs. Their influence was evident in passage of the economic stimulus package in 2009. While working to help their members adapt to the changing economy, union leaders also recognize their responsibility to the environment. The following two alliances, which bring together union leaders with environmentalists and business leaders, are examples on the national level of these partnerships.

Apollo Alliance

The slogan of the Apollo Association is "Clean Energy, Good Jobs." According to its mission statement, the Apollo Alliance is "a coalition of labor, business, environmental, and community leaders working to catalyze a clean energy revolution that will put millions of Americans to work in a new generation of high-quality, green-collar jobs. Inspired by the Apollo space program, we promote investments in energy efficiency, clean power, mass transit, next-generation vehicles, and emerging technology, as well as in education and training. Working together, we will reduce carbon emissions and oil imports, spur domestic job growth, and position America to thrive in the twenty-first–century economy."

The Board of Apollo Alliance includes the president of United Steelworkers Union, the executive vice president of Service Employees International Union, the general president of Laborers International Union of North America, and business, environmental, and community leaders. Among union supporters are the national AFL-CIO and various state affiliates. The Alliance has published numerous reports and research on environmental issues and is active in lobbying efforts to promote increasing the number of well-paying, career-track, green-collar jobs.

For more information, check the Web site http://apolloalliance.org.

Blue Green Alliance

The Blue Green Alliance is a national partnership of labor unions (blue) and environmental organizations (green) dedicated to expanding the number and quality of jobs in the green economy. The alliance, now numbering more than 6 million people, was launched in 2006 by the Sierra Club and United Steelworkers. Today, it includes the Communications Workers of America (CWA), National Resource Defense Council (NRDC), Laborers' International Union of North America (LIUNA), and Service Employees International Union (SEIU).

Among its goals, the Blue Green Alliance seeks to educate the public about solutions that "reduce global warming in the timeframe necessary to avoid the effects of climate change" and "curb the use of toxic chemicals in order to enhance public health and promote safer alternatives." The Alliance also advocates for fair "labor, environmental, and human rights standards in trade policies."

To achieve these goals, the Alliance works in partnership with the Good Jobs, Green Jobs National Conference; the Green Jobs for America campaign, including additional partners such as Working America, the community affiliate of the AFL-CIO; Green for All; the Center for American Progress; and the Labor-Climate Project, a partnership with Al Gore's Alliance for Climate Protection. The Blue Green Alliance also publishes groundbreaking research reports focused on renewable energy and green chemistry.

For more information, check the Web site www.bluegreenalliance.org.

PART III

WORKFORCE TRAINING

CHAPTER 9

STATE AND FEDERAL
WORKFORCE TRAINING

The Web site for the state of Arkansas defines "workforce development" as follows:

[E]ducation and/or training beyond high school which leads to a GED, certificate, two- to four-year degree; and/or other short-term, customized training designed to meet the needs of employers to upgrade the skills of existing, emerging, transitional, and entrepreneurial workforces.

The other forty-nine states and the District of Columbia view workforce development similarly. In every case, the emphasis is on *employer* needs and attracting new employers to the state. Training and apprenticeship programs are also geared to a state's major employers, who often receive tax incentives and access to free services for hiring employees or for implementing existing training resources. What does this mean for you, the job seeker? Workforce development emphasizes the provision of resources for finding jobs, writing resumes, and developing interview skills to satisfy the employment needs of a state's employers.

USING THE INTERNET

Every state has an Internet portal through which job seekers can post resumes, search for job openings, or apply for unemployment benefits—and where state employers can post job openings and review resumes of prospective employees. The quality and thoroughness of these portals vary by state:

Some are more user-friendly than others; some are more comprehensive than others. To access these resources, one usually needs to establish an online user ID and password, so you'll have at least a minimum level of security for the information you post.

FINDING A ONE-STOP CAREER CENTER

The Workforce Investment Act (WIA) of 1998, which took effect in 2000, was enacted to replace the Job Training Partnership Act and other federal job-training laws. The WIA aims to encourage businesses to participate in local Workforce Development Services through Workforce Investment Boards. These boards are chaired by community members in the private sector. The WIA established a national workforce preparation and employment system—called America's Workforce Network—to meet the needs of businesses and workers who are interested in furthering their careers.

A main feature of Title I of the WIA is the creation of the One-Stop Career Center system through which job seekers can access a broad range of employment-related and training services from a single point of entry. Each year, nearly 16 million Americans find job placement assistance through One-Stop Career Centers. The following programs are required by federal law to deliver their services through this system:

- Title I of WIA (adults, youth, and dislocated workers)
- Job Corps
- Native American Job Programs
- Wagner-Peyser (employment service)
- Unemployment Insurance
- Trade Adjustment Assistance
- North American Free Trade Association (NAFTA) Transitional Adjustment Assistance
- Welfare-to-Work
- Senior Community Service Employment
- Veterans Employment and Training
- Vocational Rehabilitation
- Adult Education
- Postsecondary Vocational Education
- Community Services Block Grant
- Employment and Training Activities
- Housing and Urban Development
- Migrant and Seasonal Farm Worker Programs

You'll find One-Stop Career Centers in every state and the District of Columbia. All are funded with federal money, and users are not charged for services. The number, locations, and types of resources in One-Stop Centers vary by state and are largely based on population density (for example, rural states will have fewer resources in outlying areas). One-Stop Centers play several roles: They operate as career centers, workforce centers, job centers, unemployment benefit centers, and state or regional government services centers all at once. The following is a list of general services that you may find at your local One-Stop Center:

- Assistance with filing for unemployment benefits
- Assessment of career goals, skills, interests, and abilities
- Information and guidance on choosing education and training programs
- Assistance with basic skills and GED preparation
- Assistance in developing and revising resumes
- Assistance with preparing for job interviews
- Information on the local labor market
- Job search and placement counseling
- Internet access for job searches
- Information on and referrals for childcare, transportation, and other supportive services

In many states, Workforce Development is a separate department or agency within the state government. In other states, it is part of the Departments of Labor, Commerce, or Employment. Each state is required to have a specific entity to administer the services required under WIA, to certify providers of services, and to report regularly to the federal government. The list in this chapter provides main contact information for One-Stop Centers in all fifty states and the District of Columbia, as well as a general description of the individual programs and other relevant workforce development information provided in each center. Use your state's workforce home page to find the location of the center nearest to you and the services that it offers. Not all centers or states have green training or retraining programs, but this is the place to start your search.

VETERANS' SERVICES

Services for veterans are provided through One-Stop Career Centers. For example, Helmets to Hardhats is a national program that connects National Guard, Reserve, and transitioning active-duty military members with career training and employment opportunities in the construction industry. The program is administered by the Center for Military Recruitment, Assessment, and Veterans Employment and is headquartered in Washington, DC.

Go online to www.careeronestop.org/military-transition/ and click on "Find State Resources for Veterans" under "Hot Topics." Here you can search by state for veteran-specific job and educational resources. Some are provided by the One-Stop Centers, and others by other agencies and institutions.

REGISTERED APPRENTICESHIP PROGRAMS

Your state may also participate in the Registered Apprenticeship Program supported by the Department of Labor's Employment and Training Administration Office of Apprenticeship (OA). There are close to 1,000 apprenticeship titles recognized by the OA. An apprenticeship program is a partnership of employers, labor management organizations, state and local workforce development agencies and programs, two- and four-year colleges, and economic development organizations to provide on-the-job training and classroom instruction to entry-level workers for certain skills or trades. It's a way to earn and learn at the same time.

Many of the apprenticeship programs partner with colleges, so enrollees can earn college credit, as well as experience and a paycheck. Some programs also lead to nationally recognized certification. Examples of registered apprenticeships are carpenter, construction laborer, electrician, and over-the-road truck driver. Not all apprenticeships are available in all states. It depends on the needs, interests, and capacity of sponsoring organizations.

Check www.doleta.gov/OA/stateoffices.cfm for your state's contact information for apprenticeship programs. Your One-Stop Center can help you find out what apprenticeships are available in your area, or go online to http://oa.doleta.gov/bat/cfm for apprenticeship sponsors and lists of apprenticeships.

ARRA GREEN JOB TRAINING GRANTS

Note that the American Recovery and Reinvestment Act (ARRA), which was signed into law in 2009 to stimulate the economy, included $4 billion for workforce investment initiatives in retraining and education. Your state, in partnership with local colleges and training providers, may have applied for some of this money to increase its workforce training programs. Nearly $100 million in green job training grants was dedicated to programs to help dislocated workers and others, including women, African Americans, and Latinos, find jobs in expanding green industries and related occupations. Funding also went to projects in communities impacted by auto industry restructuring. Nearly $190 million was provided to thirty-four states through the State Energy Sector Partnership and Training Grants to train workers in emerging industries including energy efficiency and renewable energy. Most of these initiatives are available through the appropriate Workforce Investment Boards.

> **About ARRA Programs and Grants**
> Check your state's Web site to see if your state won federal money for green industries and green training programs. Also look for information for programs your own state is supporting.

The following are a few examples of ARRA grants:

- *California:* Funding to train unemployed workers or upgrade skills of employed workers for jobs that reduce energy or water use in the building trades.
- *Maryland:* Funding to prepare 1,500 veterans, reservists, low-wage workers, and ex-offenders as the first wave of a goal of 100,000 workers in new green jobs in the state by 2015.
- *Michigan:* International Training Institute for Sheet Metal and Air Conditioning:

Funding to prepare 240 sheet metal workers in Michigan for careers in energy-efficient building construction, retrofitting, and manufacturing.

- *Nevada:* Funding to train workers for residential weatherization jobs.
- *New Mexico:* Funding to prepare workers for careers in green building/energy efficiency, solar energy, biofuels, and wind energy.
- *South Carolina:* Funding to train workers in the solar industry.

STATES' ONE-STOP CAREER CENTERS

About Resource Areas in One-Stop Career Centers

Many One-Stop Career Centers have resource rooms or separate areas where job seekers can access the Internet and use the printers, phones, copiers, and fax machines in their job searches. Employment professionals in these resource rooms are there to help job seekers find what they need. Some centers may have childcare areas as well, but call your local center to be sure.

ALABAMA

Office of Workforce Development
PO Box 302130
Montgomery, Alabama 36130-2130
334-293-4700
https://joblink.alabama.gov/ada

Alabama Joblink is a portal to services offered through the Alabama Career Center system, which administers the state's One-Stop Centers. CareerLink centers are located in each county and are administered by three regional centers: Central Alabama Skills Center at Southern Union State Community College, North Alabama Skills Center, and South Alabama Skills Center.

ALASKA

Alaska Workforce Investment Board
1016 West 6th Avenue
Suite 105
Anchorage, Alaska 99501
907-269-7485
www.jobs.state.ak.us/offices

Job-related training services are available to eligible youth, adults, and dislocated workers through the Alaska Job Center Network (AJCN) and select training providers and partners across the state. Funding for these training services is available primarily through WIA, the State Training Employment Program (STEP), the Trade Assistance Act (TAA), and the High Growth Job Training Initiative (HGJTI). These funds may be leveraged with federal Pell grants and/or the Alaska State Student Loan program. For Alaska Native Americans, other funding for training is available through recognized tribal organizations throughout the state. Job training resources are available for a limited number of residents of select rural locations through the Denali Training Fund via the Denali Commission.

ARIZONA

Department of Commerce, Workforce
    Development
1700 W. Washington
Suite 600
Phoenix, Arizona 85007
602-771-1100
www.azworkforceconnection.com

Arizona Workforce Connection is a statewide system of workforce development partners that provide free services to employers seeking access to skilled new hires or to existing worker training resources. Through a network of One-Stop Centers and online services, Arizona Workforce Connection provides access to employee recruitment, labor market information, job training and hiring tax credits, customized training and skills upgrading, and pre-layoff assistance.

Note that as of January 1, 2010, the state of Arizona has a new tool in advancing its solar platform and capacity in renewable energy, that is, the Arizona Renewable Energy Tax Incentive Program. The program is designed to stimulate new investments in manufacturing and in headquarter operations of renewable energy companies, including solar, wind, geothermal, and other renewable technologies. It is administered by the Department of Commerce.

ARKANSAS
Arkansas Workforce Centers
Department of Workforce Services
Two Capitol Mall
Little Rock, Arkansas 72201
501-371-1020
E-mail: arkansaswib@arkansas.gov
www.arworks.org/index.html

Arkansas Workforce Centers provide locally developed and operated services, including training and linking employers and job seekers through a statewide delivery system. Convenient One-Stop Centers are designed to eliminate the need to visit different locations. The centers integrate multiple workforce development programs into a single system, making the resources more accessible and user-friendly to job seekers and expanding services to employers.

CALIFORNIA
Employment Development Department
800 Capitol Mall, MIC 83
Sacramento, California 95814
916-654-7799
www.edd.ca.gov/Jobs_and_Training

California's Employment Development Department (EDD) provides a comprehensive range of employment and training services in partnership with state and local agencies and organizations. These services are provided statewide through the state's One-Stop Career Center system, or EDD Workforce Services Offices. Each county has at least one One-Stop Career Center.

On January 11, 2010, Southern California Edison (SCE) announced a $1 million gift to California's community colleges to launch the Green Jobs Education Initiative. This program will provide scholarship support for students with financial need who are enrolled in green job workforce preparation or training programs.

COLORADO
Department of Labor and Employment
633 17th Street
Suite 700
Denver, Colorado 80202
303-318-8000
www.colorado.gov/cs/Satellite/
    CDLE-EmployTrain/CDLE/1248095319014

In nearly all of Colorado's nine federally recognized workforce regions, program administration and service delivery of WIA and Wagner-Peyser Act programs are consolidated, providing local businesses and job seekers with easy access to a broader range of workforce center services. The centers provide an array of employment and training services at no charge to employers or job seekers.

CONNECTICUT
Department of Labor
200 Folly Brook Boulevard
Wethersfield, Connecticut 06109
860-263-6000
www.ctdol.state.ct.us/ContactInfo

The One-Stop Career Center system in Connecticut is called CTWorks. The system helps more than 80,000 state residents annually with resume writing, interviewing skills, job training, and much more. Most training results in certification and job placement.

About Funding for Training or Retraining

If you need financial help, ask your local One-Stop employment professionals about the possibility of funding while training. Some states and programs may also provide supportive funding.

DELAWARE

Department of Labor, Workforce Investment
 Board (WIB)
4425 N. Market Street
Fox Valley
Wilmington, Delaware 19802
302-761-8160
www.delawareworks.com/wib

The WIB oversees Delaware's One-Stop Centers to ensure that the state's citizens are provided with occupational training and employment service opportunities to help them gain employment that will sustain them and their families. One-Stop Centers are located within each of Delaware's Department of Labor locations: Wilmington, Newark, Dover, and Georgetown.

DISTRICT OF COLUMBIA

Department of Employment Services (DOES)
Government of the District of Columbia
64 New York Avenue NE
Suite 3000
Washington, DC 20002
202-724-7000
E-mail: does@dc.gov
http://does.dc.gov/does/site/default.asp

The Department of Employment Services administers One-Stop Career Centers in the District of Columbia. Each DOES center provides a range of services, including career counseling, career planning, resume assistance, direct job placement, classroom and on-the-job training, online and phone access to America's Job Bank, information about local and national labor markets, and unemployment compensation. In addition to the traditional One-Stop Centers, DC's Department of Employment Services has pioneered an advanced Web-based workforce development system to better serve the citizens and employers of the District. Virtual One-Stop offers job seekers, employers, training providers, benefit applicants, students, youth, and other One-Stop customers a comprehensive array of services via the Internet.

FLORIDA

Agency for Workforce Innovation
107 East Madison Street
Caldwell Building
Tallahassee, Florida 32399-4120
866-352-2345 (toll-free)
www.floridajobs.org/onestop/onestopdir

Florida's Office of Workforce Services (WFS) provides One-Stop program support services to the twenty-four Regional Workforce Boards that administer the One-Stop Centers.

Employ Florida Marketplace (www.employ-florida.com) is Florida's official online portal to virtual job-matching services and many other workforce resources. The site offers assistance in selecting a new career, finding a new job, or locating suitable education or training.

GEORGIA

Department of Labor
404-232-3540
www.dol.state.ga.us/find_one_stop_centers.htm

Most of the direct services of Georgia's Department of Labor are provided through the Internet or by staff in fifty-three local Career Centers, more than fifty local Vocational Rehabilitation Offices, and twenty Workforce Areas, offering a wide range of services to both job seekers and employers. Each county has multiple One-Stop Centers that provide individuals who seek employment with the most up-to-date tools to find and keep jobs, including resource areas, education and training services, local and national job listings, and job search and financial management workshops.

HAWAII

Department of Labor and Industrial Relations:
    Workforce Development Division
830 Punchbowl Street #329
Honolulu, Hawaii 96813
808-586-8877
http://dlir.workforce.develop@hawaii.gov
http://hawaii.gov/labor/wdd/onestops

Hawaii's One-Stop Centers provide free services to job seekers and employers, including job-search assistance; personal career-planning services; training opportunities; support for HireNet Hawaii, the online employment site; and a resource area. Centers are located on Oahu, Maui, Hila, Kona, and Kauai.

IDAHO

Department of Labor
317 W. Main Street
Boise, Idaho 83735
208-332-3570
http://labor.idaho.gov/dnn/StateCouncil/
    CareerCenters/tabid/2042/Default.aspx

The IdahoWorks Career Center is the primary point of access to a full range of labor market and education services. More than seventeen programs have been assembled under the One-Stop system to meet the needs of workers, students, and businesses. Six centers throughout the state offer a variety of self-service options, a comprehensive resource center, and highly trained staff. For those seeking employment or education, the Career Centers provide one-stop access to national, state, and local job listings; career guidance; specialized workshops; and education and training services and resources in the community. IdahoWorks also provides online access to finding jobs and applying for various services from your own computer at http://labor.idaho.gov/iw/.

The Workforce Development Training Fund helps eligible Idaho companies with up to $2000 per employee for job skills training. The fund underwrites training for new employees of companies expanding in Idaho and skills upgrade training to prevent layoffs of current workers. The application process is designed for quick response and turnaround with minimal paperwork.

ILLINOIS

Illinois Department of Employment Security
    (IDES)
33 South State Street
Chicago, Illinois 60603
www.ides.state.il.us/

IDES provides employment services and guidance to workers, job seekers, and employers through a statewide network of IDES offices and Illinois workNet local centers. The agency combines federally funded job training programs in Illinois into a "workforce development" system where individuals can find a job or train for a new career. With nearly sixty locations throughout the state, local IDES offices and Illinois workNet Centers are the primary one-stop sources for the state's workforce development services. IDES also provides an online resource to help workers and job seekers find job listings, job training information, and help with creating resumes through the Illinois workNet Web site.

INDIANA

Department of Workforce Development
Indiana Government Center South
10 North Senate Avenue
Indianapolis, Indiana 46204
800-891-6499 (toll-free)
www.in.gov/dwd/WorkOne/

Indiana's WorkOne portal provides valuable information about WorkOne and its programs. The WorkOne Center is the heart of Indiana's workforce development system and helps people find a new or better job, choose a career, find a good employee, or find training. Indiana has eleven WorkOne Regions, with centers located throughout the state. IndianaCAREERconnect .com is the state's new innovative online job-matching system.

IOWA

Iowa Workforce Development
1000 East Grand Avenue
Des Moines, Iowa 50319-0209
515-281-5387
800-JOB-IOWA (toll-free)
www.iowaworkforce.org/centers/regionalsites
.htm

Fifteen regions make up the Iowa Workforce Development network. The network provides complete one-stop services for job search, unemployment information, career guidance, and training.

KANSAS

Department of Commerce
Workforce Services Division
1000 S.W. Jackson Street
Suite 100
Topeka, Kansas 66612-1354
785-296-0607
E-mail: workforcesvcs@kansasworks.com
www.kansascommerce.com/WorkforceCenters/
tabid/160/Default.aspx

The Kansas Department of Commerce administers the KansasWorks workforce system that links businesses, job seekers, and educational institutions to ensure that the state's employers can find skilled workers. The system operates workforce centers throughout the state to help connect Kansas businesses with skilled job seekers in their area. Its online portal is https://www.kansasworks .com/ada.

KENTUCKY

Office of Employment and Training
275 East Main Street
2nd Floor
Frankfort, Kentucky 40601
502-564-7456
http://workforce.ky.gov/

The Kentucky Office of Employment and Training (OET) is part of the Department for Workforce Investment. OET staff members provide job services, unemployment insurance services, labor market information, and training opportunities. Kentucky One-Stop Career Centers, which are located throughout the state, are designed to give job seekers and employers quick, easy access to necessary services.

LOUISIANA

Louisiana Workforce Commission
1001 N. 23rd Street
Baton Rouge, Louisiana 70802
225-342-3111
https://www.voshost.com/default.asp

The Louisiana Workforce Commission, under the LaWorks network, provides an online portal to services like resume posting, career options, education, and training. It also provides access to information on youth services and administers One-Stop Career Centers throughout the state.

MAINE

Department of Labor
54 State House Station
Augusta, Maine 04333
207-623-7981
E-mail: mdol@maine.gov
www.mainecareercenter.com/

Maine's CareerCenter, the state's online workforce portal, offers a variety of job-related information, including links to One-Stop Centers located throughout the state.

MARYLAND

Department of Labor, Licensing and Regulation
Division of Workforce Development and Adult
    Learning
1100 North Eutaw Street
Baltimore, Maryland 21201
410-230-6001
E-mail: det@dllr.state.md.us
https://mwe.dllr.state.md.us

Workforce Exchange is a virtual one-stop network aimed at improving access to information about jobs, training, and workforce support throughout Maryland. The exchange connects agencies, programs, and services electronically to assist employers and individuals in making the right career decisions. The heart of Maryland's workforce system is its more than forty workforce service centers, which provide locally designed and operated services to meet local labor market needs.

MASSACHUSETTS

Labor and Workforce Development, Division of
    Career Services
Charles F. Hurley Building
19 Staniford Street
Boston, Massachusetts 02114
617-626-5300
E-mail: DCSCustomerfeedback@detma.org
https://web.detma.org/JobQuest/Default.aspx

The state's online portal, JobQuest, provides access to job-search and training programs available online. Thirty-seven One-Stop Career Centers form the foundation of the state's delivery system for employment and training services.

MICHIGAN

Department of Energy, Labor and Economic
    Growth
201 N. Washington Square
Victor Office Center
5th Floor
Lansing, Michigan 48913
888-253-6855 (toll-free)
E-mail: careerhelp@michigan.gov
www.michiganworks.org

Michigan's Employment Service program provides services to job seekers online through the Michigan Talent Bank portal and more than 100 Michigan Works! Service Centers statewide. Local Michigan Works! agencies oversee a wide variety of programs designed to help employers find skilled workers and help job seekers find satisfying careers. The programs are also designed to prepare youth and unskilled adults for entry into the labor force and to aid individuals who face serious barriers to employment to obtain the assistance necessary to get and keep a job.

MINNESOTA

Department of Employment and Economic
    Development (DEED)
1st National Bank Building
332 Minnesota Street
Suite E-200
Saint Paul, Minnesota 55101-1351
651-259-7114
http://www.positivelyminnesota.com/

There are nearly fifty WorkForce Centers throughout the state where people looking for jobs can find employment and career assistance. An online job bank "MinnesotaWorks.net" connects job seekers and employers.

MISSISSIPPI

Department of Employment Security
Office of the Governor
1235 Echelon Parkway
PO Box 1699
Jackson, Mississippi 39215-1699
601-321-6000
www.mdes.ms.gov/wps/portal

Workforce Investment Network (WIN) Job Centers, located throughout Mississippi, provide convenient, one-stop employment and training services to employers and job seekers. Online services are provided through the AccessMississippi portal.

MISSOURI

Department of Economic Development
Division of Workforce Development
421 East Dunklin Street
PO Box 1087
Jefferson City, Missouri 65102-1087
573 751-3349
888-728-JOBS (toll-free)
E-mail: wfd@ded.mo.gov
www.missouricareersource.com/mcs/mcs/default
    .seek

MissouriCareerSource.com is the portal to Internet resources available to job seekers and employers in Missouri. Missouri Career Centers provide training development services to workers and employers through the coordination of a variety of partner agencies. Career Centers are located throughout the state. A wealth of information and resources about workforce services can be found on WorkSmart Missouri, a Web site of the Division of Workforce Development.

MONTANA

Department of Labor: Workforce Services
  Division
PO Box 1728
Helena, Montana 59624-1728
406-444-4100
http://wsd.dli.mt.gov/service/officelist.asp

Montana's Workforce Services Division (WSD) is a gateway to government services in employment and training. The WSD consists of twenty-three Job Service Workforce Center sites located throughout Montana along with a team of experts who are located in a central support office. The focus is on developing and maintaining a high-quality workforce in the state. The online portal to jobs and job information is https://jobs.mt.gov.

NEBRASKA

Department of Labor: Nebraska Workforce
  Development
550 South 16th Street
Lincoln, Nebraska 68508
402-471-9000
http://nejoblink.nebraska.gov/

Joblink is Nebraska's Internet portal providing job searches, resume services, and assistance to job seekers. Seventeen Workforce Development Career Centers are located statewide, offering comprehensive services, including training programs, to job seekers.

NEVADA

Department of Employment, Training and
  Rehabilitation
500 East Third Street
Carson City, Nevada 89713-0021
E-mail: detrinfo@nvdetr.org
www.nevadajobconnect.org/

Nevada's JobConnect Career Centers provide businesses and job seekers with personalized attention and a variety of services, including access to job listings and placement; work registration; labor market information; career information, guidance, and assessment; information about education and training opportunities; unemployment insurance information; resume preparation; referrals to other partner agency services; and more.

NEW HAMPSHIRE

Department of Employment Security (NHES)
32 South Main Street
Concord, New Hampshire 03301
603-224-3311
800-852-3400 (toll-free)
www.nhworks.org

New Hampshire's Department of Employment Security offers free services, resources, and tools to help the job seeker with the entire job-search process. NH WORKS Resource Centers, located within each of the thirteen local offices, provide services, information, resources, and tools for job seekers in a one-stop setting. The NH WORKS system is a partnership of a number of government agencies and community organizations to provide services, resources, and information to job seekers and employers. NH WORKS is an online portal offering comprehensive services to job seekers and employers alike.

About the Energy Star Program

For information on the Energy Star program of the U.S. Department of Energy, go to www.energystar.gov or call 888-782-7937 (toll-free). For information on available Energy Star tax credits for energy-efficient home improvements, check out www.energystar.gov/taxcredits.

NEW JERSEY

Department of Labor and Workforce
    Development
1 John Fitch Way
PO Box 110
Trenton, New Jersey 08625-0110
http://lwd.dol.state.nj.us/labor/wnjpin/findjob/
    onestop/services.html

Located county-wide throughout New Jersey, One-Stop Career Centers assist with obtaining employment and training. The One-Stop Career Centers offer educational training programs at vocational and trade schools or on-site at the One-Stop, including on-the-job training with employers and apprenticeships in many fields.

NEW MEXICO

Department of Workforce Solutions
401 Broadway NE
Albuquerque, New Mexico 87102
E-mail: infodws@state.nm.us
www.dws.state.nm.us/index.html

The One-Stop System is intended to meet the needs of job seekers and workers through services such as access to job listings, career-planning resources, soft skills training, and training and education for high-growth industries. Workforce Offices are located throughout New Mexico.

NEW YORK

Department of Labor
Division of Employment and Workforce
    Solutions
State Campus, Building 12
Albany, New York 12240
518-457-9000
888-4-NYSDOL (toll-free)
E-mail: nysdol@labor.state.ny.us
www.labor.state.ny.us/workforcenypartners/
    osview.asp

At New York's One-Stop Career Centers, job seekers can learn resume writing and successful interviewing techniques, access apprenticeship training and training grants, search online job listings, and attend a job fair. Job seekers can research occupations on the Career Zone site and post customized resumes on Job Portfolio, part of the Job Zone section.

NORTH CAROLINA

Department of Commerce
301 North Wilmington Street
Raleigh, North Carolina 27601-1058

Mailing Address:
4301 Mail Service Center
Raleigh, North Carolina 27699-4301
919-733-4151
E-mail: info@commerce.com
www.nccommerce.com/en/WorkforceServices/

The Division of Workforce Development oversees the chartering and operation of the state's JobLink One-Stop Career Centers and administration of the federal WIA. These centers combine a variety of state and local agencies in one location to provide job seekers and businesses with information, recruitment and placement, and training opportunities. JobLink One-Stop Career Centers are located throughout the state.

About Tools for America's Job Seekers

The U.S. Department of Labor ran a challenge to find the top-rated sites for job seeker tools on the Internet. Members of the public rated more than 600 online tools over a two-week period. The top tools in each of the six categories are available through http://www.careerone stop.org/jobseekertools. The tools cover general job boards, niche job boards, career planning tools, career exploration tools, social media job search, and other job and career tools such as preparing for an interview, labor market data, and training grants.

NORTH DAKOTA

Job Service North Dakota
PO Box 5507
Bismarck, North Dakota 58506-5507
701-328-2825
www.jobsnd.com/

Job Service's online labor exchange system provides individuals with maximum flexibility in their job searches. Customers may use the online services exclusively, or they may consult with a Job Service employment professional who can assist them in a variety of ways. Job seekers may attend workshops to learn about resume writing, interviewing, and other job search techniques. They may work through an assessment of their interests and abilities to find an appropriate career path. If job seekers do not have the necessary skills to pursue their desired occupations, Job Service employment professionals offer guidance on ways to access funds for training. Fourteen full-service offices and two part-time offices are located in the state.

OHIO

Department of Jobs and Family Services (JFS)
Office of Workforce Development
PO Box 1618
Columbus, Ohio 43216-1618
614-644-0677
E-mail: Workforce@jfs.ohio.gov
http://jfs.ohio.gov/workforce/

In Ohio, there are thirty-one comprehensive, full-service One-Stop sites and fifty-nine satellite sites throughout the state's twenty workforce development areas, with at least one site in every Ohio county. The local workforce development areas are based on population, economic development, educational resources, and labor markets, and the One-Stop Centers tailor their services to meet local customer needs. Job-seeking customers can expect services like resource rooms, job-related workshops, supportive services, individual training accounts, and other activities that match job seekers to employment.

OKLAHOMA

Department of Commerce
900 North Stiles Avenue
Oklahoma City, Oklahoma 73104-3234
405-815-5125
800-879-6552 (toll free)
www.workforceok.org/locator.htm

Under the umbrella of Workforce Oklahoma, business leaders, educators, training providers, and employment professionals work together to achieve job growth, employee productivity, and employer satisfaction within the workforce system. A network of statewide offices integrates employment, education, and training to assist employers in finding qualified employees and to help workers find jobs, make career decisions, and access training opportunities.

OREGON

Employment Department
875 Union Street, NE
Salem, Oregon 97311
503-451-2400
800-237-3710 (toll-free)
http://findit.emp.state.or.us/locations/index.cfm

Through forty-seven WorkSource Center offices across the state, the department serves job seekers and employers by helping workers find suitable employment, providing qualified applicants for employers, supplying statewide and local labor market information, and offering unemployment insurance benefits to workers temporarily unemployed through no fault of their own. The department helps job seekers find jobs that match their skills and employers' needs, provides up-to-date information about trends in occupations and skills needed for success in the job market, and works with other agencies to direct workers to appropriate training programs and job experiences.

PENNSYLVANIA

Department of Labor and Industry
717-787- 3354
http://www.paworkforce.state.pa.us/portal/server
    .pt/community/contact_us/12950

The department prepares job seekers for the global workforce through employment and job-training services for adult, youth, older workers, and dislocated workers. The Commonwealth Workforce Development System (CWDS) is an Internet-based system of services for use by customers and potential customers of the PA CareerLink offices. CWDS provides online access to job openings; information about employers, services, and training opportunities for job seekers; and labor market information. The department administers a network of PA CareerLink centers around the state.

RHODE ISLAND

RI Department of Labor and Training
Center General Complex
1511 Pontiac Avenue
Cranston, Rhode Island 02920
401-462-8000
www.networkri.org/

Rhode Island's One-Stop Career Center System, netWORKri, is a partnership of professional, labor, training, and education organizations. The netWORKri Centers, located throughout the state, match job seekers and employers through high-quality employment programs and services.

SOUTH CAROLINA

Department of Commerce: Workforce
    Development
1201 Main Street
Suite 1600
Columbia, South Carolina 29201-3200
803-737-0400
800-868-7232 (toll-free)
www.sces.org/Individual/locations/1stoploc.htm

Matching the needs of businesses for skilled workers and training with the needs of individuals for education and employment, the Workforce Division seeks to provide customers with timely information and services. Through its One-Stop system, South Carolina's Workforce Division assists in finding appropriate training for adults and enables smooth coordination with industries, education, and economic development.

SOUTH DAKOTA

Department of Labor: Workforce Training
700 Governors Drive
Pierre, South Dakota 57501-2291
605-773-3101
http://dol.sd.gov/workforce_training/clcs.aspx

The South Dakota Department of Labor (DOL) offers a variety of training and education programs to ensure that employers have the skilled workforce they need and to help individuals realize their potential as employees. Some of these programs are geared toward helping target groups successfully overcome unique employment challenges, such as those for whom English is a second language or those who do not possess a high school diploma. The department also helps individuals assess their training and educational needs and identify options. Career Learning Centers (CLCs) work closely with the DOL to provide education and employment training services that meet the needs of local job seekers and businesses.

TENNESSEE

Department of Labor and Workforce
    Development
220 French Landing Drive
Nashville, Tennessee 37243
615-741-6642
E-mail: TDLWD@tn.gov
http://state.tn.us/labor-wfd/cc/

Tennessee has a network of Career Centers across the state where employers can go to find the workers they need and job seekers can get assistance and career information. In addition to job placement, recruitment, and training referrals, each center offers computerized labor market information, Internet access, workshops, and an online talent bank.

TEXAS

Employment and Labor
Texas Workforce Commission
101 E. 15th Street
Austin, Texas 78778-0001
800-832-2829 (toll free)
www.twc.state.tx.us/dirs/wdas/wdamap.html

The Texas Workforce Commission (TWC) is part of a local/state network of 240 Workforce Centers and satellite offices represented on a regional level by twenty-eight local workforce boards. TWC oversees and provides workforce development services to employers and job seekers. For job seekers, TWC offers career-development information, job-search resources, training programs, and, as appropriate, unemployment benefits. Customers can access local workforce solutions and statewide services in a single location, the Texas Workforce Centers. The TWC administers a comprehensive online job resource service at www.workintexas.com.

UTAH

Department of Workforce Services
PO Box 45249
Salt Lake City, Utah 84145-0249
801-526-WORK (9675)
E-mail: dwscontactus@utah.gov
http://jobs.utah.gov/regions/ec.asp

Utah's one-stop Employment Centers provide training information and job-search assistance. Job seekers receive assistance in determining their interests, abilities, and current skill levels; develop individual employment plans; and explore potential training options. The Department of Workforce Services sponsors access to online services through Utah's Job Connection Web site at http://jobs.utah.gov.

VERMONT

Department of Labor
5 Green Mountain Drive
PO Box 488
Montpelier, Vermont 05601-0488
802-828-4000
http://labor.vermont.gov/Default.aspx?tabid=285

Vermont's fourteen Resource Centers provide employers with interview space, assistance in posting jobs, and help with human resources issues. A Resource Room in each center provides job seekers with services and resources such as personal computers and access to the Internet. The centers are equipped with assistive technology for individuals with disabilities. Staff members are also available to provide specific resources for veterans. Vermont JobLink, www.vermontjoblink.com, is an online portal with access to resources for job seekers and employers alike.

VIRGINIA

The Virginia Employment Commission
703 East Main Street
Richmond, Virginia 23219
PO Box 1358
Richmond, Virginia 23218-1358
804-786-1485
http://www.vec.virginia.gov/vecportal/field/
    field_offices.cfm

The Virginia Workforce Centers provide one-stop access to workforce, employment, and training services of various programs and partner organizations. Each Virginia Workforce Center provides services required by federal legislation, plus services designed to meet the needs of the local community. The Virginia Workforce Connection at www.VaWorkConnect.com is an online job-seeker service that provides job search and career information, training opportunities, skill requirements, and labor market information, including wage data and industry and occupational trends.

WASHINGTON

Employment Security Department (ESD)
PO Box 9046
Olympia, Washington 98507
212 Maple Park Avenue SE
Olympia, Washington 98504
360-902-9500
E-mail: work@esd.wa.gov
https://fortress.wa.gov/esd/
    worksource/Employment.aspx

WorkSource is a partnership of Washington State's businesses, government agencies, community and technical colleges, and nonprofit organizations. It has become the cornerstone for improving access to employment and training services via One-Stop Career Centers in the state. WorkSource services are delivered to customers in a variety of ways, including self-directed efforts via the Internet or at so-called kiosks; group programs and activities, like workshops, one-on-one discussions, training programs, and business consultations.

WEST VIRGINIA

Department of Commerce
WORKFORCE West Virginia
Capitol Complex Building 6, Room 609
112 California Avenue
Charleston, West Virginia 25305-0112
304-558-7024
https://www.workforcewv.org/

WORKFORCE West Virginia, a consortium of partners, assists workers in finding suitable employment and employers in finding qualified workers. It seeks to match job seekers with employers in an efficient manner, help those in need become job ready, and analyze and disseminate labor market information. One-stop Workforce Centers are located throughout the state.

WISCONSIN

Department of Workforce Development (DWD)
201 E. Washington Avenue,
Madison, Wisconsin 53703

Mailing Address:
PO Box 7946
Madison, Wisconsin 53707-7946
608-266-3131
888-258-9966 (toll-free)
https://jobcenterofwisconsin.com/

JobCenterOfWisconsin.com, operated by the Wisconsin Department of Workforce Development and the Wisconsin Job Center system, is a Wisconsin-centered employment exchange, linking employers in all parts of the state and in communities that border Wisconsin with anyone looking for a job. The Wisconsin Job Center system delivers services through locations in fifty-seven communities throughout the state. The centers are part of the workforce system led by Wisconsin's eleven independently operated, regional Workforce Development Boards.

WYOMING

Department of Workforce Services
122 W. 25th Street
Herschler Building 2E
Cheyenne, Wyoming 82002
307-777-8728
http://wyomingworkforce.org/contact/offices.aspx

Wyoming's Department of Workforce Services (DWS) has a number of programs available for individuals seeking jobs throughout the state—whether laid off, disabled, otherwise unemployed, or simply wanting to change career direction. The DWS administers numerous education and training programs to meet a variety of needs and groups through its local Workforce Centers.

Ten Eco-Friendly Actions You Can Take Now

1. **Buy a couple of refillable water bottles and fill them with tap water.** If you don't like the taste of your local water, buy a water filter that fits on the faucet. Depending on the filter, the cost of twenty bottles of water will quickly pay for it. Remember to wash refillable bottles, so that they don't breed bacteria.

2. **Reuse shopping bags.** The debate rages over whether paper or plastic bags are worse for the environment. If you have your groceries packed in either, reuse the bags as many times as possible. Better yet, buy and use eco-friendly reusable bags that many supermarkets sell. These stores reduce your bill by a few cents for each bag you bring and use.

3. **Replace your light bulbs with compact fluorescent light bulbs (CFLs) or light emitting diodes (LEDs).** Incandescent light bulbs are due to be phased out beginning in 2012. The Energy Independence and Security Act of 2007 calls for the transition to more energy-efficient lighting starting January 1, 2012, at which time 100-watt incandescent bulbs will no longer be sold. The following year, 75-watt incandescents will be phased out, and in 2014, sales of 40- and 60-watt bulbs will end. Current CFLs have mercury in them, so you can't throw them in the trash when they burn out—in about seven years. However, this may change over time as engineers work on new ways to manufacture CFLs. The good news is that changing just 25 percent of your light bulbs to CFLs will save 50 percent on what you spend to light your house. CFLs save you about $30 in electricity costs over the life of a bulb.

4. **Repair leaky faucets.** A slow drip can fill five 10-gallon containers in a month.

5. **Install a water-saving showerhead.** Depending on what you buy, you will use one-third to one-half the water of a regular showerhead. For a family of four, that translates into 20,000 fewer gallons of water a year.

6. **Caulk windows and doors to keep air out.** Tightly sealed windows and doors will keep out heat in the summer and cold in the winter, thus saving money on your energy bills.

7. **Look for the Energy Star label and Energy Guide when you buy appliances like air conditioners and washers.** The guide shows you how much it costs to run the appliance and the range of costs for similar machines. Buying Energy Star appliances may also entitle you to a rebate. Check with your salesperson at time of purchase.

8. **Install a programmable thermostat to operate your heating and air conditioning systems.** Set it to a high of 68° in the winter and 72° in the summer. Also during the winter set it to turn down automatically at night and when everyone is out of the house during the day. In summer, do the opposite. Set it to turn up automatically when you are out during the day, so you aren't wasting energy cooling an empty house.

9. **Don't turn the car on to idle and warm up on cold mornings.** It takes only 30 seconds for the engine to warm up. It may take you longer to warm up, but consider the fewer carbon emissions your car will generate—and the money you'll save on gas.

10. **Check your car's owner's manual for the proper pressure for your tires.** Keep your tires inflated to the correct pressure and save money on gas.

PART IV

APPENDIXES

BUILDING AND LANDSCAPING JOBS BY INDUSTRY

BUILDING DESIGN AND CONSTRUCTION

- Architect
  - Architectural Engineer
  - Architectural Engineering Consultant
  - Architectural and Engineering Manager
  - Architectural Project Manager
  - Design Architect
  - Project Architect
  - Project Manager
  - Green Building and Retrofit Architect
  - Industrial Green Systems and Retrofit Designer
- Architectural Drafter
  - CAD Technician (Computer-Aided Design)
  - CADD Operator (Computer-Aided Design and Drafting)
  - Designer
  - Drafter
  - Intern Architect
  - Project Manager
  - Project Architect
- Carpenter Helper
  - Carpenter Apprentice
  - Carpenter Frame Helper
  - Formwork Carpenter Helper
  - Industrial Carpenter Helper
  - Industrial Scaffold Carpenter Helper
- Cement Mason/Concrete Finisher
  - Cement Finisher
  - Concrete Mason

- Mason
- Terrazzo Worker
- Civil Engineer
  - Architectural Engineer
  - City Engineer
  - Civil Engineering Manager
  - Design Engineer
  - Project Engineer
  - Project Manager
  - Research Hydraulic Engineer
  - Structural Engineer
- Civil Engineering Technician
  - Civil Designer
  - Civil Engineering Assistant
  - Civil Engineering Designer
  - Construction Analyst
  - Construction Technician
  - Design Technician
  - Engineering Assistant
  - Engineering Specialist
  - Engineering Technician
  - Transportation Engineering Technician
- Civil Drafter
  - Civil CAD Designer (Computer-Aided Design)
  - Civil CAD Technician (Computer-Aided Design)
  - Computer-Aided Design Designer (CAD)
  - Computer-Aided Design Operator (CAD)
  - Computer-Aided Design Technician (CAD)
  - Computer-Aided Drafting and Design Drafter (CADD)
  - Drafting Technician

- Construction Carpenter
  - Assembler
  - Concrete Carpenter
  - Construction Worker
  - Custom Stair Builder
  - Finish Carpenter
  - Installer
  - Lead Carpenter
  - Trim Carpenter
- Construction Manager
  - Construction Area Manager
  - Construction Foreman
  - Construction Superintendent
  - General Contractor
  - Job Superintendent
  - Project Manager
  - Project Superintendent
- Construction Worker
  - Construction Laborer
  - Curb and Gutter Laborer
  - Drain Layer
  - Drop Crew Laborer
  - Finisher
  - Helper
  - Post Framer
  - Punch Out Crew Member
- Cost Estimator
  - Construction Estimator
  - Cost Analyst
  - Estimator
  - Estimator Project Manager
  - Operations Manager
  - Project Manager
  - Sales Engineer
- Electrical Engineer
  - Circuits Engineer
  - Electrical and Instrument Maintenance Supervisor (E and I)
  - Electrical Controls Engineer
  - Electrical Design Engineer
  - Electrical Project Engineer
  - Electro-Mechanical Engineer
  - Project Engineer
  - Test Engineer
- Engineering Manager
  - Chief Engineer
  - Civil Engineering Manager
  - Director of Engineering
  - Principal Engineer
  - Process Engineering Manager
  - Project Engineer
  - Project Engineering Manager
  - Project Manager
  - Supervisory Civil Engineer

- Operating Engineer/Construction Equipment Operator
  - Back Hoe Operator
  - Equipment Operator
  - Excavator Operator
  - Grader Operator
  - Heavy Equipment Operator
  - Loader Operator
  - Machine Operator
  - Motor Grader Operator
  - Track Hoe Operator
- Pipe Fitter and Steamfitter
  - Equipment Service Associate (ESA)
  - Industrial Pipefitter
  - Journeyman Pipe Fitter
  - Lead Pipefitter
  - Lead Steamfitter
  - Machine Repairman
  - Mechanical Pipefitter
  - Millwright
  - Pipefitting Tradesman
  - Pipefitter Helper
  - Plumber and Steamfitter
  - Senior Steamfitter
  - Service Technician
  - Sprinkler Fitter
  - Steamfitter Foreman
  - Welder
- Plumber
  - Commercial Plumber
  - Drain Technician
  - Journeyman Plumber
  - Plumber Gasfitter
  - Plumbing and Heating Mechanic
  - Residential Plumber
  - Service Plumber
- Property/Real Estate/Community Association Manager
  - Apartment Manager
  - Community Manager
  - Concierge
  - Lease Administration Supervisor
  - Leasing Manager
  - On-Site Manager
  - Resident Manager
- Real Estate Agent
  - Associate Broker
  - Broker Associate
  - Real Estate Broker
  - Real Estate Broker Associate
  - Real Estate Sales Agent
  - Real Estate Salesperson
  - Broker in Charge

- o Realtor
- o Sales Agent
- Roofer
  - o Industrial Roofer
  - o Metal Roofing Mechanic
  - o Residential Roofer
  - o Roof Mechanic
  - o Roof Service Technician
  - o Roofing Technician
  - o Sheet Metal Roofer
- Rough Carpenter
  - o Apprentice Carpenter
  - o Carpenter
  - o Framer Rough Carpenter
  - o Journeyman Carpenter
- Sheet Metal Worker
  - o Fabricator
  - o Crew Leader
  - o Geothermal Heat Pump Fabricator
  - o Journeyman Sheet Metal Worker
  - o Machinist
  - o Project Manager
  - o Sheet Metal Apprentice
  - o Sheet Metal Lay Out Mechanic
  - o Sheet Metal Mechanic
- Structural Iron and Steel Worker
  - o Fitter/Welder
  - o Ironworker
  - o Ornamental Ironworker
  - o Reinforcing Iron and Rebar Worker
  - o Rod Buster
  - o Steel Fabricator
  - o Steel Worker
  - o Structural Steel Erector
  - o Tower Hand
- Surveyor
  - o County Surveyor
  - o Geodesist
  - o Land Surveyor
  - o Licensed Land Surveyor
  - o Professional Land Surveyor
  - o Survey Engineer
  - o Survey Party Chief
- Surveying Technician
  - o Chainman
  - o Engineering Assistant
  - o Engineering Technician
  - o Field Crew Chief
  - o Instrument Man (I-Man)
  - o Instrument Operator
  - o Rodman
  - o Survey Crew Chief
  - o Survey Party Chief
  - o Survey Technician

- Welder, Cutter, and Welder Fitter
  - o Maintenance Welder
  - o Sub Arc Operator
  - o Welder-Brazier
  - o Welder-Cutter
  - o Welder-Fitter
  - o Welding Inspector
  - o Welder/Solderer
  - o Welding Supervisor

INSTALLATION, OPERATIONS, AND ENERGY-EFFICIENCY JOBS

- Boilermaker
  - o Boilermaker Mechanic
  - o Boilermaker Pipe Fitter
  - o Boilermaker Welder
  - o Boiler Mechanic
  - o Boiler Technician
  - o Boiler Welder
  - o Service Technician
- Electrician
  - o Journeyman Electrician
  - o Commercial Electrician
  - o Maintenance Electrician
  - o Inside Wireman
  - o Journeyman Wireman
  - o Electrician Technician
  - o Electrical Systems Installer
- Energy Auditor
  - o Energy Rater
  - o Energy Consultant
  - o Home Energy Rater
  - o Home Performance Consultant
  - o Building Performance Consultant
- Energy Broker
  - o Account Executive: Energy Sales
  - o Energy Consultant
  - o Energy Sales Consultant
  - o Energy Sales Representative
- Energy Engineer
  - o Energy Efficiency Engineer
  - o Energy Manager
  - o Distributed Generation Project Manager
  - o Environmental Solutions Engineer
  - o Industrial Energy Engineer
  - o Measurement and Verification Engineer
  - o Test and Balance Engineer

- Facility Manager
  - Administrative Services Manager
  - Building Manager
  - Building Operations Manager
  - Maintenance and Operations Manager
  - Maintenance Engineer
  - Maintenance Manager
  - Energy Manager
- Geothermal Technician
  - Geothermal Installer
- Heating and Air Conditioning Mechanic and Installer
  - Air Conditioning Technician (AC Tech)
  - Commercial Service Technician
  - Field Service Technician
  - HVAC Installer (Heating, Ventilation, and Air Conditioning)
  - HVAC Specialist (Heating, Ventilation, and Air Conditioning)
  - HVAC Technician (Heating, Ventilation, and Air Conditioning)
  - HVAC/R Service Technician (Heating, Ventilation, and Air Conditioning/Refrigeration)
  - Service Manager
  - Service Technician
- Insulation Worker, Floor, Ceiling, and Wall
  - Insulation Installer
  - Installer
  - Insulation Estimator
  - Retrofit Installer
  - Insulation Mechanic
- Insulation Worker, Mechanical
  - Commercial Insulator
  - Heat and Frost Insulator
  - Industrial Insulator
  - Insulation Mechanic
  - Insulation Installer
  - Insulation Worker
  - Mechanical Insulator
- Maintenance and Repair Worker, General
  - Building Maintenance Mechanic
  - Building Mechanic
  - Equipment Engineering Technician
  - I&C Technician (Instrument and Controls)
  - Maintenance Technician
  - Maintenance Mechanic
  - Maintenance Supervisor
  - Maintenance Electrician
  - Maintenance Engineer
  - Process Technician

- Mechanical Engineer
  - Commissioning Engineer
  - Design Engineer
  - Design Maintenance Engineer
  - Equipment Engineer
  - Mechanical Design Engineer
  - Process Engineer
  - Product Engineer
  - Systems Engineer
- Refrigeration Mechanic and Installer
  - Refrigeration Mechanic
  - Refrigeration Operator
  - Refrigeration Technician
  - Service Technician
- Solar Energy Installation Manager
  - Foreman
  - Project Manager
- Solar Photovoltaic Installer
  - Solar Field Service Technician
  - Solar Installation Electrician
  - Solar Installation Technician Commercial
  - Solar Installation Technician Residential
  - Solar and PV Installation Roofer
- Solar Sales Representative and Assessor
  - Account Manager
  - Assistant Sales Manager
  - Director, Regional Sales
  - Independent Sales Representative, Solar
  - Outside Solar Energy Sales Representative
  - Outside Solar Sales Representative
  - Outside Sales Representative, Residential Solar
  - PV Sales Representative, Commercial
  - Senior Account Executive
  - Solar Account Executive
  - Solar PV Sales Representative
- Solar Thermal Installer and Technician
  - Solar Field Service Technician
  - Solar Installation Technician Commercial
  - Solar Installation Technician Residential
- Stationary Engineer and Boiler Operator
  - Boiler Engineer
  - Boiler Inspector
  - Building Manager
  - Boiler Operator
  - Building Superintendent
  - Boiler Tender

- o Chief Plant Engineer
- o Fireman
- o Operating Engineer
- o Plant Operator
- o Plant Superintendent
- o Plant Utilities Engineer
- o Stationary Engineer
- o Stationary Steam Engineer
- o Utility Operator
- Weatherization Installer and Technician
  - o Weatherization Field Technician
  - o Weatherization Crew Chief
  - o Residential Air Sealing Technician
  - o Window/Door Retrofit Technician
  - o Weatherization Operations Manager

COMMERCIAL, INDUSTRIAL, AND RESIDENTIAL DESIGN JOBS

- Bath Designer
  - o Associate Bath Designer
  - o Bath Dealer/Distributor
  - o Bath Design and Sales Consultant
  - o Builder or Remodeler
  - o Display Designer (bath furnishings)
  - o Industrial Designer
  - o Junior Designer
  - o Project Manager
- Flooring Installer
  - o Carpet Installer
  - o Carpet Journeyman
  - o Carpet Layer
  - o Flooring Installation Mechanic
  - o Flooring Mechanic
- Furniture Designer
  - o Cabinet Maker
  - o Furniture Maker
  - o Furniture Showroom Sales Representative
  - o Interior Furniture Systems Designer
  - o Office Furniture CAD Designer
  - o Office Furniture Designer
  - o Retail Furniture Sales/Design Consultant
- Interior Decorator
  - o Commercial Interior Decorator
  - o Interior Decorating Consultant
  - o Interior Decorating Director
  - o Interior Decorating Sales Consultant
  - o Interior Decorating Supervisor
  - o Retail Store Decorator

- Interior Designer
  - o Color and Materials Designer
  - o Commercial Interior Designer
  - o Design Assistant Director of Interiors
  - o Director of Interiors
  - o Interior Design Coordinator
  - o Interior Design Consultant
  - o Interior Design Director
  - o Senior Designer
- Painter
  - o Facilities Painter
  - o Maintenance Painter
  - o Industrial Painter
- Kitchen Designer
  - o Associate Industrial Designer
  - o Cabinet Designer
  - o Junior Designer
  - o Kitchen Dealer/Distributor
  - o Kitchen Design and Sales Consultant
  - o Builder or Remodeler
  - o Display Designer (kitchen furnishings)
  - o Industrial Designer
  - o Project Manager
  - o Senior Creative Designer
- Product Designer
- Commercial Designer
- Industrial Designer

LANDSCAPING, GROUNDSKEEPING, AND TURF CARE JOBS

- Arborist
  - Aerial Lift Operator
    - o Arboretum/Parks/Botanical Garden Arborist
    - o Arboriculture Consultant
    - o Climber
    - o Crew Leader
    - o Ground Worker
    - o Line Clearance Foreman
    - o Manager, Tree Care Company
    - o Municipal Arborist/Forester
    - o Plant Health Care Integrated Pest Management (PHC IPM) Monitor
    - o Plant Health Care Integrated Pest Management (PHC IPM) Technician

- o Product/Equipment Manufacturer Salesperson
- o Tree Care Foreman
- o Tree Care Salesperson
- o Tree Trimmer and Pruner
- o Urban Forester
- o Utility Forestry Manager
- First-Line Supervisor/Manager of Agricultural Crop and Horticultural Workers
  - o Farm Manager
  - o Grower
  - o Farm Owner Operator
  - o Field Operations Farm Manager
  - o Pest Management Supervisor
  - o Supervisor Grower
  - o Grove Manager
- First-Line Supervisor/Manager of Landscaping, Lawn Service, and Groundskeeping Workers
  - o Athletic Fields Superintendent
  - o Buildings and Grounds Supervisor
  - o Golf Course Superintendent
  - o Grounds Crew Supervisor
  - o Grounds Foreman
  - o Grounds Maintenance Supervisor
  - o Grounds Supervisor
  - o Groundskeeper Supervisor
  - o Landscape Manager
  - o Landscape Supervisor
- Landscape Architect
  - o Environmental Landscape Architect
  - o Golf Course Architect
  - o Land Planner
  - o Project Manager
- Landscape Designer
  - o Head Horticulturist
  - o Landscape Design Estimator
  - o Landscape Design Project Director
- Landscaping and Groundskeeping Worker
  - o Gardener
  - o Greenskeeper
  - o Groundskeeper
  - o Grounds/Maintenance Specialist
  - o Grounds Maintenance Worker
  - o Grounds Supervisor
  - o Grounds Technician
  - o Grounds Worker
  - o Landscape Technician
  - o Lawn Care Technician
  - o Outside Maintenance Worker
- Lawn Care Specialist
  - o Lawn Care Crew Leader
  - o Lawn Care Technician

- Nursery and Greenhouse Manager
  - o Farm Manager
  - o Garden Center Manager
  - o Garden Supply Store Manager
  - o Greenhouse Manager
  - o Grower
  - o Horticulturist
  - o Lawn and Garden Center Manager
  - o Nursery Manager
  - o Perennial House Manager
  - o Production Manager
  - o Propagation Manager
- Pesticide Handler, Sprayer, and Applicator
  - o Applicator
  - o Chemical Applicator
  - o Integrated Pest Management Technician (IPM)
  - o Lawn Technician
  - o Lawn Specialist
  - o Pest Control Technician
  - o Pesticides Applicator
  - o Spray Applicator
  - o Spray Technician
  - o Tree and Shrub Technician
  - o Turf and Ornamental Spray Technician
- Turf Grass Manager
  - o Assistant Golf Course Superintendent
  - o Athletic Fields Superintendent
  - o Buildings and Grounds Supervisor
  - o Golf Course Superintendent
  - o Grounds Crew Supervisor
  - o Grounds Foreman
  - o Groundskeeper Supervisor
  - o Grounds Maintenance Supervisor
  - o Grounds Supervisor
  - o Landscape Manager
  - o Landscape Supervisor
  - o Sod Farm Manager
  - o Sports Turf Manager
  - o Turf Technician

POLICY, ANALYSIS, ADVOCACY, AND REGULATORY AFFAIRS JOBS

- Chief Sustainability Officer
  - o Campus Sustainability Coordinator
  - o Chief Green Officer
  - o Director of Social and Environmental Responsibility

- o Director of Sustainability
- o Director, Sustainability Integration Office
- o Environmental Policy Manager
- o Environmental Sustainability Manager
- o Sustainability Coordinator
- o Sustainability Manager
- o Vice President, Corporate Social Responsibility
- City and Regional Planning Aide
  - o Community Planner
  - o Development Technician
  - o GIS (Geographic Information Systems) Technician
  - o Planning Aide
  - o Planning Assistant
  - o Planning Technician
  - o Transportation Planning Assistant
  - o Zoning Technician
- Compliance Manager
  - o Compliance Administrator
  - o Compliance Analyst
  - o Compliance Associate
  - o Compliance Engineer
  - o Compliance Inspector
  - o Compliance Officer
  - o Compliance Program Manager
  - o Compliance Team Manager
  - o Regulatory Compliance Manager
  - o Compliance Director
  - o Chief Compliance Officer
- Construction and Building Inspector
  - o Electrical Inspector
  - o Green Building Inspector
  - o Home Inspector
  - o Mechanical Inspector
  - o Plan Examiner
  - o Plumbing Inspector
  - o Public Works Inspector
  - o Specification Inspector
  - o Structural Inspector
- Environmental Compliance Inspector
  - o Compliance Investigator
  - o Enforcement Officer
  - o Environmental Compliance Technician
  - o Environmental Protection Specialist
  - o Environmental Quality Analyst
  - o Environmental Specialist

- o Resource Conservation and Recovery Act Enforcement Officer (RCRA Enforcement Officer
- o Toxic Program Officer
- o Waste Management Specialist
- Regulatory Affairs Specialist
  - o Compliance Manager
  - o Compliance Officer
- Training and Development Specialist
  - o Computer Training Specialist
  - o Corporate Trainer
  - o E-Learning Developer
  - o Job Training Specialist
  - o Management Development Specialist
  - o Technical Trainer
  - o Training Coordinator
  - o Training Specialist
- Urban and Regional Planner
  - o Airport Planner
  - o Building, Planning and Zoning Director
  - o City Planner
  - o Community Development Planner
  - o Community Development Director
  - o Community Planning and Development Representative
  - o Neighborhood Planner
  - o Planning Director
  - o Regional Planner
- Water Resource Specialist
  - o Natural Resource Specialist
  - o Resource Management Specialist
  - o Water Resource Management Specialist
  - o Water Technology Specialist
- Water/Wastewater Engineer
  - o Civil Engineer, Water/Wastewater
  - o Civil Water-Wastewater Engineer
  - o Engineer, Water/Wastewater Resources
  - o Senior Civil Engineer
  - o Senior Water/Wastewater Engineer
  - o Waste/Water Environmental Engineer
  - o Water Treatment Specialist
  - o Water Quality Specialist

GREEN JOB BOARDS

ABOUT GREEN JOB BOARDS

Once upon a time, just a few years ago, if you were looking for a job, you'd read the want ads in the newspaper or in trade and association publications. Today, most job listings have migrated to the Internet where you will find hundreds of job boards. How do you decide which ones to search and what to look for? Here are a few ideas to help you concentrate your search in the best places.

Remember that job boards are not just for searching when you are looking for a job. They can be helpful when you are deciding on a career to pursue. Analyzing job titles related to your interests; the regions of the country where particular jobs are most common, for example, the Plains states and the Southwest for wind power jobs; types of employers such as public or private, nonprofit, small companies or large corporations; and salaries can help direct your career choice.

Where to Look?

Major Internet sites for jobs are monster.com, careerbuilder.com, and hotjobs.yahoo.com. Type in your job area such as "architectural designer" and see what jobs come up. You can search for jobs in a specific city or nationwide. Monster.com has a green careers section. Green For All and Yahoo! Hotjobs have partnered to create a Green Jobs page at hotjobs.yahoo.com. Green For All is not a job board, but it is a great resource for information about green-collar jobs for skilled workers,

especially for those in urban centers and returning veterans.

You will also find job boards that are specific to green jobs in the construction industry, including those related to the installation and operation of new energy sources for homes and other buildings such as the following:

- www.aecjobbank.com (architect, engineering, and construction jobs)
- www.careersinwind.com (sponsored by the American Wind Energy Association)
- www.cleantech.org
- www.constructionexecutive.com
- www.constructionjobs.com
- www.constructionjobforce.com/Channel.asp
- www.jobsinsolarpower.com
- www.renewableenergyjobs.com
- www.renewableenergyjobs.net
- www.renewableenergyworld.com
- www.simplyhired.com (not just for energy, but lists many green energy jobs)
- www.solarjobs.com

There are also a number of job boards that post a variety of green jobs. Type "green job boards" into a search engine and more than two dozen will pop up. The following are ones that came up in researching this book:

- http://careercenter.usgbc.org/home
- www.americangreenjobs.com
- www.brightgreentalent.com

- www.careeronestop.org (sponsored by the U.S. Department of Labor)
- www.cleanedgejobs.com
- www.ecojobs.com
- www.environmentalcareer.com
- www.greenbiz.com
- www.greendreamjobs.com
- www.greenjobs.net
- www.greenjobsalliance.org
- www.greenjobsearch.org
- www.sustainlane.com/green-jobs
- www.veteransgreenjobs.org

Other Sources for Job Boards

Also, look at the Web site of the professional organizations and trade associations that you belong to. Many of them have job boards, and their postings will be the most closely aligned with the group's specialties.

Don't overlook your college or university career counseling or job placement office. Many schools today offer their services to alumni and alumnae, not just to seniors and graduate students. If you graduated from a large university, your department may have its own career services link on its Web site or may have links to other job boards.

APPENDIX C

"GREEN" YOUR VOCABULARY FOR A SUSTAINABLE FUTURE

Just about everywhere you turn these days, you see and hear the lingo of the new green economy: *biofuel, carbon footprint, geothermal, LEED,* just to name a few. Understanding what these words actually mean will certainly help you in your green job search—and in your everyday life. Here's a list of some key green terms and their definitions to get you started on your way to a sustainable future.

alternative energy/renewable energy: energy derived from natural resources that aren't used up over time, such as wind and sun

biodegradable: able to decompose by natural forces and without harming the environment

biodiesel: fuel made from vegetable oils, animal fats, or recycled grease that are chemically processed and blended with petroleum diesel fuel

biofuel: fuel that is produced from renewable biological resources such as plant biomass and treated municipal and industrial waste; for example, ethanol produced from sugarcane or corn

biogas: fuel made from a combination of methane gas and carbon dioxide created by the bacterial degradation of organic matter

biomass: a wide range of materials that have uses other than as food or in consumer goods such as agricultural waste, wood, treated municipal waste, and energy crops such as corn and soybeans

cap-and-trade: system of pollution credits established by the government and based on the amount of air pollution created in a region that enables a company that doesn't use all its pollution credits to sell unused ones to companies that pollute more than the credits allotted to them by the government

carbon emissions: carbon dioxide and carbon monoxide gases released by motor vehicles and industrial production that pollute the atmosphere

carbon footprint: a way to measure the impact of human activity on the environment; uses units of carbon dioxide to calculate amount of greenhouse gases produced

carbon neutral: not adding to carbon dioxide emissions

carbon trading: process by which companies can sell their unused pollution credits; see *cap-and-trade*

clean tech: economically competitive and production technology that uses fewer resources and/or energy, generates less waste, and causes less environmental damage than traditional fuels such as oil and coal

ecotravel: traveling responsibly in terms of the environment, especially to natural areas in a way "that conserves the environment and improves the well-being of local people" (The International Ecotourism Society)

energy audit: assessment of energy use to determine ways to conserve energy; first step in *weatherization*

energy efficient: denotes a product that is as good as or better than standard products, but uses less energy and costs less to operate

Energy Star: U.S. Department of Energy and EPA joint program to increase the energy efficiency of household appliances and electronic devices; adopted by other nations including the European Union

ethanol: alternate fuel made from corn or sugar cane

Fair Trade: agreement by countries in international trade to live up to standards for the fair and just treatment of labor and the environment in the production of goods; goods manufactured and sold under the agreement

feedstock: raw materials such as corn and sugarcane used to produce biofuels

geothermal: energy source; uses heat from the Earth as a clean, renewable source of electricity

global warming: increase in the average temperature of the Earth's atmosphere resulting in climate change

green building: building materials and methods used to construct homes, buildings, highways, bridges, and other structures that are environmentally responsible and energy efficient

green-collar career/job: a career/job that promotes stewardship of the environment now and for the future; some definitions also include the provision that the jobs must provide a decent living standard for workers and their families

green design: creating materials, products, buildings, services, and experiences that are energy-efficient and environmentally friendly

hybrid: motor vehicle that runs on gasoline and an electric battery

LEED: acronym for Leadership in Energy and Environmental Design, a Green Building Rating System developed by the U.S. Green Building Council (USGBC); "LEED certified" denotes that new construction, renovation, building operations, etc., meet the USGBC guidelines for building sustainability

methane: colorless, odorless, flammable gas that is a constituent of natural gas and a source of hydrogen; can be produced from the decomposition of landfills; LFG (landfill gas)

organic: product made solely from natural ingredients; farming without the use of synthetic pesticides and fertilizer

New Urbanism: urban design movement that encourages the development of walkable neighborhoods with a range of housing and jobs

photovoltaic cell: device that turns sunlight directly into electricity

PCW: stands for Post Consumer Waste; denotes product made from recycled materials

retrofit: to add new technology to an existing structure or system

solar energy system: one of two types of power systems: photovoltaic uses sunlight to produce electricity directly, and the solar water heating system uses sunlight to heat water that is used to provide electricity

solar panel/solar array: device that collects the heat of the sun for use in various types of solar energy systems

solar thermal collector: device that uses energy from sunlight to heat substances like water for use in heating

solar thermal power: energy produced by using sunlight to heat water; also known as concentrated solar power (CSP)

STARS: acronym for Sustainability Tracking Assessment & Rating System for colleges and universities, established by the Association for the Advancement of Sustainability in Higher Education, a consortium of U.S. colleges and universities

sustainability: efforts to "create and maintain conditions under which [humans] and nature can exist in productive harmony, and fulfill the social, economic, and other requirements of present and future generations of Americans" (U.S. Environmental Protection Agency)

sustainable design: the designing of objects and structures according to principles of economic, social, and environmental sustainability; also known as *green design*

VOC: stands for volatile organic compounds; carbon-based molecules that vaporize as gases and enter the atmosphere; ingredient in paint, paint thinners, paint strippers, furniture, and household cleaning products that causes the odor

waste audit: assessment of the amount of waste generated at a home or business

waste reduction: reusing materials, reducing or eliminating the amount of waste at its source by buying less, reducing the amount of toxicity in waste by using environmentally safe products

wastewater recycling: treatment of wastewater for recycling for industrial uses and agriculture

weatherization: improving the energy efficiency of a building by sealing off air leaks

wind turbine: device for harnessing the wind to create electricity

APPENDIX D

GREEN FEATURES IN THIS GUIDE